lonely planet

Best Road Trips
FRANCE

ANNA RICHARDS, ALEXIS AVERBUCK, JOEL BALSAM, OLIVER BERRY, CELESTE BRASH, STUART BUTLER, JEAN-BERNARD CARILLET, GREGOR CLARK, MARK ELLIOT, STEVE FALLON, ANITA ISALSKA, CATHERINE LE NEVEZ, CHRISTOPHER PITTS, DANIEL ROBINSON, REGIS ST LOUIS, RYAN VER BERKMOES, TASMIN WABY, NICOLA WILLIAMS

CONTENTS

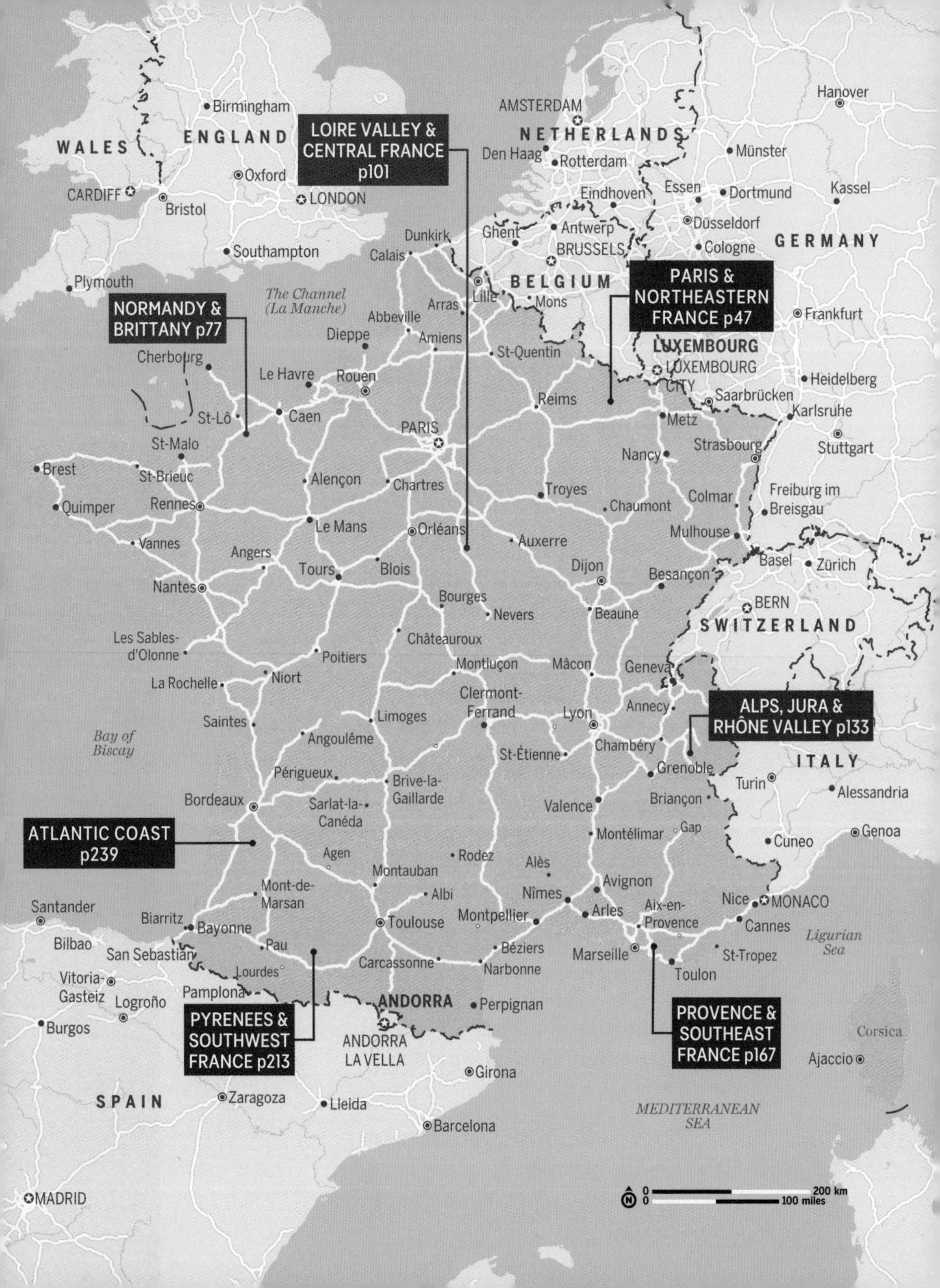

LOIRE VALLEY & CENTRAL FRANCE p101
NORMANDY & BRITTANY p77
PARIS & NORTHEASTERN FRANCE p47
ALPS, JURA & RHÔNE VALLEY p133
ATLANTIC COAST p239
PYRENEES & SOUTHWEST FRANCE p213
PROVENCE & SOUTHEAST FRANCE p167
WALES
ENGLAND
NETHERLANDS
BELGIUM
LUXEMBOURG
GERMANY
SWITZERLAND
ITALY
ANDORRA
SPAIN
Birmingham
CARDIFF
Bristol
Oxford
LONDON
Southampton
Plymouth
AMSTERDAM
Den Haag
Rotterdam
Eindhoven
Essen
Dortmund
Münster
Hanover
Kassel
Düsseldorf
Cologne
Antwerp
Ghent
BRUSSELS
Dunkirk
Calais
Lille
Mons
Frankfurt
LUXEMBOURG CITY
Saarbrücken
Heidelberg
Karlsruhe
Stuttgart
Freiburg im Breisgau
The Channel (La Manche)
Arras
Abbeville
Dieppe
Amiens
St-Quentin
Cherbourg
Le Havre
Rouen
Caen
St-Lô
Reims
Metz
Strasbourg
Nancy
PARIS
St-Malo
Brest
St-Brieuc
Alençon
Chartres
Troyes
Chaumont
Colmar
Mulhouse
Quimper
Rennes
Le Mans
Orléans
Auxerre
Vannes
Angers
Tours
Blois
Dijon
Besançon
Basel
Zürich
Nantes
Bourges
Nevers
Beaune
BERN
Les Sables-d'Olonne
Châteauroux
Poitiers
Montluçon
Mâcon
Geneva
La Rochelle
Niort
Clermont-Ferrand
Annecy
Saintes
Limoges
Lyon
Bay of Biscay
Angoulême
St-Étienne
Chambéry
Grenoble
Turin
Périgueux
Brive-la-Gaillarde
Briançon
Alessandria
Bordeaux
Sarlat-la-Canéda
Valence
Gap
Montélimar
Cuneo
Genoa
Agen
Rodez
Alès
Montauban
Avignon
Mont-de-Marsan
Albi
Nîmes
Arles
Aix-en-Provence
Nice
MONACO
Santander
Biarritz
Bayonne
Toulouse
Montpellier
Cannes
Ligurian Sea
Bilbao
San Sebastián
Pau
Béziers
Marseille
St-Tropez
Vitoria-Gasteiz
Lourdes
Carcassonne
Narbonne
Toulon
Pamplona
Logroño
Perpignan
Burgos
ANDORRA LA VELLA
Corsica
Ajaccio
Girona
Zaragoza
Lleida
MEDITERRANEAN SEA
Barcelona
MADRID
0 200 km
0 100 miles

WELCOME TO FRANCE

Mesmerising, cinematic France is where you can learn the *art de vivre* (art of living) over long lunch breaks on restaurant *terrasses,* soak in views of a sparkling Eiffel Tower from Montmartre at sunset, pick up local artisan produce at village square markets, or sip apéritifs on the celebrity-studded French Riviera.

France is also a country of proud agrarian traditions, with vast, varied and eternally photographable landscapes. Between Normandy's white cliffs and the turquoise Mediterranean Sea, you'll find hills ribboned with vines, medieval villages of golden stone, and lush river valleys dotted with châteaux, plus deciduous forests, snow-peaked mountains and west-coast surf beaches.

Let us help you navigate *l'Hexagone,* whether this is your first or fifth visit. Our expert-led road trips take you to the best of France with local insights and off-the-beaten-track detours designed to ensure a truly unforgettable experience.

Honfleur (p99)
CHRISTIAN MUELLER/SHUTTERSTOCK

P'TITE CHINE

MY PERFECT ROAD TRIP

ANNA RICHARDS

CORSICAN COAST CRUISER, p202

Road tripping Corsica makes me feel free. I first came here straight after moving to France in 2021. Arriving on the car ferry at sunrise, the cliffs and mountains were silhouettes like a shadow puppet show, and as the sun rose, the coast road plunged and climbed, and my spirits soared. I've been back every year since. There are no other views that can leave me quite as giddy as this island's, particularly the stretch of road to Porto and Les Calanques de Piana.

FROM LEFT: M. SCHAUER/SHUTTERSTOCK; LUKAS HODON/SHUTTERSTOCK

Above: Ponte Pianella, (p206); Right: Les Calanques de Piana (p206)

BEST LONG DRIVES

1. **Roman Provence** History and scenery are front of house on this drive.
2. **Southern Corsica** Be seduced by the southern coast of Corsica.
3. **Cheat's Compostela** Follow in the steps of Camino walkers.
4. **Basque Country** Take in a different France along the Spanish border.
5. **Atlantic to Med** Wind your way across the south of France over the Pyrenees.

BEAUTIFUL VILLAGES

France will spoil you with historic villages to swoon over. Wander cobbled lanes to town squares framed by cafe terraces; stumble across ornate fountains and houses clad in ivy, wisteria or roses; or join locals at *boulangeries* (bakeries) and fresh-produce markets. France is not short of the extravagant either. Its gorgeous villages are often adjoined by châteaux, palaces, abbeys and cathedrals.

① DORDOGNE'S FORTIFIED VILLAGES

Riverbank châteaux, medieval villages and market stalls groaning with local produce await. p266

② BEAUJOLAIS VILLAGES

Winding country roads lead to golden villages and manicured vineyards producing crimson-red Beaujolais. p156

③ CHÂTEAUX OF THE LOIRE

Tour picturesque villages and evocative châteaux, then hire a bicycle to explore more of the verdant Loire Valley. p104

④ MEDIEVAL BURGUNDY

Check out medieval monasteries, multicoloured tiled roofs and an ancient hilltop pilgrim site in this region steeped in history. p124

⑤ LAVENDER ROUTE

Immerse yourself in quintessential Provençal life by sipping pastis and playing pétanque between fields of flowers. p176

Left: Domme (p268), Dordogne; Right: Château de Chambord (p108), Loire Valley

CHÂTEAU STAGS

Prebook a visit to Château de Chambord (p108) in autumn to observe the bellowing antics of its mating stags during rutting season.

GO EXPLORING

Beautiful villages are everywhere. Turn off the GPS and explore. You may stumble upon the perfect village *boulangerie* for morning croissants.

BREAD AND CHEESE

Grab fresh baguettes and paired-with-your-wine cheeses (ask for local recommendations) for a perfect late-afternoon picnic.

MIND THE KIDS

Many wineries welcome children, but there's not a lot for them to do. Bring your own activities (a DIY vineyard bingo, for example).

WINE TASTING 101

If there's one thing France knows about, it's wine. Viticulture has been a cornerstone of French culture for hundreds of years, and the merest mention of the nation's top vineyards will make any sommelier go weak at the knees. On these driving tours, which take you from the effervescent Champagne to southern France's majestic red regions, you'll meander vine-ribboned hills, stopping for tours and tastings in cosy cool cellars (or you can even stay over *au château*).

① CHAMPAGNE TASTER

Taste, and learn the history of, this much-adored drop at famous brand cellars and small niche producers. p66

② HERITAGE WINE COUNTRY

Tour the world-famous wineries surrounding Bordeaux, largely known for blended reds. p248

③ ROUTE DES GRANDS CRUS

Sample some of France's most prestigious reds and whites on this epicurean adventure through Burgundy. p128

LEFT TO RIGHT: MASSIMO SANTI/SHUTTERSTOCK, BARMALINI/SHUTTERSTOCK

④ ALSACE ACCENTS

Discover centuries-old wine traditions and admire the colourful half-timbered houses of the Alsace region. p72

⑤ THE JURA

Vineyards produce distinctive *vin jaune* (golden wine) – pair it with a local Comté cheese – in this off-the-beaten-track destination. p136

Left: Château du Clos de Vougeot (p128), Burgundy; Above: *vin jaune* (golden wine) from Jura

HISTORIC SITES

REPLICA CAVE
A replica of the Lascaux cave was built in a museum at the site (p35), after the cave was closed for preservation.

With a rich history stretching back several millennia, as well as an outsized influence on the world stage, it is little wonder that France is a must-tour for history buffs. From prehistoric caves to the Roman Empire; medieval Europe to the rise of the French Court; and the Enlightenment to the Republic – the land is littered with continual reminders of this country's storied past.

1 CAVE ART OF THE VÉZÈRE VALLEY

Step back 20,000 years at the extraordinary prehistoric sites in the Dordogne region. p260

2 ROMAN PROVENCE

Follow Roman roads, cross Roman bridges and grab a seat in the stands at Roman theatres and arenas. p170

3 CAVES & CELLARS OF THE LOIRE

Discover ancient troglodyte dwellings, dating to the 4th century BCE, where locals lived – and stored their wine. p110

4 THE CATHAR TRAIL

Trace the history of the Cathars through hilltop towns and medieval ramparts in the foothills of the Pyrenees. p220

5 IN FLANDERS FIELDS

Battlefields dotted with WWI cemeteries and moving memorials are today a stark reminder of the fragility of peace. p62

Château de Foix (p222), Pyrenees
RYSAN/SHUTTERSTOCK

IMAGEDOC/ALAMY

Musée des Beaux-Arts (p81), Rouen

OUR PICKS

CULTURAL LEGACY

France's art, music, literature and cinema have had a huge impact on the world. Here you'll find thriving bookshops, plus abundant newspapers and magazine racks; the sound of live music is embedded into the fabric of town life; and the French film industry has seen a boost in investment in recent years. From prehistoric cave art to provocative street art, these drives take you to some of those sources of inspiration.

① MONET'S NORMANDY

Begin with a pilgrimage to the cradle of impressionism before finding further inspiration in Honfleur and Rouen. p80

PRINT IS KING

A whopping 80% of French readers still prefer print over digital, whether they're reading novels, art books or comics.

BALCONY VIEWS

The innovative architecture of the Centre Pompidou-Metz (p52) is best observed from inside, on the balcony outside its topmost gallery.

② A TOAST TO ART

Drive the northeast corner of France to visit regional galleries like the Louvre-Lens and Centre Pompidou-Metz. p50

③ ROMAN PROVENCE

Having nurtured countless artists, from Picasso to Gauguin and Van Gogh, Arles is a hub for creative communities. p170

④ BRETON COAST

See Brittany through the eyes of the Pont-Aven school of painters, then admire street art and sculptures in Vannes. p90

⑤ RIVIERA CROSSING

Filmmakers, writers and artists have long been inspired by the Côte d'Azur. In May they descend on Cannes. p182

THE GREAT OUTDOORS

Whether exploring the windswept *sentier du littoral* (coastal trail), scented with sea salt and herbal scrub, or walking the breathtaking summits of its highest mountains, you'll soon realise that France's natural world is both beautiful and dramatic. For outdoor adventures, there are hikes, cycle trails and surf beaches to explore. If you prefer your comforts, fear not – cable cars and mountain railways take the legwork out of many alpine sojourns.

① ALPINE ADVENTURE

Whether it is hiking, skiing, snowshoeing, mountain biking or white-water rafting, get thee to the mountains. p142

② VAR DELIGHTS

Discover deserted coves in the Calanques, hike the Massif des Maures or explore the wild hills of the Var. p188

③ THE LOT VALLEY

Zipline, climb a via ferrata or paddle a canoe to explore this river valley, which cuts through limestone cliffs. p272

④ CORSICAN COAST CRUISER

Meander Corsica's breathtaking coast, then boat around the red-rock formations of Réserve Naturelle de Scandola. p202

⑤ VOLCANOES OF THE AUVERGNE

Beyond the rugged peaks of the Parc Naturel Régional des Volcans d'Auvergne, you can find family-friendly walking trails. p116

Left: Réserve Naturelle de Scandola (p205); Right: Hikers, Bouziès (p273), Lot Valley

LEFT TO RIGHT: PI-R PHOTOS/SHUTTERSTOCK, PIERRE JEAN DURIEU/SHUTTERSTOCK

CLIFF CARVINGS

Carvings by Daniel Monnier can be seen while walking the historic *chemin de halage* (towpath), cut into the cliff side between Bouziès and St-Cirq-Lapopie.

SEE A GLACIER

Mer de Glace (p43) at Mont Blanc may be in retreat, but it's as breathtakingly beautiful as ever.

WHEN TO GO

France is most spellbinding in spring and summer, when vines and trees are lush, honey-coloured villages gleam and back roads unfurl in the sunshine.

I LIVE HERE

VAN ROAD TRIPS IN THE LOT REGION

Senny Ferreira trains barristas in Lyon. Instagram: @ferreira.senny

I love travelling around France in my Vito van. I often think about a van trip I took in the Lot region in the spring. I used to go there as a kid to visit my grandparents. This trip was my very first time driving as an adult, with time to spare to explore the region with its medieval villages and little rivers. As there's limited access to motorways, you're forced to slow down and take in the region's country roads lined with blossoming trees.

Driving gives you the freedom to get to less-visited destinations and stay in unusual tucked-away accommodation, including summer campsites. When days are long and light, you have more time to explore by foot as well as car. In the low season, plan for shorter days and prebook accommodation with parking close by (this is less likely in historic city centres). Spring and autumn can bring changeable weather, so factor in time for slower roads and potential weather-related detours. While winter snow is beautiful, it brings additional driving challenges and the need for safety gear.

Festival d'Avignon

MARIE MARCEL/SIPA/SHUTTERSTOCK

WEATHER WATCH: PARIS

JANUARY	FEBRUARY	MARCH	APRIL	MAY	JUNE
Avg. daytime max: **8°C**	Avg. daytime max: **9°C**	Avg. daytime max: **13°C**	Avg. daytime max: **17°C**	Avg. daytime max: **20°C**	Avg. daytime max: **24°C**
Days of rainfall: **9**	Days of rainfall: **8**	Days of rainfall: **9**	Days of rainfall: **8**	Days of rainfall: **9**	Days of rainfall: **8**

RADU RAZVAN/SHUTTERSTOCK

Tour de France

ACCOMMODATION

From fairy-tale châteaux to a floating pod on a lake, France has accommodation to suit every taste and pocket. In high season, the best coastal options, from campsites to B&Bs, fill up months in advance.

SPEED LIMITS

The *autoroute* speed limit is reduced to 110km/h when it's raining. Keep abreast of local weather warnings: climate change is bringing damaging winds and torrential rains, even in the country's south.

SUMMER SUN AND WINTER MOUNTAINS

Summers are hot, especially in the south. If undercover parking is unavailable, cover your steering wheel with a towel or scarf. It's light until late in June and July, which means you can stay on the road for longer, but avoid heading into the setting sun. In winter, ice and snow make for challenging driving. Plan to be on mountain roads between mid-morning and mid-afternoon when roads are cleared and ice is melting. You must carry snow chains in alpine areas even if you have winter tyres fitted.

BIG-TICKET FESTIVALS

White Night
In a last-ditch attempt to stretch out what's left of summer, museums, monuments, cultural spaces, bars and clubs rock around the clock during Paris' so-called White Night, aka a fabulous all-nighter. **October**

Festival d'Avignon
Rouse your inner thespian with Avignon's legendary performing-arts festival. Street acts in its fringe fest are as inspired as those on official stages. **July**

Fête des Lumières
France's biggest and best light show, on and around 8 December, transforms the streets and squares of Lyon into an open stage. **December**

Tour de France
The world's most prestigious cycling race ends on av des Champs-Élysées in Paris in late July. In the preceding three weeks it travels all over France – the route changes each year, but the French Alps are a hot spot. **July**

JULY
Avg. daytime max: **26°C**
Days of rainfall: **7**

AUGUST
Avg. daytime max: **26°C**
Days of rainfall: **6**

SEPTEMBER
Avg. daytime max: **22°C**
Days of rainfall: **7**

OCTOBER
Avg. daytime max: **17°C**
Days of rainfall: **8**

NOVEMBER
Avg. daytime max: **12°C**
Days of rainfall: **9**

DECEMBER
Avg. daytime max: **9°C**
Days of rainfall: **9**

GET PREPARED FOR FRANCE

Useful things to load in your bag, your ears and your brain.

CLOTHING

Your most chic outfit for meandering the streets of Paris, Lyon or the Côte d'Azur.

Sunhat, sunglasses and sunscreen for summer touring.

Swimwear for the beach or an inland lake. Controversially, burkinis are banned at public pools.

Lightweight summery clothes for the baking heat down south (think: breezy linens).

Light scarf to cover bare shoulders in churches.

Warm layers for autumn days that can turn cold by evening.

Comfortable shoes to drive in and to walk around villages.

Rainwear and an umbrella for those rare(ish) rainy days.

Wellingtons (gumboots) for muddy walks along rivers.

Hiking shoes to walk in nature.

Smart-looking shoes for going out.

Smart clothing is a must for the theatre, a winery or a restaurant in any rural village.

Jeans and a T-shirt or jumper (sweatshirt) for camping. While the French are usually more formally dressed, casual wear is fine if you're staying at camping sites or heading out for a budget meal.

WATCH

- **Être et Avoir**
  (To Be and to Have; Nicolas Philibert, 2002) Ode to childhood and early education from a single-class school in rural France.
- **La Haine**
  (Hatred; Mathieu Kassovitz, 1995) An 'explosive deconstruction of France's treatment of minorities and widening social inequality'.
- **Engrenages**
  (Spiral; TV series, 2005–20) French equivalent to *The Wire*, where police investigations are shown from a different perspective.
- **À Plein Temps**
  (Full Time; Eric Gravel, 2021) Single mother grappling with work, parenting and train strikes.

CLOCKWISE FROM TOP LEFT: LTUMMY/SHUTTERSTOCK, HEYMRPATRICK STUDIO/SHUTTERSTOCK, MARGOUILLAT PHOTO/SHUTTERSTOCK, NATALLIA PLOSKAYA/SHUTTERSTOCK, DEN ROZHNOVSKY/SHUTTERSTOCK

Hiking in the Auvergne (p116)

WORDS

aire rest area
allumez vos feux turn on your lights
arrêt stop
autoroute motorway
carrefour crossroads
cédez le passage give way
déviation detour
gazole diesel
halte péage slow down; toll area ahead
le pont bridge
péage toll
pneu à plat flat tyre
priorité à droite priority on the right
rappel reminder (usually seen with the speed limit)
le rondpont roundabout
sans plomb 95 standard unleaded petrol
sans plomb 98 higher octane unleaded petrol
sens unique one way
toutes directions all directions (the road ahead will take you in any direction, rather than only east/west etc)
travaux roadworks

LISTEN

Psycho Tropical Berlin
(La Femme; 2013) French pop/surf-rock/electro album; perfect road trip music *à la français*.

Reflets du monde lointain
(Dominique A; 2023) Latest from French artist with pop and new-wave inspirations.

FIP Radio
For contemporary jazz, *chansons*, world music and electronic tunes.

The New Paris Podcast
Insights from US journalist, and adopted Parisian, Lindsey Tramuta.

READ

The Flâneur
(Edmund White; 2015) Celebrates the diversity and freedom of big-city life.

Bonjour Tristesse
(Françoise Sagan; 1954) A classic young adult novel about jealousy and its consequences.

The Vernon Subtext Trilogy
(Virginie Despentes; 2015–17) Described as 'part social epic, part punk-rock thriller'.

France: An Adventure History
(Graham Robb; 2022) A new and entertaining perspective on French history.

Gorges de l'Ardèche (p163)

DUPONT MATTHIEU/HEMIS/ALAMY

ROAD TRIPS

CONTENTS

01

EPIC TRIP: INTO THE WILD

This route doesn't tick off France's big hitters. In my opinion, that's what makes it so epic. It takes you through the country's heartland, to paths first trodden by donkeys, and to places where myths, legend and superstition still run strong. This is an amalgamation of the two best motorbike trips my partner and I have taken recently, winding through the limestone gorges, plateaux and Roman remains of southeastern and central France. It doesn't have to be done by motorbike – a car works just as well, but I'd recommend a highly impractical little soapbox on wheels. Or just a regular car. Just avoid hiring an oversized motorhome that looks like a five-star hotel on wheels. Not only are many of the roads on this route narrow and windy, but these rural areas value every tourist they get. If you must travel by van, rent a small *van amenagé* (camper van) from a site like *wikiloc.com,* and try to eat in at least a few local *bistrots.*

The road to Gorges du Tarn (p30)

WITOLD SKRYPCZAK/ALAMY

EPIC TRIPS

★ BEST FOR:

SLOW TRAVEL

Winding your way through gorges and small villages brings the speed down a notch.

DURATION: 6+ DAYS. I ENCOURAGE YOU TO GO AS SLOWLY AS POSSIBLE.

DISTANCE: 656KM / 407 MILES

BEST TIME TO GO: MAY-JUNE OR SEPTEMBER-OCTOBER FOR LONG, WARM DAYS WITHOUT THE SUMMER HOLIDAY CROWDS.

Palais des Papes

LINK YOUR TRIP

21 Rhône Valley
Follow the Rhône north of the Ardèche, up through the fertile vineyards to foodie capital Lyon.

22 Roman Provence
Think about the Roman Empire and combine the trip with the arenas of Arles and Orange.

39 Atlantic to Med
Tack on the tail end of this ocean-to-ocean epic, heading to the French Riviera via Marseille.

01 Avignon

Avignon, historic capital of the popes and modern-day capital of theatre, is the start and end point for this trip, but it's not a particularly fun place to drive around. It's great on foot though. The walled old city is the colour of a crusty cob of sourdough and looks like a desert fort in the south of France. Inside, many of the roads are pedestrianised.

The **Palais des Papes** (Palace of the Popes; *palais-des-papes.com*), rising like a sandcastle over town, is like all your favourite medieval TV shows rolled into one. In the 14th century, during Avignon's 'golden age', seven consecutive popes ruled here, before the seat of the papacy was transferred back to Rome in 1377. Make time to visit the covered market, **Avignon Les Halles** *(avignon-leshalles.com)*, to stock up on journey snacks, before hitting the road.

Note that the *parcs relais* (park and rides) with shuttle buses or trams into the city centre are free of charge: Parking des Italiens, Parking Île Piot and P+R St-Chamand. If you're determined to get to the city centre in your vehicle, you'll find most of the car parks charge a fee. Alternatively, if you've arrived on public transport, hire your car or motorbike when you leave Avignon to save yourself a couple of days of rental costs.

THE DRIVE: Head north to the gorges of the Ardèche. This isn't the quickest way to get there – a running theme on this route – but the quickest way would be no fun! Take the D225 heading northeast out of Avignon. Turn left onto the E714 up to the pretty, riverside town of Sorgues, which then becomes the D17, and heads through the famous winemaking town of Châteauneuf-du-Pape. Spend the night here if you're planning on doing tastings.

Just before Caderousse, take the D237 left until you reach

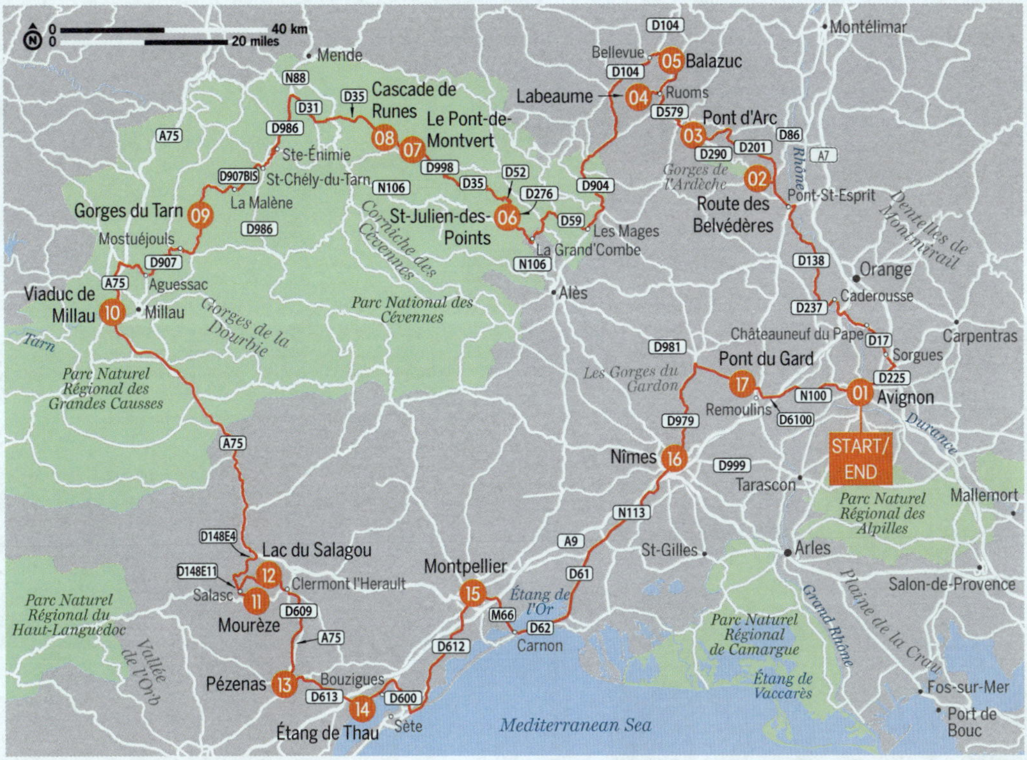

OLIVEROUGE 3/SHUTTERSTOCK

the D238, another left which crosses the River Rhône. The D238 becomes the D138A, hugging the east bank of the Rhône all the way to Pont-St-Esprit, which has a beautiful riverside church. From Pont-St-Esprit, take the D86 up to St-Just-d'Ardèche, and turn left onto the D290 to reach St-Martin-d'Ardèche, and the start of one of the most magnificent stretches of road in France. Without stops, this should take around 1½ hours (63km).

02 Route des Belvédères

The Route des Belvédères, otherwise known by the less glamorous title of the continuation of the D290, is the kind of drive that will live rent-free in your memory for years to come. Largely staying up the top of the limestone plateau, the route looks down at the Ardèche River from a lofty height of 300m, with 11 *belvédères* (viewpoints) along the way.

From each viewpoint, you can see the pockmarked cliffs of the gorges peppered with caves – used as impregnable resistance hideouts in WWII – and often vultures or Bonelli's eagles swooping. Reintroduction programs have upped the number of Bonelli's eagle couples to 42 in recent years, saved from extinction in the region after numbering just six in 1960. Watch out for cyclists along this road; with the hairpin bends they're often not visible until the last minute.

THE DRIVE: The road then swoops down, wheeling vulture-like around several more sharp bends to reach the Pont d'Arc.

03 Pont d'Arc

The Pont d'Arc is a natural rock arch over the Ardèche, created by more than 100,000 years of water erosion. What you can't see from the road is that there are caves inside the rock arch; if you have time, it's worth hiring a kayak and tackling one of the descents downriver.

To get out and see the Pont d'Arc up close, park at Parking Méandre, but know that it costs €0.80 every

15 minutes, so the cost quickly racks up! A cheaper way is to park up at the *gare routière* (bus station) in Vallon-Pont d'Arc and catch a free *navette* (shuttle bus) back to Pont d'Arc.

THE DRIVE: A straight road from the Pont d'Arc takes you to Vallon-Pont-d'Arc (all roads in Ardèche seem to lead to this rather nondescript town full of kayak rental outlets). From here, take the D579 up to Ruoms, followed by the D245 east to Labeaume (20 minutes from Vallon-Pont-d'Arc, or 18km). There's a free car park on the east side of town.

04 Labeaume

In Labeaume, the cobblestones seem to grow moss-like hair, and half-pint-sized artists' studios peep out of stone archways. Time your visit right (May, June or September) and the whole village is purple with blooming wisteria.

THE DRIVE: Double back the way you came to Ruoms, and turn left onto the D579 to Balazuc (13km).

05 Balazuc

Park up and head out on foot to explore the cobbled streets and covered walkways that cut through the buildings here. If you're sticking around for a few days, Balazuc, Labeaume and the other villages of the northern Ardèche also offer plenty of opportunities for wild swimming, kayaking and scenic bike rides. Much of the accommodation around here is in riverside campsites.

THE DRIVE: Leaving Balazuc on the D294, you'll cross the Ardèche River over a magnificent

Labeaume

THOMAS KLEE/SHUTTERSTOCK

VERA PETRUNINA/SHUTTERSTOCK

CARPOOL KARAOKE

Driving in France can be expensive. Although this particular route only has one toll (on the stretch of motorway that crosses the Viaduc de Millau), fuel costs in France are higher than the European average. Perhaps this is why the French-born car-sharing business Blablacar is so successful, with some 10 million journeys offered in France per year.

I've spent over 10 years using Blablacar as both a passenger and a driver, and I'm sure it has saved me thousands of euros. It works particularly well in parts of the country that are badly connected by trains, especially the *diagonale du vide* (empty diagonal), which is where the entire first part of this road trip, right up to Pézenas, falls. If you have spare seats in your car, efficiently using Blablacar can entirely offset your fuel and toll costs, and you might make some new friends along the way. I ended up staying with a fellow Blablacar passenger in Strasbourg after we got on so well during the journey! I've also met the likes of circus performers and musicians on journeys – even if you don't hit it off with your fellow passengers, you're guaranteed to arrive with a story to tell.

Mobicoop *(mobicoop.fr)* is a commission-free alternative to Blablacar (which takes a percentage of around 16% to 20% on each journey), but it doesn't have as many users, so it can be trickier to find rides or fill spare seats.

stone bridge dating from the late 19th century. After the bridge, carry on straight until you reach the D104. It's straightforward cruising south for the next stretch. The D104 becomes the D904: keep following it until Les Mages, to fork off right on the D59. The D59 becomes the D128 until La Grand-Combe, where a right on the N106 follows the river Le Gardon d'Alès all the way to St-Julien-des-Points, a journey of some 80km and just under two hours in total.

06 St-Julien-des-Points

So begins my favourite part of the trip.

There are two curiosities in St-Julien-des-Points. The first is an orthodox monastery, the home of Frères Jean and Joseph. The former was a fashion photographer in Paris, before becoming an orthodox monk and recipe book author. **Skite Sainte Foy** *(photo-frerejean.com)*, their home, looks like an exhibition space of Frère Jean's photography and the monks' elaborately embellished 'party' (liturgy) clothes. The vegetable garden is delightful, and visitors are welcome, provided you've been in touch and confirmed in advance.

The second is the kind of motorist's homestay that I'd have loved to include for every stop of every route in this book, but these sorts of places are red-diamond rare. Run by a couple of bikers, Alain and Nelly, **Le Relais du Motard Cévenol** is a cornucopia of beer mats, bumper stickers and motorbike paraphernalia. Meals are served at long tables with the owners and all the other guests, and Alain has a draught beer in your hand before you've even had a chance to remove your motorbike gloves.

THE DRIVE: The road that climbs up from St-Julien-des-Points, the D276, is a hairy one, with more zigzags than a heart-rate monitor, and the number of potholes might well have your heart rate matching the road map. Don't attempt it in bad weather or in winter; instead, take the less dramatic but altogether safer N106 east through the valley instead. If the weather is on your side, the D276 climbs and weaves and turns until it joins the D52, a much flatter route west along the plateau, although there are still several hairpin bends.

The D52 becomes the D35 and then the D998 all the way to Le Pont-de-Montvert, 34km from St-Julien-des-Points. Ironically, after the gnarly start to this stage, this is some of the smoothest, most relaxing driving on the route. Grazing cows and meadow flowers form most of the views, with plenty of rural *auberges* (country inns) serving as pit stops for cheese-heavy lunches.

07 Le Pont-de-Montvert

When you arrive at Le Pont-de-Montvert, a higgledy-piggledy stone village straddling the Tarn River, roughly an hour after setting off from St-Julien-des-Points, you may notice that your fellow pilgrims have come on a much slower mode of transport: donkey. Or, rather, on foot accompanied by a pack donkey. Le Pont-de-Montvert is a mid-point stop on the popular,

Balazuc (p27)
PROCHASSON FREDERIC/SHUTTERSTOCK

THE MAGIC OF THE WINDING ROAD

The Cévennes is probably the most intriguing part of France. How could I fail to be charmed by a region that many tourists choose to visit on foot with a pack donkey, walking in the footsteps of 19th-century author Robert Louis Stevenson along the 12-day Stevenson Trail (GR70)?

It's ironic, then, that it was hiking that inspired me to visit, yet it's become my favourite place for a road trip. Road trips, for me, aren't about covering huge distances. I can't think of anything worse than sitting in the car for eight hours at a time speeding along a poker-straight highway! I want to stop every hour or so in tiny little villages where a foreign tourist might as well be from another planet. I want the roads to wind and climb and plunge down again so that the scenery constantly stimulates me.

That's what happens here. The Gorges of the Tarn and the Ardèche are well-known, of course – you don't get this much nature on steroids without it attracting a fair few visitors. Similarly, the Étang de Thau is hardly under the radar, but you can still rock up on your motorbike at little oyster shacks down potholed tracks and eat to your heart's content without fear of spending your epic road trip in a traffic jam. This is France in discovery mode. Expect blank looks when you tell friends where you've been, which will just make you all the smugger.

12-day **Stevenson Trail**, which Robert Louis Stevenson undertook with his donkey Modestine in 1878.

THE DRIVE: Leaving Le Pont-de-Montvert behind, take the D35 when it forks off to your right and follow it for 15 minutes. Just before the village of Runes, there's a little car park and a waterfall signposted on your left. It's only 5km after Le Pont-de-Montvert.

08 Cascade de Runes

From the car park (free), it's a short but steep walk downhill, 600m or so, to reach a beautiful, 60m-high waterfall, **Cascade de Runes**, with a natural pool for (chilly) wild swimming at the bottom. I only put my feet in, and that was quite enough.

THE DRIVE: Continue straight on the D35, past Runes, until you come to a T-junction at the D31. Turn right here. At the D986, turn left before the road begins plunging down into the Gorges du Tarn. Here, the view risks sending your jaw down to meet the Tarn River 500m below while royal eagles and buzzards soar above. It's majestic.

I'd been before, but on the back seat of the motorbike I cried several times, not because of my partner's driving, but at the impossible beauty of it all.

09 Gorges du Tarn

The first town you arrive at in the Gorges du Tarn is medieval **Ste-Enimie**, 40km after Le Pont-de-Montvert. It has the bulk of restaurants, hotels, kayak rentals and tourist tat, but even elbow-to-elbow shops selling overpriced plush toys can't detract from the beauty of the place.

St-Chély-du-Tarn, 5km further along the D907BIS, has a mossy waterfall sprouting from the buildings in the cliff, which, even after part of the cliff eroded and fell into the Tarn in October 2025, is still one of the most scenic spots in the gorges. It's a great place for a swim, but beware the strong pull of the current, which can drag you downriver at quite a speed. There are very few accommodation options here, and they tend to get booked out well in advance in peak season.

If you're suffering from a case of saddle seat and you need to stretch your legs, I love this area for trail running. An excellent and surprisingly shady route runs downriver from the centre of the village: expect plenty of shingle climbs and descents.

La Malène, a further 9km from St-Chély-du-Tarn along the same, scenic riverside road, has a few more accommodation options, restaurants and pixie-like houses, with fewer knock-off key rings than Ste-Enimie. **Les Bateliers du Gorges du Tarn** (wooden punt boats) leave from here; these were once the only way to get across the river, or even from one village to another on the same bank.

Whichever town you choose, I recommend spending at least a night in the Gorges du Tarn. Many people just visit on a day trip, which means if you get up early enough, you can have these sublime views all to yourself.

THE DRIVE: Stay in the gorges, heading past other stone villages, including picturesque Mostuéjouls, which looks as though it's clinging to the cliff.

Cascade de Runes
JAMES1924/SHUTTERSTOCK

The road stays in the belly of the gorge, following the River Tarn for around an hour. All in all, it's around 60km entirely in the shadow of the precipitous cliffs that make up the Gorges du Tarn. At Aguessac, take the D29 right, very briefly, to join the A75, the *autoroute* (or motorway) for the first and last time on this trip. This is purely to pass over the Golden Gate–esqe bridge, Viaduc de Millau.

10 Viaduc de Millau

Viaduc de Millau is white rather than red, and it's actually significantly taller than its San Francisco counterpart. In fact, it was the tallest road bridge in the world until the Changtai Yangtze River Bridge in China stole its thunder in September 2025. Note that there's a toll to cross over the Viaduc de Millau, which costs €13.80 from mid-June to mid-September and €11.20 the rest of the year for a regular car.

THE DRIVE: Stay on the motorway south for approximately one hour, until you reach Cartels. It's only a 20-minute drive on the D148, followed by the D148E11, to reach Mourèze, your next stop, or 75km in total from the Viaduc de Millau. As the motorway heads south, the glimpses of the landscape that you'll see reveal a land of lost villages, which gradually flattens out into the vast plains of vineyards and lagoons making up a patchwork quilt until the Mediterranean Sea.

11 Mourèze

In Mourèze, towering rocks like termite hills create a landscape

Gorges du Tarn (p30)

St-Chély-du-Tarn, p30

BIKER GROVE

If you or your travel buddy has a motorbike licence, there's no better mode of transport for this route.

A helmet approved by the ECE (Economic Commission for Europe) is mandatory. Gloves are too, for both the driver and the passenger. If you're not wearing gloves, you might get a fine (but who wants to ride a motorcycle with no gloves – I would be freezing!). You also need to carry a hi-vis jacket (for both the driver and passenger) in your luggage. Headlights must always be on, even in the middle of the day.

You won't find many EV charging points in this neck of the woods. If you're renting a motorbike, **Good Motors** *(goodmotors.agency)* has outlets in several major French cities, including Avignon, where this trip starts and ends. Rentals are contactless; they are done through an application that gives you all the relevant security codes to unlock your bike and pick up your safety gear from locked garages.

You'll need a valid motorbike licence, to be over 21 and have held a driving licence for more than a year to be able to rent a bike. Licences from most countries are accepted, including the UK, US, Australia and New Zealand. Security deposits are pretty high, generally in the region of €1000. If you've got a French bank account, these tend to be in the form of an imprint of your card rather than debiting the amount, but from experience, it tends to get debited from foreign accounts, and generally takes a week or so from the end of the trip for the balance to be refunded.

♥ WHY I LOVE THIS TRIP

ANNA RICHARDS, WRITER

I love travelling around France by motorbike, and always choose the slow roads. There's nothing fun about speeding down the motorway: my partner can't hear the epic playlist I've put together, and you're going too fast to see the sights. And said sights on the motorway largely consist of toll bridges and the hard shoulder – not what you came on holiday to see.

We're also not big on city driving. Too much stop-start driving at traffic lights, too many fumes, too many Crit'Air rules (see p287 for more on that), and too much stress about leaving our rental bike when we go for lunch. Cities in France largely have wonderful public transport in the form of trams, the metro or buses. It's best to leave the car at a *parc relais* (park and ride) and make use of this.

What we seek out is the countryside. The wide open spaces, the scenery that lurches from prehistoric limestone gorges to saltwater lagoons, the views that leave your head and spirits vertiginous. Over cities, we choose little villages with one or two riverside *bistrots*, where you can dine alfresco and proudly admire the gleaming Royal Enfield Interceptor that we rent for aesthetics and not an ounce of practicality!

For the sake of honesty, I must confess to not driving the motorbike. I sit, a lady of leisure, on the back seat and blissfully take in the scenery and line up the tunes, claiming it gives me more headspace to take in all the details of our journeys and write about them. That may be true, but it's also because I have zero desire to drive a motorbike.

of limestone stalagmites, making for some excellent hiking.

THE DRIVE: Below the village, head back the way you came to Salasc, and then along the D148 and D156 for some 11km to Lac du Salagou.

12 Lac du Salagou

The Martian landscape of rust-red Lac du Salagou baffles. This reservoir was, in fact, human-made, formed by the construction of a dam in 1968. The bloody rocks and resulting red reflections in the water are due to iron ore in the soil. There are often flamingos in the lake: hire a pedalo or kayak at **Base de Plein Air du Salagou** *(basedusalagou.com)* and paddle across the otherworldly landscape to go and see them.

THE DRIVE: Follow the D156E4 southeast to Clermont-l'Hérault, to pick up the D609 all the way to Pézenas (27km).

13 Pézenas

Pézenas is the former hometown of the famous 17th-century French playwright Molière. All begonia-draped buildings, blue shutters and tight-packed Renaissance townhouses, it looks just like the setting for a Molière play – his 13 years here clearly inspired him. Pézenas is almost always lively with a *terrasse* culture to rival Paris, but it truly comes alive every Saturday morning, the town's market day. Marseille soaps, oysters and olive oil fill almost every cobbled street in town.

THE DRIVE: From here, it's a 30-minute drive (20km) along wide avenues of plane trees along the D613 to reach Le St Pierre Tarbouriech on the Étang de Thau.

14 Étang de Thau

Stop at **Le St Pierre Tarbouriech** *(tarbouriech-le-st-pierre-bouzigues.fr)* for oysters. This gorgeous, shack-like restaurant with a pontoon over the lagoon may look unassuming, but this is where many Michelin-starred restaurants source their oysters. Buy *tielle à la sétois* (octopus pies) to stash in the glove compartment for later.

The Étang de Thau, a 7500-hectare saltwater lagoon, is separated from the Mediterranean by a narrow spit of land with one road, and it's so vast it can be difficult to see the land at the other side. It's a lovely place to spend a couple of days if you have time.

THE DRIVE: Once you're ready to move on, or you've eaten your fill, take the D613 to Bouzigues, followed by the D600 past Sète. This way you can avoid the motorway, and take the D612 all the way to Montpellier. Sète to Montpellier via this route is 43km, and takes around 50 minutes. Be aware of Crit'Air rules in Montpellier; if your vehicle doesn't comply, use a

EPIC TRIP

Cave Dwelling

Step back in time some 37,000 years when the inhabitants of the Ardèche and Cévennes lived underground.

Radiocarbon dating at **Grotte Chauvet** (5km from Vallon-Pont-d'Arc) found that this particular cave may have been inhabited up to 37,000 years ago, meaning human habitation here long predates that in the famous Lascaux Cave in the Dordogne. For preservation reasons, it's not possible to visit the original site, but at the excellent replica **Grotte Chauvet 2** *(grottechauvet2ardeche.com)* next door guides walk you through all the remarkably detailed cave art. Here you'll learn how archaeologists have been able to identify which paintings were done by men and which by women, the rough ages of the artists, and even signatures and styles that allow them to see which works were done by the same artist. The paintings also provide an insight into the kind of wildlife that used to roam this area. Many of the paintings are of hunts, and show long extinct species: cave lions and cave bears, woolly mammoths and woolly rhinoceros. It's like seeing all of the characters of *Ice Age* brought to life on the walls.

Inhabitation in the caves didn't end in Palaeolithic times. The **Balmes de Montbrun**, 30 or so troglodyte caves carved into the rock face, were inhabited for some 1200 years, right up until the 1880s. They're half an hour north of Balazuc, and free to visit, with a little car park right by the entrance.

The Gorges du Tarn is home to many troglodytes, less frequented than their famous cousins in the Loire Valley, but no less charming. These hamlets seem to sprout out of the limestone cliffs, the stone buildings at one with their surroundings. You'll have to ditch the car to visit them: the troglodyte villages of **St-Marcellin** and **Eglazines** can only be reached on foot (park at Mostuéjouls). The reward is bird's-eye views over the gorges. Eglazines was inhabited right up until 1960, when its last resident, aged 80 at the time, abandoned the hamlet for the valley.

Since then, the Tarn's caves have been almost uninhabited, save for one hermit, who moved into the **Grotte des Battuts**, further southwest in Tarn, in the late 1980s. He stayed there for 25 years, until his death in 2014, and became known as the 'hermit of Penne'. Although he was living off-grid, he settled into the cave with a refrigerator (there was no electricity, so it simply served as a storage cupboard), a real bed and a wardrobe. After the hermit's death, a monumental cleanup job removed more than a tonne of rubbish to restore Grotte des Battuts to its natural state.

Eglazines

OLI HAZEL/SHUTTERSTOCK

parc relais and let the trams do the rest of the work for you.

15 Montpellier

A handsome student city with terracotta roofs, rainbow-coloured steps and trams that look as though they've been pasted in gaudy wrapping paper, Montpellier is incredibly liveable. It's worth spending at least a night here to explore some of the museums. **Musée Fabre** *(museefabre.fr)* has works by Monet, Manet and Matisse, among others, and the two **MO.CO** *(moco.art)* galleries, which belong to Montpellier's fine-arts school, have plenty of contemporary works.

For dinner, head to **Marché du Lez** *(marchedulez.com),* an ultra-cool street-food market in a car park, built in reclaimed agricultural buildings.

THE DRIVE: Drive south from Montpellier along the M66, past Montpellier's airport, to reach the Mediterranean Sea at Carnon. From here the D62 cuts through a narrow strip of land between the Étang de l'Or and the sea. Follow it until the D61 splits off to your left. Take this road north until it reaches the N113, which you can follow east all the way to Nîmes, a journey of around an hour over 56km.

16 Nîmes

The **amphitheatre** *(arenes-nimes.com)* in Nîmes, once the Roman city of Nemasus, is less frequented than the better-known amphitheatre in neighbouring Arles. There's also a wonderful urban park, **Les Jardins de la Fontaine**, which meshes almost two millennia of history, with Roman temples and classical, 18th-century sculptures. It's a short walk from here to the UNESCO-listed Roman temple, **La Maison Carrée** *(lamaisoncarredenimes.fr).*

I'm always baffled not to see more tourists in Nîmes. It has some of the most impressive Roman sites in the country, and it's cheap to stay in the city centre, yet it stays delightfully quiet.

THE DRIVE: Barely 31km north, the D979 followed by the D981 east takes you to Pont du Gard.

17 Pont du Gard

The **Pont du Gard** *(pontdugard.fr),* a three-tier Roman aqueduct with 52 arches, is in remarkably good nick for its 2000 years standing. There are car parks on both sides of the river, with the closest to this route being Parking Rive Gauche, which costs €9 no matter the season. Walk down to the river bank to swim right under the Pont du Gard, or rent a kayak from nearby **Collias** or **Remoulins** to paddle under it.

THE DRIVE: Once you're done, pick up the N100 from Remoulins, the town just east of Pont du Gard. It's the quickest way back to Avignon, where you began the trip, a 27km relatively straight road, taking just 30 minutes to the city centre.

Marché du Lez

RIEGER BERTRAND/HEMIS/ALAMY

Place du Marche
SAUF
MARCHÉ DU LEZ
SYNERG-IN

02

EPIC TRIPS

ESSENTIAL FRANCE

★ BEST FOR

FAMILIES

Braving the space-age rides and roller-coaster thrills of Futuroscope.

Place du Tertre

DURATION: 3 WEEKS

DISTANCE: 3060KM / 1902 MILES

GREAT FOR: FAMILIES, HISTORY & CULTURE, NATURE

BEST TIME TO GO: APRIL TO JUNE, FOR SUNNY WEATHER, LONGER DAYS AND FLOWERS.

This is the big one: an epic journey that travels all the way from the chilly waters of the English Channel to the gleaming blue Mediterranean. Along the way, you'll stop off at some of France's most iconic sights: the château of Versailles, the abbey of Mont St-Michel, the summit of Mont Blanc and the beaches of the French Riviera. *Allez-y!*

LINK YOUR TRIP

18 Alpine Adventure
Chamonix features on our Alps trip, so it's easy to launch a cross-mountain adventure from there.

24 Riviera Crossing
Combine this journey with a jaunt down the French Riviera, beginning in Cannes.

01 Paris

For that essentially Parisian experience, it's hard to beat Montmartre, the neighbourhood of cobbled lanes and cafe-lined squares beloved by writers and painters since the 19th century. This was once a notoriously ramshackle part of Paris, full of bordellos, brothels, dance halls and bars, as well as the city's first can-can clubs. Though its hedonistic heyday has long since passed, Montmartre still retains a villagey charm, despite the throngs of tourists.

The centre of Montmartre is **place du Tertre**, once the village's main square, now packed with buskers and portrait artists. You can get a sense of how the area would once have looked at the **Musée de Montmartre** *(museedemontmartre.fr)*, which details the area's bohemian past.

Nearby, Montmartre's finest view unfolds from the dome of

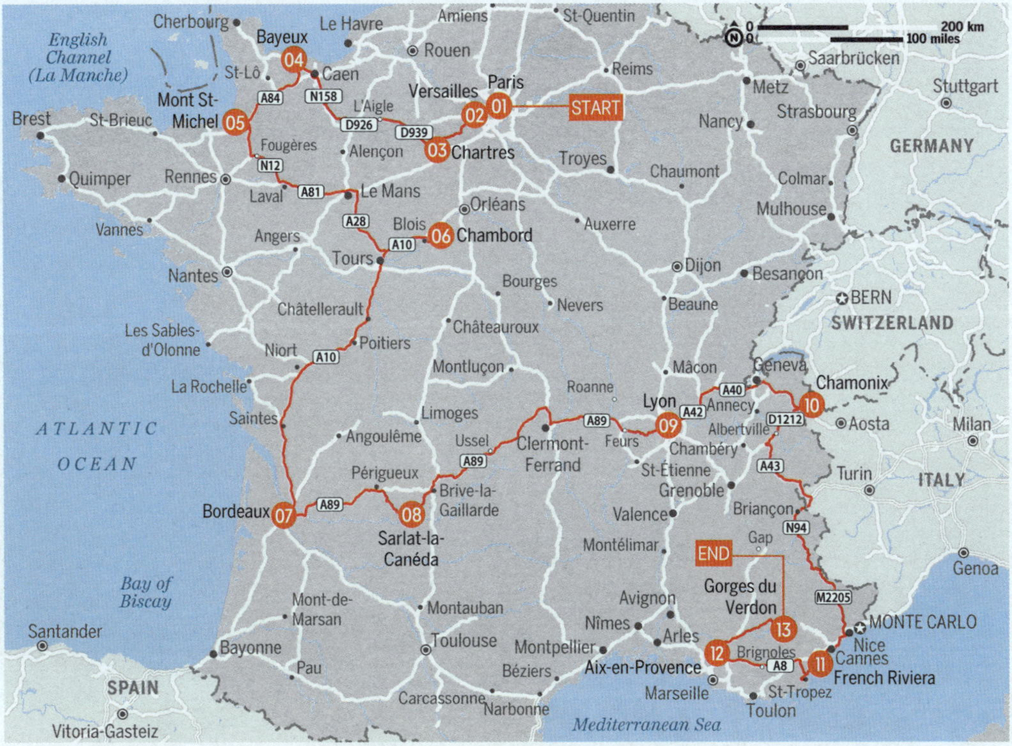

ANAMARIA MEJIA/SHUTTERSTOCK

the **Basilique du Sacré-Cœur** *(sacre-coeur-montmartre.com)*. On a clear day, you can see for up to 30km away.

It's a legal requirement to display a Crit'Air sticker on your car when driving in central Paris's low emission zone. Only cars with a Crit'Air 1 or 2 are allowed to drive here; everyone else risks a fine.

THE DRIVE: From the centre of Paris, follow the A13 west from Porte d'Auteuil and take the exit marked 'Versailles Château'. Versailles is 28km southwest of the city.

02 Versailles

Louis XIV transformed his father's hunting lodge into the **Château de Versailles** *(chateauversailles.fr)* in the mid-17th century, and it remains France's most majestic palace. The royal court was based here from 1682 until 1789, when revolutionaries massacred the palace guard and dragged Louis XVI and Marie Antoinette back to Paris, where they were ingloriously guillotined.

The architecture is truly eye-popping. Highlights include the **Grands Appartements du Roi et de la Reine** (State Apartments) and the famous **Galerie des Glaces** (Hall of Mirrors), a 75m-long ballroom filled with chandeliers and floor-to-ceiling mirrors. Outside, the vast park incorporates terraces, flower beds, paths and fountains, as well as the **Grand and Petit Canals**.

Northwest of the main palace is the **Domaine de Trianon** (Trianon Estate; *chateauversailles.fr*), where the royal family would have taken refuge from the intrigue and etiquette of court life.

THE DRIVE: The N10 runs southwest from Versailles through pleasant countryside and forest to Rambouillet. You'll join the D906 to Chartres. All told, it's a journey of 76km.

03 Chartres

You'll know you're nearing Chartres long before you reach it thanks to the twin spires of the **Cathédrale Notre Dame** *(cathedrale-chartres.org)*, considered to be one of the most important structures in Christendom.

PHOTO OPPORTUNITY

Overlooking the Parisian panorama from the Basilique du Sacré-Cœur.

The present cathedral was built during the late 12th century after the original was destroyed by fire. It has survived wars and revolutions remarkably intact, and the brilliant-blue stained-glass windows have even inspired their own shade of paint (Chartres blue). The cathedral also houses the **Sainte Voile** (Holy Veil), supposedly worn by the Virgin Mary while giving birth to Jesus.

The best views are from the 112m-high **Clocher Neuf** (North Tower).

THE DRIVE: Follow the D939 northwest for 58km to Verneuil-sur-Avre, then take the D926 west for 78km to Argentan – both great roads through typical Norman countryside. Just west of Argentan, the D158/N158 heads north to Caen, then turns northwest on the N13 to Bayeux, 94km further.

04 Bayeux

The **Bayeux Tapestry** (La Tapisserie de Bayeux; *bayeux museum.com*) is without doubt the world's most celebrated (and ambitious) piece of embroidery. Comprising over 58 panels, the tapestry recounts the invasion of England in 1066 by William I, or William the Conqueror, as he's now known.

Commissioned in 1077 by Bishop Odo of Bayeux, William's half-brother, the tapestry retells the battle in fascinating detail: look out for Norman horses getting stuck in the quicksands around Mont St-Michel, and the famous appearance of Halley's Comet in scene 32. The final showdown at the Battle of Hastings is particularly graphic, complete with severed limbs, decapitated heads, and the English King Harold getting an arrow in the eye.

The view from the Basilique du Sacré-Cœur (p39)
JOANNA URWIN PHOTOGRAPHY/SHUTTERSTOCK

ANNABARANOVA/SHUTTERSTOCK

Château de Versailles (p39)

VISITING VERSAILLES

Versailles is one of the country's most popular destinations, so planning ahead will make your visit more enjoyable. Avoid the busiest days of Tuesday and Sunday, and remember that the château is closed on Monday. Save time by pre-purchasing tickets on the château website, or arrive early if you're buying at the door – by noon queues spiral out of control.

You can also access off-limits areas (such as the Private Apartments of Louis XV and Louis XVI, the Opera House and the Royal Chapel) by taking a 1½-hour **guided tour** *(chateauversailles.fr)*.

THE DRIVE: Mont St-Michel is 125km southwest of Bayeux; the fastest route is along the D6 and then the A84 motorway.

05 Mont St-Michel

You've already seen it on a million postcards, but nothing prepares you for the real **Mont St-Michel** *(abbaye-mont-saint-michel.fr/en)*. It's one of France's architectural marvels, an 11th-century island abbey marooned in the middle of a vast bay.

When you arrive, you'll be steered into one of the Mont's huge car parks. You then walk along the causeway (or catch a free shuttle bus) to the island itself. Guided tours are included, or you can explore solo with an audio guide.

The **Église Abbatiale** (Abbey Church) is reached via a steep climb along the **Grande Rue**. Around the church, the cluster of buildings known as **La Merveille** (The Marvel) includes the cloister, refectory, guest hall, ambulatory and various chapels.

For a different perspective, take a guided walk across the sands with **Découverte de la Baie du Mont-Saint-Michel** *(decouvertebaie.com)* or **Chemins de la Baie** *(cheminsdelabaie.com)*, both based in Genêts. Don't be tempted to do it on your own – the bay's tides are notoriously treacherous.

THE DRIVE: Take the A84, N12 and A81 for 190km to Le Mans and the A28 for 102km to Tours, where you can follow a tour through the Loire Valley if you wish. Chambord is about 75km from Tours via the D952.

06 Chambord

If you only have time to visit one château in the Loire, you might as well make it the grandest – and **Chambord** *(chambord.org)* is the most lavish of them all. It's a showpiece of Renaissance architecture, from the double-helix staircase up to the turret-covered rooftop. With 426 rooms, the sheer scale of the place is mindboggling – and in the Loire, that's really saying something. If you have time, detour to the richly furnished and very elegant **Château de Chenonceau** *(chenonceau.com)*.

THE DRIVE: It's 425km to Bordeaux via Blois and the A10 motorway. You could consider breaking the journey with stop-offs at Futuroscope and Poitiers, roughly halfway between the two.

07 Bordeaux

When UNESCO decided to protect Bordeaux' medieval architecture in 2007, it simply listed half the city in one fell swoop. Covering 18 sq km, this is the world's largest urban World Heritage Site, with grand buildings and architectural treasures galore.

Top of the heap is the **Cathédrale St-André** *(cathedrale-bordeaux.fr)*, known for its stone carvings and generously gargoyled belfry, the **Tour Pey Berland** *(pey-berland.fr)*. But the whole old city rewards wandering, especially around the **Jardin Public**, the pretty squares of **esplanade des Quinconces** and **place Gambetta**, and the city's 4km-long **riverfront esplanade**, with its playgrounds, paths and paddling pools. There's also the superb **La Cité du Vin** *(laciteduvin.com)*, a must-see for wine lovers.

THE DRIVE: It's a 194km drive to Sarlat-la-Canéda via the A89 motorway, or you can take a longer but more enjoyable route via the D936.

FUTUROSCOPE

Halfway between Chambord and Bordeaux on the A10, and 10km north of Poitiers, **Futuroscope** *(futuroscope.com)* is one of France's top theme parks. It's a futuristic experience that takes you whizzing through space, diving into the ocean depths, racing around city streets and on a close encounter with creatures of the future. Note that many rides require a minimum height of 120cm.

You'll need at least five hours to check out the major attractions, or two days to see everything. The park is in the suburb of Jaunay-Clan; take exit 28 off the A10.

08 Sarlat-la-Canéda

If you're looking for France's heart and soul, you'll find it among the forests and fields of the Dordogne. It's the stuff of French fantasies: riverbank châteaux, medieval villages, wooden-hulled *gabarres* (flat-bottomed barges) and market stalls groaning with truffles, walnuts and wines. The town of **Sarlat-la-Canéda** makes the perfect base, with a beautiful medieval centre and lots of lively markets.

It's also ideally placed for exploring the Vézère Valley, about 20km to the northwest, home to France's finest cave paintings. Most famous of all are the ones at the **Grotte de Lascaux**, although to prevent damage to the paintings, you now visit a replica of the cave's main sections in a nearby **grotto** *(lascaux.fr)*.

THE DRIVE: The drive east to Lyon is a long one, covering well over 400km and travelling across the spine of the Massif Central. A good route is to follow the A89 all the way to exit 6, then turn off onto the N89/D89 to Lyon. This route should cover between 420km and 430km.

09 Lyon

Fired up by French food? Then you'll love Lyon, with its *bouchons* (small bistros), bustling markets and fascinating food culture. Start in Lyon's picturesque 1st *arrondissement* before crossing the river to **Vieux Lyon** to catch the funicular to the top of **Fourvière** to explore the city's Roman ruins and enjoy cross-town views.

Film buffs will also want to make time for the **Musée Lumière** *(institut-lumiere.org)*, where the

EQROY/SHUTTERSTOCK

Gare du Montenvers

Lumière Brothers (Auguste and Louis) shot the first reels of the world's first motion picture, *La Sortie de l'Usine Lumière à Lyon,* on 19 March 1895.

THE DRIVE: Take the A42 towards Lake Geneva, then the A40 towards St-Gervais-les-Bains. The motorway becomes the N205 as it nears Chamonix. It's a drive of at least 225km.

10 Chamonix

Snuggling among snow-clad mountains – including Europe's highest summit, Mont Blanc – adrenaline-fuelled Chamonix is an ideal springboard for the French Alps. In winter, it draws skiers and snowboarders, and in summer, once the snows thaw, the high-level trails become a trekkers' paradise.

There are two really essential Chamonix experiences. First, catch the dizzying cable car to the top of the **Aiguille du Midi** to snap a shot of Mont Blanc.

Then take the combination mountain train and cable car from the **Gare du Montenvers** *(montenvers train.com)* to the **Mer de Glace** (Sea of Ice), France's largest glacier. Wrap up warmly if you want to visit the glacier's sculptures and ice caves.

THE DRIVE: The drive to the Riviera is full of scenic thrills. An attractive route is via the D1212 to Albertville, and then via the A43, which travels over the Italian border and through the Tunnel de Fréjus. From here, the N94 runs through Briançon, and a combination of the A51, N85 and D6085 carries you south to Nice. You'll cover at least 430km.

11 French Riviera

If there's one coast road in France you simply have to drive, it's the French Riviera, with its rocky cliffs, maquis-scented air and dazzling Mediterranean views. Sun-seekers have been flocking here since the 19th century, and its scenery still never fails to seduce.

Lively **Nice** and cinematic **Cannes** make natural starts, but for the Riviera's loveliest scenery, you'll want to drive down the gorgeous **Corniche de l'Estérel** to **St-Tropez**, still a watchword for seaside glamour. Crowds can make summer hellish, but come in spring or autumn and you'll have its winding lanes and fragrant hills practically to yourself.

♥ WHY I LOVE THIS TRIP

OLIVER BERRY, WRITER

It's epic in every sense: in scale, views, time and geography. This once-in-a-lifetime journey covers France from every possible angle: top to bottom, east to west, city and village, old-fashioned and modern, coast and countryside. It links together many of the country's truly unmissable highlights, and by the end you'll genuinely be able to say you've seen the heart and soul of France.

For maximum views, stick to the coast roads: the D6098 to Antibes and Cannes, the D559 around the Corniche de l'Estérel and the D98A to St-Tropez. It's about 120km via this route.

THE DRIVE: From St-Tropez, take the fast A8 for about 125km west to Aix-en-Provence.

12 Aix-en-Provence

Sleepy Provence sums up the essence of *la douce vie* (the sweet life). Cloaked in lavender and spotted with hilltop villages, it's a region that encompasses everything that's good about France.

Cruising the back roads and browsing the markets are the best ways to get acquainted with the region. Artistic **Aix-en-Provence** encapsulates the classic Provençal vibe, with its pastel buildings and Cézanne connections, while **Mont Ste-Victoire**, to the east, makes for a superb outing.

THE DRIVE: The gorges are 140km northeast of Aix-en-Provence, via the A51 and D952.

13 Gorges du Verdon

Complete your cross-France adventure with an unforgettable expedition to the Gorges du Verdon – sometimes known as the Grand Canyon of Europe. This deep ravine slashes 25km through the plateaux of Haute-Provence; in places, its walls rise to a dizzying 700m, twice the height of the Eiffel Tower (330m).

The two main jumping-off points are the villages of **Moustiers-Ste-Marie**, in the west, and **Castellane**, in the east. Drivers and bikers can take in the canyon panorama from two vertigo-inducing cliffside roads, but the base of the gorge is only accessible on foot or by raft.

Mont Ste-Victoire

MAJONIT/SHUTTERSTOCK

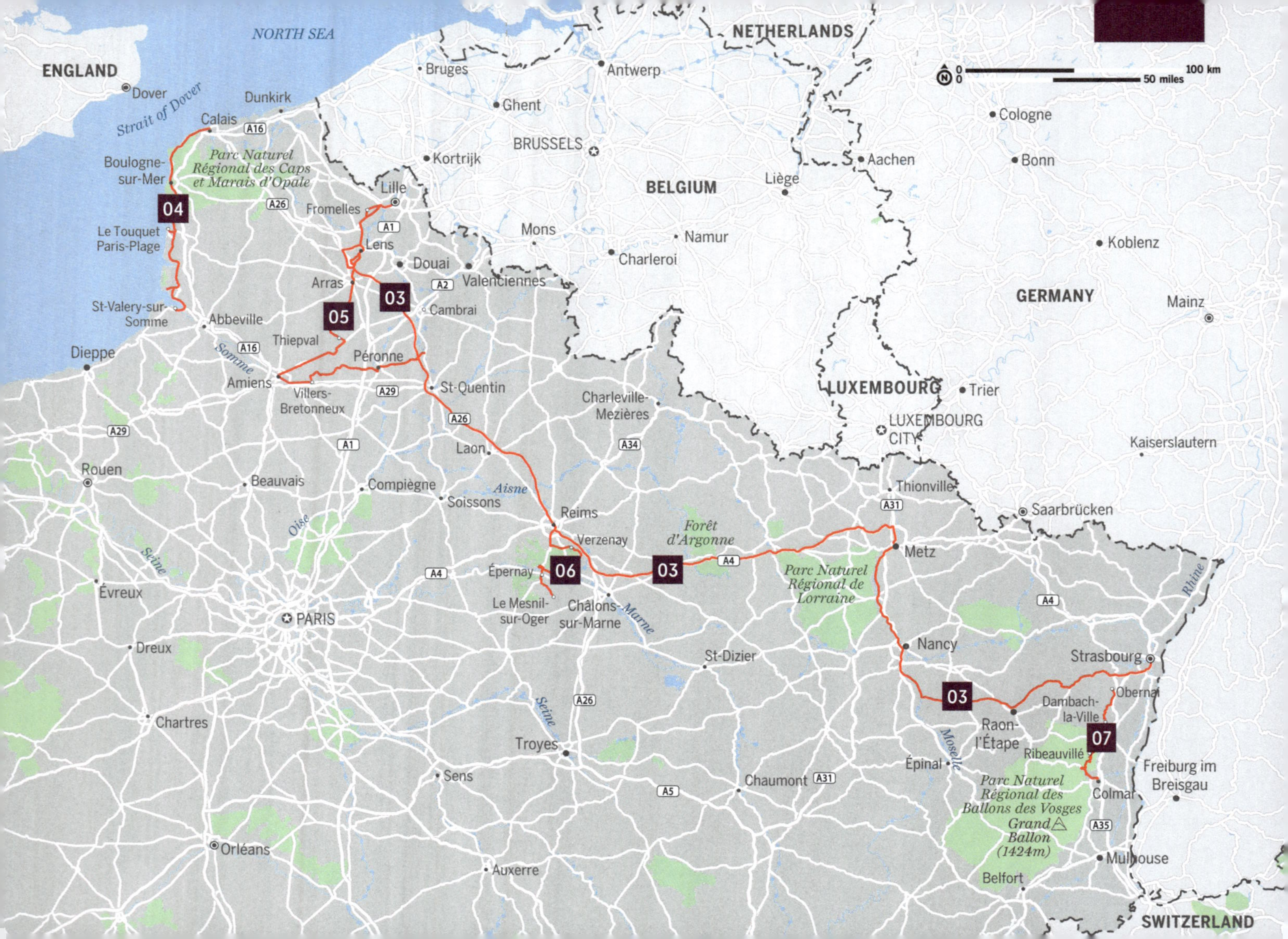

ENGLAND
NORTH SEA
NETHERLANDS
BELGIUM
LUXEMBOURG
GERMANY
SWITZERLAND
0 50 miles
0 100 km
Dover
Strait of Dover
Calais
Dunkirk
Boulogne-sur-Mer
Le Touquet Paris-Plage
St-Valery-sur-Somme
Parc Naturel Régional des Caps et Marais d'Opale
Bruges
Antwerp
Ghent
Kortrijk
BRUSSELS
Lille
Fromelles
Lens
Douai
Arras
Valenciennes
Cambrai
Mons
Namur
Charleroi
Liège
Aachen
Cologne
Bonn
Koblenz
Mainz
Trier
LUXEMBOURG CITY
Kaiserslautern
Saarbrücken
Thionville
Abbeville
Thiepval
Péronne
Amiens
Villers-Bretonneux
Somme
Dieppe
St-Quentin
Charleville-Mezières
Laon
Rouen
Beauvais
Compiègne
Soissons
Aisne
Oise
Reims
Verzenay
Forêt d'Argonne
Épernay
Le Mesnil-sur-Oger
Châlons-sur-Marne
Marne
Metz
Parc Naturel Régional de Lorraine
Nancy
Strasbourg
Rhine
Obernai
Dambach-la-Ville
Raon-l'Étape
Ribeauvillé
Colmar
Épinal
Moselle
Parc Naturel Régional des Ballons des Vosges
Grand Ballon (1424m)
Freiburg im Breisgau
Mulhouse
Belfort
Évreux
PARIS
Seine
Dreux
Chartres
St-Dizier
Troyes
Sens
Chaumont
Orléans
Auxerre
A16
A26
A1
A2
A29
A26
A34
A31
A4
A5
A35
03
04
05
06
07

Petite Place (p63), Arras

PARIS & NORTHEASTERN FRANCE

EXPLORE

PARIS & NORTH-EASTERN FRANCE

Northeastern France is a driver's dream – a memorable mix of wineries, ancient towns, art galleries and countryside that overflows with beauty, culture and historical significance. These gently paced trips take you through the vineyards and medieval cathedrals of Champagne, the tragic WWI battlefields and serene countryside of Flanders, the forested hills and Franco-Germanic *winstubs* (wine bistros) of Alsace and the artistic essentials of cities such as Nancy and Metz. Throw in some time spent strolling the storied attractions of Paris, and you've got the blueprint for a perfect France holiday in this richly rewarding region.

Paris

The French capital, obviously a world-class destination in its own right, is also a natural gateway to the northeast. Paris is served by France's largest international airport, Charles de Gaulle (CDG), which connects to destinations throughout the world and is just an hour from central Paris on the RER (train). Short-haul, budget and domestic flights may use Orly or Beauvais-Tillé Airports, 16km and 80km distant from the capital, respectively. Linked to the UK and Belgium by the Eurostar, Paris is also well served by Eurail and domestic trains. All the major car-rental firms have offices here, both at the airport and at the Gare du Nord train station. There's abundant accommodation in every price bracket (you can even choose to camp not that far from the city centre), plus supermarkets at which to get supplies.

Strasbourg

The Alsatian capital is served by Strasbourg International Airport, which connects to over 35 destinations across France, Europe and North Africa. The handsome Gare Centrale receives TGV and SNCF trains from Paris, Lyon, Lille, Nancy, Metz, towns on the Route des Vins d'Alsace (Alsace Wine Route) and other destinations. Car hire can also be found at the station, and accommodation and supply options are plentiful.

Reims

One of the major centres of the Champagne wine region, regal

WHEN TO GO

The region is at its sun-soaked best during late spring (May and June). Popular centres such as Lille, Reims, Metz and Arras can be hot and busy during the summer school holidays. Cold winters bring the consolation of Christmas markets, while the early spring and autumn months are the best times to travel without a crowd.

Reims makes an ideal base for the 'A Toast to Art' and 'Champagne Taster' drives. Connected to Paris by the high-speed TGV (45 minutes) or the slower SNCF (1½ hours), and Lille via Charleville-Mézières, it has a handful of car-rental agencies at the train station, plus plentiful accommodation options and places at which to stock up for your trip, including large supermarkets on the outer edge of town.

Metz

This thriving city in Lorraine is situated at the heart of the 'Toast to Art' route and within easy striking distance of 'Alsace Accents'. Served by the high-speed TGV line between Luxembourg and Paris, it's also easily accessible from Strasbourg and Nancy. Accommodation offerings, primarily chain hotels (with parking), are dotted around the old city perimeter. Car-hire options near the train station and grocery stores are easily found.

Lille

Handy for the 'Northern Coast', 'A Toast to Art' and 'In Flanders Fields' routes, the cultural powerhouse of Lille is served by the Aéroport de Lille, flying to domestic and southern European destinations. The city's main train stations, Gare Lille-Flandres and Gare Lille-Europe, connect it to London, Brussels and Paris via the Eurostar. It also boasts the best accommodation in the region, alongside ample car-hire and grocery suppliers.

TRANSPORT

The TGV (gleaming, high-speed trains) connects Lille with Brussels, Paris and Charles de Gaulle airport. The Eurostar also reaches London. Calais (also on the Eurostar line) is a major ferry port, receiving around 50 car ferries per day from Dover in the UK, and Le Shuttle (the Eurotunnel cars train) disembarks here.

NOTE: A Crit'Air sticker is required in Lille, Reims, Nancy and Strasbourg. See p287 for more details.

WHERE TO STAY

On the Route des Vins d'Alsace, **Villa Élyane** in Colmar is a charming, five-room B&B occupying a 19th-century villa with original art nouveau features. **Hôtel L'Arbre Voyageur** is a design hotel near Lille-Flandres station that makes creative use of the former Polish consulate building. In the village Villers-Allerand, just outside Reims, **La Bastide Champenoise** is an ideal stay for families. The renovated farmhouse has large beautifully decorated rooms and a lush garden with a BBQ. **Hôtel Marotte** in Amiens offers 12 boutique rooms across two buildings and is ideal for exploring the Cathédrale Notre Dame and the nearby Somme battlefields.

RESOURCES

Michelin Guide
An excellent place to research both fine dining and more rustic eating options along your route. *guide.michelin.com*

The Man in Seat 61
Everything to do with train travel. *seat61.com*

Lost in Cheeseland
For more on Paris life, check out this site by American Francophile Lindsey Tramuta. *lindseytramuta.com*

WHAT'S ON

La Champagne en Fête
The bubbly flows over three days in July or August at Épernay, the self-proclaimed capital of the world's most famous wine region.

La Grande Braderie de Lille
This is billed as the world's largest *marché aux puces* (flea market), filling Lille's charming streets in early September.

Marché de Noël
This Christmas market is held from November to 31 December in the lovely vineyard-wrapped Alsatian village of Colmar.

03

PARIS & NORTH-EASTERN FRANCE

A TOAST TO ART

★ BEST FOR

SHOPPING

Strasbourg's old quarters for chocolate, glassware and other souvenirs.

Palais des Beaux Arts, Lille

DURATION: 7 DAYS

DISTANCE: 650KM / 404 MILES

GREAT FOR: HISTORY & CULTURE

BEST TIME TO GO: APRIL TO JULY (AVOID THE SCHOOL-HOLIDAY CROWDS).

France's northeast is one of the country's most artistic corners, thanks to the arrival of high-profile addresses like the Louvre-Lens and Metz' Centre Pompidou. But these glitzy contemporary museums are simply the continuation of a long artistic legacy. This high-culture tour takes in Gothic cathedrals, neoclassical squares, chic crystalware and art nouveau mansions – not to mention some of Europe's most experimental art.

LINK YOUR TRIP

05 In Flanders Fields
WWI battlefields are covered in this emotional tour; looping back at the end to Lille makes an ideal combo with this trip.

07 Alsace Accents
To extend your journey, pick up the Route des Vins d'Alsace after ending this trip in Strasbourg.

01 Lille

Lille may be France's most underrated major city. In recent decades, this once-grimy industrial metropolis has morphed into a glittering and self-confident cultural and commercial hub – and a key shopping, art and culture stop with an attractive old town and a trio of renowned art museums.

Classic works find a home at the **Palais des Beaux Arts** (Fine Arts Museum; *pba-lille.fr*), an illustrious fine-arts museum with a first-rate collection of 15th- to 20th-century paintings, including works by Rubens, Van Dyck and Manet.

Contrast these with the playful – and sometimes just plain weird – works on show at the **Musée d'Art Moderne** *(musee-lam.fr)*. Big names including Braque, Calder, Léger, Miró, Modigliani and Picasso are the main draws. It's in Villeneuve-d'Ascq, 9km east of Gare Lille-Europe.

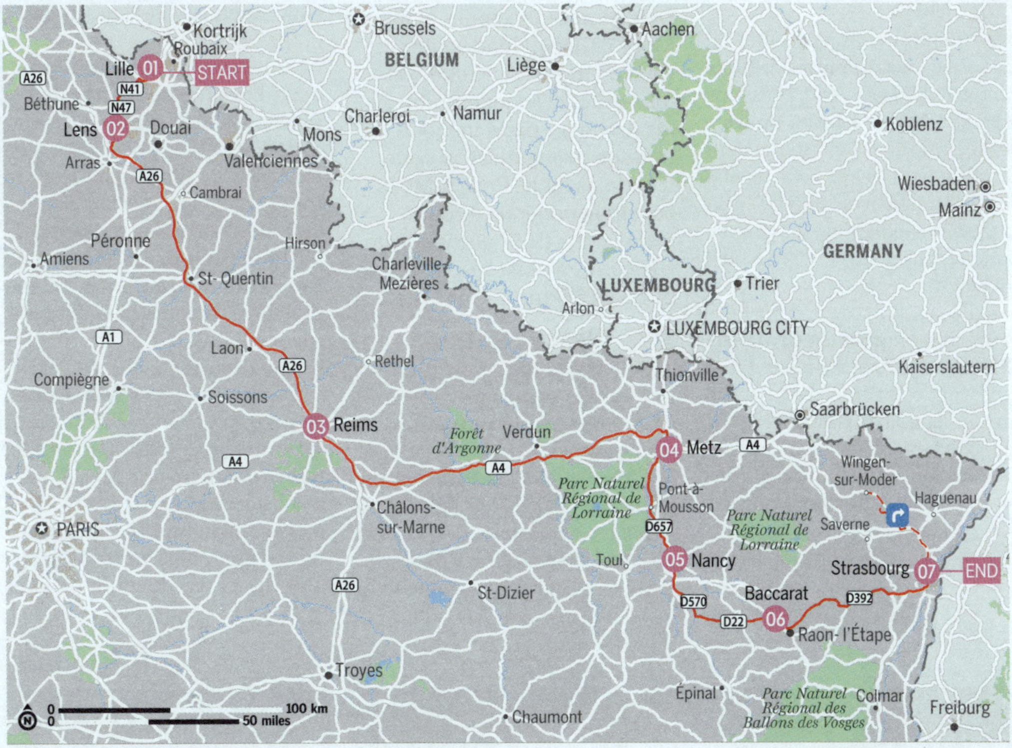

MISTERSTOCK/SHUTTERSTOCK

A few kilometres north at **La Piscine Musée d'Art et d'Industrie** *(roubaix-lapiscine.com),* the building is almost as intriguing as the art: a glorious art deco swimming pool has been beautifully converted into a cutting-edge gallery, showing contemporary paintings and sculptures.

THE DRIVE: The quickest route to Lens is via the A1, but a less hectic route takes the N41 and N47. It's a 37km drive from the outskirts of Lille.

02 Lens

A coal-mining town might not seem like the most obvious place to continue your investigation of French art, but *au contraire.* The jewel in the crown of industrial Lens is the **Louvre-Lens** *(louvrelens.fr).* An offshoot of the Paris original, this innovative gallery showcases treasures from Paris' venerable Musée du Louvre in state-of-the-art exhibition spaces. The centrepiece, the 120m-long Galerie du Temps, displays a semi-permanent collection of judiciously chosen objects – some of them true masterpieces – from the dawn of civilisation to the mid-1800s.

THE DRIVE: Follow the N17 south of town and join the A26 toll road for 178km to Reims, about a two- to 2½-hour drive away.

03 Reims

Along with its towering Gothic cathedral and Champagne connections, Reims is also worth visiting for its splendid **Musée des Beaux-Arts** *(musees-reims.fr),* located inside an 18th-century abbey. Highlights include 27 works by Camille Corot (only the Louvre has more), 13 portraits by German Renaissance painters Cranach the Elder and Younger, lots of Barbizon School landscapes, and two works each by Monet, Gauguin and Pissarro. But its most celebrated possession is probably Jacques-Louis David's world-famous *The Death of Marat,* depicting the Revolutionary leader's bloody, just-murdered corpse in the bathtub. It's one of only four known versions of the painting in the world.

THE DRIVE: Metz is 192km east of Reims via the A4 toll road, another two-hour drive.

04 Metz

The swoopy, spaceship facade of the **Centre Pompidou-Metz** *(centrepompidou-metz.fr)* fronts one of France's boldest galleries. Drawing on the Pompidou's fantastic modern art collection, it has gained a reputation for ambitious exhibitions, such as the one spotlighting the graphic works of American conceptual artist Sol LeWitt.

While you're in town, don't miss Metz' amazing **Cathédrale St-Étienne** *(cathedrale-metz.fr)*, a lacy wonder lit by kaleidoscopic curtains of stained glass. It's known as 'God's lantern' for good reason – look out for the technicolour windows created by the visionary artist Marc Chagall.

THE DRIVE: The most scenic option to Nancy is the D657, which tracks the banks of the Moselle River. Head southwest on the A31 toll road, then take exit 30a (signed to Jouy les Arches). Follow the road through rolling Alsatian countryside as far as Pont-à-Mousson, then continue through town on the D657 all the way to Nancy. It's a point-to-point drive of about 65km.

05 Nancy

Home of the art nouveau movement, Nancy has an air of grace and refinement that's all its own. Start your art appreciation at the **Musée de l'École de Nancy** (School of Nancy Museum; *musee-ecole-de-nancy.nancy.fr*), an art nouveau showpiece of dreamy interiors and curvy glass, housed in a 19th-century villa 2km southwest of the centre.

Next, head into the city's heart, magnificent **place Stanislas**, a vast neoclassical square that's now a UNESCO World Heritage Site. Designed by Emmanuel Héré in the 1750s, it's encircled by glorious buildings, including the **Hôtel de Ville** and **Opéra National de Lorraine** *(opera-nancy.fr)*, and contains a treasure trove of statues, rococo fountains and wrought-iron gateways. On one side of the square is the city's **Musée des Beaux-Arts** *(musee-des-beaux-arts.nancy.fr)*, where Caravaggio, Rubens, Picasso and Monet hang alongside works by Lorraine-born artists, including the dreamlike landscapes of Claude Lorrain and the pared-down designs of

Place Stanislas, Nancy

PETE STUART/SHUTTERSTOCK

Nancy-born architect Jean Prouvé (1901–84).

On nearby Grand Rue, the regal Renaissance Palais Ducal was once home to the dukes of Lorraine. It's now the **Musée Lorrain** *(musee-lorrain.nancy.fr)*, with a rich fine-art and history collection, including medieval statuary and faience (glazed pottery). The museum was closed for renovations at the time of research, though the church inside remains open.

THE DRIVE: Head south from Nancy on the main A330 toll road. Take exit 7, signed to Flavigny-sur-Moselle, which will take you onto the rural riverside D570. Stay on this road all the way to Bayon, then cross the river through town, following the D22 east through quiet countryside to Baccarat. It's a drive of 78km.

06 Baccarat

The glitzy glassware of Baccarat was considered the height of sophistication in 18th-century France, and its exquisite crystal could be found gracing mansions and châteaux all over Europe. The **Musée Baccarat** *(baccarat.fr)* displays 1100 pieces, and the boutique out front is almost as dazzling as the museum. Nearby crystal shops sell lesser, and less expensive, brands.

Glass aficionados will also want to stroll across the River Meurthe to the 1950s-built **Église St-Rémy**, whose austere facade conceals a blindingly bright interior containing 20,000 Baccarat panels.

THE DRIVE: Take the D590 southeast to Raon-l'Étape, then turn northeast on the D392A, a lovely back road that winds up through woodland and mountains, offering great views of the Vosges en route. Eventually you'll link up with the D1420, which will take you on to Strasbourg. It's a good two-hour drive of about 100km.

07 Strasbourg

Finish with a couple of days exploring the architectural splendour of Strasbourg and visiting the **Musée d'Art Moderne et Contemporain** (MAMCS; *musees.strasbourg.eu*), a striking glass-and-steel cube showcasing fine art, graphics and photography. The art is defiantly modern: Kandinsky, Picasso, Magritte and Monet canvases can all be found here, alongside curvaceous works by Strasbourg-born abstract artist Jean Arp.

Afterwards, have a good wander around **Grande Île**, Strasbourg's historic and UNESCO-listed old quarter, as well as **Petite France**, the canal district.

> ☑ TOP TIP
>
> ### STRASBOURG CENT SAVERS
>
> The **Strasbourg Pass Musées** *(musees.strasbourg.eu)* covers admission to all of Strasbourg's museums; buy it at the museums. Alternatively, the three-day **Strasbourg Pass** includes one museum, a trip up to the 66m-high viewing platform at the city's cathedral platform, and a boat tour.

DETOUR

Musée Lalique

Start: 07 Strasbourg

René Lalique was one of the great figures of the art nouveau movement, and the **Musée Lalique** *(musee-lalique.com)* provides a fitting tribute to his talents.

At home on the site of the old Hochberg glassworks, this museum investigates Lalique's fascination with naturalistic forms (especially flowers, insects and foliage) and the curves of the female body. The collection illustrates his astonishing breadth of work, from gem-encrusted jewellery to perfume bottles and sculpture.

The museum is 60km northwest of Strasbourg in Wingen-sur-Moder.

STAY AWHILE

STRASBOURG

BY ANNA RICHARDS

Strasbourg reminds me of an advent calendar. Not just because it's France's capital of Christmas, thanks to its 300-chalet-strong December market. It's rather because the half-timber, Alsatian houses look just like the drawings you'd get in an advent calendar, and behind every door is something completely unexpected.

Take the **Cave Historique des Hospices de Strasbourg** *(vins-des-hospices-de-strasbourg.fr)* as an example. This wine cellar, in the basement of a hospital (still a working hospital today), began in 1395 because many of the local countryfolk couldn't pay for their medical care. Since many were winemakers, they paid in liquid, or with vines, and the cellars were born. On a visit, you'll see the oldest white wine in France, dating from 1472 (tastings strictly forbidden, that stuff could kill you – aging like a fine wine is only applicable up to a point!), and the most colossal wine barrels you've ever set eyes on.

Another fascinating place is the **European Parliament** *(visiting.europarl.europa.eu/en/visitor-offer/strasbourg/hemicycle),* which is completely free to visit; just present your ID. It's pretty special to see where members of the European Parliament meet each month, and there are also exhibition spaces detailing the fascinating life of Simone Veil, the first female president of the European Parliament, who pushed through the legalisation of abortion in France.

Don't miss eating at a *winstub,* a traditional restaurant reminiscent of a British pub. Specialities include *choucroute* (cabbage and meat stew) and *tarte flambée* (similar to a thin pizza).

LINK YOUR TRIP

03 **A Toast to Art** Finish this road trip with a longer stay exploring the museums of Strasbourg.

Left: European Parliament; Right: Cave Historique des Hospices de Strasbourg

PLACES TO STAY

The People
On the banks of the Ill River, this is a great choice for budget travellers: central and sociable, with plenty of themed evenings, from drag to DJ sets. *(thepeoplehostel.com/en/destinations/strasbourg)*

Hôtel Tandem
Next to the train station and many of the car-rental outlets, this is a convenient choice for road trippers, and it has a cracking breakfast. *(hotel-tandem.fr)*

Cour du Corbeau
Easily the most atmospheric place to stay, the Cour du Corbeau has served as an inn to weary travellers since 1528. The only downside is that there's no on-site parking, and the public car park nearby is €35/day. *(mgallery.accor.com)*

04

PARIS & NORTH-EASTERN FRANCE

NORTHERN COAST

DURATION: 2–4 DAYS

DISTANCE: 148KM / 92 MILES

GREAT FOR: NATURE

BEST TIME TO GO: MAY TO AUGUST FOR LONG DAYS AND WARM WEATHER.

Named for the ever-changing interplay of greys and blues in the sea and sky, the Côte d'Opale (Opal Coast) is on spectacular display between Calais and Boulogne-sur-Mer. Further south, the relatively flat coastline is broken by the estuaries, wetlands and tidal marshes created by the Rivers Canche, Authie and Somme. The area has several attractive beach resorts and excellent spots for bird-watching and seal spotting.

LINK YOUR TRIP

05 In Flanders Fields

From Calais, drive 110km to the southeast, on the A16 and A25, to start this trip in Lille.

09 Monet's Normandy

From St-Valery-sur-Somme, it's a 170km drive south to Giverny.

01 Calais

France's premier trans-Channel port is a short hop from England by car ferry, Eurotunnel rail shuttle or fast Eurostar train. Begin the itinerary at Rodin's famous 1895 sculpture the **Burghers of Calais**, in front of Calais' Flemish- and Renaissance-style **Hôtel de Ville** (Town Hall). Then head to the city's sandy, cabin-lined **beach**, where the singularly riveting attraction is watching huge car ferries as they sail majestically to and from Dover. The sand continues westward along 8km-long, dune-lined **Blériot Plage**, broad and gently sloping. It's named for the pioneer aviator Louis Blériot, who undertook the first-ever trans-Channel flight from here – it lasted 27 minutes – in 1909.

THE DRIVE: Take the D940 west, past Blériot Plage in the commune of Sangatte, and a further 5km southwest to reach Cap Blanc-Nez.

★ BEST FOR

HISTORY

A colossal German bunker, part of Nazi Germany's Atlantic Wall, houses the WWII museum Musée du Mur de l'Atlantique.

MARC BRUXELLE/SHUTTERSTOCK

Burghers of Calais

02 Cap Blanc-Nez

Just past Sangatte, the coastal dunes give way to cliffs that culminate in windswept, 134m-high Cap Blanc-Nez, which affords breathtaking views of the Bay of Wissant, the port of Calais, the Flemish countryside (pock-marked by Allied bomb craters, such as those on the slopes of Mont d'Hubert) and the distant chalk cliffs of Kent. A grey stone obelisk honours the WWI Dover Patrol. Paths lead to a number of massive WWII German bunkers.

THE DRIVE: It's an 8km descent on the D940 from Cap Blanc-Nez to Wissant.

03 Wissant

The attractive seaside village of Wissant, long home to both fishers and farmers, is centred around a 15th-century church. It's a good base for exploring the area between Cap Blanc-Nez and Cap Gris-Nez, including a wide-at-low-tide **beach** that's long, flat and clean – perfect for young children and kitesurfers.

THE DRIVE: Take the D940 southwestward for 6km. About 700m past the centre of Audinghen, turn right onto the D191 and continue northwest for 3.5km.

04 Cap Gris-Nez

Topped by a lighthouse and a radar station that keeps track of the more than 500 ships that pass by here each day, the 45m-high cliffs of **Cap Gris-Nez** are only 28km from the white cliffs of the English coast. The name, which means 'grey nose' in French, is a corruption of the archaic English 'craig ness', meaning 'rocky promontory'. The area is a stopping-off point for millions of migrating birds. The parking lot is a good starting point for hikes, such as along the **GR120 du Littoral** coastal trail (marked with red and white blazes).

THE DRIVE: From Cap Gris-Nez, take the D191 3.5km southeast back to the D940 and turn right. After about 100m, at the Maison du Site des Deux Caps tourist office, turn right again and continue for 400m for the Musée du Mur de l'Atlantique.

PHOTO OPPORTUNITY

The Channel panorama from atop Cap Blanc-Nez.

05 Audinghen

Oodles of WWII hardware, including a massive, rail-borne 283mm German artillery piece with a range of 86km (more than enough to hit the English coast), are on display at Audinghen's well-organised **Musée du Mur de l'Atlantique** (Atlantic Wall Museum; *batterietodt.com*). It is housed in Batterie Todt, a colossal, round German pillbox.

THE DRIVE: From Audinghen it's 5.5km south along the D940 to Ambleteuse. On the way you'll pass the colourful village of Audresselles, still active as a fishing port. It's a great place to dine on super-fresh seafood.

06 Ambleteuse

The seaside village of Ambleteuse is home to **Fort Mahon** (Fort d'Ambleteuse), a small fortress built by Louis XIV in the 1680s, and a pebbly beach. At the modern **Musée 39–45** *(musee3945.com)*, popular period songs accompany visitors as they stroll past dozens of life-size tableaux of WWII military and civilian life. The museum screens archival films. The dashing but wildly impractical French officers' dress uniforms of 1931 hint at possible reasons why France fared so poorly on the battlefields of 1940.

THE DRIVE: From Ambleteuse drive 1.5km southeast along the D940 to reach the Dunes de la Slack.

07 Dunes de la Slack

Just south of Ambleteuse along the estuary of the tiny River Slack, wind-sculpted sand dunes are covered with – and stabilised by – clumps of marram grass and brambles such as privet and wild rose. The best way to appreciate the undulating landscape of Dunes de la Slack is to follow the marked walking paths that criss-cross the area.

THE DRIVE: From the Dunes de la Slack head south on the D940 for 10km to reach Boulogne-sur-Mer.

Cap Blanc-Nez (p57)
MISTERSTOCK/SHUTTERSTOCK

BRASSERIE 2 CAPS

Brasserie Artisanale des 2 Caps

BRASSERIE ARTISANALE DES 2 CAPS

Historic farm buildings deep in the countryside house the **Brasserie Artisanale des 2 Caps** *(2caps.fr)*, one of northern France's best microbreweries. Sample and buy here, or look for 2 Caps, Blanche de Wissant and Noire de Slack in area pubs. Brewmaster Christophe Noyon offers occasional 1½-hour tours. It's situated 1.5km along the D249 from the church in the village of Tardinghen, which is midway between Wissant and Audinghen.

08 Boulogne-sur-Mer

France's most important fishing port, Boulogne-sur-Mer is home to **Nausicaá** *(nausicaa.fr)*, one of Europe's premier aquariums. Boulogne-sur-Mer's **Basse-Ville** (Lower City) is a bustling but uninspiring assemblage of postwar structures, but the attractive **Haute-Ville** (Upper City), perched high above the rest of town and girded by a 13th-century wall, is an island of centuries-old buildings and cobblestone streets. You can walk all the way around this **Ville Fortifiée** (Fortified City) atop the ancient stone walls – look for signs for the **Promenade des Remparts**.

THE DRIVE: From Boulogne-sur-Mer, take the D940 south for 28km. At Les Étaples, turn west onto the D939 and continue for 4km.

09 Le Touquet-Paris-Plage

This leafy beach resort was hugely fashionable in the interwar period, when the British upper crust found it positively smashing. The town was a favourite of Noël Coward, and in 1940 a politically oblivious PG Wodehouse was taken prisoner here by the Germans. These days it remains no less posh and no less British, though it also attracts plenty of chic Parisians.

THE DRIVE: From Les Étaples, take the D940 south for 34km. Just past the village of Rue, turn right onto the D4, continuing westward on the D204, for a total of 6km.

10 Parc du Marquenterre Bird Sanctuary

An astonishing 300 species of bird have been sighted at the 2-sq-km **Parc du Marquenterre** *(parcdumarquenterre.fr)*, an important migratory stopover between the UK, Iceland, Scandinavia and Siberia and the warmer climes of West Africa. Marked **walking circuits** (2km to 6km) take you to marshes, dunes, meadows, freshwater ponds, a brackish lagoon and 13 observation posts. Year-round, the park's friendly guides – they're the ones carrying telescopes on tripods – are happy to help visitors, especially kids, spot and identify birds.

THE DRIVE: From the Parc du Marquenterre, take the D204 east for 4km to the D4 and turn right. After 4.5km continue onto the D104 for the 2km to Le Crotoy.

> ☑ TOP TIP
>
> ### TWO CAPES TOURIST INFORMATION
>
> The **Maison du Site des Deux Caps** *(lesdeuxcaps.fr)* serves as a visitor information centre for the 'two capes', ie the area around and between Cap Blanc-Nez and Cap Gris-Nez. Staff have English brochures, rent out bicycles – both regular and electric – and sell hiking maps.

11 Le Crotoy

Occupying a wonderfully picturesque spot on the northern bank of the Baie de Somme (Somme estuary), laid-back Le Crotoy is a lovely place in which to relax. Attractions include scenic walks around the Somme estuary – vast expanses are exposed at low tide – and the only sandy beach in northern France that faces south; restaurants and cafes can be found nearby. Jules Verne wrote *Twenty Thousand Leagues Under the Sea* (1870) while living here.

THE DRIVE: St-Valery-sur-Somme is 16km around the Somme estuary from Le Crotoy. Take the D104 to the D940, follow it for 11km and then turn right onto the D3.

12 St-Valery-sur-Somme

This old port town has a charming maritime quarter, a pocket-sized walled city and an attractive seaside promenade. The colours of St-Valery-sur-Somme are the colours of maritime Picardy: the deep brick reds of the houses and the sea hues that range from a sparkling blue to overcast grey are accented by dashes of red, white and blue from flapping French flags, just like in an impressionist seascape. Grey and harbour seals can often be spotted off **Pointe du Hourdel**, 8km northwest of town.

Maritime quarter, St-Valery-sur-Somme

OLIVEROUGE 3/SHUTTERSTOCK

☑ TOP TIP

NATURE WALKS

Non-profit **Eden 62** *(eden62.fr)* organises two-hour nature walks several times a week. They're in French, but tourists, including families, are welcome. There's no need to reserve – just show up at the meeting point.

05

★ BEST FOR

HISTORY

Historial de la Grande Guerre, Péronne's first-rate WWI museum.

PARIS & NORTH-EASTERN FRANCE

IN FLANDERS FIELDS

DURATION: 3 DAYS

DISTANCE: 235KM / 146 MILES

GREAT FOR: HISTORY & CULTURE

BEST TIME TO GO: MARCH TO NOVEMBER; A FEW SITES CLOSE IN DECEMBER AND JANUARY.

War memorial, Vimy Ridge

Shortly after WWI broke out in 1914, Allied troops established a line of resistance against further German advances in the northern French countryside near Arras, initiating one of the longest and bloodiest standoffs in military history. This tour of Flanders and Picardy takes in some of France's most important WWI battle sites and memorials, along with the charming cities of Lille, Arras and Amiens.

LINK YOUR TRIP

03 A Toast to Art
From Vimy, detour 9km to Lens for this tour of northern France's arts scene.

04 Northern Coast
From Bony, head northwest to Calais (200km) to begin this spectacular drive along the Channel coast.

01 Lille

A convenient gateway to northern France's WWI battlefields, cosmopolitan Lille offers an engaging mix of grand architecture and Flemish culture. Stop in for dinner at an *estaminet* (traditional Flemish restaurant) and stroll around the bustling pedestrianised centre, whose highlights include the **Vieille Bourse** (place du Général de Gaulle), a 17th-century Flemish Renaissance extravaganza decorated with caryatids and cornucopia, and the neighbourhood of **Vieux Lille** (Old Lille), where restored 17th- and 18th-century brick houses are home to chic boutiques.

THE DRIVE: Take the westbound A25, the southbound N41, the D207 and finally the D141B to Fromelles, a distance of 17km.

02 Fromelles

The death toll was horrific – 1917 Australians and 519 Britons killed in just one day of fighting –

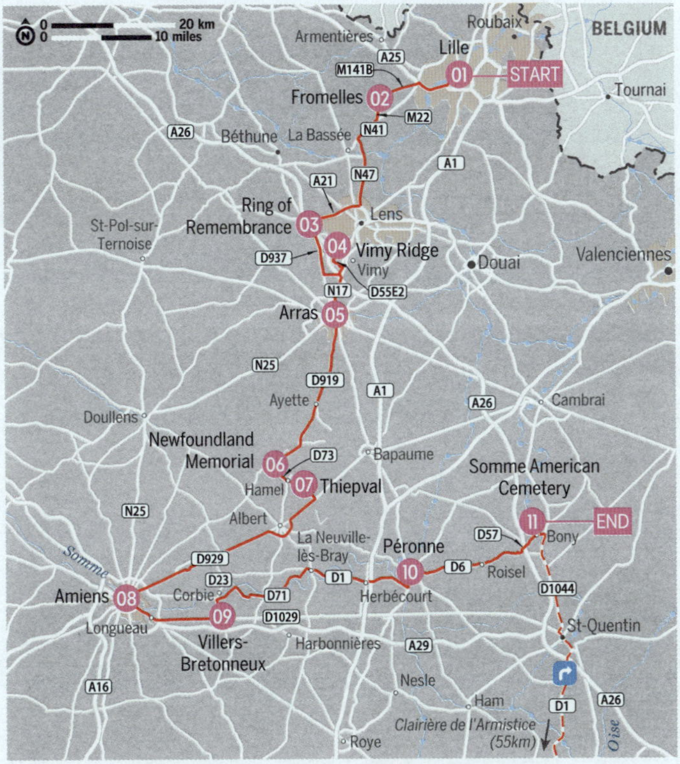

NIGEL JARVIS/SHUTTERSTOCK

yet the 1916 Battle of Fromelles was largely forgotten until 2008, when the remains of 250 of the fallen were discovered. They are now buried in the **Fromelles (Pheasant Wood) Cemetery**; 144 have been identified thanks to DNA testing. The adjoining and excellent **Musée de la Bataille de Fromelles** *(musee-bataille-fromelles.fr)* evokes life in the trenches with reconstructed bunkers, photos and biographies.

THE DRIVE: Take the D22 4km south to the N41, turn southwest and after 3km turn south onto the N47; continue for 12km before turning west onto the A21. Get off at the D937, drive southeast for 5km and then follow the signs to Notre-Dame de Lorette. Total distance: 37km.

03 Ring of Remembrance

It's hard not to be overwhelmed by the folly and waste of the Western Front at the **Ring of Remembrance** (L'Anneau de la Mémoire; *memorial 1418.com*) as you walk past panel after panel engraved with almost 580,000 names: WWI dead from both sides who are listed in strict alphabetical order, without reference to nationality, rank or religion.

THE DRIVE: Return to the D937 and drive south for 6km. Then take the D49 east for 3km, the D917 north for 1km and finally the D55E2 northwest. Total distance: 12.5km.

04 Vimy Ridge

Right after the war, the French attempted to erase all signs of battle and return northern France to agriculture and normalcy. The Canadians took a different approach, deciding that the most evocative way to remember their fallen was to preserve part of the crater-pocked battlefield exactly the way it looked when the guns fell silent. As a result, the best place to get some sense of the hell known as the Western Front is the chilling, eerie moonscape of **Vimy Ridge** *(cheminsdememoire.gouv.fr)*. During visitor centre opening hours, bilingual Canadian students lead free guided tours of reconstructed tunnels and trenches.

THE DRIVE: Follow the D55E2, N17 and D917 12km into Arras.

05 Arras

Contemplating the picture-perfect Flemish-style facades of Arras' two gorgeous market squares, the **Grand' Place** and the **Petite Place** (Place des Héros), it's hard to believe that almost the entire city centre was reduced to rubble during WWI (it was reconstructed in the 1920s). To understand life in wartime Arras, head 1.5km south to **Carrière Wellington** (Wellington Quarry; *carrierewellington.com*), a subterranean quarry that served as a staging area for the Allies' 1917 spring offensive. Prior to the attack, 500 New Zealand soldiers worked round the clock for five months expanding medieval quarries to accommodate kitchens, a hospital and several thousand Commonwealth troops. Reminders of these events are everywhere, from Māori-language graffiti to candle burn marks from the Easter Mass celebrated underground the day before the troops stormed German front lines.

THE DRIVE: Take the D919, D174 and D73 31km southwest to the Newfoundland Memorial, detouring briefly at Km 15 to the Ayette Indian and Chinese Cemetery, a Commonwealth cemetery where Hindi, Arabic and Chinese inscriptions mark the graves of Indian soldiers and Chinese labourers recruited by the British government.

06 Newfoundland Memorial

On 1 July 1916 the volunteer Royal Newfoundland Regiment stormed entrenched German positions and was nearly wiped out. The evocative **Beaumont-Hamel Newfoundland Memorial** *(veterans.gc.ca)* preserves the battlefield much as it was at fighting's end. Climb to the bronze caribou statue, on a hillside surrounded by native Newfoundland plants, for views of the shell craters, barbed-wire barriers and zigzag trenches that still fill with mud in winter. The on-site welcome centre offers guided tours.

THE DRIVE: Head 5km east-southeast on the D73 through tiny Beaumont-Hamel, across a pretty valley, past the 36th (Ulster) Division Memorial (site of a Northern Irish war monument and a homey tearoom) and on to the easy-to-spot arches of the Thiepval Memorial.

07 Thiepval

On a lonely, windswept hilltop, the towering **Thiepval Memorial** *(historial.fr)* to 'the Missing of the Somme' marks the site of a German stronghold that was stormed on 1 July 1916 with unimaginable casualties. Thiepval catches visitors off guard, both with its monumentality and its staggering simplicity: inscribed below the enormous arch, which is visible from kilometres around, are the names of over 72,000 British and South African soldiers whose remains were never recovered or identified. The **Museum at Thiepval**, run by Péronne's outstanding Historial de la Grande Guerre, has good large-scale displays.

THE DRIVE: A 44km ride on the D73 and the D929 brings you to Amiens.

08 Amiens

Amiens' attractive, pedestrianised city centre offers a relaxing break from the battlefields. Climb the north tower of breathtaking, 13th-century **Cathédrale Notre Dame** *(cathedrale-amiens.fr)*, a UNESCO World Heritage Site, for stupendous views of the town; a free, 45-minute **light show** bathes the cathedral's facade in vivid medieval colours nightly in summer.

Across the Somme River, gondola-like boats offer tours of Amiens' vast market gardens, the **Hortillonnages** *(hortillonnages-amiens.fr)*, which have supplied the city with vegetables and flowers since the Middle Ages.

Literature buffs will love the **Maison de Jules Verne** (Maisons des Illustres; *amiens.fr*), the turreted home where Jules Verne wrote some of his best-known works of science fiction.

THE DRIVE: Take the D1029 19km east to Villers-Bretonneux.

09 Villers-Bretonneux

During WWI, 46,000 of Australia's 313,000 volunteer soldiers met their deaths on the Western Front (14,000 others perished elsewhere). In the village of Villers-Bretonneux, the **Musée Franco-Australien** (Franco-Australian Museum; *museeaustralien.com*) displays a collection of highly personal WWI Australiana, including letters and photographs that evoke life on the front. The names of 10,722 Australian soldiers whose remains were never found are engraved on the base of the 32m-high **Australian National War Memorial** *(sjmc.gov.au)*, 2km north of town.

THE DRIVE: From the Australian National War Memorial, take the D23 briefly north, then meander east through pretty rolling country, roughly paralleling the Somme River, along the D71 and D1 via La Neuville-lès-Bray for 41km into Péronne.

10 Péronne

Housed in a fortified medieval château, Péronne's **Historial de la Grande Guerre** (Museum of the Great War; *historial.fr*) provides a superb overview of WWI's historical and cultural context, telling the story of the war chronologically, with equal space given to the French, British and German perspectives. Visually engaging exhibits, including period films and bone-chilling engravings by Otto Dix, capture the aesthetic sensibilities, enthusiasm, naive patriotism and unimaginable violence of the time.

For excellent English-language brochures about the battlefields, visit Péronne's **tourist office** (Office of Haute Somme Tourism; *peronnehautesomme-tourisme.com*), opposite the museum.

THE DRIVE: The American cemetery is 24km east-northeast of Péronne via the D6, D406 and D57.

TODAMO/SHUTTERSTOCK

PHOTO OPPORTUNITY

The staggering list of missing soldiers' names at Thiepval.

Thiepval Memorial

11 Somme American Cemetery

In late September 1918, six weeks before the end of WWI, American units – flanked by their Commonwealth allies – launched an assault on the Germans' heavily fortified Hindenburg Line. Some of the fiercest fighting took place near the village of Bony, on the sloping site now occupied by the 1844 Latin crosses and Stars of David of the **Somme American Cemetery** *(abmc.gov)*; the names of 333 other soldiers whose remains were never recovered are inscribed on the walls of the **Memorial Chapel**.

DETOUR

Clairière de l'Armistice

Start: 11 Somme American Cemetery

On the 11th hour of the 11th day of the 11th month of 1918, WWI officially ended at **Clairière de l'Armistice** (Armistice Clearing), 7km northeast of the city of Compiègne, with the signing of an armistice inside the railway carriage of Allied supreme commander Maréchal Ferdinand Foch. In the same forest clearing, in an almost identical railroad car, the **Mémorial de l'Armistice** *(musee-armistice-14-18.fr)* commemorates these events with memorabilia, newspaper clippings and stereoscopic photos that capture – in 3D – all the mud, muck and misery of WWI; some of the furnishings, hidden away during WWII, were the ones actually used in 1918.

From the Somme American Cemetery, take the D1044, D1 and D1032 94km southwest towards Compiègne, then follow signs 8km east along the N1031 and D546 to Clairière de l'Armistice.

06

PARIS & NORTH-EASTERN FRANCE

CHAMPAGNE TASTER

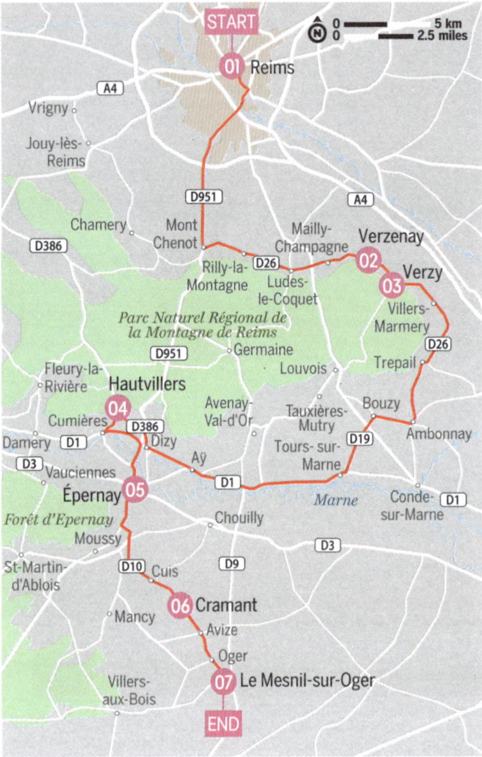

DURATION: 3 DAYS

DISTANCE: 85KM / 53 MILES

GREAT FOR: FOOD & DRINK, HISTORY & CULTURE

BEST TIME TO GO: APRIL TO JUNE FOR SPRING SUNSHINE; SEPTEMBER AND OCTOBER TO SEE THE HARVEST.

'My only regret in life is that I didn't drink enough Champagne,' wrote the economist John Maynard Keynes; unlike him, by the end of this tour, you'll have drunk enough bubbly to last several lifetimes. Starting at the prestigious Champagne centre of Reims, passing through Épernay and ending in Le Mesnil-sur-Oger, this fizz-fuelled trip includes stops at some of the world's most famous producers – with ample time for tasting en route.

LINK YOUR TRIP

02 Essential France
Lying 150km west of Épernay, Paris marks the beginning of our epic journey around France's most essential sights.

03 A Toast to Art
Pick up our art-themed tour in Reims, where it takes in the city's renowned Musée des Beaux-Arts.

01 Reims

There's nowhere better to start your Champagne tour than the regal city of Reims. Several big names have their *caves* (wine cellars) nearby. **Mumm** *(mumm.com)*, pronounced 'moom', is the only *maison* (house) in central Reims. Founded in 1827, it's the world's third- or fourth-largest Champagne producer, depending on the year. One-hour tours explore its enormous cellars, filled with 25 million bottles of bubbly, and include tastings of several vintages.

North of town, **Taittinger** *(cellars-booking.taittinger.fr)* provides an informative overview of how Champagne is actually made – you'll leave with a good understanding of the production process, from grape to bottle. Parts of the cellars occupy Roman stone quarries dug in the 4th century.

Before you leave town, don't forget to drop by **Waïda**, an

GAMJAI/SHUTTERSTOCK

★ BEST FOR

CULTURE

Sip Champagne in the cellars of Moët & Chandon.

Montagne de Reims Champagne Route

old-fashioned confectioner that sells Reims' famous *biscuits roses* (pink biscuits), a sweet treat traditionally nibbled with a glass of Champagne.

THE DRIVE: The countryside between Reims and Épernay is carpeted with vineyards, fields and back roads that are a dream to drive through. From Reims, head south along the D951 for 13km. Near Mont Chenot, turn onto the D26, signposted to Rilly and the 'Route Touristique du Champagne'. The next 12km take you through the pretty villages of Rilly-la-Montagne and Mailly-Champagne en route to Verzenay.

02 Verzenay

Reims marks the start of the 70km **Montagne de Reims Champagne Route**, the prettiest (and most prestigious) of the three signposted road routes that wind their way through the Champagne vineyards. Of the 17 *grand cru* villages in Champagne, nine lie on and around the Montagne, a hilly area whose sheltered slopes and chalky soils provide the perfect environment for viticulture.

Most of the area's vineyards are devoted to the pinot noir grape. You'll pass plenty of producers offering *dégustation* (tasting) en route. It's up to you how many you visit – but don't miss the panorama of the vineyards of Verzenay from the top of the **Phare de Verzenay**

♥ WHY I LOVE THIS TRIP

KERRY CHRISTIANI, WRITER

You can sip Champagne anywhere, but a road trip really slips under the skin of these UNESCO-listed vineyards. Begin with an eye-opening, palate-awakening tour and tasting at *grande maison* cellars in Épernay and Reims. I love the far-reaching view from Phare de Verzenay and touring the back roads in search of small producers, especially when the aroma of new wine hangs in the air and the vines are golden in autumn.

PHOTO OPPORTUNITY

Overlooking glossy vineyards from the Phare de Verzenay.

(Verzenay Lighthouse; *phare-verzenay.com*), which was constructed as a publicity gimmick in 1909.

THE DRIVE: Continue south along the D26 for 3km.

03 Verzy

This village is home to several small vineyards that provide an interesting contrast to the big producers. **Étienne and Anne-Laure Lefevre** *(champagne-etienne-lefevre.com)* run group tours of their family-owned vineyards and cellars – if you're on your own, call ahead to see if you can join a pre-arranged tour. There are no flashy videos or multimedia shows – the emphasis is firmly on the nitty-gritty of Champagne production.

For a glass of fizz high above the treetops, seek out the sleek **Perching Bar** *(perchinglife.com)* deep in the forest.

THE DRIVE: Stay on the D26 south of Verzy and enjoy wide-open countryside views as you spin south to Ambonnay. Detour west onto the D19, signed to Bouzy, and bear right onto the D1 along the northern bank of the Marne River. When you reach the village of Dizy, follow signs onto the D386 to Hautvillers. It's a total drive of 32km, taking around 45 minutes.

04 Hautvillers

Next stop is the hilltop village of Hautvillers, a hallowed name among Champagne aficionados: it's where a Benedictine monk by the name of Dom Pierre Pérignon is popularly believed to have created Champagne in the late 16th century.

Phare de Verzenay (p67)

BARMALINI/SHUTTERSTOCK

DAAN KLOEG/SHUTTERSTOCK

Champagne in a cellar at De Castellane (p71)

THE SCIENCE OF CHAMPAGNE

Champagne is made from the red pinot noir (38%), the black pinot meunier (35%) or the white chardonnay (27%) grape. Each vine is vigorously pruned and trained to produce a small quantity of high-quality grapes. Indeed, to maintain exclusivity (and price), the designated areas where grapes used for Champagne can be grown and the amount of wine produced each year are limited.

Making Champagne according to the *méthode champenoise* (traditional method) is a complex procedure. There are two fermentation processes, the first in casks and the second after the wine has been bottled and had sugar and yeast added. Bottles are then aged in cellars for two to five years, depending on the *cuvée* (vintage).

For two months in early spring, the bottles are aged in cellars kept at 12°C and the wine turns effervescent. The sediment that forms in the bottle is removed by *remuage*, a painstakingly slow process in which each bottle, stored horizontally, is rotated slightly every day for weeks until the sludge works its way to the cork. Next comes *dégorgement:* the neck of the bottle is frozen, creating a blob of solidified Champagne and sediment, which is then removed.

The great man's tomb lies in front of the altar of the **Église Abbatiale**.

The village itself is well worth a stroll, with a jumble of lanes, timbered houses and stone-walled vineyards. On place de la République, the **tourist office** *(tourisme-hautvillers.com)* hands out free maps detailing local vineyard walks.

Steps away is **Au 36** *(au36.net)*, a wine boutique with a 'wall' of Champagne quirkily arranged by aroma. There's a tasting room upstairs.

THE DRIVE: From the centre of the village, take the rte de Cumières for grand views across the vine-cloaked slopes. Follow the road all the way to the D1, turn left and follow signs to Épernay's *centre-ville*, 6km to the south.

05 Épernay

The prosperous town of Épernay is the self-proclaimed *capitale du Champagne* and is home to many of the most illustrious Champagne houses. Beneath the streets are an astonishing 110km of subterranean cellars, containing an estimated 200 million bottles of vintage bubbly.

Most of the big names are arranged along the grand Avenue

CHAMPAGNE KNOW-HOW

Types of Champagne

- **Blanc de Blancs**
  Champagne made using only chardonnay grapes. Fresh and elegant, with very small bubbles and a bouquet reminiscent of 'yellow fruits' such as pear and plum.

- **Blanc de Noirs**
  A full-bodied, deep golden Champagne made solely with black grapes (despite the colour). Often rich and refined, with great complexity and a long finish.

- **Rosé Pink Champagne**
  Mostly served as an apéritif, it has a fresh character and summer-fruit flavours. Made by adding a small percentage of red pinot noir to white Champagne.

- **Prestige Cuvée**
  The crème de la crème. Usually made with grapes from *grand cru* vineyards and priced and bottled accordingly.

- **Millésimé Vintage**
  Champagne produced from a single crop during an exceptional year. Most Champagne is nonvintage.

Sweetness

- **Brut (Dry)**
  Most common style; pairs well with food.

- **Extra Sec**
  Fairly dry but sweeter than Brut; nice as an apéritif.

- **Demi Sec**
  Medium sweet; goes well with fruit and dessert.

- **Doux**
  Very sweet; a dessert Champagne.

Serving & Tasting

- **Chilling**
  Chill Champagne in a bucket of ice for 30 minutes before serving. The ideal serving temperature is 7°C to 9°C.

- **Opening**
  Grip the bottle securely and tilt it at a 45-degree angle facing away from you. Rotate the bottle slowly to ease out the cork – it should sigh, not pop.

- **Pouring**
  Hold the flute by the stem at an angle and let the Champagne trickle gently into the glass – less foam, more bubbles.

- **Tasting**
  Admire the colour and bubbles. Swirl your glass to release the aroma and inhale slowly before tasting the Champagne.

BARMALINI/SHUTTERSTOCK

Cramant

de Champagne. **Moët & Chandon** *(moet.com)* offers frequent and fascinating one-hour tours of its prestigious cellars, while at nearby **Mercier** *(champagnemercier.fr)* tours take place aboard a laser-guided underground train.

Finish with a climb up the 237-step tower at **De Castellane** *(castellane.com),* which offers knockout views over the town's rooftops and vine-clad hills.

THE DRIVE: Head south of town along av Maréchal Foch or av du 8 Mai 1945, following 'Autres Directions' signs across the roundabouts until you see signs for Cramant. The village is 10km southeast of Épernay via the D10.

06 Cramant

You'll find it hard to miss this quaint village, as the northern entrance is heralded by a two-storey-high Champagne bottle. From the ridge above the village, views stretch out in all directions across the Champagne countryside, taking in a patchwork of fields, farmhouses and row upon row of endless vines. Pack a picnic and your own bottle of bubbly for the perfect Champagne country lunch.

THE DRIVE: Continue southeast along the D10 for 7km, and follow signs to Le Mesnil-sur-Oger.

07 Le Mesnil-sur-Oger

Finish with a visit to the excellent **Musée de la Vigne et du Vin** *(museedelavigneetduvin.com),* where a local wine-growing family has assembled a collection of century-old Champagne-making equipment. Among the highlights is a massive 16-tonne oak-beam grape press from 1630. Reservations must be made by phone or online; ask about the availability of English tours when you book.

Round off your trip with lunch at **La Gare** *(lagarelemesnil.com),* which prides itself on serving bistro-style grub prepared with seasonal produce, simple as pork tenderloin with cider and potatoes. There's a €13 menu for *les petits.*

07

PARIS & NORTH-EASTERN FRANCE

ALSACE ACCENTS

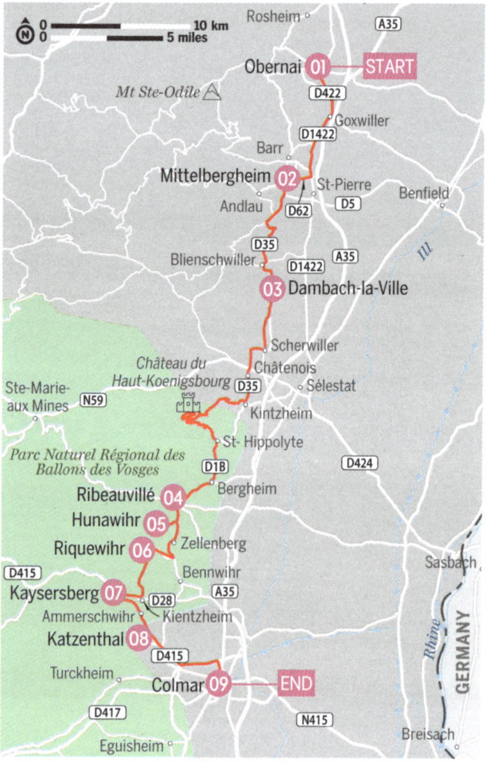

DURATION: 3 DAYS

DISTANCE: 105 KM / 66 MILES

GREAT FOR: FAMILIES, HISTORY & CULTURE, WINE

BEST TIME TO GO: MAY TO OCTOBER FOR THE BEST CHANCE OF SUNSHINE.

Gloriously green and reassuringly rustic, the Route des Vins d'Alsace (Alsace Wine Route) is one of France's most evocative drives. Vines march up the hillsides to castle-topped crags and the mist-shrouded Vosges, and every kilometre or so a roadside cellar or half-timbered village invites you to stop and raise a toast. The official route runs between Marlenheim and Thann, but we've factored in a stop at Colmar, too.

LINK YOUR TRIP

03 A Toast to Art
Our art tour ends in Strasbourg, so it's a natural addition to this trip along the Route des Vins d'Alsace.

17 The Jura
Travel 170km southwest to Besançon to take a jaunt through the mountains and plateaux of the Jura.

01 Obernai

Sitting 31km south of Strasbourg (take the A35 and turn off at exit 11) is the typically Alsatian village of Obernai. Life still revolves around the **Place du Marché**, the market square where you'll find the 16th-century town hall, the Renaissance **Puits aux Six Seaux** (Six Bucket Well) and the bell-topped **Halle aux Blés** (Corn Exchange). Visit on Thursday mornings for the weekly market.

There are lots of flower-decked alleyways to explore – don't miss **ruelle des Juifs** – and you can access the town's 13th-century ramparts in front of the **Église St-Pierre et St-Paul**.

THE DRIVE: Follow the D422 and D1422 for 9km south of Obernai, then turn off onto the D62. Mittelbergheim is another 1.5km west, among dreamy vine-covered countryside.

VLAD PROKOPENKO/SHUTTERSTOCK

★ BEST FOR

FAMILIES

Watching the storks at the NaturOparC.

A stork at NaturOparC (p74)

02 Mittelbergheim

Serene and untouristy, hillside Mittelbergheim sits amid a sea of grapevines and wild tulips, its streets lined with red-roofed houses.

Like most Alsatian towns, it's home to numerous wineries, each marked by a wrought-iron sign. **Domaine Gilg** *(domaine-gilg.com)* is a family-run winery that's won many awards for its *grand cru* sylvaners, pinots and rieslings.

From the car park on the D362 next to the cemetery, a vineyard trail, the **Sentier Viticole**, winds towards the twin-towered **Château du Haut Andlau** and the forested Vosges.

THE DRIVE: Follow rue Principale onto the D425, signed to Eichhoffen. The road winds through lush Alsatian countryside and becomes the D35 as it travels to Dambach-la-Ville, 12km south.

03 Dambach-la-Ville

This is another chocolate-box village, with lots of pre-1500 houses painted in ice-cream shades of pistachio, caramel and raspberry. To the southwest is the **Château du Haut Kœnigsbourg** *(haut-koenigsbourg.fr)*, a turreted castle hovering above vineyards and hills. The castle dates back nine centuries, but it was rebuilt (with typical grandiosity) by Kaiser Wilhelm II in 1908. The wraparound panorama from its pink-granite ramparts alone is worth the admission fee.

THE DRIVE: Stay on the D35, which becomes the D1B as it nears Ribeauvillé, 22km south. It's a truly lovely drive, travelling through carpets of vines and quiet villages. You'll see the turn-off to the château about halfway to Ribeauvillé.

04 Ribeauvillé

Nestled snugly in a valley and presided over by a castle, medieval Ribeauvillé is a Route des Vins must – so you'll definitely share it with crowds during the busy season. Along the main street, keep an eye out for the 17th-century **Pfifferhüs** *(Fifers' House)*, which once housed the town's fife-playing minstrels; the **Hôtel de Ville** and its Renaissance fountain; and the nearby clock-topped **Tour des Bouchers** (Butchers' Bell Tower).

It's also worth stopping in at the **Cave de Ribeauvillé**

(vins-ribeauville.com), France's oldest winegrowers' cooperative, founded in 1895. It has an interesting viniculture museum and offers free tastings of its excellent wines. It's located two roundabouts north from the tourist office.

THE DRIVE: Hunawihr is 2.5km south of Ribeauvillé.

05 Hunawihr

Cigognes (white storks) are Alsace's most emblematic birds. They feature in many folk tales and are believed to bring good luck (as well as newborn babies). They've been roosting on rooftops here for centuries, but their numbers fell dramatically during the 20th century as a result of environmental damage and habitat loss.

Thankfully, conservation programs have helped revive the birds' fortunes. **NaturOparC** *(naturoparc.fr)* houses more than 200 storks, plus cormorants, penguins, otters and sea lions.

THE DRIVE: Backtrack to the D1B and travel 4km south, following signs to Riquewihr. Distant hills unfold to the south as you drive.

06 Riquewihr

Competition is stiff, but Riquewihr just may be the most enchanting town on the Route des Vins. Medieval ramparts enclose a maze of twisting lanes and half-timbered houses, each brighter and lovelier than the last.

The **Tour des Voleurs** (Thieves' Tower; *musee-riquewihr.fr*) houses a gruesome torture chamber that's guaranteed to enthral the kids.

The late-13th-century, half-timbered **Dolder** *(musee-riquewihr.fr),* topped by a 25m bell tower, is worth a look for its panoramic views and small local-history museum.

THE DRIVE: A scenic minor road winds 7km south from av Méquillet in Riquewihr to Kientzheim, then joins the D28 for another 1km to Kaysersberg.

07 Kaysersberg

Just 10km northwest of Colmar, Kaysersberg is another instant heart-stealer with its backdrop of vines, castle and 16th-century bridge. An old-town saunter through the **Vieille Ville** brings you to the Renaissance Hôtel de Ville and the red-sandstone **Église Ste-Croix**, whose altar has 18 painted panels of the Passion and the Resurrection.

Kaysersberg was also the birthplace of Albert Schweitzer (1875–1965), a musicologist, doctor and winner of the Nobel Peace Prize.

THE DRIVE: Take the N415 southeast of Kaysersberg for 7km, passing through Ammerschwihr and then following signs to Katzenthal.

08 Katzenthal

Katzenthal is great for tiptoeing off the tourist trail. *Grand cru* vines ensnare the hillside, topped by the medieval ruins of **Château du Wineck**, where walks through forest and vineyard begin.

It's also a great place for some wine tasting thanks to **Vignoble Klur** *(klur.net),* an organic, family-run winery that also offers cookery classes, vineyard walks and back-to-nature holidays.

THE DRIVE: Rejoin the D415. Colmar is another 8km south and is clearly signed.

09 Colmar

At times the Route des Vins d'Alsace fools you into thinking it's 1454, but in Colmar the illusion is complete.

Mosey around the canal quarter of **Petite Venise** (Little Venice), then head along **rue des Tanneurs**, with its rooftop verandahs for drying hides, and **quai de la Poissonnerie**, the former fishers' quarter. Afterwards, hire a **rowing boat** beside the rue de Turenne bridge for that Venetian vibe.

The town also has some intriguing museums. The star attraction at the **Musée d'Unterlinden** *(musee-unterlinden.com)* is the Rétable d'Issenheim (Issenheim Altarpiece), a medieval masterpiece that depicts scenes from the New Testament.

Meanwhile, the **Musée Bartholdi** *(musee-bartholdi.fr)* is the birthplace of sculptor Frédéric Auguste Bartholdi, architect of the Statue of Liberty. Highlights include a full-sized model of Lady Liberty's left ear (the lobe is watermelon-sized!) and the family's sparklingly bourgeois apartment.

Look out for the miniature version of the statue on the rte du Strasbourg (N83), erected to mark the centenary of Bartholdi's death.

DRIVING THE ROUTE DES VINS

The Route des Vins d'Alsace is signposted, but local tourist offices have maps, which come in handy. Among these are free English-language maps – *The Alsace Wine Route* and *Alsace Grand Cru Wines* – detailing Alsace's prestigious AOC regions. There is info online at *routedesvins.alsace.*

Parking can be a nightmare in the high season, especially in Ribeauvillé and Riquewihr; your best bet is to park outside the town centre and walk for a few minutes.

Petite Venise, Colmar

SINA ETTMER PHOTOGRAPHY/SHUTTERSTOCK

PHOTO OPPORTUNITY

Punting along the flower-decked canals of Colmar in a romantic rowboat.

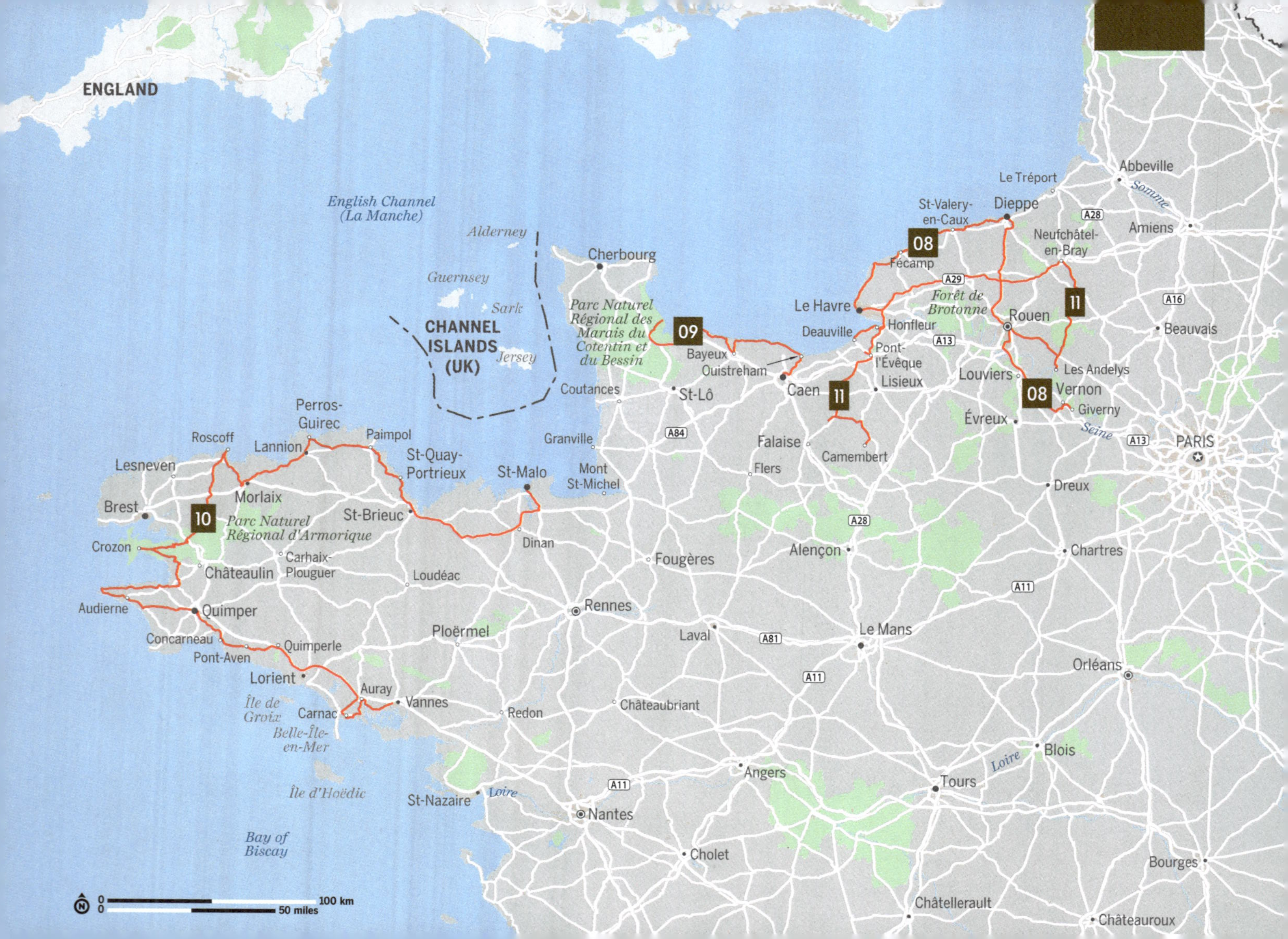

ENGLAND
English Channel (La Manche)
Alderney
Guernsey
Sark
Jersey
CHANNEL ISLANDS (UK)
Cherbourg
Parc Naturel Régional des Marais du Cotentin et du Bessin
09
Bayeux
Ouistreham
Caen
St-Lô
Coutances
Granville
Mont St-Michel
St-Malo
Dinan
Le Havre
Deauville
Honfleur
Pont-l'Évêque
Lisieux
11
Falaise
Camembert
Flers
Fécamp
08
St-Valery-en-Caux
Dieppe
Le Tréport
Abbeville
Somme
Amiens
Neufchâtel-en-Bray
A28
A29
Forêt de Brotonne
Rouen
A13
A16
Beauvais
Les Andelys
Louviers
Vernon
Giverny
Évreux
Seine
PARIS
Dreux
Chartres
Alençon
Fougères
Rennes
Laval
A81
Le Mans
A11
Orléans
Blois
Loire
Tours
Angers
Châteaubriant
Redon
Nantes
Cholet
Châtellerault
Châteauroux
Bourges
A84
St-Nazaire
Bay of Biscay
Île d'Hoëdic
Belle-Île-en-Mer
Île de Groix
Carnac
Auray
Vannes
Lorient
Quimperle
Pont-Aven
Concarneau
Quimper
Audierne
Châteaulin
Crozon
Brest
Lesneven
Roscoff
10
Morlaix
Parc Naturel Régional d'Armorique
Carhaix-Plouguer
Lannion
Perros-Guirec
Paimpol
St-Quay-Portrieux
St-Brieuc
Loudéac
Ploërmel
0 100 km
0 50 miles

MALOFF/SHUTTERSTOCK

Musée de Dieppe (p81)

NORMANDY & BRITTANY

EXPLORE

NORMANDY & BRITTANY

Abutting the English Channel, Normandy and Brittany offer some of France's most diverse and delightful touring. From the sombre WWII memorials and chalk cliffs of Normandy's coast to the gastronomic joys of some of the world's most famous cheese appellations, a bumper crop of scenic châteaux, the distinctive Celtic culture of Brittany and the aesthetic apogee of Monet's back garden, you'll find it almost impossible to tire of these regions. With good roads branching out from stately, historic towns through verdant countryside to a varied coastline dotted with appealing villages, they're ideal for driving at any time of the year.

Paris

The French capital lies within easy reach of the 'Monet's Normandy' and 'Tour des Fromages' drives. Charles de Gaulle airport (CDG), a mere two hours' drive from Rouen and 2½ hours from Dieppe, is Europe's third busiest, handling huge volumes of long-haul flights from the US and around the world. Paris also sits at the centre of the extensive French train network, with TER, TGV and Eurostar connections to London, Brussels, Rouen, Rennes and throughout France and Europe. All the major car-rental companies are represented at CDG and within Paris itself, and there are abundant accommodation and grocery supply options.

Rouen

The capital of Normandy is a logical inland staging point for all three driving trips within the region. Of Roman origin, with a proud medieval past, it's around an hour's drive from either Dieppe or Le Havre (with train links to both) plus other centres including Paris (Gare St-Lazare) and Caen. Car-rental firms cluster around the station and the southern bank of the Seine and there are hotels aplenty in the centre of town.

Le Havre

The UNESCO-listed Norman port of Le Havre, its modernist centre completely rebuilt by the Belgian architect Auguste Perret following destruction in WWII, is a major ferry terminus handy for

WHEN TO GO

July and August, the high season, bring heat to northern France. Everything is open and bustling, but you should anticipate higher prices, competition for accommodation, busier roads and possible delays. Winter brings seasonal closures, especially of seaside attractions and businesses. The shoulder months, April to June and September, can be the best bets for milder weather and thinner crowds.

the 'Monet's Normandy' and 'Tour des Fromages' drives. The ferry dock, where regular car ferries to Portsmouth and other destinations put in, is just 1km south of central Le Havre. With good rail connections to Rouen (one hour) and Paris Gare St-Lazare (2¼ hours), it also boasts plenty of budget and midrange hotels within its historic centre and around the train station. Car rental is available in the streets immediately north and south of the station, while supermarkets for road supplies dot the city and its main arterial approaches.

Rennes

Rennes is the best-equipped major centre for the eight-day 'Breton Coast' drive. A crossroads since Roman times, it still occupies the centre of the network of roads connecting the major centres of northwestern France. Only 1½ hours from Paris Montparnasse by TGV, Rennes is also the local rail hub for Breton towns like Brest, Nantes and Quimper. Rennes airport, serving mainly domestic and nearby European destinations, offers plenty of car-rental options, while accommodation and supplies are easily found in this city of more than 200,000.

TRANSPORT

Normandy and, to a lesser extent, Brittany are easy to access. Assuming most visitors come through Paris, either through Charles de Gaulle or Orly airports, Normandy can be reached in two hours or less by car, train or bus. Those touring Brittany should aim for Rennes, either flying in from Paris, Frankfurt or Gatwick, or taking the TGV from Paris.

NOTE: A Crit'Air sticker is required in Rouen, Le Havre and Caen. See p287 for more details.

WHERE TO STAY

A welcoming B&B situated above an excellent, traditional bakery, **La Boulangerie** is on the northern side of Rouen's historic heart. **La Maison de Famille** is a sensitively appointed four-room B&B in a 17th-century townhouse in the heart of historic Caen. **Vent d'Ouest Hotel**, on Le Havre seafront, is a stylish four-star hotel with a great restaurant and a full spa on-site. A gorgeously redeveloped medieval townhouse in the heart of Dinan, **La Maison Pavie** is one of the loveliest places to stay on Brittany's Côtes d'Armor.

RESOURCES

- **Normandy Tourism**
  A one-stop shop for all visits to Normandy, offering touring itineraries, details of events and activities, and restaurant and accommodation listings. *en.normandie-tourisme.fr*

- **Brittany Tourism**
  You'll find information, bookings and events alongside comprehensive guides to each Breton subregion. *brittanytourism.com*

WHAT'S ON

- **Fête de la Bretagne**
  Hundreds of thousands attend this two-week, province-wide celebration of Breton culture in the second half of May.

- **D-Day Festival**
  Commemorating the Allied Landings in Normandy, this festival spans all five D-Day beaches (late May to mid-June).

- **Les Médiévales de Bayeux**
  For a weekend in late June or early July, Bayeux skips back to the Middle Ages, with a medieval market, street performers, a parade and more.

08

NORMANDY & BRITTANY

MONET'S NORMANDY

★ BEST FOR

CULTURE

Rouen has plenty of top-quality museums and historic buildings.

DURATION: 4 DAYS

DISTANCE: 290KM / 180 MILES

GREAT FOR: FOOD & DRINK, HISTORY & CULTURE

BEST TIME TO GO: ANY TIME FROM SEPTEMBER TO JUNE FOR PERFECTLY NUANCED LIGHT.

St-Valery en Caux

Be prepared for a visual feast on this four-day trip around the eastern part of Normandy – the cradle of impressionism. Starting from Giverny, location of the most celebrated garden in France, you'll follow in the footsteps of Monet and other impressionist megastars, taking in medieval Rouen, the dramatic Côte d'Albâtre, Le Havre, Honfleur and Trouville-sur-Mer.

LINK YOUR TRIP

11 Tour des Fromages
From Honfleur or Rouen you can embark on a gastronomic drive, and taste and learn about some of the best cheese in France at various cheese museums.

09 D-Day's Beaches
From Trouville, it's an easy 50km drive west to Caen, the obvious starting point for the D-Day beaches.

01 Giverny

The tiny country village of Giverny is a place of pilgrimage for devotees of impressionism. Claude Monet lived here from 1883 until his death in 1926, in a rambling house – surrounded by flower-filled gardens – that's now the immensely popular **Maison et Jardins de Claude Monet** *(claudemonetgiverny.fr)*. His pastel-pink house and Water Lily studio stand on the periphery of the garden (called 'Clos Normand'), with its symmetrically laid-out gardens bursting with flowers.

THE DRIVE: It's a 71km trip (one hour) to Rouen. Head to Vernon and follow signs to Rouen along the A13. A more scenic (but slower) route is the D313 via Les Andelys, along the east bank of the Seine.

02 Rouen

With its elegant spires and atmospheric medieval quarter

TRAVELLER70/SHUTTERSTOCK

complete with narrow lanes and wonky half-timbered houses, it's no wonder that Rouen has inspired numerous painters, including Monet. Some of his works, including one of his studies of the stunning Gothic **Cathédrale Notre Dame** *(cathedrale-rouen.net)*, are displayed at the splendid **Musée des Beaux-Arts** *(mbarouen.fr)*. Feeling inspired? Sign up for an art class with the **tourist office** *(rouentourisme.com)* and create your own Rouen Cathedral canvas from the very room in which Monet painted his series of that building.

If you're at all interested in architectural glories, the 14th-century **Abbatiale St-Ouen** *(rouen.fr/abbatiale-saint-ouen)*, which is a marvellous example of the Rayonnant Gothic style, is a must-see abbey. There's also much Joan of Arc lore in Rouen (she was executed here in 1431). For the story of her life don't miss the spectacular audiovisual displays in the **Historial Jeanne d'Arc** *(historial-jeannedarc.fr)*.

THE DRIVE: Follow signs to Dieppe. Count on 45 minutes for the 64km trip via the A151 and N27.

03 Dieppe

Sandwiched between limestone cliffs, Dieppe is a small-scale fishing port with a pleasant seafront promenade. Still used by fishing vessels but dominated by pleasure craft, the port makes for a bracing sea-air stroll. High above the city on the western cliff, the 15th-century **Musée de Dieppe** *(dieppe.fr)* is the town's most imposing landmark. Monet immortalised **Pourville**, a seaside village on the western outskirts of Dieppe.

THE DRIVE: Take the scenic coastal roads (D75 and D68), rather than the inland D925, via the resort towns of Pourville, Varengeville-sur-Mer, Quiberville, St-Aubin-sur-Mer, Sotteville-sur-Mer and Veules-les-Roses. The 35km journey takes 45 minutes.

04 St-Valery en Caux

You're now in the heart of the scenic Côte d'Albâtre (Alabaster Coast), which stretches from Dieppe southwest to Étretat. With its lofty bone-white cliffs, this wedge of coast is a geological wonderworld that charmed a generation of impressionists, including Monet. Once you get a glimpse of sweet little St-Valery en Caux, with its delightful port, lovely stretch of stony beach and majestic cliffs, you'll see why.

THE DRIVE: Take the coastal road (D79) via Veulettes-sur-Mer. Count on an hour for the 36km trip.

05 Fécamp

After all that driving along the Côte d'Albâtre, it's time to stop for a glass of Bénédictine at the **Palais de la Bénédictine** *(benedictinedom.com)*. Opened in 1900, this unusually ornate factory is where all the Bénédictine liqueur in the world is made.

Be sure to drive up north to **Cap Fagnet**, which offers gobsmacking views of the town and the coastline.

THE DRIVE: Follow signs to Étretat (17km, along the D940). You could also start on the D940 and turn off onto the more scenic D11 (via Yport).

06 Étretat

Étretat might be the most enticing town in Normandy. It's picture-postcard everywhere you look and the dramatic white cliffs that bookend the town, the **Falaise d'Aval** to the southwest and the **Falaise d'Amont** to the northeast, will stick in your memory. Once at the top, you'll pinch yourself to see if it's real – the views are sensational. Such irresistible scenery made Étretat a favourite of painters, especially Monet, who produced more than 80 canvases of the scenery here.

THE DRIVE: Follow signs to Le Havre (28km, along the D940 and the D147). Count on about half an hour for the journey.

07 Le Havre

It was in Le Havre that Monet painted the defining impressionist view. His 1873 canvas of the harbour at dawn was entitled *Impression: Sunrise*. Monet wouldn't recognise present-day Le Havre: all but obliterated in September 1944 by Allied bombing raids, the city centre was totally redesigned after the war by Belgian architect Auguste Perret. Make sure you visit the **Musée d'Art Moderne André Malraux** (MuMa; *muma-lehavre.fr*), which houses a truly fabulous collection of impressionist works, with canvases by Monet, Eugène Boudin, Camille Corot and many more. Then take in the **Église St-Joseph** (*lehavre-etretat-tourisme.com/decouvrir/les-incontournables/eglise-saint-joseph-du-havre*), a modern church whose interior is a luminous work of art – thanks to 13,000 panels of coloured glass on its walls and tower. For doses of Baroque ecclesiastical architecture, stop by **Cathédrale Notre-Dame**.

THE DRIVE: Follow the A131 and A29 for 25km, which link Le Havre to Honfleur.

08 Honfleur

Honfleur is exquisite to look at. (No, you're not dreaming!) Its heart is the highly picturesque **Vieux Bassin** (Old Harbour), from where explorers once set sail for the New World. Marvel at the extraordinary 15th-century wooden **Église Ste-Catherine**, complete with a roof that from the inside resembles an upturned boat, then

Étretat

PHOTO OPPORTUNITY

The truly extraordinary coastal vista from the clifftop in Étretat.

ZIYE/SHUTTERSTOCK

wander the warren of flower-filled cobbled streets lined with wooden and stone buildings.

Honfleur's graceful beauty has inspired numerous painters, including Eugène Boudin, an early impressionist painter born here in 1824, and Monet. Their works are displayed at the **Musée Eugène Boudin** *(musees-honfleur.fr)*. Honfleur was also the birthplace of composer Erik Satie. The fascinating **Les Maisons Satie** *(musees-honfleur.fr/maison-satie.html)* is packed with surrealist surprises, all set to his ethereal compositions.

THE DRIVE: From Honfleur it's a 14km trip to Trouville-sur-Mer along the D513 (about 20 minutes).

09 Deauville-Trouville

Finish your impressionist road trip in style by heading southwest to the twin seaside resorts of Deauville and Trouville-sur-Mer, which are only separated by a river bridge but maintain distinctly different personalities. Exclusive, expensive and brash, **Deauville** is packed with designer boutiques, deluxe hotels and public gardens of impossible neatness, and is home to two racetracks and a high-profile American **film festival** *(festival-deauville.com)*.

Trouville-sur-Mer, another veteran beach resort, is more down to earth. During the 19th century the town was frequented by writers and painters, including Monet, who spent his honeymoon here in 1870. No doubt he was lured by the picturesque port, the 2km-long sandy beach lined with opulent villas, and the laid-back seaside ambience.

SUSAN MONTGOMERY/SHUTTERSTOCK

Giverny (p80)

CLAUDE MONET

The undisputed leader of the impressionists, Claude Monet was born in Paris in 1840 and grew up in Le Havre, where he found an early affinity with the outdoors.

From 1867 Monet's distinctive style began to emerge, focusing on the effects of light and colour and using the quick, undisguised broken brushstrokes that would characterise the impressionist period. His contemporaries were Pissarro, Renoir, Sisley, Cézanne and Degas. The young painters left the studio to work outdoors, experimenting with the shades and hues of nature, and arguing and sharing ideas. Their work was far from welcomed by critics; one of them condemned it as 'impressionism', in reference to Monet's *Impression: Sunrise* when it was exhibited in 1874.

From the late 1870s Monet concentrated on painting in series, seeking to recreate a landscape by showing its transformation under different conditions of light and atmosphere. In 1883 Monet moved to Giverny, planting his property with a variety of flowers around an artificial pond, the Jardin d'Eau, in order to paint the subtle effects of sunlight on natural forms. It was here that he painted the *Nymphéas* (Water Lilies) series.

For more info on Monet and his work, visit *claude-monet.com*.

09

NORMANDY & BRITTANY

D-DAY'S BEACHES

★ BEST FOR

HISTORY

The Caen-Normandie Mémorial provides you with a comprehensive D-Day overview.

Sword Beach

DURATION: 3 DAYS

DISTANCE: 142KM / 88 MILES

GREAT FOR: HISTORY & CULTURE

BEST TIME TO GO: APRIL TO JULY, TO AVOID SUMMER-HOLIDAY TRAFFIC AROUND THE BEACHES.

The beaches and bluffs are quiet today, but on 6 June 1944 the Normandy shoreline witnessed the arrival of the largest armada the world has ever seen. This patch of the French coast will forever be synonymous with D-Day (known to the French as Jour J), and the coastline is strewn with memorials, museums and cemeteries – reminders that though victory was won on the Longest Day, it came at a high price.

LINK YOUR TRIP

02 Essential France
The island abbey of Mont St-Michel is about 140km from the Normandy coastline, about two hours' drive via the A84 motorway.

08 Monet's Normandy
From the end of our Monet-themed trip at Trouville-sur-Mer, drive southwest on the D677 and A13 to Caen, a journey of just over 60km.

01 Caen

Situated 3km northwest of Caen, the award-winning **Caen-Normandie Mémorial** *(memorial-caen.fr)* is a brilliant place to begin with some background on the historic events of D-Day and the wider context of WWII. Housed in a purpose-designed building covering 14,000 sq metres, the memorial offers an immersive experience, using sound, lighting, film, animation and audio testimony to evoke the grim realities of war, the trials of occupation and the joy of liberation.

The visit begins with a whistle-stop overview of Europe's descent into total war, tracing events from the end of WWI through to the rise of fascism in Europe, the German occupation of France and the Battle of Normandy. A second section focuses on the Cold War. There's also the well-preserved original bunker used by German command in 1944.

PETE STUART/SHUTTERSTOCK

On your way around, look out for a Hawker Typhoon fighter plane and a full-size Sherman tank.

THE DRIVE: From the museum, head northeast along Esplanade Brillaud de Laujardière, and follow signs to Ouistreham. You'll join the E46 ring road; follow it to exit 3a (Porte d'Angleterre), and merge onto the D515 and D84 to Ouistreham. Park on the seafront on bd Aristide Briand. In all, it's a trip of 18km.

02 Ouistreham

On D-Day, the sandy seafront around Ouistreham was codenamed **Sword Beach** and was the focus of attack for the British 3rd Infantry Division.

There are precious few reminders of the battle now, but on D-Day the scene was very different: most of the surrounding buildings had been levelled by artillery fire, and German bunkers and artillery positions were strung out along the seafront. Sword Beach was the site of some of the most famous images of D-Day – including the infamous ones of British troops landing with bicycles, and bagpiper Bill Millin piping troops ashore while under heavy fire.

THE DRIVE: Follow the seafront west onto rue de Lion, following signs for 'Overlord – L'Assaut' onto the D514 towards Courseulles-sur-Mer, 18km west. Drive through town onto rue de Ver, and follow signs to 'Centre Juno Beach'.

03 Juno & Gold Beaches

On D-Day, Courseulles-sur-Mer was known as Juno Beach, and was stormed mainly by Canadian troops. It was here that the exiled French General Charles de Gaulle came ashore after the landings – the first 'official' French soldier to set foot in mainland Europe since 1940. He was followed by Winston Churchill on 12 June and King George VI on 16 June. A Cross of Lorraine marks the historic spot.

The area's only Canadian museum, the **Juno Beach Centre** *(junobeach.org)*, has exhibits on Canada's role in the war effort and the landings, and offers guided tours of Juno Beach, including the bunker there, from April to October.

D-DAY DRIVING ROUTES

There are several signposted driving routes around the main battle sites – look for signs for 'D-Day-Le Choc' in the American sectors and 'Overlord – L'Assaut' in the British and Canadian sectors. A free booklet called *The D-Day Landings and the Battle of Normandy*, available from tourist offices, has details on the main routes.

Maps of the D-Day beaches are widely available in the region.

A short way west is **Gold Beach**, attacked by the British 50th Infantry on D-Day.

THE DRIVE: Drive west along the D514 for 14km to Arromanches. You'll pass a car park and viewpoint marked with a statue of the Virgin Mary, which overlooks Port Winston and Gold Beach. Follow the road into town and signs to Musée du Débarquement.

04 Arromanches

This seaside town was the site of one of the great logistical achievements of D-Day. In order to unload the vast quantities of cargo needed by the invasion forces without capturing one of the heavily defended Channel ports, the Allies set up prefabricated marinas off two landing beaches, code named **Mulberry Harbour**. These consisted of 146 massive cement caissons towed over from England and sunk to form a semicircular breakwater in which floating bridge spans were moored. In the three months after D-Day, the Mulberries facilitated the unloading of a mind-boggling 2.5 million soldiers, four million tonnes of equipment and 500,000 vehicles.

At low tide, the stanchions of one of these artificial quays, **Port Winston** (named after Winston Churchill), can still be seen on the sands at Arromanches.

Beside the beach, the **Musée du Débarquement** (Landing Museum; *musee-arromanches.fr*) explains the logistics and importance of Port Winston.

THE DRIVE: Continue west along the D514 for 6km to the village of

Mulberry Harbour, Arromanches

OLRAT/SHUTTERSTOCK

Longues-sur-Mer. You'll see the sign for the Batterie de Longues on your right.

05 Longues-sur-Mer

At Longues-sur-Mer you can get a glimpse of the awesome firepower available to the German defenders in the shape of a row of 150mm artillery guns, still housed in their concrete casements. On D-Day they were capable of hitting targets over 20km away – including Gold Beach (to the east) and Omaha Beach (to the west). Parts of the classic D-Day film *The Longest Day* (1962) were filmed here.

THE DRIVE: Backtrack to the crossroads and head straight over onto the D104, signed to Vaux-sur-Aure/Bayeux, for 8km. When you reach town, turn right onto the D613, and follow signs to the 'Musée de la Bataille de Normandie'.

06 Bayeux

Though best known for its medieval tapestry, Bayeux has another claim to fame: it was the first town to be liberated after D-Day (on the morning of 7 June 1944).

It's also home to the largest of Normandy's 18 Commonwealth military cemeteries – the **Bayeux War Cemetery** *(cwgc.org)*, situated on bd Fabien Ware. It contains 4848 graves of soldiers from the UK and 10 other countries, including Germany. Across the road is a memorial for 1807 Commonwealth soldiers whose remains were never found. The Latin inscription reads: 'We, whom William once conquered, have now set free the conqueror's native land'.

Nearby, the **Musée Mémorial de la Bataille de Normandie** (Battle of Normandy Memorial Museum; *bayeuxmuseum.com*) explores the battle through photos, personal accounts, dioramas and film.

♥ WHY I LOVE THIS TRIP

OLIVER BERRY, WRITER

You'll have heard the D-Day story many times before, but there's nothing quite like standing on the beaches where this epic struggle played out. D-Day marked the turning point of WWII and heralded the end for Nazism in Europe. Paying your respects to the soldiers who laid down their lives in the name of freedom is an experience that will stay with you forever.

THE DRIVE: After overnighting in Bayeux, head northwest of town on the D6 towards Port-en-Bessin-Huppain. You'll reach a supermarket after about 10km. Go round the roundabout and turn onto the D514 for another 8km. You'll see signs to the 'Cimetière Americain' near the hamlet of Le Bray. Omaha Beach is another 4km further on, near Vierville-sur-Mer.

07 Omaha Beach

If anywhere symbolises the courage and sacrifice of D-Day, it's Omaha – still known as 'Bloody Omaha' to US veterans. It was here, on the 7km stretch of coastline between Vierville-sur-Mer, St-Laurent-sur-Mer and Colleville-sur-Mer, that the most brutal fighting on D-Day took place. US troops had to fight their way across the beach towards the heavily defended cliffs, exposed to underwater obstacles, hidden minefields and withering crossfire. The toll was heavy: of the 2500 casualties at Omaha on D-Day, more than 1000 were killed, most within the first hour of the landings.

High on the bluffs above Omaha, the **Normandy American Cemetery & Memorial** *(abmc.gov)* provides a sobering reminder of the human cost of the battle. Featured in the opening scenes of *Saving Private Ryan* (1998), this is the largest American cemetery in Europe, containing the graves of 9387 American soldiers, and a memorial to 1557 comrades 'known only unto God'.

Start off in the very thoughtfully designed visitor centre, which has moving portrayals of some of the soldiers buried here. Afterwards, take in the expanse of white marble crosses and Stars of David that stretch off in seemingly endless rows, surrounded by an immaculately tended expanse of lawn.

THE DRIVE: From the Vierville-sur-Mer seafront, follow the rural D514 through quiet countryside towards Grandcamp-Maisy. After about 10km you'll see signs to 'Pointe du Hoc'.

08 Pointe du Hoc

West of Omaha, this craggy promontory was the site of D-Day's most audacious military exploit. At 7.10am, 225 US Army Rangers commanded by Lt Col James Earl Rudder scaled the sheer 30m cliffs, where the Germans had stationed a battery of artillery guns trained onto the beaches of Utah and Omaha. Unfortunately, the guns had already been moved inland, and Rudder and his soldiers spent the next two days repelling counterattacks. By the time they were finally relieved on 8 June, 81 of the rangers had been killed and 58 more had been wounded.

Today the **Pointe du Hoc Ranger Memorial** *(abmc.gov)*, which France turned over to the US government in 1979, looks much as it did on D-Day, complete with shell craters and crumbling gun emplacements.

THE DRIVE: Stay on the D514 to Grandcamp-Maisy, then continue south onto the D13. Stay on the road until you reach the turn-off for the D913, signed to St-Marie-du-Mont/Utah Beach. It's a drive of 44km.

09 Utah Beach

The D-Day tour ends at Ste-Marie-du-Mont, aka Utah Beach, assaulted by soldiers of the US 4th and 8th Infantry Divisions. The beach was relatively lightly defended, and by midday the landing force had linked with paratroopers from the 101st Airborne. By nightfall, some 20,000 soldiers and 1700 vehicles had arrived on French soil, and the road to European liberation had begun.

Today the site is marked by military memorials and the **Musée du Débarquement** (Utah Beach Landing Museum; *utah-beach.com*), a modern and impressive museum just inland from the beach.

DETOUR

Coutances
Start: 09 Utah Beach

The lovely old Norman town of Coutances makes a good detour when travelling between the D-Day beaches and Mont St-Michel. At the town's heart is its Gothic **Cathédrale Notre-Dame de Coutances** *(cathedralecoutances.free.fr)*. Interior highlights include several 13th-century windows, a 14th-century fresco of St Michael skewering the dragon, and an organ and high altar from the mid-1700s. You can climb the lantern tower on a tour.

Coutances is 50km south of Utah Beach by the most direct route via the D913 and D971.

D-DAY IN FIGURES

Code named 'Operation Overlord', the D-Day landings were the largest military operation in history. On the morning of 6 June 1944, swarms of landing craft – part of an armada of over 6000 ships and 13,000 aeroplanes – hit the northern Normandy beaches, and tens of thousands of soldiers from the USA, the UK, Canada and elsewhere began pouring onto French soil. The initial landing force involved some 45,000 troops; 15 more divisions were to follow once successful beachheads had been established.

The majority of the 135,000 Allied troops stormed ashore along 80km of beaches north of Bayeux code named (from west to east) Utah, Omaha, Gold, Juno and Sword. The landings were followed by the 76-day Battle of Normandy, during which the Allies suffered 210,000 casualties, including 37,000 troops killed. German casualties are believed to have been around 200,000; another 200,000 German soldiers were taken prisoner. About 14,000 French civilians also died.

For more background and statistics, see *normandie44lamemoire.com, dday.org* and *6juin1944.com*.

Normandy American Cemetery & Memorial (p87)

MIKE WORKMAN/SHUTTERSTOCK

PHOTO OPPORTUNITY

The forest of white marble crosses at the Normandy American Cemetery & Memorial.

10

NORMANDY & BRITTANY

BRETON COAST

DURATION: 8 DAYS

DISTANCE: 642KM / 399 MILES

GREAT FOR: FAMILIES, HISTORY & CULTURE, NATURE

BEST TIME TO GO: APRIL AND MAY, FOR FINE, SUNNY WEATHER AND NO CROWDS.

★ BEST FOR

HISTORY

Walking through the prehistoric megalithic sites at Carnac.

St-Malo

This is a trip for explorers who want to experience a very different slice of French life. Instead of the Eiffel Tower, fine wines and *haute couture* (high fashion), you'll take in a dramatic coastline, excellent seafood, medieval towns, prehistoric mysticism and Celtic pride.

LINK YOUR TRIP

09 D-Day's Beaches
Combining a drive around the Breton coast with the war memorials of Normandy is easy. Caen is 170km along the A84 from St-Malo.

13 Caves & Cellars of the Loire
From Vannes it's 268km to Montsoreau, where you can pick up our tour of the Western Loire's cave dwellings and wine cellars.

01 St-Malo

Once a haven for pirates and adventurers, the impressive walled town of St-Malo is today a genteel mast-filled port hemmed by pretty beaches and guarded by an array of offshore islands. The walled quarter of **Intra-Muros** is arguably the most interesting urban centre in Brittany, but it's not as old as it appears. Most of the town was flattened in WWII and has since been painstakingly rebuilt.

THE DRIVE: The 35km, half-hour drive along the D137 between St-Malo and Dinan is through a largely built-up area and offers little of interest. Expect heavy traffic and delays.

02 Dinan

Set high above the fast-flowing Rance River, the narrow (and sometimes plunging) cobblestone streets of Dinan are lined with crooked, creaking

ANTOINEZK/SHUTTERSTOCK

half-timbered houses straight out of the Middle Ages. All of this guarantees a tourist bonanza in the warmer months, of course, but choose anything slightly off-season and you may find the place deserted.

THE DRIVE: Take the wiggly and very slow (count on a 3½-hour drive) coastal D786 between Dinan and Roscoff. Highlights include the pretty port of Paimpol and the breathtaking Côte de Granit Rose, which extends west of the town of Perros-Guirec. This leg is 220km.

03 Roscoff

Set around an arcing harbour studded with granite cottages and seafront villas, Roscoff is one of the more captivating cross-channel ferry ports.

After you've explored the town, set sail for the peaceful **Île de Batz**, which sits a short way offshore. The mild island climate supports the luxuriant **Jardins Georges Delaselle** *(jardin-georgesdelaselle.bzh)*, with over 1500 plants from all five continents.

Ferries run every 30 minutes in July and August, but less frequently the rest of the year.

THE DRIVE: Taking the D69, D30 and D791, drive the 88km between Roscoff and Crozon, the main town on the Presqu'île de Crozon. You'll follow the western edge of the Parc Naturel Régional d'Armorique. Visit famous Breton parish closes (enclosed churches with special architecture) at St-Thégonnec, Guimiliau and/or Sizun.

04 Presqu'île de Crozon

Anchor-shaped Crozon Peninsula is without doubt one of the most scenic spots in Brittany.

At the western extremity of the peninsula, **Camaret-sur-Mer** is a classic fishing village that lures artists. Three kilometres south of the village is the spectacular **Pointe de Pen-Hir** headland.

Nearby **Morgat** is one of the prettier resorts in this part of Brittany, with colourful houses clustered at one end of a long sandy beach.

THE DRIVE: Using the D63 it's just over 50km from Crozon town to Quimper. But if you turn off onto the D7 at Plonévez-Porzay after 30km and head west for another 46km, you'll reach **Pointe du Raz**, one of Brittany's most spectacular rocky points. Then you can swing back east on the D784 via Audierne for the 53km to Quimper.

05 Quimper

At the centre of the Finistère region's thriving capital is the **Cathédrale St-Corentin** *(diocese-quimper.fr)*, with its distinctive dip, said to symbolise Christ's inclined head as he was dying on the cross. Next door, the **Musée Départemental Breton** *(musee-breton.finistere.fr)* showcases Breton history, furniture, costumes, crafts and archaeology.

THE DRIVE: Rather than taking the faster N165 between Quimper and Concarneau, meander along the more scenic D783. Even on this slower road you only need 30 minutes to travel the 23km.

06 Concarneau

The sheltered harbour of Concarneau is one of the busiest fishing ports in Brittany and is a hugely popular summer holiday destination with numerous attractive **beaches** and coves. In the middle of the harbour is the old quarter of the **Ville Close**, encircled by medieval walls and crammed with enchanting old stone houses.

MIGHTY MEGALITHS

This entire region is rich in neolithic menhirs, dolmens, cromlechs, tumuli and cairns. Just north of Carnac there is a vast array of monoliths set up in several distinct alignments, all visible from the road, though fenced for controlled admission. The main information point for the Carnac alignments is the **Maison des Mégalithes** *(menhirs-carnac.fr)*, which explores the history of the site and has a rooftop viewpoint overlooking the alignments. The Maison organises one-hour guided visits several times daily in French and weekly in English during the summer.

Across the road from the Maison des Mégalithes, the largest menhir field – with 1170 stones – is the **Alignements du Ménec**, 1km north of Carnac-Ville. From here, the D196 heads northeast for about 1.5km to the equally impressive **Alignements de Kermario**, parts of which are open year-round. Climb the stone observation tower midway along the site to see the alignment from above.

The **Tumulus de Kercado** lies just east of Kermario and 500m to the south of the D196. It's the massive burial mound of a neolithic chieftain dating from 3800 BCE. Deposit your fee (€1) in an honour box at the entry gate. The easternmost of the major groups is the Alignements de Kerlescan.

Be sure to visit the **Musée de Préhistoire** *(museedecarnac.fr)* in Carnac-Ville to see incredible neolithic artefacts found throughout the region.

THE DRIVE: Cross the picturesque Moros River on the D783 and trundle on for 17km (30 minutes) through rural scenery to Pont-Aven.

07 Pont-Aven

Long ago discovered by artists like Paul Gauguin (1848–1903), the tiny village of Pont-Aven is brimming with galleries. For an insight into the town's place in art history, stop by the excellent **Musée de Pont-Aven** *(museepontaven.fr)*. The town also has excellent eateries, so it's perfect for a pit stop.

THE DRIVE: From Pont-Aven to Carnac it's a fast but dull one-hour (81km) drive down the N165 dual carriageway past the large industrial city of Lorient.

08 Carnac

With enticing beaches and a pretty town centre, Carnac would be a popular tourist town even without its collection of magnificent megalithic sites. The area surrounding the town has 3000 of these upright stones – the world's largest concentration – erected between 5000 and 3500 BCE.

THE DRIVE: Rather than taking the N165 to Vannes (31km), opt for the beautiful coastal route. From Carnac head south to Carnac Plage and then east to pretty La Trinité-sur-Mer. Join the D781 and then the D28 inland to Auray. From here join the D101, which leads into Vannes. This 40km route takes just over an hour.

09 Vannes

Street art, sculptures and intriguing galleries pop up unexpectedly through the half-timbered, lively cobbled city of Vannes. Surrounding the pretty

BILDAGENTUR ZOONAR GMBH/SHUTTERSTOCK

PHOTO OPPORTUNITY

Standing on the precipice of the cliffs of the Pointe du Raz.

Pointe du Raz

walled old town is a broad moat; within the ramparts explore the web of narrow alleys ranged around the 13th-century Gothic **Cathédrale St-Pierre**.

The nearby **Golfe du Morbihan** is one of France's most attractive stretches of coastline. From April to September, **Navix** *(navix.fr)* and other companies run a range of cruises.

DETOUR

Josselin

Start: 09 Vannes

In the shadow of an enormous, cone-turreted, 14th-century castle, the storybook village of Josselin lies on the banks of the Oust River, 45km northeast of Vannes. Place Notre Dame, a beautiful square of 16th-century half-timbered houses, is the little town's heart, but the magnificent **Château de Josselin** *(chateaudejosselin.com)* is the real reason for this detour.

From Vannes it's an easy one-hour drive along the D126 through an increasingly green and rural landscape of cows and forests.

STAY AWHILE

PRESQU'ÎLE DE CROZON

BY ANNA RICHARDS

Although the Presqu'île de Crozon is, as the name suggests, a peninsula rather than an island, there's a sense of otherness here that you won't find even on many of Brittany's true islands. **Morgat** is the most polished town, drawing visitors with a long, sandy beach and easy access to Île Vierge's sea arch; you can hire a kayak from the **Centre Nautique de Crozon Morgat** *(cncm.fr)* to paddle right underneath it. It's also well placed for some beautiful and pretty challenging clifftop hiking around Cap de la Chèvre.

It is creative little **Camaret-sur-Mer**, though, that could turn just about anyone into an aspiring artiste. Here, artists' studios are plentiful, and paintings of the gorse, rock formations and sea birds are propped up against every wall. In **Rostellec**, you can go shipwreck diving without leaving land at the boat cemetery, where the skeletons of old fishing vessels litter the shoreline.

Between kayaking, hiking and eating as many Breton *galettes* (savoury buckwheat crêpes) as you possibly can, there are dozens of beaches to explore, from shingle to soft, golden sand. The most spectacular are those backed with sand dunes: the beaches of Aber, Goulien, La Palue and Lostmarc'h.

If you happen to be visiting in late July or early August, don't miss **Le Festival du Bout du Monde** *(festivalduboutdumonde.com),* a three day celebration of world music with plenty of patriotic Breton flag flying.

LINK YOUR TRIP

10 **Breton Coast** Great half-way stop on the Brittany coast.

Left: Rostellec; Right: Le Festival du Bout du Monde

PLACES TO STAY

The Presqu'Île de Crozon is riddled with small, characterful, family-run properties.

- **Le Styvel**
  Canary-yellow Le Styvel, right on the port in Camaret-sur-Mer, has spectacular sea views from most of the rooms, plus a restaurant on-site. *(hotel-du-styvel.com)*

- **Kermaria**
  On the other side of the peninsula, Kermaria is just metres from Morgat's sandy beach, with gorgeous wood panelling in all the communal areas and a large garden. *(kermaria.com)*

- **Lodg'Ing Crozon**
  Glampers should head to Lodg'Ing Crozon, whose 20 upmarket bell tents look right across the bay towards Brest.

11

NORMANDY & BRITTANY

TOUR DES FROMAGES

★ BEST FOR

HISTORY

Pay your respects to the memory of Joan of Arc in Rouen.

DURATION: 5 DAYS

DISTANCE: 315KM / 196 MILES

GREAT FOR: FOOD & DRINK, HISTORY & CULTURE

BEST TIME TO GO: IN MAY PONT-L'ÉVÊQUE CELEBRATES ALL THAT IS CHEESE DURING THE FÊTE DU FROMAGE.

Camembert cheese

More cheese, please! It's said that in France there is a different variety of cheese for every day of the year. On this culinary extravaganza, you'll taste – and learn about – some of the very finest of French cheeses. Cheese cravings sated, explore the backstreets of Rouen, build castles made of sand on the seashore and clamber up to castles made of stone in the interior.

LINK YOUR TRIP

05 In Flanders Fields
The war memorials of northern France are a powerful symbol of the wastefulness of war. Amiens, on our Flanders Fields drive, is 120km from Rouen.

06 Champagne Taster
From Rouen it's 284km to Reims and the start of another culinary adventure – this one fuelled by the bubbly stuff.

01 Camembert

The delicious soft cheese Camembert is known the world over. Therefore, it can come as a surprise to learn that Camembert is also a small, but very picturesque, classic Norman village of half-timbered buildings. The big attraction here is, of course, its cheese, and you can learn all about it during a guided tour of the **Maison du Camembert** *(maisonducamembert.com)*, an early-19th-century farm restored by Président, one of the region's largest Camembert producers.

THE DRIVE: It's a 5km, 10-minute drive along the D246 and then the D16 from Camembert village to the Musée du Camembert in Vimoutiers.

02 Musée du Camembert

Make a stop in the tiny village of Vimoutiers to visit the small **Musée du Camembert**

JIRI HERA/SHUTTERSTOCK

(museeducamembert.fr), which gives you the lowdown on the history and culture of the smelly stuff. Needless to say, you'll get to do plenty of sampling of a variety of regional cheeses and ciders.

THE DRIVE: It's another 10-minute drive north to Livarot along the D579.

03 Livarot

Although not as famous internationally as Camembert, Livarot is a big deal in France, where this traditional soft cheese is beloved for its nutty flavour. The town where the namesake cheese originated is home to probably the best cheese tour in Normandy. **Le Village Fromager** (L'Atelier Fromager; *graindorge.fr*) offers free tours and tastings at the Graindorge factory. A self-guided walk accompanied by multimedia displays leads through a series of aromatic viewing rooms where you can watch Livarot, Camembert and Pont-l'Évêque being made.

After you've deepened your *fromage* knowledge on the tour, work up an appetite for more on a walk around the town. Its wobbly-wiggly half-timbered buildings make it a real charmer.

THE DRIVE: Head west along the D4 from Livarot to the village of St-Pierre-sur-Dives. The D271 leads to Les Arpents du Soleil winery a little south of the village en route to Grisy.

04 Les Arpents du Soleil

From Livarot, you're detouring a little further west. Just outside the village of St-Pierre-sur-Dives is something a little different for Normandy – not a cider farm, but a renowned vineyard, **Les Arpents du Soleil** *(arpents-du-soleil.com)*, a winemaker since medieval times. The current crop includes three dry whites and a fruity, oaky pinot noir. The shop is open year-round and offers the chance to try the estate's wines, but guided tours only run on certain days, so phone ahead.

THE DRIVE: A gentle countryside cruise of about 45 minutes (42km) up the D16 via St-Pierre-sur-Dives will see you easing into Pont-l'Évêque.

05 Pont-l'Évêque

Since the 13th century this unpretentious little town with rivers meandering through its centre has been known for its eponymous cheese. Although two-thirds of the town was destroyed in WWII, careful reconstruction has brought much of it back to life. Half-timbered buildings line the main street, and 1960s stained glass bathes the 15th-century **Église St-Michel** in coloured light.

There is no shortage of **cheese shops** in town, and if you're passing through over the second weekend in May, don't miss the **Fête du Fromage**, when the town throws a little party for cheese.

THE DRIVE: To get to the Distillerie Christian Drouin, head out of Pont-l'Évêque in a northeasterly direction on the D675. At the roundabout on the edge of the town, take the third exit (rue St-Mélaine/D677) and continue for about 2.5km until you see the farm on your left.

06 Distillerie Christian Drouin

In case you were starting to wonder if Normandy was merely a

PHOTO OPPORTUNITY

The Seine through the ruined windows of Château Gaillard.

one-cheese pony, pay a visit to the **Distillerie Christian Drouin** *(calvados-drouin.com)*, which will let you in on the delights of Norman cider and *calvados* (apple-flavoured brandy, that other classic Norman tipple). Entrance is free.

THE DRIVE: It's a simple 17km drive along the D579 to Honfleur and your first sea views.

07 Honfleur

Long a favourite with painters, Honfleur is arguably Normandy's most charming seaside town.

On the west side of the **Vieux Bassin**, with its many pleasure boats, **quai Ste-Catherine** is lined with tall, taper-thin houses – many protected from the elements by slate tiles – dating from the 16th to the 18th centuries. The **Lieutenance**, at the mouth of the old harbour, was once the residence of the town's royal governor.

Initially intended as a temporary structure, the **Église Ste-Catherine** has been standing in the square for more than 500 years. The church is particularly notable for its double-vaulted roof and twin naves, which from the inside resemble a couple of overturned ships' hulls.

THE DRIVE: Switching from nice, mellow country lanes, hit the gas for the 111km run down the A29 to Neufchâtel-en-Bray.

08 Neufchâtel-en-Bray

The small market town of Neufchâtel-en-Bray is renowned for its heart-shaped cheese called, imaginatively, Neufchâtel. To buy it in the most authentic way, try to time your arrival to coincide with the Saturday-morning **market**.

Appetite satisfied, it's now time for some culture. Check out the **Musée Mathon-Durand** inside a 16th-century half-timbered building that once belonged to a knight. He's long since gone off to fight dragons in the sky, and today the house contains a small museum of local culture.

THE DRIVE: The most obvious route between Neufchâtel-en-Bray and Les Andelys is along the A28, but that means skirting around Rouen – time it badly and you'll be stuck in noxious traffic. Instead, take the more serene D921 country road. Going this way should take you about 80 minutes to cover the 75km.

09 Les Andelys

On a hairpin curve in the Seine lies Les Andelys (the 's' is silent), the old part of which is crowned by the noble ruin of Château Gaillard, the 12th-century hilltop fastness of Richard the Lionheart.

Built in 1196–1197, **Château Gaillard** *(nouvelle-normandie-tourisme.com/decouvrir-nouvelle-normandie/chateau-gaillard-le-medieval)* once secured the western border of English territory along the Seine until Henry IV ordered its destruction in 1603. Fantastic views of the Seine's white cliffs can be enjoyed from the platform a few hundred metres up the one-lane road from the castle.

THE DRIVE: It's a 45km, 50-minute jaunt (assuming you don't hit rush-hour traffic) down the D6014 to your final stop, Rouen.

10 Rouen

With its elegant spires, beautifully restored medieval quarter and soaring Gothic cathedral, the ancient city of Rouen is one of Normandy's highlights. It was here that the young French heroine Joan of Arc (Jeanne d'Arc) was tried for heresy.

Rouen's stunning **Cathédrale Notre Dame** *(cathedrale-rouen.net)* is the famous subject of a series of paintings by Monet.

Rue du Gros Horloge runs from the cathedral west to **Place du Vieux Marché**, where you'll find the arresting **Église Ste-Jeanne-d'Arc**, with its fish-scale exterior and vast, sublime wall of stained glass. It sits on the spot where the 19-year-old Joan was burned at the stake.

Château Gaillard

MAX LEBEDEV/GETTY IMAGES

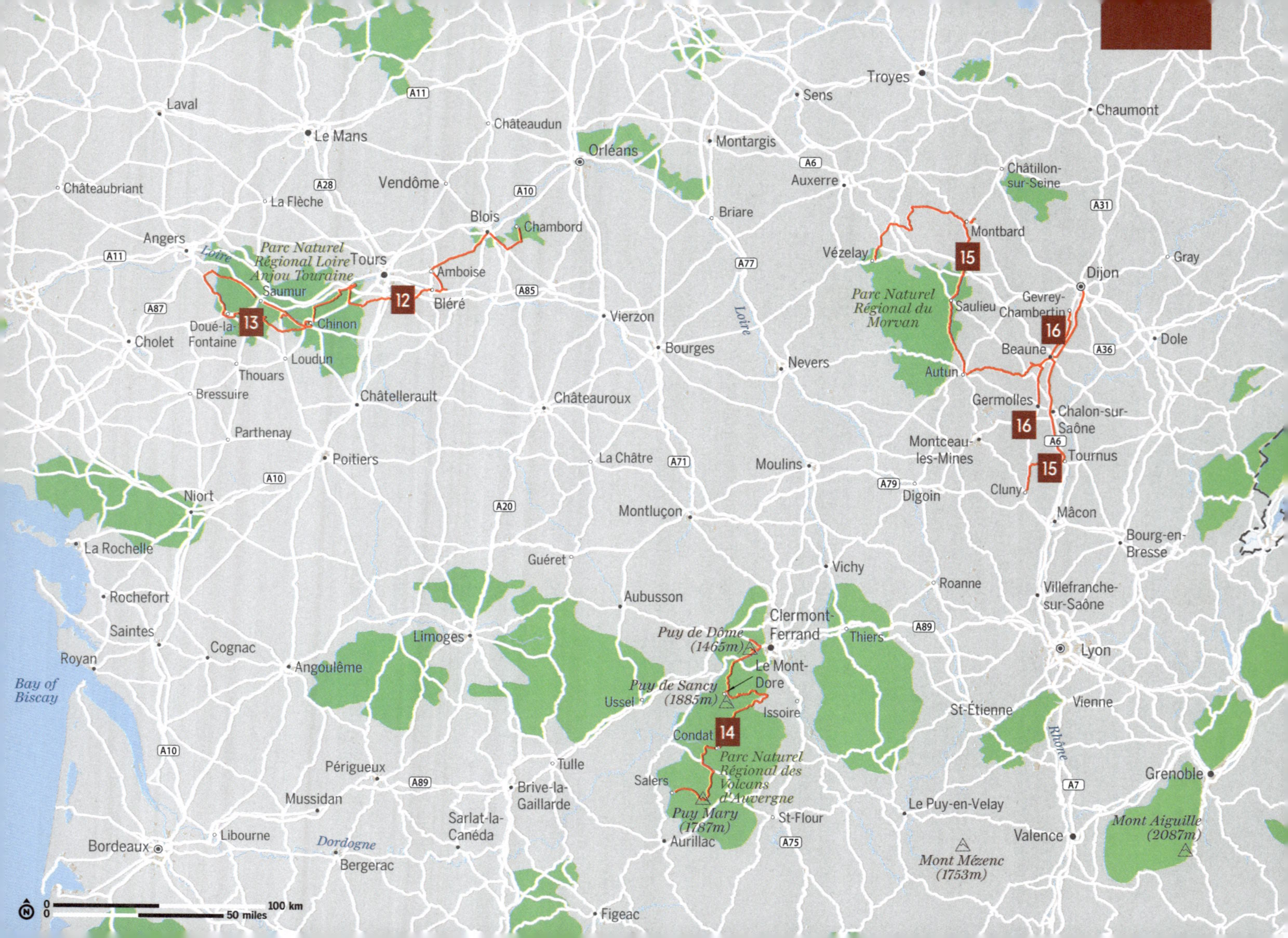

Troyes
Sens
Chaumont
Laval
Le Mans
Châteaudun
Orléans
Montargis
Châtillon-sur-Seine
Châteaubriant
La Flèche
Vendôme
Auxerre
Blois
Chambord
Briare
Montbard
Angers
Loire
Parc Naturel Régional Loire Anjou Touraine
Tours
Amboise
Vézelay
Gray
Dijon
Saumur
Bléré
Parc Naturel Régional du Morvan
Saulieu
Gevrey-Chambertin
Doué-la-Fontaine
Chinon
Vierzon
Cholet
Loudun
Bourges
Nevers
Beaune
Dole
Thouars
Autun
Bressuire
Châtellerault
Châteauroux
Germolles
Chalon-sur-Saône
Parthenay
Montceau-les-Mines
Poitiers
La Châtre
Moulins
Tournus
Cluny
Digoin
Niort
Montluçon
Mâcon
La Rochelle
Bourg-en-Bresse
Guéret
Vichy
Roanne
Rochefort
Aubusson
Villefranche-sur-Saône
Saintes
Clermont-Ferrand
Cognac
Limoges
Puy de Dôme (1465m)
Thiers
Lyon
Royan
Angoulême
Le Mont-Dore
Bay of Biscay
Puy de Sancy (1885m)
Ussel
Vienne
Issoire
St-Étienne
Condat
Parc Naturel Régional des Volcans d'Auvergne
Rhône
Périgueux
Tulle
Salers
Brive-la-Gaillarde
Grenoble
Mussidan
Puy Mary (1787m)
Le Puy-en-Velay
St-Flour
Sarlat-la-Canéda
Mont Aiguille (2087m)
Libourne
Valence
Bordeaux
Dordogne
Aurillac
Bergerac
Mont Mézenc (1753m)
Figeac
A11
A28
A10
A87
A85
A77
A6
A31
A36
A71
A79
A20
A89
A75
A7
12
13
14
15
16
0
100 km
50 miles
N

DMITRY DEMKIN/SHUTTERSTOCK

Château de Chenonceau (p107)

LOIRE VALLEY & CENTRAL FRANCE

EXPLORE

LOIRE VALLEY & CENTRAL FRANCE

The Loire Valley and central region is the France of your childhood imagination. Multi-turreted châteaux bask in the sun amid sprawling carpets of grape vines. Broad rivers flow through cherry orchards and manicured gardens. The harmonious architecture of medieval towns also nods to the contributions of the Romans and the Gauls. The unforgettable dining here spans the spectrum from peasant classics to haute cuisine. And the ancient forests and volcanic uplands of Auvergne are complemented by the distinctive history and culture of the Burgundians. These driving tours take in the best of these quintessential regions.

Lyon

France's third-largest city is a natural gateway to both Burgundy and Auvergne. A handsome, prosperous and confident city with Roman roots, it's served by Lyon–Saint Exupéry international airport, France's third largest. Connecting Lyon with numerous European destinations, the airport is 30 minutes from the city centre via the Rhônexpress tramway, which terminates at Part-Dieu station. Fast TGV trains connect Lyon and Saint Exupéry with Paris, Marseille, Dijon and other destinations, while local trains run to Clermont-Ferrand. There are plenty of accommodation choices, car-rental firms and supermarkets in central Lyon and near the airport, but be aware that parking in town is scarce and expensive.

Clermont-Ferrand

The natural base for the 'Volcanoes of the Auvergne' road trip, Clermont-Ferrand is the region's largest city. Don't plan on arriving by plane, as the airport here only services a handful of destinations. Rely instead on long-distance bus services, or trains, including TER services to Lyon, Paris, Nantes, Marseille and other French cities. There are plenty of accommodation options, car rentals and places to buy supplies near the train station and in the twin centres of the conjoined town Clermont and Montferrand.

Dijon

The historic capital of the former Duchy of Burgundy, perfectly situated for tackling the 'Medieval Burgundy' and 'Route des Grands

WHEN TO GO

Spring brings both warming weather and a quickening of activity to the Loire Valley and central France, although snow can linger until late May on the volcanoes of the Auvergne. It's also time for the transhumance of alpine dairy herds – an occasion marked by festivals. Summer brings reliably warm weather alongside crowds, especially during school holidays. Autumn is mellower, in both temperature and busyness, while winter usually delivers snow in the uplands.

Crus' drives, Dijon is an appealing destination in its own right. Its pedestrianised heart is packed with historic churches, free museums and accommodation options in every price range. Dijon's principal station, a short stroll from the city centre, offers direct trains to Paris, Lyon, Auxerre, Autun and other regional destinations. Car-rental offices cluster around the station, while grocery stores dot the city and larger supermarkets can be found in its outer reaches.

Tours

One of the largest urban centres in the Loire Valley, Tours is the perfect base for launching into the 'Châteaux of the Loire' and 'Caves & Cellars of the Loire' routes. An important Gallo-Roman settlement and now a university town, it's also a pleasant place to stay in its own right, offering excellent museums, lofty cathedrals, plentiful accommodation and great dining. Tours Val de Loire Airport only services a few destinations, but as the main rail hub in the Loire Valley, the city offers easy access to Paris, Blois, Orléans, Loches and other centres. Car rental and groceries are also readily available.

TRANSPORT

Central France is easily accessed from outside the country by flying into either Lyon or Paris. The country's excellent rail system provides plenty of onward options from both cities, including express TGV trains to Marseille, Dijon and Tours. Just pick a convenient hub town for your intended route, and either hire a car there or at your chosen international airport.

NOTE: A Crit'Air sticker is required in Dijon. See p287 for more details.

RESOURCES

- **Destination Dijon**
  For city passes, guided tours and more. *destinationdijon.com*
- **La Route des Vins de Loire**
  Has all the information you could need on vineyards and wineries in this famous region. *laroutedesvinsdeloire.fr*
- **Auvergne Volcanoes Park**
  For background information, activities and events. *auvergnevolcansancy.com*

WHAT'S ON

- **Fêtes de Jeanne d'Arc**
  The city of Orléans celebrates the liberation of the city by France's patron saint in late April and May, as it has done every year since 1430.
- **Transhumance**
  The mountain culture of the Auvergne is celebrated in late May in tiny Salers, with herds of local dairy cattle driven through the centre of town before being taken to fatten on alpine pastures.

WHERE TO STAY

A contemporary B&B spread over three floors of a townhouse, **5 Chambres en Ville** is close to the station in Clermont-Ferrand. In central Dijon, **La Cour Berbisey** is a classically decorated B&B, offering three huge, parquet-floored suites in a charming, ivy-clad building. **Hôtel SY Les Glycines** in Vézelay is a wisteria-cloaked 18th-century townhouse with boutique hotel rooms filled with old-world charm. **Château de Beaulieu**, on the banks of the Loire 10 minutes from Tours, will satisfy château fantasies. Book for lunch too. **Hôtel Anne de Bretagne** is an ivy-clad hotel in central Blois on the Loire à Vélo, perfect for local cycling adventures.

12

LOIRE VALLEY & CENTRAL FRANCE

CHÂTEAUX OF THE LOIRE

★ BEST

TWO DAYS

The stretch between Chenonceau and Chambord takes in the true classics.

Château de Villandry

DURATION: 5 DAYS

DISTANCE: 189KM / 118 MILES

GREAT FOR: FAMILIES, HISTORY & CULTURE

BEST TIME TO GO: MAY AND JUNE FOR GOOD CYCLING WEATHER; JULY FOR GARDENS AND SPECIAL EVENTS.

From warring medieval warlords to the kings and queens of Renaissance France, a parade of powerful men and women have left their mark on the Loire Valley. The result is France's most magnificent collection of castles. This itinerary visits nine of the Loire's most evocative châteaux, ranging from austere medieval fortresses to ostentatious royal pleasure palaces. Midway through, a side trip leads off the beaten track to four lesser-known châteaux.

LINK YOUR TRIP

13 Caves & Cellars of the Loire
Tour wineries and centuries-old cave dwellings between Chinon and Saumur.

15 Medieval Burgundy
Three hours east of Blois, steep yourself in the world of Burgundy's medieval churches and abbeys.

01 Chinon

Tucked between the medieval **Forteresse Royale de Chinon** *(forteressechinon.fr)* – a magnificent hilltop castle – and the Vienne River, Chinon is known to French schoolchildren as the venue of Joan of Arc's first meeting with Charles VII, future king of France, in 1429. Highlights include superb panoramas from the castle's ramparts and, down in the medieval part of town (along rue Voltaire), several fine buildings dating from the 15th to 17th centuries.

THE DRIVE: Follow the D16 north of Chinon for 10km, then head 15km east on the riverside D7 past the fairy-tale Château d'Ussé (the inspiration for the fairy tale *Sleeping Beauty*) to Lignières, where you catch the D57 3km north into Langeais.

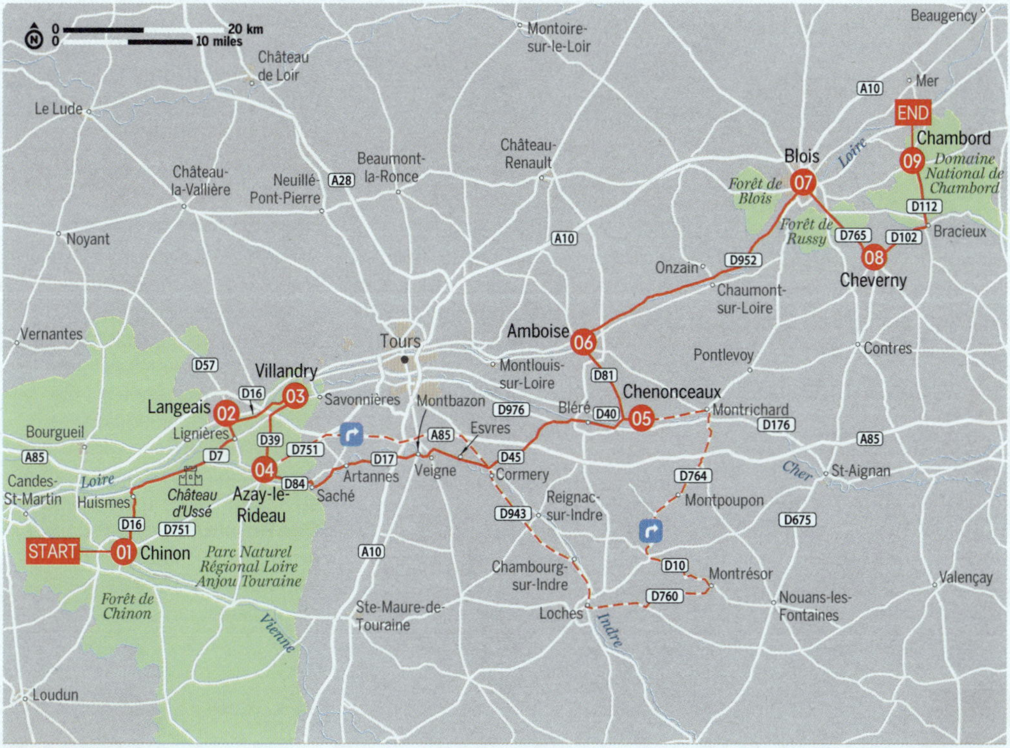

KATE_GPS/SHUTTERSTOCK

02 Langeais

The most medieval of the Loire châteaux, the **Château de Langeais** *(chateau-de-langeais.com)* – built in the 1460s – is superbly preserved inside and out, looking much as it did at the tail end of the Middle Ages, with crenellated ramparts and massive towers dominating the surrounding village. Original 15th-century furniture and Flemish tapestries fill its flagstoned chambers. In one room, a life-size wax-figure tableau portrays the marriage of Charles VIII and Anne of Brittany, held here on 6 December 1491, which brought about the historic union of France and Brittany.

Langeais presents two faces to the world. From the town you see a fortified castle, nearly windowless, with machicolated walls rising forbiddingly from the drawbridge. But the newer sections facing the courtyard have large windows, ornate dormers and decorative stonework designed for more refined living.

Behind the château stands a ruined stone keep constructed in 994 by the warlord Foulques Nerra, France's first great château builder. It is the oldest such structure in France.

THE DRIVE: Backtrack south across the Loire River on the D57, then follow the riverbank east 10km on the D16 to Villandry.

03 Villandry

The six glorious landscaped gardens at the **Château de Villandry** *(chateauvillandry.com)* are among the finest in France, with over 6 hectares of cascading flowers, ornamental vines, manicured lime trees, razor-sharp box hedges and tinkling fountains. Try to visit when the gardens are blooming, between April and October; midsummer is the most spectacular.

Wandering the pebbled walkways, you'll see the classical **Jardin d'Eau** (Water Garden), the **Labyrinthe** (Maze) and the **Jardin d'Ornement** (Ornamental Garden), which depicts various kinds of love (fickle, passionate, tender and tragic). But the highlight is the 16th-century-style **Potager Décoratif** (Decorative Kitchen Garden), where cabbages, leeks and carrots are laid out to create nine geometrical, colour-coordinated squares.

For bird's-eye views across the gardens and the nearby Loire and Cher Rivers, climb to the top of the **donjon** (keep), the only medieval remnant in this otherwise Renaissance-style château.

THE DRIVE: Go southwest 4km on the D7, then turn south 7km on the D39 into Azay-le-Rideau.

04 Azay-le-Rideau

Romantic, moat-ringed **Azay-le-Rideau** *(azay-le-rideau.fr)*, built in the early 1500s on a natural island in the middle of the Indre River, is wonderfully adorned with elegant turrets, Renaissance-style dormer windows, delicate stonework and steep slate roofs. Its most famous feature is an Italian-style loggia staircase overlooking the central courtyard, decorated with the royal salamanders and ermines of François I and Queen Claude. The interior furnishings are mostly 19th century. Outside, the lovely English-style gardens are great for a stroll. A sound-and-light spectacular, **Les Nuits Fantastiques**, is usually projected on the château's walls in July and August.

THE DRIVE: Follow the D84 east 6km through the tranquil Indre valley, then cross the river south into Saché, home to an attractive château and Balzac museum. From Saché continue 26km east on the D17, 11km northeast on the D45 and 9km east on the D976. Cross north over the Cher River and follow the D40 east 1.5km to Chenonceaux village and the Château de Chenonceau.

DETOUR

South of the Loire River

Start: 04 Azay-le-Rideau

Escape the crowds by detouring to four less-visited châteaux between Azay-le-Rideau and Chenonceaux. First stop: **Loches**, where Joan of Arc, fresh from her victory at Orléans in 1429, famously persuaded Charles VII to march to Reims and claim the French crown. The undisputed highlight here is the walled **Cité Royale** *(citeroyaleloches.fr)*, a vast citadel that spans 500 years of French château

Le Clos Lucé

ANTONELLO ARINGHIERI/SHUTTERSTOCK

architecture in a single site, from Foulques Nerra's early-11th-century donjon to the Flamboyant Gothic and Renaissance styles of the **Logis Royal**. To get here from Azay-le-Rideau, head 55km east and then southeast along the D751, A85 and D943.

Next comes the quirky **Château de Montrésor** *(chateaudemontresor.fr)*, 19km east of Loches on the D760, still furnished much as it was 160 years ago, when it belonged to Polish-born count, financier and railroad magnate Xavier Branicki. The eclectic Second Empire decor includes a Cuban mahogany spiral staircase, a piano once played by Chopin and a sumptuous library. Next, head 20km north on the D10 and D764 to the turreted **Château de Montpoupon** *(montpoupon.com)*, idyllically situated in rolling countryside. Furnished in the late 19th and early 20th centuries by the family that still resides there, it has an intimate, lived-in feel. Continue 12km north on the D764 to the ruins of the hilltop **Château de Montrichard**, another massive fortress constructed in the 11th century by Foulques Nerra. You can picnic in the park by the Cher River or taste sparkling wines at **Caves Monmousseau** *(monmousseau.com)*. From Montrichard, head 10km west on the D176 and D40 to rejoin the main route at Chenonceaux.

05 Chenonceaux

Spanning the languid Cher River atop a supremely graceful arched bridge, the **Château de Chenonceau** *(chenonceau.com)* is one of France's most elegant castles. It's hard not to be moved and exhilarated by the glorious setting, the formal gardens, the magic of the architecture and the château's fascinating history. The interior is decorated with rare furnishings and a fabulous art collection.

This extraordinary complex is largely the work of several remarkable women (hence its nickname, Le Château des Dames). The distinctive arches and the eastern formal garden were added by Diane de Poitiers, mistress of King Henri II. Following Henri's death, Catherine de Médici, the king's scheming widow, forced Diane (her second cousin) to exchange Chenonceau for the rather less grand Château de Chaumont. Catherine completed the château's construction and added the yew-tree maze and western rose garden. Chenonceau had an 18th-century heyday under the aristocratic Madame Dupin, who made it a centre of fashionable society; guests included Voltaire and Rousseau.

The château's pièce de résistance is the 60m-long, chequerboard-floored **Grande Gallerie** over the Cher. From 1940 to 1942 it served as an escape route for Jews and other refugees fleeing from German-occupied France (north of the Cher) to the Vichy-controlled south.

THE DRIVE: Follow the D81 north 13km into Amboise; 2km south of town, you'll pass the Mini-Châteaux theme park *(parcminichateaux.com)*, whose intricate scale models of 41 Loire Valley châteaux are great fun for kids.

06 Amboise

Towering above town, the **Château Royal d'Amboise** *(chateau-amboise.com)* was a favoured retreat for all of France's Valois and Bourbon kings. The ramparts afford thrilling views of the town and river, and you can visit the furnished **Logis** (Lodge) and Flamboyant Gothic **Chapelle St-Hubert** (1493), where Leonardo da Vinci's presumed remains have been buried since 1863.

Amboise's other main sight is **Le Clos Lucé** *(vinci-closluce.com)*, the grand manor house where da Vinci (1452–1519) took up residence in 1516 and spent the final years of his life at the invitation of François I.

The most exciting Loire château to open to visitors in years, the **Château Gaillard** *(chateau-gaillard-amboise.fr)* is the earliest expression of the Italian Renaissance in France.

♥ WHY I LOVE THIS TRIP

DANIEL ROBINSON, WRITER

Travel doesn't get more splendidly French – or elegantly sumptuous – than this tour of the most famous Loire Valley châteaux, which bring together so many of the things I love most about France: supremely refined architecture, dramatic history, exquisite cuisine and delectable wines. My kids especially enjoy the forbidding medieval fortresses of Langeais and Loches, which conjure up a long-lost world of knights, counts and court intrigue.

THE DRIVE: Follow the D952 northeast along the Loire's northern bank, enjoying 35km of beautiful river views en route to Blois. The Château de Chaumont-sur-Loire, renowned for its world-class contemporary art and magnificent international garden festival (April to early November), makes a wonderful stop.

07 Blois

Seven French kings lived in the **Château Royal de Blois** *(chateaudeblois.fr)*, whose four grand wings were built during four distinct periods in French architecture: Gothic (13th century), Flamboyant Gothic (1498–1501), early Renaissance (1515–20) and classical (1630s). You can easily spend a half-day immersing yourself in the château's dramatic and bloody history and its extraordinary architecture.

In the Renaissance wing, the most remarkable feature is the spiral **loggia staircase**, decorated with fierce salamanders and curly Fs, heraldic symbols of François I. The **King's Chamber** was the setting for one of the bloodiest episodes in the château's history. In 1588 Henri III had his arch-rival, Duke Henri I de Guise, murdered by royal bodyguards. Dramatic and very graphic oil paintings illustrate this gruesome event next door in the **Council Chamber**.

THE DRIVE: Cross the Loire and continue 16km southeast into Cheverny via the D765 and, for the final 1km, the D102.

08 Cheverny

Perhaps the Loire's most elegantly proportioned château, **Cheverny** *(chateau-cheverny.fr)* represents the zenith of French classical architecture: the perfect blend of symmetry, geometry and aesthetic order. Inside are some of the most elegantly furnished rooms in the Loire Valley. Highlights include the dining room, with panels depicting the story of Don Quixote; the king's bedchamber, with murals and tapestries illustrating Greek myths; and a children's playroom complete with toys from the time of Napoléon III.

Cheverny's **kennels** house about 100 pedigreed hunting dogs. Feeding time, known as the **Soupe des Chiens**, takes place on Monday, Wednesday, Thursday and Friday at 11.30am (daily from April to mid-September).

Behind the château, the 18th-century **orangerie**, which sheltered priceless artworks – including (apparently) the *Mona Lisa* – during WWII, is now a tearoom (open April to mid-November).

Fans of Tintin may recognise the château's facade as the model for Captain Haddock's ancestral home, Marlinspike Hall. **Les Secrets de Moulinsart** has interactive exhibits about the comics hero.

THE DRIVE: Take the D102 10km northeast into Bracieux, then turn north on the D112 for the final 8km run through the forested Domaine National de Chambord, the largest walled park in Europe. Catch your first dramatic glimpse of France's most famous château on the right as you arrive in Chambord.

09 Chambord

One of the crowning achievements of French Renaissance architecture, **Château de Chambord** *(chambord.org)* – with 426 rooms, 282 fireplaces and 77 staircases – is the largest, grandest and most visited château in the Loire Valley.

Rising through the centre, the world-famous **double-helix staircase** – very possibly designed by the king's chum Leonardo da Vinci – ascends to the great **lantern tower** and the rooftop, where you can marvel at a veritable skyline of cupolas, domes, turrets, chimneys and lightning rods, and gaze out across the vast grounds.

Château de Chambord
LAPAS77/SHUTTERSTOCK

13

★ BEST FOR

WINE TASTING

The 15km stretch between St-Hilaire-St-Florent and Montsoreau.

LOIRE VALLEY & CENTRAL FRANCE

CAVES & CELLARS OF THE LOIRE

DURATION: 3 DAYS

DISTANCE: 160KM / 100 MILES

GREAT FOR: FOOD & DRINK, HISTORY & CULTURE

BEST TIME TO GO: MAY FOR GREENERY; SEPTEMBER AND OCTOBER FOR GRAPE HARVEST.

Château de Saumur

The Loire Valley's easily excavated *tuffeau* (soft limestone) has been central to the area's culture for millennia. From Merovingian quarries that did a booming long-distance trade in Christian sarcophagi, to medieval and Renaissance châteaux, and to modern restaurants and wine cellars ensconced in one-time cave dwellings, this tour offers an introduction to local troglodyte culture and opportunities to savour the region's renowned gastronomy and wines.

LINK YOUR TRIP

02 Essential France
Head east to Chambord to join this country-wide circuit of iconic French sights.

12 Châteaux of the Loire
In Chinon, connect to this classic tour of the Loire Valley's most famous châteaux.

01 Saumur

Start your tour in sophisticated Saumur, one of the Loire Valley's great gastronomic and viticultural centres.

For an overview of the region's wine producers, along with tastings (for a small fee), head to the **Maison des Vins d'Anjou et de Saumur** *(instagram.com/maison_des_vins_anjou_saumur)*, right next to the **tourist office** *(ot-saumur.fr)*.

Next, explore Saumur's other claim to fermented fame at **Distillerie Combier** *(combier.fr)*, where triple sec liqueur was invented in 1834; one-hour tours offer an engaging, behind-the-scenes look at vintage architecture by Eiffel, gleaming century-old copper stills and fragrant vats full of Haitian bitter oranges. Combier also produces absinthe, legal in France since 2011 – you can taste it for no charge in the shop. Around town, make sure to

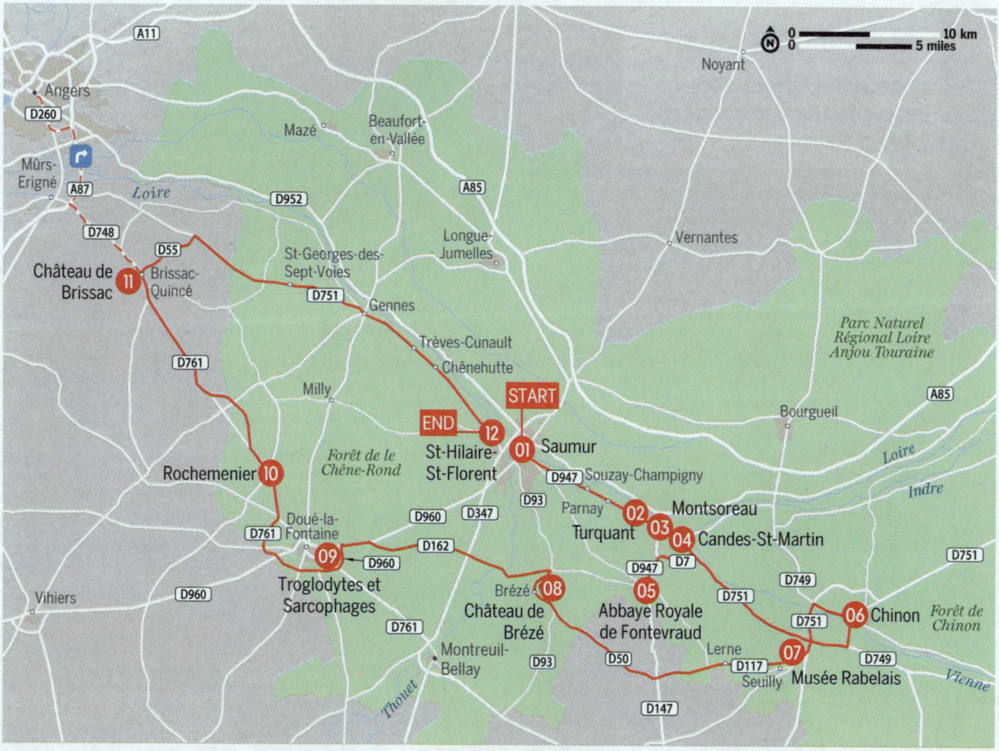

WINDCOLORS/SHUTTERSTOCK

try Saumur's iconic apéritif, *soupe saumuroise* – made with triple sec, lemon juice and sparkling wine.

The **École Nationale d'Équitation** *(ifce.fr/cadre-noir)* is a renowned equestrian academy that trains France's Olympic teams and the Cadre Noir, an elite group of riding instructors. Take a one-hour guided visit, or book ahead for one of the not-to-be-missed **Cadre Noir performances** *(ifce.fr/cadre-noir)*, 'horse ballets' that show off the horses' astonishing acrobatic capabilities and discipline.

Saumur also has several excellent museums, including the **Musée des Blindés** *(museedesblindes.fr)*, home to one of the world's largest collections of 'armoured cavalry' vehicles and tanks, and, soaring above the town's rooftops, the **Château de Saumur** *(chateau-saumur.fr)*.

THE DRIVE: Southeast of Saumur on the south bank of the Loire, the D947 meanders for 10km through the villages of Souzay-Champigny and Parnay, home to several wineries offering tastings, including the Château Villeneuve, Clos des Cordeliers, Château de Parnay and Château de Targé. Troglodyte dwellings burrow into the cliff face to your right as a hilltop windmill signals your arrival in Turquant.

02 Turquant

Backed by chalk-coloured cliffs riddled with caves, picturesque Turquant is a showcase for the creative adaptation of historic troglodyte dwellings. The town's 'main street' runs parallel to the D947, past a handful of art galleries, restaurants and other enterprises featuring bespoke windows and colourful doors wedged into the cliff face. Turn right off the main road to **Les Pommes Tapées du Val de Loire** *(pommes-tapees.fr)*, one of the last places in France producing the traditionally made dried apples known as *pommes tapées*. Tours begin at 10am, 11am, 2pm, 3pm and 4pm. Turquant's *tuffeau* cliffs have also been adapted for use as wine cellars by producers such as **La Grande Vignolle** *(domaine-filliatreau.com)* and **Domaine des Amandiers** *(domainedesamandiers-viticulteur.fr)*.

PHOTO OPPORTUNITY

Turquant's cliff face, with converted cave dwellings and a windmill.

THE DRIVE: It's just a 3km hop, skip and jump southeast to Montsoreau along the D947 and D751. Alternatively, follow the narrow Route des Vins (parallel and slightly south of the D947) to the 16th-century windmill Moulin de la Herpinière, then continue northeast into Montsoreau via tiny Chemin de la Herpinière.

03 Montsoreau

A surprising warning, written in huge letters in the gravel of the courtyard, greets you as you enter the Renaissance-style **Château de Montsoreau-Musée d'Art Contemporain** *(chateau-montsoreau.com)*, home to a museum of conceptual art specialising in the UK- and US-based Art & Language movement. Many works feature words, often in English, with intellectual and theoretical pretensions that range from profound to silly. For spectacular river views, climb to the roof of the tower.

Nearby, the **Regional Park Visitors Centre** *(parc-loire-anjou-touraine.fr)* provides information on activities throughout the 2708-sq-km **Parc Naturel Régional Loire-Anjou-Touraine**, established to protect the region's landscape, architecture and culture.

THE DRIVE: Follow the D751 1km southeast into Candes-St-Martin, enjoying pretty river views on your left.

04 Candes-St-Martin

The picturesque village of Candes-St-Martin occupies an idyllic spot at the confluence of the Vienne and Loire Rivers. St Martin died here in 397, and the village's 12th- to 13th-century church is a major pilgrimage destination.

For great panoramas, climb the tiny streets above the church, past inhabited cave dwellings, or head down to the benches and path along the waterfront.

THE DRIVE: Snake 6km southwest along the D751, D7 and D947, following signs for Fontevraud-l'Abbaye.

05 Abbaye Royale de Fontevraud

The highlight of the 12th-century **Fontevraud-l'Abbaye** *(fontevraud.fr)* – turned into one of France's toughest prisons in the 19th century – is the vast but movingly simple church, notable for its soaring pillars, Romanesque domes and the polychrome stone tombs of four illustrious Plantagenets: Henry II, King of England (r 1154–89); his wife, Eleanor of Aquitaine (who retired to Fontevraud following Henry's death); their son Richard the Lionheart; and the wife of his brother King John, Isabelle of Angoulème. The cloister is surrounded by one-time dormitories, workrooms, prayer halls and a wonderful Gothic-vaulted refectory, while outside there are medieval-style gardens and a multi-chimneyed kitchen (restored in 2020).

A major modern art museum opened here in 2021, the **Musée d'Art Moderne de Fontevraud**, and features paintings and sculptures by Toulouse-Lautrec, Degas and many more.

THE DRIVE: Backtrack 5km to the D751 and follow it 13km southeast and then north towards Chinon. Immediately after crossing the Vienne River, take the D749 east 3km, paralleling the riverfront into town.

06 Chinon

Dominated by the vast **Forteresse Royale de Chinon** *(forteressechinon.fr)*, Chinon is etched into France's collective memory both as the favourite redoubt of Henry II (1133–89), king of England, and as the venue for Joan of Arc's first meeting with Charles VII, in 1429. Below the castle is an appealing **medieval quarter**, a warren of narrow lanes whose white tufa houses are topped with black slate roofs, giving the town its characteristic high-contrast aspect.

Surrounding the town is one of the Loire's main wine-producing areas; **Chinon AOC** *(chinon.com)* cabernet-franc vineyards stretch along the Vienne River. Chinon makes a good base for wine-cellar visits.

THE DRIVE: Zigzag 8km southwest of Chinon through lovely rolling farmland along the D749A, D751E, D759, D24 and D117, following signs for La Devinière.

07 Musée Rabelais

The prosperous farm in **La Devinière** where François Rabelais (1483 or 1494–1553) – doctor, Franciscan friar, theoretician, author and all-around Renaissance man – lived for part of his childhood inspired settings for some of his five satirical, erudite *Gargantua and Pantagruel* novels. Surrounded by vineyards and open farmland, the farmstead is now the **Musée Rabelais** *(musee-rabelais.fr)*, with exhibits on Rabelais' life and genius and an original 1951 Matisse charcoal portrait.

THE DRIVE: Follow the D117 west through the gorgeous village of Seuilly, home to an 11th-century abbey. After 8km, cross the D147 and continue another 13km west-northwest along the D48, D50, D310, D110 and D93 into Brézé.

Turquant (p111)

ANDIA/UNIVERSAL IMAGES GROUP VIA GETTY IMAGES

08 Château de Brézé

The **Château de Brézé** *(chateaudebreze.com)* sits on top of a network of subterranean rooms and passages (1.5km of them open to the public) that encompass a bakery, wine cellars, defensive bastions and a troglodyte dwelling dating from at least the time of the Norman invasions (early 10th century). The dry moat is the deepest (15m to 18m) in Europe that completely encircles a castle. Above ground, much of the U-shaped château dates from the 19th century, as do the many intricately painted neogothic and neo-Renaissance interiors.

THE DRIVE: Chart a meandering 22km course through relatively flat farm country into Doué-la-Fontaine via the D93, D162, D163 and D960.

09 Troglodytes et Sarcophages

At the southeastern edge of this small industrial town, stop to visit the fascinating **Troglodytes et Sarcophages** *(troglo-sarcophages.fr)*, a Merovingian quarry where stone coffins were produced from the 5th to the 9th centuries and exported all over western France. Tours, in French with printed information in six languages, last one hour.

Nearby at **Le Mystère des Faluns** *(le-mystere-des-faluns.com)*, creative lighting and sound effects illustrating the origins of *falun* stone and its fossils turn the entire 600m walking route here, through ancient quarries (nicknamed 'cathedral caves' for their lofty sloping walls), into a glowing, ever-changing work of art.

THE DRIVE: Skirt the southern edge of Doué-la-Fontaine via the D960 for 4km, then continue 5km north on the D761 to the Rochemenier exit. Follow signs the remaining 1.5km into Rochemenier.

10 Rochemenier

One of the Loire's most evocative examples of troglodyte culture is **Rochemenier Village Troglodytique** *(troglodyte.fr)*. You can explore the remains of two adjacent farmsteads, complete with dwellings, stables and a chapel, that were originally excavated to provide lime fertiliser. Farm tools and photos of former residents bring alive the hard-working spirit and simple pleasures that defined life here for many generations.

Château de Brissac

LEOKS/SHUTTERSTOCK

THE DRIVE: Return to the D761, then follow it 15km northwest to Brissac-Quincé, where signs direct you 1.5km further to the château.

11 Château de Brissac

One of the Loire Valley's most opulent castles, the seven-storey **Château de Brissac** *(brissac.net)* – France's tallest – has been owned by the Brissac family for 18 generations (since 1502). Many of the 204 rooms are sumptuously furnished with antique furniture, Flemish tapestries and twinkling chandeliers. The serene 70-hectare grounds, whose vineyards boast four AOC vintages, can be visited on five themed paths.

THE DRIVE: Follow the D55 6km northeast, then wind 15km east-southeast on the D751 through forests and sunflower fields to rejoin the Loire at Gennes. From here, a particularly scenic stretch of the D751 follows the Loire's sandy banks 12km to St-Hilaire-St-Florent, passing by the villages of St-Georges-des-Sept-Voies and Chênehutte-Trèves-Cunault.

DETOUR

Angers

Start: 11 Château de Brissac

Angers' forbidding medieval **Château d'Angers** *(chateau-angers.fr)* – historic seat of the once-mighty counts and dukes of Anjou – is ringed by moats, 2.5m-thick walls made of dark schist, and 17 massive round towers. Inside is one of Europe's great medieval masterpieces, the stunning **Tenture de l'Apocalypse** (Apocalypse Tapestry), a 104m-long series of tapestries commissioned in 1375 to illustrate the story of the final bloody battle between good and evil, as prophesied in the New Testament's book of Revelation.

Just outside the château, learn about the region's 26 AOC wines – and taste them – at the **Maison des Vin de l'Anjou**. Afterwards stroll through Angers' (pronounced ahn-ZHAY) pedestrianised centre, where you'll find cafes, restaurants, excellent museums and, behind the cathedral, the whimsical **Maison d'Adam** (place Ste-Croix), a medieval house decorated with bawdy carved figurines. Across the river, don't miss the stunning modern tapestries at the **Musée Jean Lurçat de la Tapisserie Contemporaine** *(musees.angers.fr)*.

To get here, head 28km northwest from Brissac on the D748, A87 and N260, following signs for Angers-Centre.

Le Mystère des Faluns

12 St-Hilaire-St-Florent

This western suburb of Saumur is home to a number of wineries and cave-based attractions. Get acquainted with some fabulous fungi at the **Musée du Champignon** *(musee-du-champignon.com)*, where a dozen varieties of mushroom grow in glowing shades of orange, yellow, tan, brown and white.

East towards Saumur, a short stretch of the D751 is home to a number of wineries offering cellar tours and *dégustation* (wine tasting), among them (from northwest to southeast) **Ackerman** *(ackerman.fr)*, **Langlois-Chateau** *(langlois-chateau.fr)*, **Bouvet Ladubay** *(bouvet-ladubay.fr)* and **Veuve Amiot** *(veuveamiot.fr)*. Look for Crémant de Loire and Saumur Brut, the region's very own bubblies.

14

LOIRE VALLEY & CENTRAL FRANCE

VOLCANOES OF THE AUVERGNE

DURATION: 4 DAYS

DISTANCE: 200KM / 125 MILES

GREAT FOR: FAMILIES, FOOD & DRINK

BEST TIME TO GO: MAY TO SEPTEMBER FOR WARM WEATHER AND SNOW-FREE TRAILS.

IMPORTANT: SNOW TYRES/CHAINS/SOCKS REQUIRED 1 NOVEMBER – 31 MARCH.

Aeons ago, Europe's biggest volcanoes shaped the landscape of south-central France, blowing their tops with awe-inspiring force. Experience the wild beauty of the Auvergne's vestigial volcanoes – Puy de Dôme, Puy de Sancy and Puy Mary – and discover a tamer Auvergne whose picturesque patchwork of eroded cinder cones and verdant pastures is home to family-friendly walking trails, symphonies of cowbells and some of France's finest cheese.

LINK YOUR TRIP

36 Cave Art of the Vézère Valley
Detour three hours west of Le Mont-Dore to discover France's oldest cave art.

37 Dordogne's Fortified Villages
Explore centuries-old castles and fortified villages along the Dordogne River, three hours downstream from Le Mont-Dore.

01 Volcan de Lemptégy

Fifteen kilometres west of Clermont-Ferrand, year-round guided walks lead visitors through the Auvergne's scorched-earth history. In summer, at weekends and during school holidays, a motorised 'train' chugs through the scarlet dust of **Volcan de Lemptégy** *(auvergne-volcan.com)*, weaving past boulders flung from the belly of this ancient volcano. Lemptégy's geological forces are further explained through a short **dynamic 3D film** (available in multiple languages) – expect bumps and jolts! If the kids are keen for more volcanic fun, rock on to **Vulcania** *(vulcania.com)*, 2km south. This educational theme park, the brainchild of two French geologists, includes the **Cité des Enfants** (Kids' City), with activities specially geared towards three- to seven-year-olds.

THE DRIVE: Head southeast 7km along the D941 to the

★ BEST FOR

FAMILIES

Geological site Volcan de Lemptégy and the Vulcania theme park.

TOMMY LAREY/SHUTTERSTOCK

Volcan de Lemptégy

D942, where full-on views of Puy de Dôme beckon you 2km southwest to the junction with the D68 at the mountain's base.

02 Puy de Dôme

Towering above the surrounding landscape, the distinctive volcanic cone of **Puy de Dôme** (1465m) was an icon long before the Romans built a temple to Mercury on its summit in the 1st century. Hop aboard the **Panoramique des Dômes** *(panoramiquedesdomes.fr)*, a spiffy cog railway inaugurated in 1907, to reach the summit. On clear days take in sublime views of the pouting cinder cones of the 40km **Chaîne des Puys**. If you're feeling fit, there are bracing hikes to the top of Puy de Dôme. The steep, 6km **Chemin des Muletiers** takes roughly 1½ hours. A longer traverse with spectacular views is the north-facing **Chemin des Chèvres** (allow two to 2½ hours for the ascent). The summit is also prime hang-gliding territory; operators such as **Aero Parapente** *(parapente-puy-de-dome.fr)* will take you soaring over the surrounding countryside.

THE DRIVE: The 20km drive to Orcival weaves through the Chaîne des Puys on the D942, then continues southwest on the D216 and D27, passing through increasingly hilly and pastoral countryside dotted with lovely stone and slate barns.

03 Orcival

Backed by a leafy green hillside and bisected by a rushing stream, photogenic Orcival clusters around a gorgeous Romanesque **basilica** that houses one of the Auvergne's most famous *Vierges noires* (black Madonnas, icons typical of the region). An object of veneration throughout the year, she's paraded through the streets with special fanfare on Assumption Day (15 August). The **tourist office** *(auvergnevolcansancy.com)* just opposite loans tablets for lively self-guided tours of the basilica's hidden details (with a version suitable for kids). If you're sticking around, **Aluna Voyages** *(aluna-voyages.com)* offers food-foraging tours

PHOTO OPPORTUNITY

The symmetrical crags of Roches Tuilière and Sanadoire framing the forests and farmland below Col de Guéry.

into the meadows surrounding Orcival, along with donkey-accompanied walks geared towards young adventurers.

THE DRIVE: The D27 climbs 8km through verdant hills and evergreen forest to a spectacular viewpoint just before Col de Guéry (1268m), where the dramatic volcanic crags Roche Tuilière (1288m) and Roche Sanadoire (1286m) rise in symmetry from the land below.

04 Col de Guéry

This mountain pass, flanked by the Auvergne's highest lake, is enticing for walkers, fishers and winter sports fans; check in with the **Centre Montagnard Cap Guéry** *(capguery.com)* for maps of the wild hiking terrain. The countryside around picturesque **Lac de Guéry** (1268m) is laced with walking trails, some of them suitable for snowshoeing in winter. Book a table at lakeside **Auberge du Lac de Guéry** for lunch with a view.

THE DRIVE: Spellbinding mountain views unfold as you approach the Massif du Sancy, with soaring peaks that are often snowcapped late into the spring. A sinuous 9km drive along the D983 and D996 drops you straight into central Le Mont-Dore.

05 Le Mont-Dore

Ringed by rugged peaks at the heart of the Parc Naturel Régional des Volcans d'Auvergne, this historic spa town makes a great base for exploring the surrounding high country. A **téléphérique** (cable car) whisks hikers through a landscape of precipitous crags to the foot of **Puy de Sancy** (1886m), the tallest peak in the Massif Central mountain range. Across town, a tortoise-slow but creakily atmospheric 1890s-vintage **funiculaire** lumbers up to Les Capucins, an upland plateau (1245m) where well-marked trails fan out in all directions.

Several fine hikes and mountain-biking routes also start in the centre of Le Mont-Dore, including the **Chemin de la Grande Cascade**, which leads to a 32m-high waterfall. For trail info and high-resolution topo maps, visit Le Mont-Dore's **tourist office** *(sancy.com)*, in a town-centre riverside park. Nearby streets are filled with outdoors-oriented shops and purveyors of local charcuterie and cheeses, such as dried sausage specialist **La Petite Boutique du Bougnat**.

THE DRIVE: Begin with a spectacular traverse of 1451m Col de la Croix St-Robert, passing through 17km of wide-open high country along the D36. Next, trundle along the D996 for 12km, enjoying pretty views of Lac Chambon, popular with boaters, hikers and campers, and Murol's hilltop castle, before reaching St-Nectaire.

06 St-Nectaire

Tiny St-Nectaire is famous for its 12th-century Romanesque church, stunningly set against a mountain backdrop, and its herds of happy bovines, who make this one of the Auvergne's dairy capitals. Buy a round of delectably creamy St-Nectaire cheese from **Maison du Fromage** *(maison-du-fromage.com)*, along with terrines, jams and other picnic nibbles. To learn the secrets of how the cheese is made, stay for a 35-minute guided tour of the cellars, complete with a swoony video presentation and cheese sampling.

THE DRIVE: Follow the D996 7km downstream to tiny Rivallet, then head southwest 15km on the D978 into Besse. Overshoot the town centre by 4km to enjoy a scenic walk by Lac Pavin.

Roches Tuilière and Sanadoire, Col de Guéry

PATRIZIA MOLINARI/SHUTTERSTOCK

CHEESE COUNTRY

The Auvergne produces some of France's finest cheeses, including five Appellation d'Origine Protégée (AOP) varieties: the semihard, cheddar-like Cantal and nutty Salers, both made from the milk of high-pasture cows; St-Nectaire, creamy, tangy and semisoft; Fourme d'Ambert, a mild, smooth blue cheese; and Bleu d'Auvergne, a powerful, creamy blue cheese with a Roquefort-like flavour.

To taste them on their home turf, follow stretches of the signposted **Route des Fromages** *(fromages-aop-auvergne.com)*, which links local farms and producers. A downloadable map is available on the website.

Local cheeses figure strongly in many traditional Auvergnat dishes. *Aligot* is a smooth blend of puréed potato with garlic and *tomme fraîche* or Cantal cheese. Heartier *truffade* mingles diced or crushed potatoes with melted Cantal cheese, usually accompanied by a generous helping of *jambon d'Auvergne* (local cured ham).

07 Besse-et-St-Anastaise

Basalt-brick cottages, cobbled lanes and a majestic old belfry are reason enough to visit this pretty mountain village. Hikers and bikers will also appreciate the fine network of trails uphill in **Super-Besse** and serene **Lac Pavin**, a crater lake 4km west of town. For a taste of mountain culture, visit during the **Transhumance de la Vierge Noire**: on 2 July, a black Madonna icon is carried amid great fanfare from Besse-et-St-Anastaise up to the little village of Vassivière.

THE DRIVE: Leave the Massif du Sancy behind and head south 75km towards the wilder, less populated Monts du Cantal. A curvy course through farmland and river valleys along the D978 and D678 leads to a supremely scenic, sustained climb along the D62 and D680, bringing you face to face with Puy Mary, the southernmost of the Auvergne's three classic peaks.

08 Puy Mary

Barely wide enough to accommodate parked cars, the vertiginous mountain pass of Pas de Peyrol (1589m) hugs the base of pyramid-shaped Puy Mary (1787m), the Cantal's most charismatic peak. A trail, complete with staircases for the steeper sections, leads to the summit (about one hour round-trip). Find walking routes for all abilities on *puymary.fr*.

THE DRIVE: The 20km descent along the D680 switchbacks steeply through a wonderland of high-country scenery before plunging into fragrant evergreen forest and following a long ridgeline into Salers.

09 Salers

Pretty Salers perches on a hilltop surrounded by fields full of long-horned brown cattle that produce the region's eponymous AOP cheese. With a compact core of 16th-century stone buildings and long views up towards Puy Mary, it's a relaxing place to linger. Central **place Tyssandier d'Escous** is lined with boutiques selling knives and handicrafts and characterful restaurants that slosh Côtes d'Auvergne wine into glasses and sizzle up famously rich Salers beef. Learn more about the region's hallowed cattle, as well as its nutty local cheese, at **Maison de la Salers** (*maisondelasalers.fr*). Day hikes range from an easy 75-minute circuit of the stone-walled pastures surrounding the town to high-mountain rambles through wide-open country around the base of 1592m-high **Puy Violent**.

View from the summit of Puy Mary
SUSANN GUENTHER/SHUTTERSTOCK

STAY AWHILE

SALERS

BY ANNA RICHARDS

Salers looks like a film set, with turreted grey stone houses straight out of a fairy tale, and indeed it's been used as the backdrop for several French films and series. Fortunately, though, outside of the summer holidays, its inaccessibility keeps it pretty quiet.

Salers is a hotbed of creation, with knife makers, glass blowers and makers of wooden children's toys among the numerous, cave-like little boutiques in town, and it's also perfectly positioned for many an emerald-green hike. Bag yourself the summits of **Puy Violent** or **Puy Chavaroche**, the two closest extinct volcanoes to town, or one of the waterfalls: forested **Cascade du Marilhou** or the mossy, tiered **Cascades du Biaguin**.

The overriding reason to visit Salers, though, is for the cheese. One of the five AOP cheeses from the Auvergne, strong, crumbly, tangy Salers cow's cheese is everywhere, and you only need to step foot in one of the numerous cheese shops or wine bars in town to taste it. For a fondue that trumps any Savoyard or Swiss equivalent, head to **Bulle de Salers** *(bulledesalers.fr)*, a 45-minute drive away. From the outside, this stone *buron* (shepherd's hut) may look like no more than a cowshed (an impression exacerbated by all the grazing cows outside), but this hidden restaurant won best fondue in France a few years back. Not only is the atmosphere incredibly inviting – with a roaring fire, walls stacked with liquor bottles and fur throws on all the seats – but I can confirm that my taste buds danced a tango upon eating the fondue here.

LINK YOUR TRIP

14 Volcanoes of the Auvergne Last stop on this trip through Auvergne.

Left: Puy Violent; Right: Salers

PLACES TO STAY

Salers is hardly overrun with accommodation options, which means it's wise to book well in advance, especially if visiting in the summer holidays. There are plenty of campsites in the Cantal region, which are easier to book at the last minute. For four walls and a roof close to town, **L'Auberge de l'Aspre** *(auberge-aspre.fr)* is easily the best of the bunch, a characterful guesthouse 5km from Salers in a village of just 200 people; it has an outdoor pool too. **Hôtel Le Bailliage** *(salers-hotel-bailliage.com)* is within the town itself and has lovely rooms in earthy tones, although service in the restaurant can be rather slow.

15

★ BEST FOR

OUTDOORS

The riverside walking trails around Noyers-sur-Serein.

LOIRE VALLEY & CENTRAL FRANCE

MEDIEVAL BURGUNDY

DURATION: 6 DAYS

DISTANCE: 407KM / 252 MILES

GREAT FOR: HISTORY & CULTURE, NATURE

BEST TIME TO GO: FROM THE MAY WILDFLOWER SEASON TO THE OCTOBER WINE HARVEST.

Abbaye de Cluny

Between the Middle Ages and the 15th century, Burgundy saw a tremendous flowering of ecclesiastical architecture accompanied by active patronage of the arts by the powerful Dukes of Burgundy. This medieval journey shows you the highlights while mixing in opportunities for wine tasting and walking in the gorgeous, rolling countryside that makes Burgundy one of France's most alluring regions.

LINK YOUR TRIP

12 Châteaux of the Loire
Three hours west of Vézelay, explore the Loire Valley's classic châteaux.

16 Route des Grands Crus
Switch gears in Beaune to discover Burgundy's best wines.

01 Cluny

The remains of Cluny's great **abbey** *(cluny-abbaye.fr)* – Christendom's largest church until the construction of St Peter's Basilica in the Vatican – are fragmentary and scattered, barely discernible among the houses and green spaces of the modern-day town. But with a bit of imagination, it's possible to picture how things looked in the 12th century, when Cluny's Benedictine abbey, renowned for its wealth and power and answerable only to the pope, held sway over 1100 priories and monasteries stretching from Poland to Portugal.

Get oriented at the **Musée d'Art et d'Archéologie**, with its scale model of the Cluny complex and 3D 'virtual tour' of the abbey's original medieval layout, then climb the **Tour des Fromages** for a bird's-eye view of the abbey's remnants, including the striking octagonal **Clocher de l'Eau Bénite** (Tower of

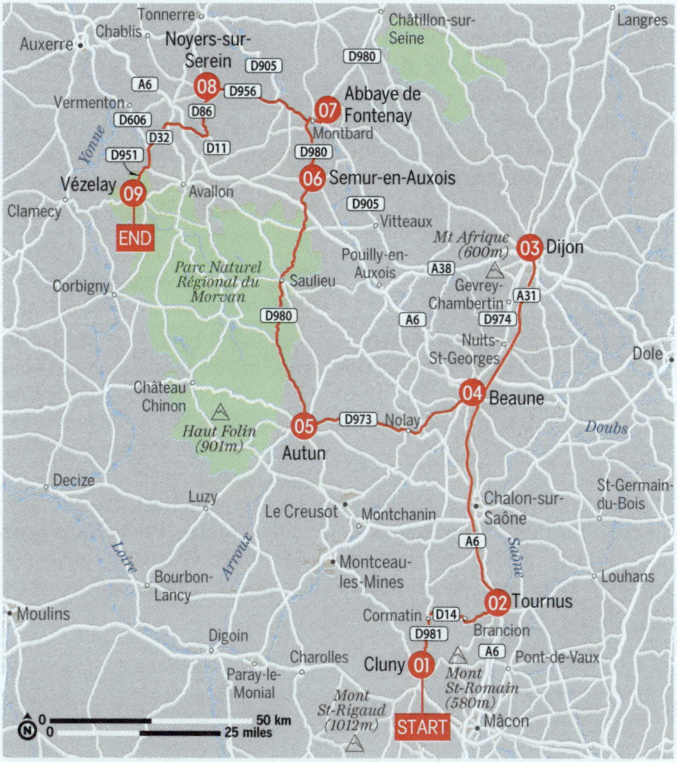

NATURSPORTS/SHUTTERSTOCK

the Holy Water) and the **Farinier** (Granary), where eight splendid capitals from the original church are displayed.

THE DRIVE: Head 13km north along the D981 to Cormatin, with its Renaissance-style château, then squiggle 25km east along the D14 past Chapaize's 11th-century Église St-Martin, Ozenay's château and the medieval hill village of Brancion before descending into Tournus.

02 Tournus

Tournus' superb 10th- to 12th-century Benedictine abbey, **Abbatiale St-Philibert** *(tournus-tourisme.com)*, makes a striking first impression, with its austere Romanesque facade peeking out through a medieval stone gate flanked by twin rounded towers. Its apse holds an extremely rare 12th-century **floor mosaic** of the calendar and the zodiac, discovered by chance in 2002. The medieval centre also boasts fine restaurants – good for a lunch stop.

THE DRIVE: From Tournus, zip 96km straight up the A6 and A31 to Dijon.

03 Dijon

Long-time capital of medieval Burgundy, Dijon was the seat of power for a series of enlightened dukes who presided over the region's 14th- and 15th-century golden age, filling the city with fine art and architecture and a wonderful medieval centre, best explored by foot.

Topping the list of must-see attractions are the early-13th-century **Église Notre Dame**, with its remarkable facade of pencil-thin columns and leering gargoyles; the **Palais des Ducs et des États de Bourgogne** (Palace of the Dukes & States of Burgundy), the Burgundy dukes' monumental palace, which also houses Dijon's extraordinary fine arts museum, the **Musée des Beaux-Arts** *(musees.dijon.fr)*; and the historic mansions that line surrounding streets, especially rue des Forges, rue Verrerie, rue Vannerie and rue de la Chouette.

THE DRIVE: Zip 44km south on the A31 to Beaune, or take the slower but much more scenic Route des Grands Crus through the Côte de Nuits vineyards.

04 Beaune

Burgundy's supremely appealing viticultural capital, Beaune (pronounced 'bone') is surrounded by vineyards producing some of the most renowned Côte d'Or appellations, grown on the slopes of the Côte de Nuits and Côte de Beaune (some AOC definitions were tweaked in 2020). Sipping local vintages at sunset on a cafe terrace here is one of France's great pleasures.

The architectural jewel of Beaune's historic centre is the **Hôtel-Dieu des Hospices de Beaune** *(hospices-de-beaune.com)*, a 15th-century charity hospital topped by stunning turrets and pitched rooftops covered in multicoloured tiles. Interior highlights include the barrel-vaulted Grande Salle, with dragon-embellished beams; an 18th-century pharmacy lined with ancient flasks; and the mesmerising *Polyptych of the Last Judgement*, a 15th-century Flemish masterpiece that depicts the glory and utter terror of Judgement Day.

THE DRIVE: A super-scenic 49km drive along the D973 weaves southwest through gorgeous vineyard country, climbing past La Rochepot's striking 13th-century castle before turning west to Autun.

05 Autun

Two millennia ago, Autun (Augustodunum) was one of Roman Gaul's most important cities. Its next heyday came 1100 years later, when **Cathédrale St-Lazare** was built to house St Lazarus' sacred relics. Climb through the old city's narrow cobblestone streets to see the cathedral's fantastical Romanesque capitals and famous 12th-century tympanum depicting the Last Judgement, carved by Burgundy's master sculptor Gislebertus. Across the street, the **Musée Rolin** *(museerolin.fr)* houses Gislebertus' sensual masterpiece *Temptation of Eve,* alongside Gallo-Roman artefacts and modern paintings. At the time of writing, the museum was closed for renovations, and due to reopen in 2028.

Roman treasures around town include the town gates, **Porte d'Arroux** and **Porte St-André**; the 16,000-seat **Théâtre Romain**; the **Temple de Janus**; and the **Pierre de Couhard**, the 27m-high remnant of a Gallo-Roman pyramid.

Autun makes an excellent base for exploring the hills, forests, lakes and hamlets of the nearby **Parc Naturel Régional du Morvan** *(parcdumorvan.org);* there's a visitor centre in St-Brisson.

THE DRIVE: The D980 runs 70km north from Autun to Semur-en-Auxois; halfway along, there's a fine collection of Romanesque capitals at Saulieu's 12th-century Basilique de St-Andoche.

06 Semur-en-Auxois

Perched on a granite spur, surrounded by a hairpin turn in the Armançon River and guarded by four massive pink-granite bastions, Semur was once an important religious centre boasting no fewer than six monasteries.

Pass through the two concentric medieval gates, **Porte Sauvigne** and **Porte Guillier**, onto pedestrianised **rue Buffon**; then

Basilique Ste-Madeleine

PHOTO OPPORTUNITY

Vézelay's sinuous sweep of stone houses crowned by a hilltop basilica.

PHOTOFORT 77/SHUTTERSTOCK

meander west through the old town to **Promenade du Rempart** for panoramic views from atop Semur's medieval battlements. Semur is especially atmospheric at night, when the ramparts are illuminated.

Be sure to stop in at the historic **Pâtisserie Alexandre** for some *granit rose de l'auxois* (a local pink confection laden with sugar, orange-infused chocolate, cherries, almonds and hazelnuts).

THE DRIVE: Follow the D980 20km north into Montbard, then hop 2km east on the D905 before joining the sleepy northbound D32 for the idyllic 3km home stretch into Fontenay.

07 Abbaye de Fontenay

Founded in 1118 and restored to its medieval glory a century ago, the UNESCO-listed **Abbaye de Fontenay** (Fontenay Abbey; *abbayedefontenay.com*) offers a glimpse of the austere, serene surroundings in which Cistercian monks lived lives of contemplation, prayer and manual labour. Set in a bucolic wooded valley, the abbey includes an unadorned Romanesque church, a barrel-vaulted monks' dormitory, landscaped gardens and Europe's first metallurgical forge, with a reconstruction of a hydraulic hammer used by 13th-century monks.

From the parking lot, the **GR213 trail** forms part of two verdant walking circuits: one to Montbard (13km return), the other (11.5km) through Touillon and Le Petit Jailly. Maps and botanical field guides are available in the abbey shop.

THE DRIVE: Backtrack to the D905, follow it 14km west-northwest to Rougemont, then take the westbound D956 21km into Noyers.

08 Noyers-sur-Serein

Tucked into a sharp bend in the Serein River, picturesque medieval Noyers is surrounded by pastureland and wooded hills. The town's cobbled streets, accessed via two imposing **stone gateways**, lead past 15th- and 16th-century gabled houses, wood and stone archways and several art galleries.

Noyers is a superb base for walking. Just outside the clock-topped southern gate, **Chemin des Fossés** threads its way between the Serein and the village's 13th-century fortifications, 19 of whose original 23 towers still remain. Continue along the Serein's right bank, joining the **Balade du Château** and climbing past Noyer's utterly ruined château to a series of belvederes with dreamy views over the town and the surrounding countryside.

THE DRIVE: Snake 14km southward through the peaceful Serein valley via the D86, then head 11km west on the D11 from Dissangis to Joux-la-Ville before charting a southwest course down the D32, D9, D606 and D951 for the final 24km run into Vézelay.

09 Vézelay

Rising from lush rolling countryside and crowned by a fabulous medieval basilica, Vézelay is one of France's loveliest hilltop villages. Founded in the 9th century on a one-time Roman and then Carolingian site, **Basilique Ste-Madeleine** *(basiliquedevezelay.org)* has served for almost a millennium as the starting point for one of the pilgrimage routes to Santiago de Compostela. Among its treasures are a 12th-century tympanum, with a carving of an enthroned Jesus radiating his holy spirit to the Apostles; several beautifully carved Romanesque capitals, including the Mystical Mill, which depicts Moses grinding grain into a flour sack held by St Paul; and a mid-12th-century crypt reputed to house one of Mary Magdalene's bones.

The **park** behind the basilica affords wonderful views of, and walking access to, the verdant Vallée de Cure. From **Porte Neuve**, Vézelay's old town gate, a footpath descends via the 12th-century chapel of **La Cordelle** to the village of **Asquins**. Another nice walk is the **Promenade des Fossés**, which circumnavigates Vézelay's medieval ramparts.

16

LOIRE VALLEY & CENTRAL FRANCE

ROUTE DES GRANDS CRUS

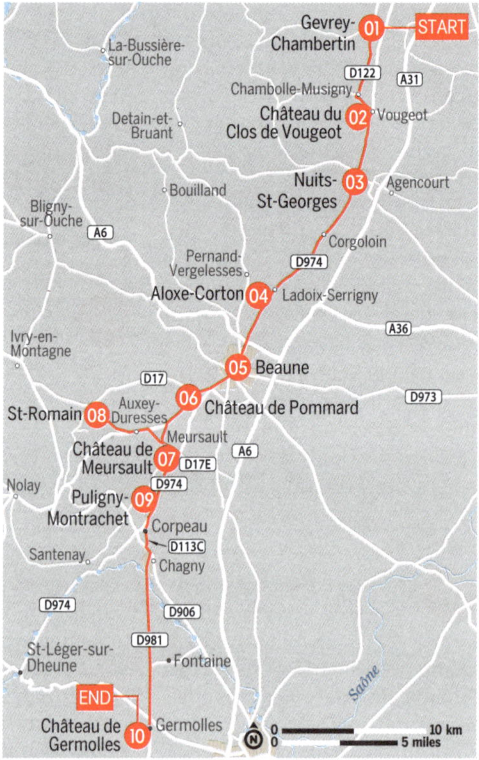

DURATION: 2 DAYS

DISTANCE: 72KM / 45 MILES

GREAT FOR: FOOD & DRINK, HISTORY & CULTURE

BEST TIME TO GO: MAY, JUNE, SEPTEMBER AND OCTOBER FOR A SYMPHONY OF COLOUR AND QUIET ROADS.

Meandering through Burgundy's vine-carpeted countryside takes you to some of the most storied vineyards in the world and to ancient wine-growing villages whose names – engraved on labels or whispered during a romantic dinner – make oenophiles swoon. You'll visit legendary wine châteaux and wine cellars, redolent with the bouquet of fermenting grapes, that offer a golden opportunity to sample some of France's most prestigious reds and whites.

LINK YOUR TRIP

15 Medieval Burgundy
It's easy to combine this trip with the itinerary focusing on medieval Burgundy, either from Beaune or La Rochepot.

20 Beaujolais Villages
In the mood for more full-bodied wines? Motor 1¼ hours south to Villefranche-sur-Saône and make your way up to Roche de Solutré.

01 Gevrey-Chambertin

Kick off your epicurean adventure by visiting this picturesque village, which enjoys a world-class reputation among wine enthusiasts – it produces nine out of the 32 *grands crus* wines from Burgundy, all of them reds made from pinot noir.

THE DRIVE: It's a relaxed 7km drive south along the tertiary D122, via Morey-St-Denis and Chambolle-Musigny, to the Château du Clos de Vougeot.

02 Château du Clos de Vougeot

The magnificent **Château du Clos de Vougeot** *(closdevougeot.fr)*, regarded by some as the birthplace of Burgundian wines, was originally the property of the Abbaye de Cîteaux, 12km southeast from here. Tours reveal the workings of enormous wine presses and casks.

THE DRIVE: Pick up the D974 to Nuits-St-Georges, 4.5km south via Vosne-Romanée.

★ BEST FOR

FOODIES

Beaune is a great place to try Burgundian specialities such as snails.

Vineyard in Gevrey-Chambertin

03 Nuits-St-Georges

It's worth spending a little time in attractive Nuits-St-Georges. Splashed around town are a dozen *domaines* (houses) selling superb reds and whites, but an informative port of call on any wine-tasting itinerary is **L'Imaginarium** *(imaginarium-bourgogne.com)*. This gleaming modern museum is a great place to learn about Burgundy wines and winemaking techniques. It's fun and entertaining, with movies, exhibits, interactive displays and tastings.

Architecture buffs might want to mosey over to the 17th-century **belfry** of the former town hall and the Romanesque **Église St-Symphorien**, slightly away from the town centre.

THE DRIVE: Continue along the D974 southwestward towards Beaune. Pass through the village of Ladoix-Serrigny and look for the sign to Château Corton-André on the right. The 11.5km drive takes about 10 minutes.

04 Aloxe-Corton

Surrounded by manicured vineyards, tiny Aloxe-Corton is a real charmer. Wine producers are handily scattered around the village. A good starting point is the **Caveau d'Aloxe Corton** *(caveaualoxecorton.com)*, a wine shop representing eight producers of terrific local reds and whites.

The high-flying **Château Corton-André** *(domainefrey.com)*, aka Château Corton C, with its splendid cellars and multicoloured tile roof, is a wonderful place for a tasting session in atmospheric surrounds.

THE DRIVE: Pick up the busy D974 to Beaune, 5.5km to the south.

05 Beaune

Attractive Beaune's *raison d'être* and the source of its unmistakable *joie de vivre* is wine: making it, ageing it, selling it, but most of all, drinking it. It's one of the best places in all of France for wine tasting.

The amoeba-shaped old city is enclosed by thick stone **ramparts** lined with overgrown gardens and ringed by a pathway that makes for a lovely stroll. The most striking attraction of Beaune's old city is the magnificent **Hôtel-Dieu des Hospices de Beaune** *(hospices-de-beaune.com)*.

Underneath Beaune, millions of dusty bottles of wine are being aged to perfection in cool, dark cellars.

Stop in at **Patriarche Père et Fils** *(patriarche.com)*, Burgundy's largest cellars, where 5km of corridors are lined with about three million bottles, the oldest a Beaune Villages AOC from 1904. Tour the premises in 60 to 90 minutes, sampling 10 wines along the way and taking the *tastevin* (tasting cup) home. Another excellent option for tours and *dégustation* is **Oenothèque Joseph Drouhin** *(drouhin.com)*.

THE DRIVE: Take the D974 (direction Autun), then the D973 to Pommard (5km).

06 Château de Pommard

For many red-wine lovers, a visit to the superb **Château de Pommard** *(chateaudepommard.com)* – established in 1726 and American-owned since 2014 – is a true Burgundian pilgrimage.

THE DRIVE: Take the D973 southwest, via Volnay, and follow the signs along the D23 to Meursault (5km). The Château de Meursault is signposted in the village centre.

07 Château de Meursault

One of the prettiest of the Côte de Beaune châteaux, the **Château de Meursault** *(chateau-meursault.com)* has beautiful grounds and produces some of the most prestigious white wines in the world. Tours visit the estate's vast labyrinth of underground caves, the oldest dating to the 12th century.

THE DRIVE: From the château, drive northwest on the D17E back to the D973. Turn left and head west on the D973 for 1.3km,

BURGUNDY WINE BASICS

Burgundy's epic vineyards extend approximately 250km from Chablis in the north to Beaujolais (almost!) in the south and comprise 84 Appellations d'Origine Contrôlée (AOC), some of which were changed slightly in 2020. Each micro-region has its own unique combination of characteristics – latitude, altitude, climate, sun exposure and, of course, soil – embodied in a concept called *terroir* (tair-WAHR) because it is the earth itself that imbues grapes with their unique, ethereal qualities.

Here's an ever-so-brief survey of some of Burgundy's major growing regions (from north to south):

- **Chablis & Grand Auxerrois**
  Four renowned chardonnay white-wine appellations from 20 villages around Chablis. Part of the Auxerrois vineyards, Irancy produces excellent pinot noir reds.
- **Châtillonnais**
  Approximately 20 villages around Châtillon-sur-Seine producing red and white wines.
- **Côte d'Or**
  The northern section, the Côte de Nuits, stretches from Marsannay-la-Côte (near Dijon) south to Corgoloin and produces reds known for their robust, full-bodied character. The southern section, the Côte de Beaune, lies between Ladoix-Serrigny and Santenay and produces great reds and whites. Appellations from the area's hilltops are the Hautes-Côtes de Nuits and Hautes-Côtes de Beaune.
- **Côte Chalonnaise**
  The southernmost continuation of the Côte de Beaune's slopes is noted for its excellent reds and whites.
- **Mâconnais**
  Known for rich or fruity white wines, like Pouilly-Fuissé chardonnay.

Want to Know More?

- **Sensation Vin**
  Offers introductory tasting sessions (no appointment needed) as well as vineyard excursions and tailor-made courses. *(sensation-vin.com)*
- **École des Vins de Bourgogne**
  Offers a variety of courses to refine your palate. *(ecoledesvins-bourgogne.com)*

PISTOLESI ANDREA/HEMIS/ALAMY

PHOTO OPPORTUNITY

Panoramic views of the countryside from the cliffs above St-Romain are exquisite.

The cliffs above St-Romain

through Auxey-Duresses, before turning right to rejoin the D17E for 2.8km. Total distance: 6.5km.

08 St-Romain

Vineyards meet pastureland, forests and cliffs in the bucolic hamlet of St-Romain. For drop-dead views over the village and the valley, drive up to the panoramic viewpoint (it's signposted), perched atop a cliff near the ruins of a castle. Hiking trails from here include the spectacular **Sentier des Roches** circuit (13.9km).

THE DRIVE: From the centre of St-Romain, head southeast on the D17E. As the road changes to the D973, you'll pass the tree-lined main street of Petit Auxey, with its pockmarked stone buildings surrounded by vines. At the fork in the road, take a right to rejoin the D17E through Meursault, before taking a hard right on the D974. Total distance: 12km.

09 Puligny-Montrachet

Beloved of white-wine aficionados (no reds in sight), this bijou appellation of Puligny-Montrachet is revered thanks to five extraordinary *grands crus*. At the relaxed **Caveau de Puligny-Montrachet** *(caveau-puligny.com)*, a comfortable wine bar and cellar, you can sample the town's namesake vintages along with other fine local wines. Knowledgeable hosts Julien and Emilien provide excellent advice.

THE DRIVE: Head south on the D974. Fork left onto the D113C just before Corpeau, a tiny commune whose church is covered in glazed Burgundy tiles, like Beaune's hospices in miniature. At the end of the town, turn left onto the D906, then double back northwest onto Route de Chalon to take the D981 all the way to Germolles. Total distance: 18km.

10 Château de Germolles

A fortified house built in the 12th century by feudal lords, **Château de Germolles** *(chateaudegermolles.fr)* is often considered the best-preserved former residence of the Dukes of Bourgogne. Many parts of the building, including the cellar and low chapel, are original. Don't miss the intricately painted tiles and frescoes.

0
0
50 miles
100 km
Dijon
A6
Besançon
Dole
A36
Beaune
Autun
Pontarlier
BERN
Lac de Neuchâtel
Arbois
Saône
Le Creusot
Chalon-sur-Saône
17
SWITZERLAND
Montceau-les-Mines
Lons-le-Saunier
Parc Naturel Régional du Haut-Jura
Lausanne
Lake Geneva (Lac Léman)
Digoin
A39
Les Rousses
A79
A6
Loire
Mâcon
Thonon-les-Bains
Rhône
Beaujeu
Geneva
A40
A40
20
Roanne
Villefranche-sur-Saône
Ambérieu-en-Bugey
St-Gervais-les-Bains
Chamonix
Annecy
Courmayeur
A89
A42
Rhône
Mont Blanc (4810m)
Aosta
Lyon
Parc Régional du Massif des Bauges
Bourgoin-Jallieu
Chambéry
Grande Casse (3855m)
Vienne
Val d'Isère
St-Étienne
A7
A43
Parc National de la Vanoise
Isère
St-Michel de Maurienne
18
Susa
Turin
Lans-en-Vercors
Grenoble
Le Puy-en-Velay
21
A49
ITALY
Barre des Écrins (4102m)
A51
Parc Naturel Régional du Vercors
Valence
Briançon
Mont Mézenc (1753m)
Parc Naturel Regional du Queyras
Parc National des Écrins
Die
St-Véran
Gap
Montélimar
Serres
A51
Cuneo
Vallon-Pont-d'Arc
Nyons
19
A7
Sisteron
Rhône
Orange
Mont Ventoux (1910m)
Alès
Peyruis
A9
Avignon
Moustiers-Ste-Marie
Menton
Nîmes
MONACO
A51
Parc Naturel Régional du Verdon
Nice

JEAFISH PING/SHUTTERSTOCK

Pont des Amours (p143), Annecy

ALPS, JURA & RHÔNE VALLEY

EXPLORE

ALPS, JURA & RHÔNE VALLEY

From Europe's ceiling to some of France's prettiest wine and dairy country, these regions promise abundant rewards to touring drivers. Best explored when the summer warmth melts the snow from alpine passes, it's a place to encounter France in all its natural splendour and human sophistication. Featuring natural parks bursting with emerald alpine meadows and coniferous forests, medieval abbeys, prehistoric cave dwellings, sun-soaked vineyards and mountain strongholds, the Alps, the Jura and the Rhône Valley promise seemingly endless varieties of delight. Gourmands, nature lovers and history buffs will find plenty to tempt them here.

Lyon

France's third-largest city provides a natural base for tackling any of our five routes, but is particularly handy for the 'Beaujolais Villages' and 'Rhône Valley' drives. Lyon–Saint Exupéry Airport, linked to Part-Dieu train station in the city centre by the 30-minute Rhônexpress tramway, operates two terminals servicing over 40 airlines and 120 international and domestic destinations. Lyon itself is a wonderful place to rest up and explore before hitting the road: a university city with excellent museums, plus historic sights, harmonious architecture and busy nightlife, it's also renowned as France's gastronomic capital.

Lyon sits at the middle of an extensive rail network, with fast TGV and regional services to Paris Gare de Lyon, Paris Charles de Gaulle, Marseille, Grenoble, Chambéry, Annecy and numerous other destinations. You'll find a wide variety of accommodation options, alongside plenty of car-rental firms in both the airport and the city itself, plus numerous supermarkets and *épiceries* (specialist grocers) in which to stock up for your trip.

Geneva

Just over the French–Swiss border, Geneva is a useful entry point for the 'Jura' and 'Alpine Adventure' drives. Geneva International Airport handles regular flights from over 50 major airlines, offering easy connections with cities throughout France and Europe

WHEN TO GO

The French Alps, synonymous with ski holidays, are difficult to access in winter, when snow, ice and even avalanches can close roads and tunnels. Summer is possibly the best time to visit, promising mild sunny days and a tourist industry operating at full throttle. For a quieter experience, consider touring in the shoulder months of May and September, but keep an eye on the weather and check high mountain passes are open. It's a good idea to have snow chains, even in shoulder season.

and as far afield as Beijing. Central Geneva is just seven minutes by train from the airport and offers a broad selection of (mainly expensive) accommodation options. Gare CFF de Cornavin has regular trains to Lyon, Annecy, Besançon and other destinations in the Alps and Jura regions. Cars can be rented from the airport, train station or Geneva proper, and there are plenty of supermarkets both within the city's centre and on its outskirts, along the major routes into France.

Grenoble

The former capital of the historical province of Dauphiné, Grenoble has been a crossroads since Roman times. With plenty of accommodation options across the price spectrum and abundant opportunities to stock up for your trip, it makes a handy base for the 'Alpine Adventure', 'Foothills of the Alps' and 'Rhône Valley' drives. Little Alpes–Isère Airport, 45km northwest of the city, offers connections to the UK and domestic centres in winter, and is linked to the city by regular coaches. Grenoble has direct train connections to Annecy, Chambéry and Lyon, and there is a good selection of car-rental agencies underneath the train station or across the street.

TRANSPORT

Lyon is the natural gateway to the southern Alps and Rhône Valley. Its busy airport connects to centres across Europe and beyond, and it has excellent rail links with Paris, Geneva, Marseille and (via the Eurostar) London. Geneva is worth considering as your point-of-entry for touring the northern French Alps and Jura, despite lying (just) over the border with Switzerland.

NOTE: A Crit'Air sticker is required in Lyon and Annecy. See p287 for more details.

RESOURCES

- **Vins Rhones**
  Provides a complete guide to the vineyards, wineries and wine-producing villages of the Rhône Valley. *vins-rhone.com*
- **Gorges de l'Ardèche**
  Plan and book visits to the Ardèche. *gorges-ardeche-pontdarc.fr*
- **Parc du Haut-Jura**
  Events, activities and attractions in this upland nature reserve. *parc-haut-jura.fr*

WHAT'S ON

- **La Percée du Vin Jaune**
  (The Opening of the Yellow Wine) This two-day festival is held in a different Jura village every February.
- **Sarmentelles de Beaujeu**
  The imminent arrival of the year's Beaujolais Nouveau is celebrated with five days of drinking, music and dancing in November.
- **Fête des Lumières**
  (Festival of Lights) Held in Lyon over four days around early December's Feast of the Immaculate Conception.

WHERE TO STAY

The Clef Verte (Green Key)–certified **SLO Hostel** is a budget hostel in central Lyon with parking nearby. Just outside the impressive bulk of the Château d'Annecy, the **Hôtel du Château Annecy** is a charming 15-room hotel with a rooftop terrace. Close to UNESCO-listed Chauvet Cave, **Prehistoric Lodge, Vallon-Pont-d'Arc** offers luxury tents and rooms with views of the Gorges de l'Ardèche, plus river access. In the Jura town of Arbois, you'll find **La Closerie des Capucines**, a 17th-century convent converted into a beautifully decorated B&B with a small pool.

17

ALPS, JURA & RHÔNE VALLEY

THE JURA

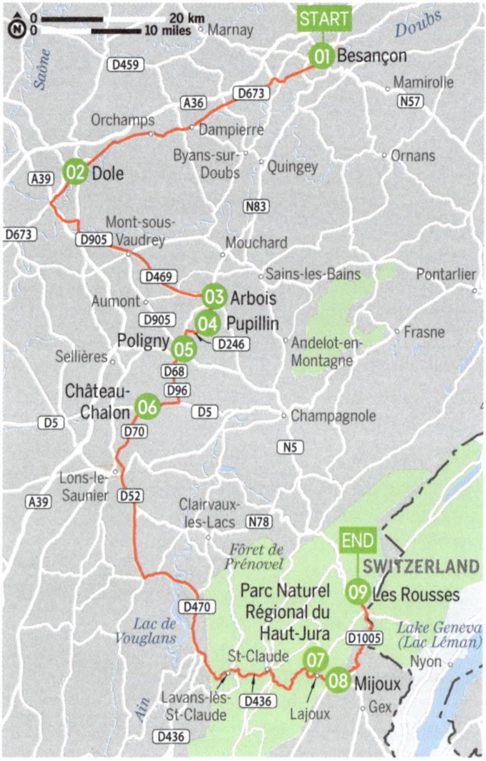

DURATION: 5 DAYS

DISTANCE: 227KM / 141 MILES

GREAT FOR: FOOD & DRINK, NATURE

BEST TIME TO GO: JUNE AND SEPTEMBER FOR SUNNY DAYS; WINTER FOR SNOW SPORTS.

IMPORTANT: SNOW TYRES/CHAINS/SOCKS REQUIRED 1 NOVEMBER – 31 MARCH

The high Jura mountains contrast starkly with the surrounding rolling, bucolic lowlands, famed for Comté cheese and golden wine. In fact, this trip is full of contrasts: one day you might check out Egyptian mummies, the next you'll be eating with vignerons at a cheery *bistrot,* and beyond that dangling above limestone escarpments in a chairlift. Despite such abundance, the Jura remains one of France's least visited territories.

LINK YOUR TRIP

16 Route des Grands Crus
Need a drink before starting the Jura tour? Combine it with the 'Route des Grands Crus' drive; its starting point of Gevrey-Chambertin is 62km from Dole along the A39.

18 Alpine Adventure
If the heights of the Jura appeal, then link up with the 'Alpine Adventure', which begins in Annecy, an 80km drive from Mijoux on the other side of Switzerland.

01 Besançon

Home to a monumental Vauban citadel and France's first public museum, birthplace of Victor Hugo and the Lumière brothers, Besançon has an extraordinary background. Somehow, though, despite its graceful 18th-century old town and first-rate restaurants, it remains something of a secret.

The UNESCO-listed **Citadelle de Besançon** *(citadelle.com)* is a formidable feat of engineering, designed by the prolific Marquis de Vauban for Louis XIV in the late 17th century. Inside (and included in the ticket price) are a number of museums.

The **Musée des Beaux-Arts et d'Archéologie** *(mbaa.besancon.fr)* houses France's oldest public art collection, founded in 1694. The stellar displays include such archaeological exhibits as Egyptian mummies, neolithic tools and Gallo-Roman mosaics, as well as a wide range of paintings and drawings, including

★ BEST FOR

FAMILIES

Camping and tramping in the Parc Naturel Régional du Haut-Jura.

Chemin des Vignes

works by Dürer, Delacroix, Rubens, Goya, Cranach and Bonnard.

THE DRIVE: From Besançon you can opt for the fast A36 (51km, 45 minutes) or the marginally slower but more enjoyable D673 (46km, 55 minutes) to Dole.

02 Dole

Almost every town in France has at least one street, square or garden named after Louis Pasteur, the great 19th-century chemist who invented pasteurisation and developed the first rabies vaccine. The Jura takes this veneration further: the illustrious man was a local lad, born in 1822 in the well-preserved medieval town of Dole.

A scenic stroll along the Canal des Tanneurs in Dole's historic tanners' quarter brings you to Pasteur's childhood home, **La Maison Natale de Pasteur** *(terredelouispasteur.fr)*, now an atmospheric museum housing exhibits including his cot, first drawings and university cap and gown.

THE DRIVE: It's a 45-minute, 36km doddle down the D905 and D469 to Arbois.

03 Arbois

The charming village of Arbois is well worth a visit. In 1827 the Pasteur family settled here, and Louis' laboratory and workshops are on display at **La Maison de Louis Pasteur** *(terredelouispasteur.fr)*.

If science is a bit too dusty for you, then may we tempt you with a glass of wine? Arbois sits at the heart of the Jura wine region, renowned for its *vin jaune*. The history of this nutty 'yellow wine' is told in the **Musée de la Vigne et du Vin du Jura** *(arbois.fr)*, housed in the whimsical, turreted Château Pécauld. Afterwards clear your head by walking the 2.5km-long **Chemin des Vignes** trail, which wends its way through the vines, starting from the steps next to the Château Pécauld.

THE DRIVE: Clamber steeply uphill for five minutes (3km) along the D246 to reach the spectacularly situated village of Pupillin.

04 Pupillin

High above Arbois is tiny Pupillin, a cute yellow-brick village famous for its wine production. Some 10 *caves* (wine cellars) are open to visitors.

THE DRIVE: Head southwest out of Pupillin on the N83 and in 15 minutes (9km) you'll have dropped to the small town of Poligny.

05 Poligny

Need a little cheese to accompany all that wine? Comté is the pre-eminent AOC cheese of the Jura, and the small town of Poligny is the 'capital' of an industry that produces 40 million tonnes of its sweet, nutty goodness a year. Learn how 450L of milk is transformed into a 40kg wheel, smell some of its 83 aromas, and have a nibble at the **Maison du Comté** *(maison-du-comte.com)*. Dozens of *fruitières* (cheese cooperatives) are open to the public. Poligny's **tourist office** *(coeurdujura-tourisme.com)* stocks an abundance of info on cheesemakers and wineries in the region.

THE DRIVE: Take the D68 out of town, and after about 4km veer right onto the D96. After a further 4km, make a sharp right onto the D5 and cruise through pretty countryside into Château-Chalon. It's 15km in total.

06 Château-Chalon

Despite a name that conjures up images of grand castles, Château-Chalon is actually a pocket-sized medieval village of honey-coloured stone perched on a hilltop and surrounded by vineyards known for their legendary *vin jaune*.

THE DRIVE: Leave Château-Chalon northeastwards on the D5 and then double back to the D70 and the town of Lons-le-Saunier. From here the D52, D470 and D436 will be your route into the high-mountain bliss of the Parc Naturel Régional du Haut-Jura and the village of Lajoux. In total it's 90km and 1½ hours.

07 Parc Naturel Régional du Haut-Jura

Experience the Jura at its rawest in the Haut-Jura Regional Park, an area of 757 sq km stretching from Chapelle-des-Bois in the north almost to the western tip of Lake Geneva.

A great place to learn more is the **Maison du Parc** *(parc-haut-jura.*

Château-Chalon
SLOOT/GETTY IMAGES

BONCHAN/SHUTTERSTOCK

Vacherin Mont d'Or

SPECIALITY FOOD & DRINK

It's hot, it's soft and it's packed in a box. Vacherin Mont d'Or is the only French cheese to be eaten with a spoon – hot. Made between 15 August and 15 March with *lait cru* (unpasteurised milk), it derives its unique nutty taste from the spruce bark in which it's wrapped. Connoisseurs top the soft-crusted cheese with chopped onions, garlic and white wine, wrap it in aluminium foil and bake it for 45 minutes to create a *boîte chaude* (hot box). Only 11 factories in the Jura are licensed to produce Vacherin Mont d'Or.

Mouthe, 15km south of Métabief Mont d'Or, is the mother of *liqueur de sapin* (fir-tree liqueur). *Glace de sapin* (fir-tree ice cream) also comes from Mont d'Or, known as the North Pole of France due to its seasonal subzero temperatures (record low: -38°C). Sampling either is rather like ingesting a Christmas tree. Then there's *Jésus* – a small, fat version of *saucisse de Morteau* (Morteau sausage), easily identified by the wooden peg on its end, attached after the sausage is smoked with pinewood sawdust in a traditional *tuyé* (mountain hut).

fr), a visitor centre that also has a kid-focused museum that explores the region and its history through sound, touch and smell. The Maison du Parc is in the village of Lajoux, 19km east of St-Claude and 5km west of Mijoux.

THE DRIVE: From the Maison du Parc, the D436 will have you switchbacking 5km down the valley into the village of Mijoux.

08 Mijoux

Close to the small ski resort of Mijoux there are some fabulous panoramas of Lake Geneva, framed by the French Alps and Mont Blanc. For the best views, drive to the **Col de la Faucille** (7km along the D936), high above the village. A 4km round-trip hike from the parking area up the Petit Montrond (1533m) makes the stop even better.

THE DRIVE: It's a 20-minute, 20km drive along the D936 and D1005 to Les Rousses through forest and pastureland.

09 Les Rousses

The driving tour comes to a close in the resort of Les Rousses, on the northeastern edge of the park and hard up against the Swiss border. This is the Haut-Jura's prime sports hub for both winter (skiing) and summer (walking and mountain biking) sports. The resort comprises four small, predominantly cross-country ski areas: Prémanon, Lamoura, Bois d'Amont and the village Les Rousses. Find out more at the Maison du Tourisme, home to the **tourist office** *(lesrousses.com)*.

LIQUID GOLD

Legend has it that *vin jaune* (yellow wine) was invented when a winemaker found a forgotten barrel, six years and three months after he'd initially filled it, and discovered its contents miraculously transformed into a gold-coloured wine.

A long, undisrupted fermentation process gives Jura's signature wine its unique characteristics. Savagnin grapes are harvested late and their sugar-saturated juices left to ferment for a minimum of six years and three months in oak barrels. A thin layer of yeast forms over the wine, which prevents it from oxidising, and there are no top-ups to compensate for evaporation (called *la part des anges* – 'the angels' share'). In the end, 100L of grape juice ferments down to 62L of *vin jaune* (lucky angels), which is then bottled in special 0.62L bottles called *clavelin*. *Vin jaune* is renowned for its ageing qualities, with prime vintages easily keeping for more than a century. A 1774 vintage, a cool 220 years old at the time, was sipped by an awestruck committee of experts in 1994.

La Percée du Vin Jaune *(percee-du-vin-jaune.com)* festival takes place annually in early February to celebrate the first tasting of the vintage produced six years and three months earlier. Villages take it in turn to hold the two-day celebrations, at which the new vintage is blessed and rated, and street tastings, cooking competitions, cellar visits and auctions keep *vin jaune* aficionados fulfilled.

Col de la Faucille
ANATOLI LAPTEV/SHUTTERSTOCK

PHOTO OPPORTUNITY

The hawks' view from the Col de la Faucille.

18

ALPS, JURA & RHÔNE VALLEY

ALPINE ADVENTURE

DURATION: 6 DAYS

DISTANCE: 363KM / 225 MILES

GREAT FOR: FAMILIES, NATURE

BEST TIME TO GO: MID-JUNE TO MID-SEPTEMBER, WHEN MOUNTAIN PASSES ARE SNOW FREE.

IMPORTANT: SNOW TYRES/CHAINS/SOCKS REQUIRED 1 NOVEMBER – 31 MARCH

This outdoorsy ramble through the heart of the French Alps runs from Annecy (perhaps France's prettiest lakeside city) via Mont Blanc (Western Europe's highest peak), Col de l'Iseran (its highest mountain pass) and Bonneval-sur-Arc (an alpine village of incomparable charm) to St-Véran (France's highest village). Along the way, you'll have ample opportunity for adrenaline-laced mountain adventures.

LINK YOUR TRIP

17 The Jura
Discover the gentler pleasures of eastern France's 'other' mountains, 1½ hours north of Annecy.

19 Foothills of the Alps
Join this nature-lover's jaunt through high-country plateaux and dramatic canyons, two hours west of Briançon.

01 Annecy

There's no dreamier introduction to the French Alps than Annecy. The mountains rise steep, wooded and snowcapped above startlingly turquoise Lac d'Annecy, providing a sublime setting for the medieval town's photogenic jumble of geranium-strewn houses, romantic canals and turreted rooftops.

Summer is the prime time to visit, when everyone is outdoors, socialising at pavement cafes, swimming in the lake (among Europe's purest) and boating, walking or cycling around it. Evening street performers feature during July's **Les Noctibules** festival, and there are lakeside fireworks during August's **Fête du Lac**.

Wander through the narrow medieval streets of the **Vieille Ville** (Old Town) to find the whimsical 12th-century **Palais de l'Isle** *(musees.annecy.fr)* on a triangular islet in the Canal du Thiou. Next stroll the tree-fringed lakefront through the flowery **Jardins de l'Europe**, linked to the

JEANLUCICHARD/SHUTTERSTOCK

★ BEST

TWO DAYS

The section between Annecy and Chamonix, for classic French alpine scenery.

Annecy

popular picnic spot **Champ de Mars** by the graceful **Pont des Amours** (Lovers' Bridge) and presided over by the dour, commanding **Château d'Annecy** *(musees.annecy.fr)*.

Cycling paths encircle the lake, passing by several pretty beaches en route. Boats can be hired along the canal-side quays, and several companies offer adventure sports. For details, visit Annecy's **tourist office** *(lac-annecy.com)*.

THE DRIVE: This 70km drive starts with a pretty southeastwards run along Annecy's lakefront, passing through the wildlife-rich wetlands of Bout du Lac on the lake's southern tip before continuing east on the D1508, then northeast on the D1212 and D909 into St-Gervais.

02 St-Gervais-les-Bains

Basking in the shadow of Mont Blanc, St-Gervais-les-Bains is a peaceful Savoyard village, centred on a Baroque church and an old-fashioned carousel.

Panoramic hiking trails in the Bettex, Mont d'Arbois and Mont Joly areas head off from town. Some of the best mountain-biking terrain is marked between Val d'Arly, Mont Blanc and Beaufortain.

For spirit-soaring mountain views with zero effort, board the **Tramway du Mont Blanc** *(montblancnaturalresort.com)*, France's highest train. Since 1913 it has been labouring up to Bellevue (1800m) in winter and Mont Lachat (2113m) in summer.

☑ TOP TIP

WINTER DRIVING

Parts of this route (notably the northern stretches around Annecy and Chamonix) are accessible to drivers in winter, but the high mountain passes further south are strictly off-limits outside summer.

Train buffs will also love the narrow-gauge **Mont Blanc Express**, which trundles along a century-old rail line from St-Gervais to Martigny in Switzerland.

THE DRIVE: The 24km route to Chamonix follows the D902, N205 and D243 into the heart of the Alps.

03 Chamonix

An outdoors playground of epic proportions, Chamonix sits directly at the foot of Western Europe's highest peak, the bone-white dome of Mont Blanc (4810m).

Climbers with the necessary skill and stamina flock here to tackle any number of iconic alpine routes, including the incomparable **Mont Blanc ascent**. If you're not quite ready to scale the big one, consider circumnavigating it on the classic eight- to 11-day **Tour du Mont Blanc**, which takes in majestic glaciers and peaks in France, Italy and Switzerland; local outfitters organise excursions including half-board in *refuges* (mountain huts), lift tickets and luggage transport. Other peak experiences include Chamonix' dozens of day hikes, the unforgettable cable-car ascent to **Aiguille du Midi** and the **Montenvers train ride** *(montblancnaturalresort.com)* to France's largest glacier, the 200m-deep **Mer de Glace** (Sea of Ice).

Chamonix has an unparalleled menu of adrenaline sports including rafting, canyoning, mountain biking and paragliding down from Planpraz (2000m) or Aiguille du Midi (3842m). For details, visit the **tourist office** *(chamonix.com)*.

THE DRIVE: Take the E25/N205 southeast 17km through the Mont Blanc Tunnel into Italy. From the Aosta/Courmayeur exit, continue 31km southwest back towards France along the SS26. Once across the border, follow the D1090 and D84 southwest, then the D902 southeast for a total of 40km into Val d'Isère.

04 Val d'Isère

This world-renowned, end-of-the-valley resort is home to the gargantuan **Espace Killy** *(espacekilly.com)* skiing area, named after French triple Olympic gold medallist Jean-Claude Killy. Even in July, you can ski the **Pisaillas Glacier** above town, though many summer visitors also come to hike, mountain bike and enjoy off-season hotel discounts.

The trails weaving into the nearby valleys of **Parc National de la Vanoise** are a hiker's dream. For more of a challenge, play among the peaks at neighbouring La Daille's two **vie ferrate** (assisted climbing routes).

Mountain biking (VTT) is big here. Five lifts offer cyclists access to 16 downhill routes, seven endurance runs and two cross-country circuits. Bike rental is available at local sport

Aiguille du Midi

PHOTO OPPORTUNITY

Jagged peaks and glacial valleys from the top of the Aiguille du Midi.

MS VECTORPLUS/SHUTTERSTOCK

shops. **Bureau des Guides** *(guides-montagne-valdisere.com)* arranges guided hiking, mountain biking, canyoning and rock-climbing excursions.

Ask at the **tourist office** *(valdisere.com)* about family-friendly activities, from donkey trekking to farm visits.

THE DRIVE: Prepare for a dizzying climb as you leave Val d'Isère, steeply switchbacking 17km up the D902 to Col de l'Iseran.

05 Col de l'Iseran

No doubt about it, you've gained some serious altitude here. Indeed, the D902 over Col de l'Iseran (2770m) is the highest paved through road in Europe. Meteorological conditions at the summit are notoriously fickle – take, for example, the Tour de France stage that was supposed to pass through here on 8 July 1996 but had to be rerouted due to snow and -5°C temperatures.

THE DRIVE: Spellbinding views unfold as you navigate the D902's hairpin turns 14km downhill into Bonneval-sur-Arc.

06 Bonneval-sur-Arc

Heralded as one of the *plus beaux villages de France* (prettiest villages in France), this high mountain hamlet is filled with stone and slate cottages that wear their winter preparations proudly (notice all the woodpiles up on 2nd-floor porches).

Bonneval makes a tranquil base for exploring the 530-sq-km **Parc National de la Vanoise** *(vanoise-parcnational.fr)*, whose rugged snowcapped peaks, mirror-like lakes and vast glaciers dominate the landscape between the Tarentaise and Maurienne Valleys. This incredible swath of wilderness was designated France's first national park in 1963, protecting habitat for marmots, chamois and France's largest colony of ibexes, along with 20 pairs of golden eagles and the odd bearded vulture.

ROBERTO MOIOLA/SYSAWORLD/GETTY IMAGES

Lac Blanc

HIKING CHAMONIX

Chamonix boasts 350km of spectacular high-altitude trails, many reached by cable car. In late June and July there's enough light to walk until at least 9pm. Here are a few recommended walks to start you off.

Lac Blanc

From the top of **Télésiège de l'Index** *(montblancnaturalresort.com)* or at **Télécabine de la Flégère**, the line's midway point, gentle 1¼- to two-hour trails lead to 2352m Lac Blanc, a turquoise-coloured lake ensnared by mountains. Stargazers can overnight at the **Refuge du Lac Blanc** *(refugelacblanc.com)*, a wooden chalet favoured by photographers for its top-of-Europe Mont Blanc views.

Grand Balcon Sud

This easy-going trail skirts the western side of the valley, stays at around 2000m and commands a terrific view of Mont Blanc. Reach it on foot from behind Le Brévent's *télécabine* station.

Grand Balcon Nord

Routes starting from the Plan de l'Aiguille include the challenging Grand Balcon Nord, which takes you to the dazzling Mer de Glace. From there, walk or take the **Montenvers** train down to Chamonix.

The park is a hiker's heaven between June and September. The **Grand Tour de Haute Maurienne** *(haute-maurienne-vanoise.com)*, a seven-day hike around the upper reaches of the valley, takes in national park highlights. For information on local day hikes, visit

Bonneval-sur-Arc's **tourist office** *(bonneval-sur-arc.com)*.

THE DRIVE: Cruise 55km down the Arc River valley on the D902/D1006 through Lanslebourg and Modane to St-Michel de Maurienne, then climb 35km through the ski resort of Valloire to the ethereal heights of Col du Galibier.

07 Col du Galibier

The signposts say you're simply crossing the departmental border from Savoie into the Hautes Alpes. The landscape says that you've entered another universe. Col du Galibier (2642m) is a staggeringly beautiful alpine pass, whose forbidding remoteness may make you feel like the last living person on Earth. To the west lies the Parc National des Écrins, a 918-sq-km expanse of high-country wilderness. Stop and savour the top-of-the-world feeling before returning to the squiggling ribbon of roadway below.

THE DRIVE: Despite the distance on the signpost (35km), the incredibly twisty and scenic descent into Briançon on the D902 and D1091 feels longer; stupendous views will stop you in your tracks every couple of minutes. Enjoy every horn-tooting, head-spinning, glacier-gawping moment, with views of thundering falls, sheer cliffs and jagged peaks razoring above thick larch forests.

08 Briançon

Perched astride a high rocky outcrop, the fairy-tale walled city of Briançon affords views of the snowcapped Écrins peaks from almost every corner. The centre's Italian ambience is no coincidence; Italy is just 20km away.

Briançon's old town is a late-medieval time capsule, its winding cobbled lanes punctuated by shuttered, candy-coloured townhouses and shops selling whistling marmots. The steep main street, **Grande Gargouille**, links two town gates, **Porte de Pignerol** and **Porte d'Embrun**. Crowning the old city is the massive **Fort du Château**. Daily guided walks (sometimes in English) are run by the **Service du Patrimoine** *(ville-briancon.fr)*.

Briançon's biggest drawcard is its ensemble of 17th- and early-18th-century structures designed by pioneering French military architect Vauban, including the old town's signature star-shaped fortifications, the coral-pink **Collégiale Notre Dame et St Nicolas**, several nearby **forts** and the **Pont d'Asfeld**.

There are outstanding hiking opportunities in the mountains of nearby **Parc National des Écrins** *(ecrins-parcnational.fr)*. Pick up maps and info at the **Maison du Parc**. For guided treks, glacier traverses, mountain biking, rafting, kayaking, canyoning and vie ferrate, check with **Bureau des Guides et Accompagnateurs** *(guides-briancon.com)*.

THE DRIVE: From Briançon resume your way southeast along the D902, then via the D947 and D5 to your final stop, St-Véran. Only 28km as the crow flies, this last section of tightly folded mountain road works out to 55km, and around 1¾ hours behind the wheel.

09 St-Véran

What more fitting place to wind up a tour of the roof of Europe than France's highest village? Nestled a cool 2040m above sea level, in the midst of the Parc Naturel Régional du Queyras, St-Véran is listed as one of France's most beautiful villages and offers serene hiking in all directions.

AIGUILLE DU MIDI

A great broken tooth of rock rearing above glaciers, snowfields and rocky crags, 8km from the hump of Mont Blanc, the Aiguille du Midi (3842m) is one of Chamonix' most distinctive landmarks. If you can handle the height, don't miss taking a trip up here – the 360-degree views of the French, Swiss and Italian Alps are breathtaking.

All year round the vertiginous **Téléphérique de l'Aiguille du Midi** *(montblancnaturalresort.com)*, one of the world's highest cable cars, climbs to the summit. Halfway up, Plan de l'Aiguille (2317m) is a terrific place to start hikes or paraglide. In summer you'll need to obtain a boarding card (marked with the number of your departing and returning cable car) in addition to a ticket. Bring warm clothes, as even in summer the temperature can drop below 0°C up top!

From the Aiguille du Midi, between late June and early September you can continue for a further 30 minutes of mind-blowing scenery – suspended glaciers, spurs, seracs and shimmering ice fields – in the smaller bubbles of the **Télécabine Panoramique Mont Blanc** to Pointe Helbronner (3466m) on the France–Italy border. From there, the **SkyWay Monte Bianco** *(montebianco.com)* can take you all the way to Courmayeur, in Italy's Val d'Aosta.

Col du Galibier
JEAN-RAOUL BIANCO/SHUTTERSTOCK

♥ WHY I LOVE THIS TRIP

CHRISTOPHER PITTS, WRITER

That a glacier's softly curving snowfields can hide fathomless crevasses and a sea of deep-blue ice shards sums up all the drama contained in this magnificent mountain range. It's irresistibly beautiful, but with just enough danger lurking beneath the surface to send a frisson down your spine. Snowy pistes, jagged peaks, glittering alpine lakes and pots of bubbling fondue – here, you truly do feel like you're on top of the world.

STAY AWHILE

PARÇ NATIONAL DES ÉCRINS

BY ANNA RICHARDS

If nature made a theme park, it would look like the **Parc National des Écrins** *(ecrins-parcnational.fr)*. Turquoise lakes accessible only on foot, immense glaciers, chamois, marmots, ermine and ibex – it stuns everywhere you look.

Winters here are filled with snow sports: get acquainted with the gnarly off-piste descents at **La Grave** and **La Meije**, or the groomed slopes of **Serre-Chevalier**, where skiing and snowboarding are just the tip of the iceberg. A particularly memorable experience for me was trying to pilot a three-wheel tricycle down an icy slope – I couldn't figure out how the brakes worked! At **Les Deux Alpes** *(les2alpes.com)*, the altitude of the resort means skiing is often possible right up until early July.

In summer, that same craggy terrain turns into a playground for hiking, mountain biking, vie ferrate, canyoning and even white-water rafting. The **Tour des Écrins** *(grand-tour-ecrins.fr)*, a hiking trail otherwise known as the GR54, is a 10- to 15-day loop around the entire national park, but many of the sections are perfectly achievable as a day hike. Those who've undertaken it (and I count myself among their number) rate it as more beautiful and more challenging than the famous Tour du Mont Blanc. It's also far less crowded.

If you're road-tripping here, summer is the best season to visit. In winter, take snow chains and park down in the Serre-Chevalier valley (Le Monêtier-les-Bains has an excellent thermal spa) and speed up and down slopes on the fringes of the Écrins on skis.

LINK YOUR TRIP

18 Alpine Adventure Take in the outdoors on this trip along the top of France.

FROM LEFT: SERAPHP/SHUTTERSTOCK; MARTIN BLAZICEK/SHUTTERSTOCK

Left: Les Deux Alpes; Right: La Meije

PLACES TO STAY

Hotel le Monêtier *(lemonetier.com)* is the most iconic place to stay, with a spa whose waters are naturally heated by thermal springs. The mountain views from the pool are straight out of a nature documentary, and it's open in both summer and winter. Winter stays are much more expensive, but **BodyGo Hostel** *(bodygohostel.com)* in the hilltop town of Briançon, just outside of the national park limits, is a good choice for travellers on budgets. Briançon has lots of different hotels at all price ranges, all within easy walking distance of restaurants.

19

ALPS, JURA & RHÔNE VALLEY

FOOTHILLS OF THE ALPS

DURATION: 6 DAYS

DISTANCE: 475KM / 295 MILES

GREAT FOR: FAMILIES, NATURE

BEST TIME TO GO: JUNE AND SEPTEMBER, FOR GOOD WEATHER WITHOUT PEAK SUMMER CROWDS.

IMPORTANT: SNOW TYRES/CHAINS/SOCKS REQUIRED 1 NOVEMBER – 31 MARCH

In the transition zone between the Alps and Provence lie some of France's most magnificent and least-explored landscapes. Extending from the Vercors plateau to the Verdon River, this trip starts in poppy-strewn pastures, where cowbells jingle beneath limestone peaks, and ends among the lavender fields and arid gorges of Haute-Provence. Along the way, there's plenty of outdoorsy excitement for the entire family.

LINK YOUR TRIP

18 Alpine Adventure
Head northeast from Lans-en-Vercors to explore France's most awe-inspiring peaks.

23 Lavender Route
Wander the purple-fringed back roads of Provence, west of Moustiers-Ste-Marie.

01 Lans-en-Vercors

Lans-en-Vercors (elevation 1020m) is idyllically set among the sloping pastures, plateaux and chiselled limestone formations of the 1750-sq-km **Parc Naturel Régional du Vercors**, 28km southwest of Grenoble. With stunning vistas and wildlife, including marmots, ibex and chamois, the park draws families seeking low-key outdoor adventure. Hikers of any age will enjoy the easy, supremely scenic 7km high-country loop from **La Molière** to **Pas de Bellecombe**, with its built-in lunch stop at **Gîte d'Alpage de la Molière**. To reach the trailhead, go 20km north of Lans-en-Vercors via Autrans, following the D106 and a partly unpaved forest road. Alternatively, **Les Accompagnateurs Nature et Patrimoine** (*curieux2vercors.fr*) offers guided walks throughout the Vercors.

THE DRIVE: Follow the D531 southwest, descending to enter the magnificent Gorges de la Bourne after about 10km.

★ BEST

FAMILY HIKE

The high-country loop from La Molière, near Lans-en-Vercors.

JEAFISH PING/SHUTTERSTOCK

Chichilianne, with Mont Aiguille behind

02 Gorges de la Bourne

Cliff walls up to 600m high crowd around the road through these deep and dramatic gorges, cut by the eponymous Bourne as it rushes off the Vercors plateau. Watch for narrow turnouts alongside the roadway where you can pull off and admire the views.

THE DRIVE: Near the end of the gorges, bear left on the D103 and proceed 20km south through the pretty mountain villages of St-Julien-en-Vercors and St-Martin-en-Vercors. At St-Agnan-en-Vercors continue 5km south on the D518 to the Grotte de la Luire.

03 Grotte de la Luire

The Vercors was a hotbed of the French Resistance in WWII. This **cave** *(grottedelaluire.com)* outside the town of St-Agnan-en-Vercors served as a field hospital for Resistance fighters for five days in July 1944 before German troops raided it, killing many patients on-site and taking the rest to Grenoble to be shot or deported. Memorial plaques mark the site, and lantern-lit tours are offered in summer.

THE DRIVE: The D518 travels 30km south to Die, culminating in a switchbacking descent from Col de Rousset. The D93 and D539 continue southeast 14km through sun-drenched farmland to Châtillon-en-Diois, a good lunch stop. The final 31km stretch along the D120 and D7 snakes over Col de Menée (1457m) to Chichilianne, affording spellbinding views of Mont Aiguille en route.

04 Chichilianne

Its lovely hayfields strewn with red poppies in late spring, Chichilianne has deep roots in mountaineering history, dating back to 1492 when Antoine de Ville scaled massive cube-shaped Mont Aiguille by order of King Charles VIII (accompanied by stonemasons and master carpenters who helped build ladders and attach ropes). Long nicknamed the 'inaccessible mountain', and celebrated by writers such as Rabelais, Mont Aiguille continues to capture the imagination of all who venture near.

Superb high-country hikes around Chichilianne include the **Sentier des Charenches** up Mont

Aiguille's southern flanks, and the six-hour loop to the Vercors plateau via **Pas de l'Essaure** and **Pas de l'Aiguille** (look for the monument to Resistance fighters who battled the Nazis at these high altitudes). Lower-elevation walks in surrounding valleys include the themed, family-oriented 5km walk, **Sentier des Artisans de la Terre**.

THE DRIVE: Follow the D7 and D526 east 17km to Mens, then cruise another 19km east on the D66 through hayfields backed by the Dévoluy massif's sawtooth ridgeline. Wind 8km south on the D66A and D537, descending to the Souloise River. Just before the bridge, turn left onto the D217, following signs for 'Sources des Gillardes' and parking at the trailhead.

05 Défilé de la Souloise

Forming the border between the *départements* of Isère and Hautes-Alpes, the sheer-faced **Souloise Gorge** is an idyllic spot to get out and stretch your legs. From the parking area, an easy there-and-back hike (200m each way) leads to the **Sources des Gillardes**, France's second-largest natural spring. Alternatively, continue downriver on the delightful **Canyon de l'Infernet** trail, through fragrant evergreen forest sandwiched between grey and orange rock walls. About 1km along, cross a bridge and loop back up the opposite bank to the parking area.

THE DRIVE: Follow the D537 and D937 south through tiny St-Disdier, enjoying stunning views of the Massif de Dévoluy's austere rocky face, punctuated by the pencil-shaped spire of the 11th-century Mère Église. Zigzag south along the D117 (5km southeast), D17 (7km southwest) and D937 (16km south over Col de Festre). From here, follow the D994, D1075 and D4075 south 54km into Sisteron.

Sources des Gillardes

PHOTOFORT 77/SHUTTERSTOCK

LERNER VADIM/SHUTTERSTOCK

Pont de l'Artuby

DRIVING THE GORGES DU VERDON

This spine-tingling drive is one of France's classic road trips. A complete circuit of the Gorges from Moustiers-Ste-Marie involves 140km (about four hours without stops) of relentless hairpin turns on precarious rim-side roads, with spectacular scenery around every bend. The only village en route is **La Palud-sur-Verdon** (930m). Expect slow traffic and scant opportunities to overtake in summer.

From Moustiers, aim first for the **Route des Crêtes** (D952 and D23), a 23km-long loop with 14 lookouts along the northern rim – ensure you drive the loop clockwise, as there's a one-way portion midway. En route, the most thrilling view is from **Belvédère de l'Escale**, an excellent place to spot vultures. After rejoining the D952, the road corkscrews eastward, past **Point Sublime**, which overlooks serrated rock formations dropping to the river.

Return towards Moustiers via the **Corniche Sublime** (D955 to D90, D71 and D19), a heart-palpitating route along the southern rim, passing landmarks including the **Balcons de la Mescla** (Mescla Terraces) and **Pont de l'Artuby**, Europe's highest bridge.

06 Sisteron

Perched on a promontory high above the Durance River, Sisteron's stunner is its **citadel** *(citadelledesisteron.fr)*. For centuries this imposing fortress guarded the strategic narrow passage between Dauphiné and Provence – though Napoléon did somehow sneak past here with 1200 soldiers after escaping Elba in 1815. Today it still commands bird's-eye perspectives of Sisteron's medieval streets, the eye-catching stratified rock face **Rocher de Baume** and the Durance Valley beyond. Architectural highlights include a 13th-century *chemin de ronde* (parapet walk) and a powder magazine designed by French military architect Vauban. On summer evenings the hilltop comes alive with open-air dance and classical-music concerts performed during the **Festival des Nuits de la Citadelle** *(nuitsdelacitadelle.fr)*.

THE DRIVE: Zip 39km down the A51 to Oraison. Take the D4 (5km), D907 (10km) and D108 (4km) southeast, climbing through Brunet to the Valensole plateau. Cruise 7km east through lavender fields on the D8, take the D953 (4km) into Puimoisson (passing roadside lavender stand Maison du Lavandin), and wind 14km into Moustiers-Ste-Marie along the D56 and D952.

07 Moustiers-Ste-Marie

Nicknamed Étoile de Provence (Star of Provence), enchanting Moustiers-Ste-Marie straddles the base of towering limestone cliffs – the beginning of the Alps and the end of Haute-Provence's rolling prairies. Winding streets climb past tile-roofed houses, connected by arched stone bridges spanning the picturesque creek (Le Riou) that courses through the village centre.

A 227m-long chain bearing a shining gold star stretches high above the village, legendarily placed there by the Knight of Blacas upon his safe return from the Crusades. Below the star, the 14th-century **Chapelle Notre Dame de Beauvoir** clings to the cliff ledge like an eagle's nest. A steep trail climbs beside a waterfall to the chapel, passing 14 stations of the cross. On 8 September, a 5am Mass celebrates the Virgin Mary's nativity, followed by flutes, drums and breakfast on the square.

THE DRIVE: The trip to Gorges du Verdon is a classic. Follow the D952 19km southeast to La Palud-sur-Verdon, then the D23, winding from 9km above the western flank of the Verdon to your final destination.

08 Gorges du Verdon

Dubbed the Grand Canyon of Europe, the breathtaking Gorges du Verdon slice 25km through Haute-Provence's limestone plateau. The narrow canyon bottom, carved by the Verdon's emerald-green waters, is only 8m to 90m wide; its steep, multihued walls, home to griffon vultures, rise as high as 700m – it's twice as tall as the Eiffel Tower (330m)! One of France's most scenic drives takes in staggering panoramas from the vertigo-inducing cliff-side roads on either side.

The canyon floors are accessible only by foot or raft. Dozens of blazed trails traverse untamed countryside between Castellane and Moustiers, including the classic **Sentier Martel**, which uses occasional ladders and tunnels to navigate 14km of riverbanks and ledges. For details on 28 walks, pick up the excellent English-language *Canyon du Verdon* at Moustiers' **tourist office** *(moustiers.fr)*. Rafting operators include **Guides pour l'Aventure** *(guidesaventure.com)* and **Aboard Rafting** *(rafting-verdon.com)*.

Gorges du Verdon

LUISA PUCCINI/SHUTTERSTOCK

PHOTO OPPORTUNITY

The dizzying view of the Gorges du Verdon from Belvédère de l'Escale.

20

ALPS, JURA & RHÔNE VALLEY

BEAUJOLAIS VILLAGES

DURATION: 2 DAYS

DISTANCE: 99KM / 61 MILES

GREAT FOR: FOOD & DRINK, HISTORY & CULTURE

BEST TIME TO GO: APRIL TO JUNE, SEPTEMBER AND OCTOBER FOR A PATCHWORK OF COLOURS.

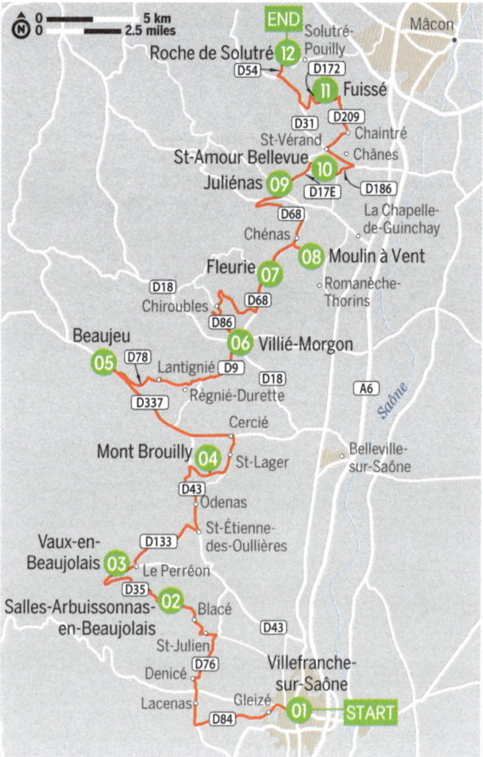

Ah, Beaujolais, where the unhurried life is complemented by rolling vineyards, beguiling villages, old churches, splendid estates and country roads that twist into the hills. Once you've left Villefranche-sur-Saône, a rural paradise awaits and a sense of escapism is within reach. Be sure to factor in plenty of time for wine tasting.

LINK YOUR TRIP

16 Route des Grands Crus
For more wine tasting and rolling vineyards, make a beeline for the Route des Grands Crus, which unfolds south of Dijon. Head to Mâcon and follow signs to Dijon.

21 Rhône Valley
For a change of scene, head to Lyon (via Mâcon) and discover the hidden gems of the Rhône Valley.

01 Villefranche-sur-Saône

Stroll along lively rue Nationale, where you'll find most of the shops and the Gothic **Collégiale Notre-Dame des Marais**, which boasts an elegant facade and a soaring spire. An excellent starting point for oenophiles would be a visit to one of several wine bars and shops in town.

THE DRIVE: At a roundabout about 800m south of the Collégiale, look out for the brown sign to 'Route des Vins du Beaujolais'. Pass through Gleizé, Lacenas, Denicé, St-Julien and Blacé before reaching Salles-Arbuissonas-en-Beaujolais. Count on a good half hour to cover the 16km trip.

02 Salles-Arbuissonnas-en-Beaujolais

As you pass through Salles-Arbuissonnas, keep an eye out for the

RICOCHET64/SHUTTERSTOCK

★ BEST FOR

FOODIES

The Beaujolais region prides itself on its Michelin-starred restaurants.

Salles-Arbuissonnas-en-Beaujolais

superb 10th-century **priory** (Musée le Prieuré; *salles-arbuissonnas.fr*) and the adjoining Roman **cloister**.

THE DRIVE: Drive along the D35 to Vaux-en-Beaujolais (6.5km).

03 Vaux-en-Beaujolais

The village of Vaux-en-Beaujolais emerges like a hamlet in a fairy tale. You can't but be dazzled by the fabulous backdrop – it's perched on a rocky spur ensnared by a sea of vineyards. Don't leave Vaux without enjoying the fruity aroma of Beaujolais-Villages (the local appellation) at **La Cave de Clochemerle** *(cavedeclochemerle.com)*, housed in atmospheric cellars.

THE DRIVE: Take the D133 to Le Perréon, then follow signs to St-Étienne-des-Oullières and Odenas. In Odenas, follow signs to Mont Brouilly (13km from Vaux-en-Beaujolais).

04 Mont Brouilly

It would be a crime to explore the Beaujolais and not take the scenic road that leads to Mont Brouilly (485m), crowned with a small chapel. Hold on to your hat and lift your jaw off the floor as you approach the lookout at the summit – the view over the entire Beaujolais region and the Saône valley will be etched in your memory forever.

THE DRIVE: Drive down to St-Lager, then take the D68 to Cercié and continue along the D337 to Beaujeu (12km from Mont Brouilly).

05 Beaujeu

The historic Beaujolais wine capital, Beaujeu is an enchanting spot to while away a few hours. **Le Comptoir Beaujolais** *(comptoirbeaujolais.fr)* is a great place to sip some excellent Beaujolais-Villages and Brouilly. It's also worth popping your head into the rewarding **La Maison du Terroir Beaujolais** *(lamaisonduterroirbeaujolais.com)*. Housed in a wonderful Renaissance building, this produce shop has a wide array of Beaujolais wines, cheeses, jams and charcuterie, among other items.

THE DRIVE: Head to Lantignié along the D78 and continue to Régnié-Durette, where you'll see signs to Villié-Morgon. The full drive covers just over 10km.

06 Villié-Morgon

Morgon wine, anybody? Expand your knowledge of the local appellation with a tasting session at the vaulted **Caveau de Morgon**, which occupies a grandiose 18th-century château in the heart of town – it can't get more atmospheric than that.

THE DRIVE: From Villié-Morgon, it's a relaxed 10km drive to Fleurie via Chiroubles. Follow the D18 and D86 to Chiroubles, then signs to Fleurie.

07 Fleurie

Beaujolais' rising star, Fleurie red wines are said to be sensuous, offering a combination of floral and fruity notes. A superb fine-dining experience, **Auberge du Cep** *(aubergeducep.com)* features traditional Beaujolais cooking at its best with a range of regional specialities in a rustic dining room.

THE DRIVE: Take the D68 towards Chénas; after about 3km turn right onto the D68e towards Romanèche-Thorins and you'll soon reach Moulin à Vent. It's a 4km drive from Fleurie.

08 Moulin à Vent

Reason itself to visit this drowsy hamlet is the heritage-listed **Moulin à Vent** (Windmill). Dubbed the 'King of Beaujolais', the Moulin à Vent appellation is a particularly charming wine to sample in situ: its **Caveau du Moulin à Vent** *(moulin-a-vent.fr)*, across the road from the windmill, provides a prime wine-tasting opportunity.

THE DRIVE: From Moulin à Vent retrace your route back towards Chénas and take the D68 to Juliénas. It's an easy 6.6km drive.

09 Juliénas

One of the best-kept secrets in Beaujolais is this delightful village famed for its eponymous vintage. A beauty of a castle, the 16th-century **Château de Juliénas** *(chateaudejulienas.com)* occupies a delightful estate; tours can be arranged by phoning ahead. No doubt you'll be struck by the cellars, the longest in the region. Tours can be followed by an *aperi'vin* (tasting and snacks) or a picnic among the grapes. Another atmospheric venture set in a disused church, **Cellier de la Vieille Église** is a great place to sip wines of the Juliénas appellation.

THE DRIVE: Follow the road to St-Amour Bellevue along the D17e and the D169 (3km from Juliénas).

10 St-Amour Bellevue

Not to be missed in St-Amour: the **Domaine des Vignes du Paradis – Pascal Durand** *(saint-amour-en-paradis.com)*. This award-winning *domaine* (estate) run by the fifth generation of vintners welcomes visitors to its intimate cellars and sells St-Amour wines at unbeatable prices.

THE DRIVE: Follow the D186 towards Chânes. In Bourgneuf, take the D31 to St-Vérand. From St-Vérand, follow signs to Chaintré and continue to Fuissé. It's a 10km trip from St-Amour.

WHEN BEAUJEU GOES WILD

A colourful time to motor in Beaujeu is around the third week in November. At the stroke of midnight on the third Thursday (ie Wednesday night), the *libération* (release) or *mise en perce* (tapping; opening) of the first bottles of cherry-bright Beaujolais Nouveau is celebrated around France and the world. In Beaujeu there's free Beaujolais Nouveau for all as part of the **Sarmentelles de Beaujeu** – a giant street party that kicks off on the Wednesday leading up to the Beaujolais Nouveau's release. Expect five days of wine tasting, live music and dancing.

11 Fuissé

If you like peace, quiet and sigh-inducing views, you'll love this absolutely picturesque stone town nestled in a small valley carpeted by manicured vineyards. You've now left Beaujolais – Fuissé is part of Burgundy. It's famous for its prestigious Chardonnay whites of the Pouilly-Fuissé appellation, parts of which were given Premier Cru status in 2020. You can attend tastings at various cellars around town or, for the ultimate experience, at the magnificent **Château de Fuissé** *(chateau-fuisse.fr)*.

THE DRIVE: From Fuissé follow signs to Chasselas along the D172. After about 3.5km, turn right onto the D31 (direction Tramayes). Drive another 2km to a right-hand turn onto the D54 (direction Solutré-Pouilly). Count on 15 minutes for the 7km trip.

12 Roche de Solutré

A lovely 20-minute walk along the **Sentier des Roches** will get you to the top of the rocky outcrop known as the Roche de Solutré (493m), from where Mont Blanc can sometimes be seen, especially at sunset. For some cultural sustenance, make a beeline for the nearby **Musée Départemental de Préhistoire de Solutré** *(rochedesolutre.com)*, which displays finds from one of Europe's richest prehistoric sites.

Mont Brouilly (p157)
LDGFR PHOTOS/SHUTTERSTOCK

PHOTO OPPORTUNITY

Enjoy a panorama over the entire region from Mont Brouilly.

21

ALPS, JURA & RHÔNE VALLEY

RHÔNE VALLEY

DURATION: 5 DAYS

DISTANCE: 293KM / 182 MILES

GREAT FOR: FOOD & DRINK, HISTORY & CULTURE, NATURE

BEST TIME TO GO: JUNE AND JULY, FOR FESTIVALS IN THE ROMAN THEATRES OF LYON, VIENNE AND ORANGE.

Food and history are recurring themes on this multifaceted meander down the Rhône, from the fabled eateries of Lyon to the Gallo-Roman museum at Vienne, the nougat factories of Montélimar and the ancient theatre at Orange. As you work your way downriver to Provence, you'll also encounter imposing hilltop fortresses, slow-paced southern villages and one of France's prettiest river gorges.

LINK YOUR TRIP

14 Volcanoes of the Auvergne
Head west of Lyon for this pastoral meander among ancient green peaks.

22 Roman Provence
From Orange, head northeast and further south to delve deeper into Roman ruins.

01 Lyon

This strategic spot at the confluence of the Rhône and Saône Rivers has been luring people ever since the Romans named it Lugudunum in 43 BCE. Climb **Fourvière hill** west of town to witness the successive waves of human settlement, spread out in chronological order at your feet: a pair of Gallo-Roman theatres in the foreground, Vieux Lyon's medieval cathedral on the Saône's nearby banks, the 17th-century Hôtel de Ville (Town Hall) on the peninsula between the rivers, and, beyond the Rhône, modern Lyon's skyscrapers backed by the distant Alps.

With its illustrious history and renowned gastronomy, France's third-largest city merits at least a two-day visit. Supplement a walking tour of Lyon's quintessential sights with a visit to **Croix Rousse**, the 19th-century silk-weavers' district where Jacquard looms still restore

FREDERIC PROCHASSON/GETTY IMAGES

★ BEST FOR

FOODIES

Lyon's beloved *bouchons* (convivial neighbourhood bistros).

A *bouchon* in Lyon

fabrics for France's historical monuments, and don't leave town without eating in at least one of the city's incomparable *bouchons*.

As of 2025, parts of Lyon's 1st *arrondissement* (district) are car-free. It's best to park outside the city centre (in one of several *parc relais*) and take public transport.

THE DRIVE: Shoot 33km down the A7 to Vienne, enjoying close-up views of the Rhône en route.

02 Vienne

France's Gallo-Roman heritage is alive and well in this laid-back riverfront city, whose back streets hide a trio of jaw-dropping ruins: the 1st-century-BCE **Temple d'Auguste et de Livie**, with its splendid Corinthian columns; the **Pyramide du Cirque**, a 15.5m-tall obelisk that once pierced the centre of a hippodrome; and the 1st-century-CE **Théâtre Romain** *(theatreantiquevienne.com)*, which relives its glory days as a performance venue each summer during Vienne's two-week **jazz festival** *(jazzavienne.com)*.

Across the river, a treasure trove of Gallo-Roman artefacts is displayed at the **Musée Gallo-Romain** *(musees-gallo-romains.com)*.

THE DRIVE: Follow the D386, D1086 and D86 for 48km south, threading the needle between the Rhône and the pretty mountains of the Parc Naturel Régional du Pilat. At Sarras cross the bridge to St-Vallier, then continue 32km south on the N7 through classic Côtes du Rhône wine country around Tain l'Hermitage into Valence.

03 Valence

With its warm weather, honey-coloured light and relaxed cadence, it's easy to see why Valence advertises itself as the northern gateway to Provence. At lunchtime, make a beeline for **André**, a stylish eatery with an excellent wine list that's part of the Pic family's award-winning, multigenerational restaurant empire. Afterwards visit **Maison Nivon** *(nivon.com)* for a *suisse*, Valence's classic orange-rind-flavoured pastry in the shape of a Swiss Vatican guard.

In the old town, gawk at the allegorical sculpted heads adorning the facade of the wonderful 16th-century **Maison des Têtes** *(valenceromansagglo.fr)*.

THE DRIVE: Cruise 28km south along the N7, then wind 4.5km through orchard-covered hills on the D57 into Mirmande.

04 Mirmande

Surrounded by pretty orchard country, this hilltop of stone houses and sleepy medieval streets was once a major centre of silkworm production. It then became an artists' colony in the 20th century, when cubist painter André Lhote made his home here. Volcanologist-cinematographer Haroun Tazieff later served as the town's mayor, adding to Mirmande's cultural cachet and earning it recognition as one of *les plus beaux villages de France*.

With a couple of charming hotels, Mirmande makes an inviting overnight stop. Wander up to the 12th-century Romanesque **Église de Ste-Foy**, where concerts and art exhibits are held in summertime and beautiful Rhône Valley views unfold year-round.

THE DRIVE: Snake 12km southeast on the D57 over Col de la Grande Limite (515m) into medieval Marsanne, then continue 15km southwest into Montélimar on the D105 and D6.

05 Montélimar

An obligatory stop for those with a sweet tooth, Montélimar is famous for its delectable nougat made from almonds, lavender honey, pistachios, sugar, egg white and vanilla. To taste this sweet delight at the source, visit one of Montélimar's small producers, such as **L'Artisan Nougatier** *(lartisannougatier.fr)*. Afterwards burn off the calories with a climb to **Château de Montélimar** *(chateaux.ladrome.fr)*, whose 12th-century fortifications hold a Romanesque chapel and a rotating series of art exhibits.

THE DRIVE: Take the D73 southwest for 10km across the Rhône into Viviers, follow the river 15km south into Bourg-St-Andéol, then squiggle 30km along the D4 past St-Remèze's lavender museum to Vallon-Pont-d'Arc, the western gateway to the Gorges de l'Ardèche.

06 Gorges de l'Ardèche

These steep and spectacular limestone gorges cut a curvaceous swath through the high scrubland along the Ardèche River, a tributary of the Rhône. The real showstopper, near the gorges' western entrance, is the **Pont d'Arc**, a sublimely beautiful natural stone arch. Stop here to camp, swim or join one of the many paddling tours down the river.

BOUCHONS

A *bouchon* might be a 'bottle stopper' or 'traffic jam' elsewhere in France, but in Lyon it's a cosy, traditional bistro specialising in regional cuisine. *Bouchons* originated in the first half of the 20th century when many bourgeois families had to let go their in-house cooks, who then set up their own restaurants.

Kick-start your meal with a *communard,* an apéritif of red Beaujolais wine and *crème de cassis* (blackcurrant liqueur), then move on to a pot – a 46cL glass bottle adorned with an elastic band to prevent wine drips – of local Brouilly, Beaujolais, Côtes du Rhône or Mâcon.

Next comes the entrée, perhaps *salade lyonnaise* (green salad with bacon, croutons and poached egg), or lentils in creamy sauce. Hearty main dishes include *boudin noir aux pommes* (blood sausage with apples), *quenelles de brochet* (pike dumplings served in a creamy crayfish sauce), *tablier de sapeur* (breaded, fried tripe) and *andouillette* (sausage made from pigs' intestines).

For the cheese course, choose between a bowl of *fromage blanc* (a cross between cream cheese and natural yoghurt); *cervelle de canut* ('brains of the silk weaver'; *fromage blanc* mixed with chives and garlic, a staple of Lyon's 19th-century weavers); or local St-Marcellin ripened to gooey perfection.

Desserts are grandma-style: think *tarte aux pommes* (apple tart), or the Lyonnais classic *tarte aux pralines,* a brilliant rose-coloured confection made with crème fraiche and crushed sugar-coated almonds.

Little etiquette is required in *bouchons*. Mopping your plate with a chunk of bread is fine, and you'll usually sit elbow-to-elbow with your fellow diners at tightly wedged tables (great for practising your French).

Mirmande
PI-R PHOTOS/SHUTTERSTOCK

Further east, the **Sentier Aval des Gorges** descends steeply for 2km to the heart of the gorges, granting hikers access to two primitive campgrounds at Bivouac de Gournier and Bivouac de Gaud. Allow some time to visit the sensational **Grotte Chauvet 2** *(grottechauvet2ardeche.com)* museum, which houses replicas of amazing prehistoric paintings.

THE DRIVE: From Vallon-Pont-d'Arc, the breathtaking D290 zigzags for 29km along the canyon's rim, with 11 viewpoints revealing dazzling vistas of horseshoe bends and kayakers in formation far below. Exiting the gorges, take the D200 for 2km south through pretty medieval Aiguèze, then continue 22km southeast across the Rhône into Mornas via the D901, D6086, D994 and N7.

07 Mornas

Perched on some precipitous cliffs, the 11th- to 14th-century **Forteresse de Mornas** *(forteresse-mornas.fr)* makes a dramatic backdrop for the pretty village below. Built by the medieval Counts of Toulouse, it commands outstanding views west to the Rhône and east to Mont Ventoux. A trail climbs 137 vertical metres from the village past the 12th-century Romanesque **Église Notre-Dame du Val-Romigier** to the fortress, where costumed guides offer historical re-enactments. Medieval fever also grips Mornas in July during **La Médiévale de Mornas**, a popular annual festival and crafts market.

THE DRIVE: Zip 12km southeast down the N7 into Orange, whose magnificent 2000-year-old Arc de Triomphe provides a fitting welcome.

08 Orange

Sun-drenched Orange is a dream destination for fans of ancient ruins. The city's outstanding **Théâtre Antique** (Ancient Roman Theatre; *theatre-antique.com*), one of only three Roman theatres in the world with a perfectly preserved stage wall, shines brightest during summer performances such as the epic international opera festival **Chorégies d'Orange** *(choregies.fr)*. North of town, Orange's second Roman treasure is the exquisitely carved 1st-century-CE **Arc de Triomphe**.

Pont d'Arc (p163), Gorges de l'Ardèche

PASCAL RATEAU/SHUTTERSTOCK

PHOTO OPPORTUNITY

The Pont d'Arc, a stunning stone archway over the Ardèche River.

ITALY
Cuneo
San Remo
Ventimiglia
Menton
MONACO
Roquebrune
Beaulieu-sur-Mer
St-Jean-Cap Ferrat
Villefranche-sur-Mer
Nice
Vence
Antibes
Juan-les-Pins
Cannes
Grasse
Ligurian Sea
Cime du Gélas (3143m)
Mont Mounier (2817m)
Tête de Siguret (3032m)
Barcelonnette
Gap
Durance
Sisteron
Château-Arnoux St-Auban
Digne-les-Bains
Peyruis
Forcalquier
Banon
Parc Naturel Régional du Verdon
Moustiers-Ste-Marie
Castellane
Manosque
Valensole
Draguignan
Fréjus
St-Raphaël
St-Maxime
St-Tropez
Le Lavandou
Hyères
Toulon
Cuers
Brignoles
St-Maximin-la-Ste-Baume
Bandol
Sanary-sur-Mer
St-Cyr-les-Lecques
Cassis
Aubagne
Marseille
L'Estaque
Vitrolles
Aix-en-Provence
Martigues
Étang de Berre
Port de Bouc
Istres
Port St-Louis du Rhône
Parc Naturel Régional de Camargue
Stes-Maries-de-la-Mer
Aigues-Mortes
St-Gilles
Arles
Salon-de-Provence
Cadenet
Parc Naturel Régional du Luberon
Apt
Coustellet
Cavaillon
Gordes
St-Saturnin-lès-Apt
Sault
Mont Ventoux (1910m)
Carpentras
Vaison-la-Romaine
Nyons
Orange
Avignon
Noves
St-Rémy de Provence
Beaucaire
Pont du Gard
Nîmes
Alès
Pont-St-Esprit
Rhône
Pierrelatte
Montélimar
A7
A9
A51
A8
A57
A50
22
23
24
25
28
MEDITERRANEAN SEA
Corsica (50km)
0 50 km
0 25 miles
CORSICA
Ligurian Sea
Bastia
Île Rousse
Calvi
T30
Monte Cinto (2706m)
Corte
Porto
Parc Naturel Régional de la Corse
T20
T10
27
Ajaccio
T40
Solenzara
26
Propriano
Sartène
Bonifacio
0 50 km
0 25 miles

SCSTOCK/SHUTTERSTOCK

Abbaye Notre-Dame de Sénanque (p177)

PROVENCE & SOUTHEAST FRANCE

EXPLORE

PROVENCE & SOUTHEAST FRANCE

The smell of lavender and the buzzing of ***cigales*** (cicadas) will linger with you long after you've shaken off the dust from these superlative driving tours of Provence and southeast France. This fabled corner of France, named for the Roman province it once was, unrolls like a tapestry of craggy wave-washed ***calanques*** (inlets); historic cities and towns; glittering harbours bobbing with yachts and fringed by perfect waterside bistros; hills blanketed with ancient chestnut forests and olive groves; the rugged coast and maquis of Corsica; and, of course, sun-soaked vineyards.

Marseille

France's second-largest city sits on a natural harbour that has provided access to Provence and the Côte d'Azur since it was founded by Greek colonists around 600 BCE. Often characterised as 'gritty', it's a lively, multicultural place that mixes historic and contemporary appeal. Marseille-Provence Airport, a hub for around 40 airlines flying to French domestic centres, the UK, Europe and beyond, lies 25km northwest and is served by regular buses to Gare St-Charles (30 minutes). This station is also the terminus for Eurostar, TGV and TER trains to London, Paris, Nice, Avignon and other destinations in the southwest.

Central Marseille offers plenty of accommodation around the Vieux Port, the train station and its suburbs. Car hire is easily found at the airport, near the train station and dotted around the centre of town. Grocery options are similarly abundant – from small neighbourhood *épiceries* (specialist grocers), *boulangeries* (bakeries) and North African delis to big modern supermarkets. It's the most convenient base for the 'Var Delights' itinerary.

Nice

Handy for both the 'Var Delights' and 'Riviera Crossing' routes, Nice can also trace its foundation to Greek colonists. A magnet for

WHEN TO GO

Provence can be hot in summer, when hotels and restaurants along the Côte d'Azur are at their busiest and most expensive. Conversely, a good proportion of tourist-focused businesses in towns such as St Tropez close in winter. For uncongested roads and milder temperatures, consider the shoulder months of April to May and September to October.

visitors since the 18th century, it's notably Ligurian (read: 'Italian') in many respects. It caters better to all accommodation budgets than many other centres on the Côte d'Azur, although prices and competition rise in the summer.

Nice-Côte d'Azur Airport, France's second busiest, offers connections with domestic, European and Middle Eastern destinations, and is linked to the old town and Nice Ville Train Station by tram and train. TGV and regional trains run to Paris, Marseille, Monaco, Cannes and other destinations; there are plenty of car-rental offices near the airport and train station and in the centre of town. Opportunities to get supplies are abundant.

Arles

The Roman-founded town of Arles is a convenient and appealing base for the 'Roman Provence', 'Camargue' and 'Lavender Route' drives. It boasts a good spread of accommodation in every price bracket, has a sprinkling of car-rental offices near the station and on its outer reaches, and is well served by groceries and supermarkets. Trains from Arles run to Nîmes, Marseille and Avignon, while buses run to Stes-Maries-de-la-Mer in the Camargue.

TRANSPORT

Most visitors arrive here through either Nice-Côte d'Azur or Marseille-Provence Airports. Rail connections spread out from these cities to regional hubs such as Arles, Avignon and Toulon (for ferries to Corsica). Longer-distance trains also provide links to Paris, London and other European destinations. Car rentals are available in the main centres, airports and train stations.

NOTE: A Crit'Air sticker is required in Marseille and Nice. See p287 for more details.

Ajaccio

You can fly into the Corsican capital for the 'Corsican Coast Cruiser' and 'Southern Corsica' drives, or get a ferry from Toulon. You'll find car rental (including international operators), groceries and accommodation here, too.

WHERE TO STAY

Just back from Nice's seafront and west of the old town, **Hostel Meyerbeer Beach** has family rooms as well as dorm bunks. In Moustiers-Ste-Marie, the loveliest town in the Gorges du Verdon, **Clos des Iris** is a picturesque little *hôtel de charme* decked out in Provençal colours. **Le Mas Julien**, on the road south from Orange to Châteauneuf-du-Pape, is perhaps the perfect Provençal stay – quiet, swathed in wisteria and with a pool (under-16s aren't allowed). In the Corsican capital of Ajaccio, **Hôtel Demeure Les Mouettes** is the perfect waterside hotel, housed in a colonnaded, peach-coloured 19th-century mansion.

RESOURCES

- **Festival de Cannes**
  Has all the details on the world's most famous film festival. *festival-cannes.com*

- **Vins de Provence**
  Info on the region's many vineyards and appellations. *vinsdeprovence.com*

- **La Routes de la Lavande**
  Research Provence's famous 'lavender routes' and associated towns and vineyards. *routes-lavande.com*

WHAT'S ON

- **Carnaval de Nice**
  This has been enlivening Nice for five days in late February and early March since 1294.

- **Festival de Cannes**
  The world's most famous and prestigious film festival is held every May.

- **Les Suds**
  The Roman amphitheatre and other Arles venues host this wonderful world-music festival over a week in July.

- **Foire aux Santons**
  Traditional hand-crafted *santons* (ceramic figurines) have been showcased each Christmas in Marseille since 1803.

22

PROVENCE & SOUTHEAST FRANCE

ROMAN PROVENCE

★ BEST FOR

CULTURE

Balmy nights at Orange's Théâtre Antique are magical; July includes the Chorégies d'Orange.

Théâtre Antique (p174), Orange

DURATION: 7 DAYS

DISTANCE: 205KM / 127 MILES

GREAT FOR: FOOD & DRINK, HISTORY & CULTURE, NATURE

BEST TIME TO GO: RUINS OPEN YEAR-ROUND, BUT AVOID AUGUST'S HEAT AND CRUSH.

Provence was where Rome first truly flexed its imperial muscles. Follow Roman roads, cross Roman bridges and grab a seat in the bleachers at Roman theatres and arenas. Thrillingly, you'll discover that most of Provence's ancient ruins aren't ruins at all. Many are exceptionally well preserved, and some are also evocatively integrated into the region's modern cities. With Provence's knockout landscape as a backdrop, history never looked so good!

LINK YOUR TRIP

21 Rhône Valley
Join up with this trip in Orange for several great Roman sites in Vienne, as well as Lyon's Roman theatres and a great Gallo-Roman museum.

24 Riviera Crossing
The Côte d'Azur shares in the Roman treasures, and many of them are in superb locations; head east from Arles to Aix, then take the E80 to Cannes to join this trip.

01 Nîmes

Although Nîmes isn't strictly speaking in modern Provence, a long, shared regional history means it has to feature in this Roman tour. The city's bizarre coat of arms – a crocodile chained to a palm tree! – recalls the region's first, but definitely not last, horde of sun-worshipping retirees. Julius Caesar's loyal legionnaires were granted land here to settle after hard years on the Nile campaigns. Two millennia later, their ambitious town blends seamlessly with the bustling, workaday French streetscapes of the modern city. **Les Arènes** (Amphithéâtre; *arenes-nimes.com*), an impressively intact 1st-century-CE amphitheatre, lies across the road from the outstanding **Musée de la Romanité** *(museedelaromanite.fr)*, which houses more than 5000 archaeological exhibits uncovered around Nîmes. North of here, locals nonchalantly skateboard or

GERHARD ROETHLINGER/SHUTTERSTOCK

window-shop on the elegant plaza that's home to a beautiful and preciously intact 1st-century-CE temple, the UNESCO-listed **Maison Carrée** *(maisoncarree.eu)*. Afterwards, stroll over to the pleasant **Jardins de la Fontaine**. The remains of the **Temple de Diane** are in its lower northwest corner and a 10-minute uphill walk brings you to the crumbling, 30m-high **Tour Magne** overlooking the gardens. Built in 15 BCE as a watchtower and display of imperial might, it is the only one that remains of several that once spanned the 7km-long ramparts.

THE DRIVE: The D6086 is direct, but sacrifice 15 minutes and take route d'Uzès (D979). This way, you'll leave Nîmes' snarly traffic behind and suddenly find yourself on a quiet stretch of winding road skirting grey rocky gorges and honey-stone villages. Cut east via Sanilhac-Sagriès on the D112, then turn off at Begude's roundabout.

02 Pont du Gard

You'll get a glimpse of the **Pont du Gard** *(pontdugard.fr)* as you approach. Nature (and clever placement of car parks and visitor centres) has created one bravura reveal. Spanning the gorge is a magnificent three-tiered aqueduct, a marvel of 1st-century engineering. During the Roman period, the Pont du Gard was (like Nîmes) part of the Roman province of Gallia Narbonensis. It was built around 19 BCE by Agrippa, Augustus' deputy, and it's huge: the 275m-long upper tier, 49m above the Gard, has over 50 arches. Each block (the largest weighs over 5 tonnes) was hauled in by cart or raft. It was once part of a 50km-long system that carried water from nearby Uzès down to thirsty Nîmes. It's a 400m wheelchair-accessible walk from car parks on both banks of the river to the bridge itself, with a shady cafe en route on the right. Swim upstream for unencumbered views, though downstream is also good for summer dips, with shaded wooden platforms set in the flatter banks. Want to make a day of it? There's an interactive, high-tech museum, a hands-on discovery space for kids, and a peaceful 1.4km botanical walk, **Mémoires de Garrigue**.

THE DRIVE: Kayaking to the next stop would be more fun, and more direct, but you'll need to return south via the D986L to Beaucaire, then the D90 and D15 to Arles.

> ☑ TOP TIP
>
> ### PADDLING THE GARD RIVER
>
> Get your first glimpse of the Pont du Gard from the river by paddling 8km downstream from Collias, 4km west of the D981. **Kayak Vert** *(kayakvert.com)* and **Canoë Le Tourbillon** *(canoeletourbillon.com)*, both based near the village bridge, run guided river trips by canoe or kayak from March/April to October.

03 Arles

Arles, formerly known as Arelate, was part of the Roman Empire from as early as the 2nd century BCE. It wasn't until the 49–45 BCE civil war, however, when nearby Massalia (Marseille) supported Pompey (ie backed the wrong side), that it became a booming regional capital.

The town today is delightful, Roman cache or no, but what a living legacy it is. Its **Les Arènes** (Amphithéâtre; *arenes-arles.com*) is not as large as Nîmes', but it is spectacularly sited and occasionally still sees blood spilled, just like in the old gladiatorial days (it hosts gory bullfights and *courses Camarguaises,* which is the local variation). Likewise, the 1st-century **Théâtre Antique** is still regularly used for open-air performances.

Just as social, political and religious life revolved around the forum in Arelate, the busy plane-tree-shaded **Place du Forum** buzzes with cafe life today. Sip a pastis (aniseed-flavoured apéritif) here and spot the remains of a 2nd-century temple embedded in the facade of the **Hôtel Nord-Pinus**. Under your feet are **Cryptoportiques** – subterranean foundations and buried arcades. Access the underground galleries, 89m long and 59m wide, at the **Hôtel de Ville** (Town Hall).

Emperor Constantine's partly preserved 4th-century private baths, the **Thermes de Constantin**, are a few minutes' stroll away, next to the quai. Southwest of the centre is **Les Alyscamps**, a necropolis founded by the Romans and adopted by Christians in the 4th century. It contains the tombs of martyr St Genest and Arles' first bishops. You may recognise it: Van Gogh and Gauguin both captured the avenues of cypresses on canvas (though only melancholy old Van Gogh painted the empty sarcophagi).

THE DRIVE: Take the D17 to Fontvielle, follow the D78F/D27A to Baux-de-Provence, then the D5. This detour takes you past beautiful dry white rocky hills dotted with scrubby pine; the trip will still only take around 45 minutes. There's on-site parking at Glanum. If heading into St-Rémy, there's parking by the tourist office (place Jean-Jaurès) and north of the periphery (place Général-de-Gaulle).

04 Glanum

Such is the glittering allure of the gourmet delis, interior boutiques and smart restaurants that line St-Rémy-de-Provence's circling boulevards and place de la République that a visit to the **Site Archéologique de Glanum** *(site-glanum.fr)* is often an afterthought. But the triumphal arch (20 CE) that marks Glanum's

ROMAN PROVENCE READING GUIDE

The Roman Provence Guide (Edwin Mullins; 2012)

The Roman Remains of Southern France (James Bromwich; 1993)

Southern France: An Oxford Archaeological Guide (Henry Cleere; 2001)

Ancient Provence: Layers of History in Southern France (Jeffrey Wolin; 2003)

Pont du Gard (p171)

JOSEF SOBOTKA/SHUTTERSTOCK

PHOTO OPPORTUNITY

The Pont du Gard, illuminated every night in summer.

entrance, 2km south of St-Rémy, is far from insignificant. It's pegged as one of France's oldest and is joined by a towering **mausoleum** (30–20 BCE). Walk down the main street and you'll pass the mainstays of Roman life: baths, a forum and marketplace, temples and town villas. And beneath all this Roman handiwork lie the remnants of an older Celtic and Hellenic settlement, built to take advantage of a sacred spring. Van Gogh, as a patient of the neighbouring asylum, painted the olive orchard that covered the site until its excavation in the 1920s.

THE DRIVE: It's the A7 all the way up to Orange; 50km of nondescript driving if you're not tempted by a detour to Avignon on the way.

05 Orange

It's often said if you can only see one Roman site in France, make it Orange. And, yes, the town's Roman treasures are gobsmacking and unusually old; both are believed to have been built during Augustus Caesar's rule (27 BCE–14 CE). Plus, while Orange may not be the Provençal village of popular fantasy, it's a cruisy, decidedly untouristy town, making for good-value accommodation and hassle-free sightseeing (such as plentiful street parking one block away from the theatre).

At a massive 103m wide and 37m high, the stage wall of the **Théâtre Antique** (Ancient Roman Theatre; *theatre-antique.com*) dominates the surrounding streetscape. Minus a few mosaics, plus a new roof, it's one of three in the world still standing in their entirety, and originally seated 10,000 spectators. Admission includes an informative audioguide and access to the **Musée d'Art et d'Histoire** across the road. Its collection includes friezes from the theatre with the Roman motifs we love: eagles holding garlands of bay leaves, and a cracking battle between cavalry and foot soldiers.

For bird's-eye views of the theatre – and phenomenal vistas of rocky Mont Ventoux and the Dentelles – follow montée Philbert de Chalons, or montée Lambert, up **Colline St-Eutrope**, once the ever-vigilant Romans' lookout point.

To the town's north, the **Arc de Triomphe** stands on the ancient Via Agrippa (now the busy N7),

Pont Romain

JO JONES/SHUTTERSTOCK

19m high and wide, and a solid 8m thick. Restored in 2009, its richly animated reliefs commemorate 49 BCE Roman victories with images of battles, ships, trophies, and chained, naked and utterly subdued Gauls.

THE DRIVE: Northeast, the D975 passes through gentle vineyard-lined valleys for 40 minutes, with views of the Dentelles de Montmirail's limestone ridges along the way (the D977 and D23 can be equally lovely). Parking in Vaison can be a trial; park by the tourist office (place du Chanoine Sautel), or west of the Cité Médiévale (along Chemin de la Haute-Ville), if you don't mind walking.

SALVE, PROVINCIA GALLIA TRANSALPINA

It all starts with the Greeks. After founding the city of Massalia, now Marseille, around 600 BCE, they spent the next few centuries establishing a long string of ports along the coast, planting olives and grapes as they went. When migrating Celts from the north joined forces with the local Ligurians, resistance to these booming colonies grew. The Celto-Ligurians were a force to be reckoned with; unfortunately, they were about to meet ancient history's biggest bullies. In 125 BCE the Romans helped the Greeks defend Massalia, and swiftly took control.

Thus begins the Gallo-Roman era and the region of Provincia Gallia Transalpina, the first Roman *provincia* (province), from which Provence takes its name. Later Provincia Narbonensis, it embraced all of southern France from the Alps to the Mediterranean and the Pyrenees.

Roads made the work of empire possible, and the Romans quickly set about securing a route that joined Italy and Spain. Via Aurelia linked Rome to Fréjus, Aix-en-Provence, Arles and Nîmes; the northbound Via Agrippa followed the Rhône from Arles to Avignon, Orange and onwards to Lyon. The Via Domitia linked the Alps with the Pyrenees by way of the Luberon and Nîmes.

With Julius Caesar's conquest of Gaul (58–51 BCE), the region truly flourished. Under the emperor Augustus, vast amphitheatres, triumphal arches and ingenious aqueducts – the ones that propel this trip – were constructed. Augustus celebrated his final defeat of the ever-rebellious Ligurians in 14 BCE, with the construction of the monument at La Turbie on the Côte d'Azur.

The Gallo-Roman legacy may be writ large and loud in Provence, but it also persists in the everyday. Look for it in unusual places: recycled into cathedral floors or hotel facades, in dusty cellars or simply buried beneath your feet.

06 Vaison-la-Romaine

Is there anything more telling of Rome's smarts than a sturdy, still-used Roman bridge? Vaison-la-Romaine's pretty little **Pont Romain** has stood the test of time and severe floods. Stand at its centre and gaze up at the walled, cobbled-street hilltop **Cité Médiévale**, or down at the fast-flowing Ouvèze River.

Vaison-la-Romaine is tucked between seven valleys and has long been a place of trade. The ruined remains of **Vasio Vocontiorum**, the Roman city that flourished here between around 100 BCE and 450 CE, fill two central **Gallo-Roman sites** *(provenceromaine.com)*. Two ancient neighbourhoods lie on either side of the tourist office and av du Général-de-Gaulle. The Romans shopped at the colonnaded boutiques and bathed at **La Villasse**, where you'll find **Maison au Dauphin**, which has splendid marble-lined fish ponds.

In **Puymin**, see nobles' houses, mosaics, a workers' quarter, a temple and the still-functioning 6000-seat **Théâtre Antique** (c 20 CE). To make sense of the remains (and gather your audioguide), head for the **archaeological museum**, which revives Vaison's Roman past with an incredible swag: superb mosaics, carved masks, and statues that include a 3rd-century silver bust and marble renderings of Hadrian and his wife, Sabina. Admission includes entry to the soothing 12th-century Romanesque cloister at **Cathédrale Notre-Dame de Nazareth**, a five-minute walk west of La Villasse and, like much of Provence, built on Roman foundations.

23

PROVENCE & SOUTHEAST FRANCE

LAVENDER ROUTE

DURATION: 4-5 DAYS

DISTANCE: 217KM / 135 MILES

GREAT FOR: FOOD & DRINK, HISTORY & CULTURE, NATURE

BEST TIME TO GO: JULY IS PURPLE PRIME TIME, BUT JUNE'S BLOOMS STILL IMPRESS.

★ BEST FOR

OUTDOORS

Mont Ventoux has brilliant hiking trails and is hallowed ground for cycling enthusiasts.

Bastide de Gordes

The Luberon and Vaucluse may be well-trodden (and driven) destinations, but you'll be surprised at how rustic they remain. This trip takes you to the undoubtedly big-ticket (and exquisitely beautiful) sights, but also gets you exploring back roads, sleepy villages, big skies and one stunner of a mountain. And, yes, past fields and fields of glorious purple blooms.

LINK YOUR TRIP

19 Foothills of the Alps
Swap rolling hills for spectacular gorges and then alpine air: take the D6 and D852 to Moustiers-Ste-Marie, or drop in at Sisteron from Forcalquier.

22 Roman Provence
From Roman Provence's last stop in Vaison-la-Romaine, it's a gorgeous drive to Gordes via Carpentras and Venasque.

01 Coustellet

Our lavender trail begins just outside the village of Coustellet at the **Musée de la Lavande** *(museedelalavande.com)*, an excellent eco-museum and working lavender farm, where you can immerse yourself in the traditions and history of the Provençal icon and buy lavender goodies in the on-site boutique. Afterwards the hilltop village of **Gordes** is worth a detour, especially at sunset, followed perhaps by a drink on the panoramic terrace at the lavish **Bastide de Gordes** *(airelles.com)* hotel.

THE DRIVE: The museum is just off the D2. From here, it's another 7km to Gordes along the D2, then a turn-off onto the D177 for 4km till you reach the abbey. You'll pass plenty of lavender photo ops en route, so feel free to stop if you can find an appropriate spot.

PVINCE73/SHUTTERSTOCK

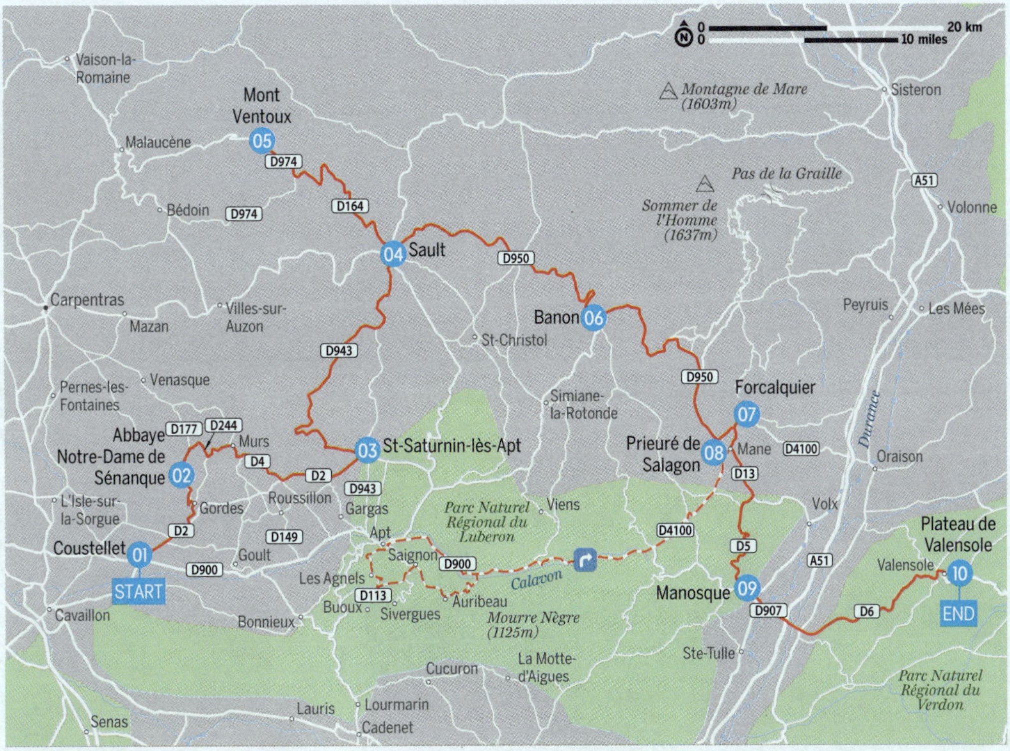

02 Abbaye Notre-Dame de Sénanque

Isolated and ridiculously photogenic, this 12th-century Cistercian **abbey** *(senanque.fr)* is famously framed by lavender from mid-June through July. The abbey was founded in 1148 and is still home to a small number of monks. The cloisters have a haunting, severe beauty; reservations are essential whether on a guided tour or independently (in the latter, visitors borrow an info-packed tablet that shows what abbey life was like in the 13th century). Conservative dress and silence are required. Be sure to build in some extra time to enjoy the meditative beauty of the lavender fields.

THE DRIVE: The more scenic route from the abbey heads north. Continue up the D177 then turn right onto the D244 and follow the signs to Murs, a very winding 9.5km drive accompanied by wheat fields and vineyards. From here it's about 25 minutes to the next stop.

03 St-Saturnin-lès-Apt

St-Saturnin-lès-Apt is a refreshingly ungentrified village, with marvellous views of the surrounding Vaucluse plateau punctuated by purple fields – climb to the **ruins** atop the village for a knockout vista. At **Moulin à Huile Jullien** *(moulin-huile-jullien.com)* see how olives are milled into oil (with honey and oil tastings thrown in).

THE DRIVE: Take the scenic, narrow D943 west and north towards Sault. Along the way, look out for the magnificent views of the red-tinged escarpment and the rust-coloured village of Roussillon. The views of Mont Ventoux only get more spectacular as you approach Sault, a 35-minute drive away.

04 Sault

This drowsily charming, isolated hilltop town mixes its lavender views with plum orchards and scattered forest. The town hot spot is **André Boyer** *(nougat-boyer.fr)*, which has kept farmers, cyclists and mountaineers in honey and almond nougat

PHOTO OPPORTUNITY

The road just north of Sault is a particularly stunning spot.

since 1887; its lavender marshmallows and the local speciality *pognes* (an orange-scented brioche) are also must-tries. Head to **Les Lavandes de Champelle** *(lavandes-champelle.fr)*, a roadside farm stand northwest of town, whose products include great buys for cooks. The lavender up here is known for its deep purple hue.

THE DRIVE: Exit town on the D164; when you hit the D974, fields give way to dense, fragrant forest. Above the treeline, strange spots of alpine scrub are gradually replaced by pale bald slopes. These steep gradients have often formed a hair-raising stage of the Tour de France – the road is daubed with Tour graffiti and many fans make a brave two-wheeled homage.

05 Mont Ventoux

If fields of flowers are intoxicating, Mont Ventoux (1910m) is awe-inspiring. Nicknamed *le géant de Provence* – Provence's giant – its great white hulk is visible from much of the region. *Le géant* sparkles all year round – once the snow melts, its lunar-style limestone slopes glimmer in the sun. From its peak, clear-day vistas extend to the Alps and the Camargue.

Even summer temperatures can plummet by 20°C at the top; it's also twice as likely to rain, and the relentless mistrals blow 130 days a year, sometimes exceeding 90km/h.

THE DRIVE: Go back the way you came to Sault, then head east to Banon on the D950 for another 40 minutes.

A village north of Sault (p177)
BORIS STROUJKO/SHUTTERSTOCK

06 Banon

A tasty, nonfloral diversion: little village, big cheese. Bustling Banon is famous for its *chèvre de Banon*, a goat's-milk cheese wrapped in a chestnut leaf. **Fromagerie de Banon** sells its cheese at the Tuesday morning market and at wonderful cheese-and-sausage shop **Brindille Melchio**, which is unbeatable for picnic supplies. Wash it all down with local vintages from wine shop **Panem o' Vinum**.

THE DRIVE: Follow the D950 southeast for 25km to Forcalquier, as the scenery alternates between gentle forested slopes and fields.

07 Forcalquier

Forcalquier has an upbeat, slightly bohemian vibe, a holdover from the 1960s and '70s, when artists and back-to-the-landers arrived, fostering a now-booming organics (*'biologiques'*, or bio) movement. Saffron is grown here, absinthe is distilled, and the town is also home to L'Université Européenne des Senteurs & Saveurs (UESS; European University of Scents and Flavours). To see it all in action, time your visit for the Monday morning market.

Climb the steep steps to Forcalquier's gold-topped **citadel** and octagonal **chapel** for more sensational views; on the way down note the once-wealthy seat's ornately carved wooden doorways and grand bourgeois townhouses. Pop in for a drink, a Michelin-starred meal and (if budget allows) an overnight stay at the luxurious **Couvent des Minimes**, owned by fragrance house L'Occitane.

THE DRIVE: Find yourself in a gentle world, all plane-tree arcades, wildflowers and, yes, lavender. Around 4km south on the D4100 you'll come to our next stop, just before the pretty town of Mane.

08 Prieuré de Salagon

This beautiful 13th-century priory, located on the outskirts of Mane, is today home to lovely gardens and a **museum** *(musee-de-salagon.com)*. This is ethnobotany at its most poetic and sensual: wander through recreated medieval herb gardens, fragrant with native lavender, mints and mugworts. Inside the medieval walls, the museum's permanent and temporary exhibitions provide a fascinating insight into rural life in Haute-Provence.

The walled town of **Mane** is lovely for strolling. The **Pont Roman de Mane** is also worth a look. This triple-arched stone bridge over the trickling Laye dates from the 12th or 13th century and makes a fine spot for a picnic. Head 800m south of Mane to the Hôtel Mas du Pont Roman, then turn right and look for the tiny lane just after passing the hotel.

THE DRIVE: Get on the D13, then follow the signs to the D5 for the forest-lined drive to Manosque (roughly 30 minutes in total).

DETOUR

The Luberon

Start: 08 Prieuré de Salagon

The Luberon's other, southern, half is equally florally blessed. Lavender carpets the **Plateau de Claparèdes** between Buoux (west), **Sivergues** (south), **Auribeau** (east) and **Saignon** (north). Cycle, walk or motor through the lavender fields and along the northern slopes of

Mourre Nègre (1125m) – the Luberon's highest point, accessible from Auribeau. The D113 climbs to idyllic lavender distillery **Les Agnels** *(lesagnels.com)*, which distils lavender, cypress and rosemary. The small on-site spa has a lavender-scented swimming pool. Stay at **L'Auberge du Presbytère** *(aubergesaignon.com)* in tiny Saignon, which perches on high rocky flanks, its narrow streets crowning a hill ringed with craggy scrub and petite lavender plots, with incredible vistas across the Luberon to Mont Ventoux.

09 Manosque

Manosque has two lovely fountains and a historic cobblestoned core, but the traffic and suburban nothingness make visiting a nuisance. Why swing by? Just southeast is the home of **L'Occitane** *(fr.loccitane.com)*, the company that turned traditional lavender-, almond- and olive-oil-based Provençal skincare into a global phenomenon. Factory tours can be booked online; the shop offers a flat 10% discount and there's also a small Mediterranean garden to peruse.

THE DRIVE: Leave the freeways and ring roads behind and cross the Durance River towards the quieter D6. You'll pass farmland and lavender fields on the 20-minute drive to the town of Valensole.

10 Plateau de Valensole

Things get very relaxed once you hit the D6, and the road begins a gentle climb. With picnic provisions packed, wind down your windows. This dreamily quiet plateau has Provence's greatest concentration of lavender farms. Once you reach **Valensole** village, make your way to **MEA Provence** *(lavande-valensole.com)*. Here you'll find lavender fields, an aromatic garden and a few exhibition panels about the history of lavender growing on the Valensole plateau. At the shop, you can browse essential oils, soaps, skincare products, dried bouquets, honey, candy, ice cream and other lavender-tinged products.

Plateau de Valensole

SCSTOCK/SHUTTERSTOCK

24

PROVENCE & SOUTHEAST FRANCE

RIVIERA CROSSING

★ BEST FOR

GLAMOUR

Strolling La Croisette in Cannes and fulfilling your film-star dreams.

DURATION: 4 DAYS

DISTANCE: 110KM / 68 MILES

GREAT FOR: FAMILIES, FOOD & DRINK, HISTORY & CULTURE

BEST TIME TO GO: ANYTIME, BUT AVOID THE CROWDS OF JULY AND AUGUST.

Boulevard de la Croisette, Cannes

Cruising the Côte d'Azur is as dazzling and chic as road trips get. From film town Cannes to sassy Nice via the corkscrew turns of the Corniches and into millionaires' Monaco, it's a drive you'll remember forever. Filmmakers, writers, celebs and artists have all had their hearts stolen by this glittering stretch of coastline, and by the end of this trip, you'll understand why.

LINK YOUR TRIP

23 Lavender Route
After the coast, head into the lavender-filled hills of Haute-Provence.

25 Var Delights
Mediterranean coast and Provençal countryside: a natural extension west.

01 Cannes

What glitzier opening could there be to this Côte d'Azur cruise than Cannes, as cinematic as its reputation suggests. Come July during the film festival, the world's stars descend on **boulevard de la Croisette** (aka La Croisette) to stroll beneath the palms, plug their latest opus and hobnob with the media and movie moguls. Getting your picture snapped outside the **Palais des Festivals** (Festival & Congress Palace; *palaisdesfestivals.com*) is a must-do, as is a night-time stroll along the boulevard, illuminated by coloured lights.

Outside festival time, Cannes still feels irresistibly ritzy. Private beaches and grand hotels line the seafront; further west lies old Cannes. Follow rue St-Antoine and snake your way up **Le Suquet**, Cannes' atmospheric original village. Pick up the region's best produce at

4KCLIPS/SHUTTERSTOCK

Marché Forville *(marcheforville.com)*, a couple of blocks back from the port.

Need nature? Then head to the **Îles de Lérins**, two islands located a 20-minute boat ride away. Tiny and traffic-free, they're perfect for walks or a picnic. Boats for the islands leave from quai des Îles, on the western side of the harbour.

THE DRIVE: The most scenic route to Antibes is via the coastal D6007. Bear right onto av Frères Roustan before Golfe Juan. With luck and no traffic jams, you should hit Juan-les-Pins in 30 minutes or so.

DETOUR

Corniche de l'Estérel

Start: 01 Cannes

West of Cannes, the winding coast road known as the **Corniche de l'Estérel** (sometimes known as the Corniche d'Or, the Golden Road) is well worth a side trip if you can spare the time. Opened in 1903 by the Touring Club de France, this twisting road is as much about driving pleasure as getting from A to B; it runs for 30 unforgettable coastal kilometres all the way to St-Raphaël. En route you'll pass seaside villages, secluded coves (sandy, pebbled, nudist, you name it) and the rocky red hills of the Massif de l'Estérel, dotted with gnarly oaks, juniper and wild thyme. Wherever you go, the blue Mediterranean shimmers alongside, tempting you to stop for just one more swim. It's too much to resist.

02 Juan-les-Pins & Antibes

A century or so ago, Antibes and Juan-les-Pins were a refuge for artists, writers, aristocrats and hedonistic expats looking to escape the horrors of post-WWI Europe. They came in their droves – F Scott Fitzgerald wrote several books here, and Pablo Picasso rented a miniature castle (it's now a museum dedicated to him).

First stop is the beach resort of **Juan-les-Pins**. It's a long way from the fashionable resort of Fitzgerald's day, but the beaches are still good for sun-lounging (even if you do have to pay).

Then it's on around the peninsula of **Cap d'Antibes**, where many of the greats had their holiday villas: the Hotel Cap du Eden Roc was one of their favourite fashionable haunts. Round the peninsula is pretty **Antibes**, with a harbour full of pleasure boats and an old town ringed by medieval ramparts. Aim to arrive before lunchtime, when the atmospheric **Marché Provençal** will still be in full swing, and then browse the nearby **Musée Picasso** *(antibes-juanlespins.com/culture/musee-picasso)* to see a few of the artist's Antibes-themed works.

THE DRIVE: Brave the traffic on the D6007 and avoid signs to turn onto the A8 motorway: it's the D2 you want, so follow signs for Villeneuve-Loubet. When you reach the town, cross the river. You'll pass through a tunnel into the outskirts of Cagnes-sur-Mer; now start following signs to St-Paul de Vence.

DETOUR

Biot

Start: 02 Juan-les-Pins & Antibes

About an 8km drive from Antibes along the coast road and the D4, this 15th-century hilltop village was once an important pottery-manufacturing centre. The advent of metal containers brought an end to this, but Biot is still active in handicraft production, especially glassmaking. At the foot of the village, the **Verrerie de Biot** *(verreriebiot.com)* produces bubbled glass by rolling molten glass into baking soda; bubbles from the chemical reaction are then trapped by a second layer of glass. You can watch skilled glass-blowers at work and browse the adjacent art galleries and shop. There are also guided tours, during which you get the chance to try your hand at a spot of glass-blowing – and learn why it's probably best left to the professionals.

03 St-Paul de Vence

Once upon a time, hilltop St-Paul de Vence was just another village like countless others in Provence. But then the artists moved in: painters such as Marc Chagall and Pablo Picasso sought solitude here, painted the local scenery and traded canvases for room and board. This is how the hotel **La Colombe d'Or** *(la-colombe-dor.com)* came by its stellar art collection.

It's now one of the Riviera's most exclusive locations, a haven for artists, film stars and celebrities, not to mention hordes of sightseers, many of whom are here to marvel at the incredible art collection at the **Fondation Maeght** *(fondation-maeght.com)*. Created in 1964 by collectors Aimé and Merguerite Maeght, it boasts works by all the big 20th-century names – including Miró sculptures, Chagall mosaics, Braque windows and canvases by Picasso, Matisse and others.

While you're here, it's worth taking a detour northwards to Vence, where the marvellous **Chapelle du Rosaire** (Rosary Chapel; *chapellematisse.fr*) was designed by an ailing Henri Matisse. He had a hand in everything here, from the stained-glass windows to the altar and candlesticks.

THE DRIVE: Return the way you came, only this time follow the

PERFUME IN GRASSE

Up in the hills to the north of Cannes, the town of **Grasse** has been synonymous with perfumery since the 16th century, and the town is still home to around 30 makers – several of whom offer guided tours of their factories, and the chance to hone your olfactory skills.

It can take up to 10 years to train a *perfumier,* but since you probably don't have that much time to spare, you'll have to make do with a crash course. Renowned maker **Molinard** *(molinard.com)* runs workshops where sessions range from 30 minutes to two hours, during which you create your own custom perfume (sandalwood, vanilla, hyacinth, lily of the valley, civet, hare and rose petals are just a few of the potential notes you could include). At the end of the workshop, you'll receive a bottle of *eau de parfum* to take home. **Galimard** *(galimard.com)* and **Fragonard's Usine Historique** *(fragonard.com/fr/usines/musee-du-parfum)* offer similar workshops.

For background, make time to visit the excellent **Musée International de la Parfumerie** (MIP; *museesdegrasse.com*) and its nearby gardens, where you can see some of the many plants and flowers used in scent-making. Needless to say, the bouquet is overpowering.

ARTMEDIAFACTORY/SHUTTERSTOCK

Marché Provençal, Antibes

blue signs onto the A8 motorway to Nice. Take exit 50 for Promenade des Anglais, which will take you all the 18km along the Baie des Anges. The views are great, but you'll hit nightmare traffic at rush hour.

04 Nice

With its mix of real-city grit, old-world opulence and year-round sunshine, Nice is the undisputed capital of the Côte d'Azur. Sure, the traffic is horrendous and the beach is made entirely of pebbles (not a patch of sand in sight!), but that doesn't detract from its charms. It's a great base, with loads of hotels and restaurants, and character in every nook and cranny.

Start with a morning stroll through the huge food and flower markets on **cours Saleya**, then delve into the winding alleyways of the old town, **Vieux Nice**, where there are many back-street restaurants at which you can try local specialities such as *pissaladière* (onion tart topped with olives and anchovies) and *socca* (chickpea-flour pancake). Stop for an ice cream at famous **Fenocchio** – flavours include tomato, lavender, olive and fig – then spend the afternoon sunbathing on the beaches along the seafront **Promenade des Anglais** before catching an epic sunset.

If you have the time, the city has some great museums too – you'll need at least an afternoon to explore all of the modern masterpieces at the **Musée d'Art Moderne et d'Art Contemporain** (MAMAC; *mamac-nice.org*). The part of the museum housing the permanent collection is currently undergoing renovation work and is due to reopen in 2029.

THE DRIVE: Exit the city through Riquier on the D2564. You don't want the motorway – you want bd Bischoffsheim, which becomes bd de l'Observatoire as it climbs to the summit of Mont Gros. The next 12km are thrilling, twisting past the Parc Naturel Régional de la Grande Corniche. Stop for a picnic or a hilly hike, then continue towards La Turbie.

05 La Grande Corniche

Remember that scene from Hitchcock's *To Catch a Thief,* when Grace Kelly and Cary Grant cruised the hills in a convertible, enjoying sparkling banter and searing blue Mediterranean views? Well, you're about to tackle the very same drive – so don your shades, roll down the windows and hit the asphalt.

It's a roller coaster of a road, veering through hairpins and switchbacks as it heads into the hills above Nice. There are countless picnic spots and photo opportunities along the way, including the **Col d'Èze**, the road's highest point at 512m. Further on you'll pass the monumental Roman landmark known as the **Trophée des Alpes** *(trophee-auguste.fr)*, a magnificent triumphal arch built to commemorate Augustus' victory over the last remaining Celtic-Ligurian tribes who had resisted conquest. The views from here are jaw-dropping, stretching all the way to Monaco and Italy beyond.

THE DRIVE: Monte Carlo may sparkle and beckon below, but keep your eyes on the road; the principality will keep for another day. Stay on the D2564 to skirt Monaco for another amazing 10km, then turn right into the D52 to Roquebrune.

06 Roquebrune-Cap-Martin

This village of two halves feels a world away from the glitz of nearby Monaco: the coastline around **Cap Martin** remains relatively unspoilt, as if Roquebrune had left its clock on medieval time. The historic half of the town, **Roquebrune** itself, sits 300m high on a pudding-shaped lump. It towers over the Cap, but they are, in fact, linked by innumerable, very steep steps.

The village is delightful and free of tack, and there are sensational views of the coast from the main village square, **place des Deux Frères**. Of all Roquebrune's steep streets, **rue Moncollet** – with its arcaded passages and stairways carved out of rock – is the most impressive. Scurry upwards to find architect Le Corbusier's grave at the cemetery at the top of the village (in section J, and, yes, he did design his own tombstone).

THE DRIVE: Continue along the D52 towards the coast, following promenade du Cap-Martin all the way along the seafront to Menton. You'll be there in 10 minutes, traffic permitting.

Jardin Exotique d'Èze

KIM HONGGYU/SHUTTERSTOCK

07 Menton

Last stop on the coast before Italy, the beautiful seaside town of Menton offers a glimpse of what the Riviera once looked like, before the high-rises, casinos and property developers moved in. It's ripe for wandering, with peaceful gardens and Belle Époque mansions galore, as well as an attractive yacht-filled harbour. Meander the historic quarter all the way to the **Cimetière du Vieux Château** for the best views in town.

Menton's miniature microclimate enables exotic plants to flourish here, many of which you can see at the **Jardin Botanique Exotique du Val Rahmeh** *(jardin botaniquevalrahmehmenton.fr)*, where terraces overflow with fruit trees, and at the beautiful, once-abandoned **Jardin de la Serre de la Madone** *(serredelamadone.com)*, overgrown with rare plants. Spend your second night in town.

THE DRIVE: Leave Menton on the D6007, the Moyenne Corniche, skirting the upper perimeter of Monaco. When you're ready, turn off into Monaco. All the car parks charge the same rate. Good options include the Chemin des Pêcheurs and Stade Louis II for old Monaco, or the huge underground Casino car park by allèes des Boulingrins for central Monte Carlo.

08 Monaco

This pint-sized principality (covering barely 200 hectares) is ridiculous, absurd, ostentatious and fabulous all at once.

♥ WHY I LOVE THIS TRIP

CELESTE BRASH, WRITER

With light that inspired Picasso and Matisse, history you can feel in your soul and a view over the Mediterranean at every hairpin turn, this drive takes in every dreamy hue of the Côte d'Azur. Each kilometre is special, from the glamour of Cannes and perfumeries of Grasse to the brassiness of Nice, audaciousness of Monaco and all the hilltop villages between.

A playground of the super-rich, with super-egos to match, it's the epitome of Riviera excess – especially at the famous **Casino de Monte Carlo** *(montecarlosbm.com/en/casino-monaco/casino-monte-carlo)*, where cards turn, roulette wheels spin and eye-watering sums are won and lost.

For all its glam, Monaco is not all show. Up in the hilltop quarter of **Le Rocher**, shady streets surround the **Palais Princier de Monaco** *(palais.mc)*, the wedding-cake castle of Monaco's royal family (time your visit for the pomptastic changing of the guard at 11.55am).

Nearby is the impressive **Musée Océanographique de Monaco** *(oceano.mc)*, stocked with all kinds of deep-sea denizens. It even has a 6m-deep lagoon complete with circling sharks.

Round things off with a stroll around the cliff-side **Jardin Exotique** *(jardin-exotique.mc)* and the obligatory photo of Monaco's harbour, bristling with over-the-top yachts.

THE DRIVE: Pick up where you left off on the Moyenne Corniche (D6007), and follow its circuitous route back up into the hills all the way to Èze.

09 Èze

This rocky little village perched on an impossible peak is outrageously romantic. The main attraction is technically the medieval village, with small higgledy-piggledy stone houses and winding lanes (with galleries and shops). It's undoubtedly delightful, but it's the ever-present views of the coast that are truly mesmerising. They just get more spectacular from the **Jardin Exotique d'Èze** *(jardinexotique-eze.fr)*, a surreal cactus garden at the top of the village, so steep and rocky it may have been purpose-built for mountain goats. It's also where you'll find the old castle ruins; take time to sit, draw a deep breath and gaze, as few places on earth offer such a panorama.

Èze gets very crowded between 10am and 5pm; if you prefer a quiet wander, plan to be here early in the morning or before dinner. Or even better, treat yourself to a night and supper at the swish **Château Eza**, a fitting finish to this most memorable of road trips.

25

PROVENCE & SOUTHEAST FRANCE

★ BEST FOR

FAMILIES

Snorkelling in sapphire waters at the Domaine du Rayol.

VAR DELIGHTS

DURATION: 5 DAYS

DISTANCE: 310KM / 192 MILES

GREAT FOR: FOOD & DRINK, NATURE

BEST TIME TO GO: EARLY SPRING AND LATE AUTUMN TO DODGE SUMMER TRAFFIC.

Vieux Port, Marseille

This is the other side of the Côte d'Azur: snazzy in spots, stark and wild in others, taking in everything from seaside towns to hilltop villages and big, busy cities. While parts of the coast have been heavily developed, finding solitude is still possible – you can hike to deserted coves in the Calanques, explore the forested trails of the Massif des Maures or get lost in the wild hills of the Var.

LINK YOUR TRIP

19 Foothills of the Alps
From Haute-Provence on into the wilds of the Vercors.

24 Riviera Crossing
Cut out the gorges and stick to the coast for Cannes.

01 Marseille

Long dismissed as the Riviera's troublesome cousin – crime-ridden, industrial, downright dirty – Marseille has enjoyed a long-overdue renaissance since its stint as European Capital of Culture in 2013. Though it retains its grittier, rough-and-ready feel compared to the coast's more genteel towns, it also has character in abundance.

Take a stroll around the **Vieux Port**, then swing by the city's spangly Mediterranean-themed museum, **Musée des Civilisations de l'Europe et de la Méditerranée** (MuCEM, Museum of European & Mediterranean Civilisations; *mucem.org*), which helped kick-start the city's revival in 2013. It's attached to the formidable **Fort St-Jean**, which once protected the city's harbour from attack. Afterwards, head uphill to the city's oldest quarter, **Le Panier** (from the French for 'basket'), which is criss-crossed

HANS ENGBERS/SHUTTERSTOCK

by graffiti-clad alleyways and full of quirky shops and neighbourhood cafes. Reward yourself with a black vanilla ice cream from **Vanille Noire** *(vanillenoire.com)*, then head off for dinner at one of the city's excellent bistros around rue Sainte.

THE DRIVE: To get to the Calanques, follow av du Prado south from the Vieux Port; it winds up into the hills and becomes the D559, the main road through the national park. There are loads of places to stop, but you'll have to do some walking to see any coves. It gets hot in summer, so set out early.

02 The Calanques

East of Marseille, a range of bone-white, parched cliffs towers above glittering turquoise coves. Known as the **Calanques** *(calanques-parcnational.fr)*, these craggy inlets run for around 20km all the way to the seaside village of Cassis. They've been protected since 1975 and were designated as a national park in 2014. They're a favourite place for Marseillais to hike and picnic; Marseille's tourist office runs regular guided hikes, although trails are closed in July and August due to fire risk.

Of the many *calanques* along the coastline, the most accessible are **Calanque de Sormiou** and **Calanque de Morgiou**, while remote inlets such as **Calanque d'En Vau** and **Calanque de Port-Miou** take dedication and time to reach – either on foot or by kayak. In July and August visitor numbers are usually limited; book in advance. The roads into each *calanque* are usually closed to drivers, but a sneaky workaround is to make a booking at one of the cove restaurants: good options are **Le Château** *(lechateausormiou.fr)* in Sormiou and **Nautic Bar** in Morgiou.

THE DRIVE: You'll see signs for Cassis not long after you drive out of the national park. Bandol is another 25km along the D559, and Sanary-sur-Mer is 8km further on.

03 Cassis, Bandol & Sanary-sur-Mer

East of Marseille, the coast road passes a handful of lovely seaside villages, all with their own reason for a stop, not least the area's excellent wines. First comes **Cassis**, nestled at the foot of a dramatic rocky outcrop crowned by a 14th-century château (now a pricey hotel). Still a working fishing port, its harbourside is crammed with seafood restaurants, perfect for a plate of grilled sardines or a copious shellfish platter. Neighbouring **Bandol** is well-known for its wines, too: stop in at the **Maison des Vins de Bandol** *(vinsdebandol.com)*, where knowledgeable staff will happily give you a crash course on recommended wines, vineyards and vintages. Last comes seaside **Sanary-sur-Mer**, perhaps the prettiest and most authentic of all: here you can still watch the fishers unload their catch on the quayside, and pick up local produce at the lively **Wednesday morning market**.

THE DRIVE: There's no compelling reason to stop in Toulon, so skip it and zoom past on the motorway (A50, A57 and A570).

04 Hyères

The coastal town of Hyères is split in two: there's the attractive old town, centring on a medieval castle, and the T-shaped peninsula, home to a busy pleasure port and some fine sandy beaches (perfect for a day's leisurely swimming and sunbathing). In between are several lagoons that are great for birdwatchers. But the main reason to visit Hyères is (rather ironically) to leave: it's the main harbour for trips over to the idyllic **Îles d'Hyères**, a tiny archipelago fringed by white sand and criss-crossed by nature trails. **Transport Littoral Varois** *(tlv-tvm.com)* runs ferries, including a two-island day trip to Île de Port-Cros and Le Levant.

THE DRIVE: It's an easy 22km along the D98 to Bormes-les-Mimosas, although the climb up to the village can be trafficky in summer. There's a large free car park on place St-François off rte de Baguier, a short walk from the village centre.

05 Bormes-les-Mimosas

This 12th-century hilltop village is heralded for its horticultural splendour: dazzling yellow mimosas in winter, deep-fuchsia bougainvilleas in summer. Generally, though, it's just a lovely place to stop for a wander: a browse around the many art galleries, a spot of

Calanque d'En Vau (p189)

PHOTO OPPORTUNITY

Standing on the dazzling white cliffs above the Calanque d'En Vau.

300DPI/SHUTTERSTOCK

souvenir shopping in the smart boutiques, or a leisurely lunch at a village bistro. On the peninsula, there's also an 11th-century fortress to visit, the **Fort de Brégançon** *(bormeslesmimosas.com)*, used as a private state residence for the French president since 1968 and opened to the public in 2014. Book a ticket at Bormes' tourist office, which also arranges guided nature walks in the nearby forests.

THE DRIVE: Pick up the coast road again (D559) and follow its curves as it becomes the Corniche des Maures. There are numerous swimming spots along here, so keep your eyes peeled and your bathing suit handy. The Domaine du Rayol is clearly signed when you hit Le Rayol-Canadel.

06 Domaine du Rayol

East of Bormes, the coastal Corniche des Maures twists past sandy beaches and seaside settlements like Le Lavandou and **Rayol-Canadel-sur-Mer**, where you'll find one of the gems of this stretch of the coastline: the dazzling gardens of the **Domaine du Rayol** *(domainedurayol.org)*, filled with plants from Mediterranean climates from across the globe. It's a riot of fragrance and colour, most impressive in April and May when the flowers are in full bloom. In summer, the estate's lovely beach also runs guided snorkelling sessions, during which you will spot some of the colourful flora and sea life that lie beneath the Mediterranean waves; reserve ahead for snorkelling.

THE DRIVE: The D559 meanders nearly all the way to swish St-Tropez, although, unfortunately, if you're here in summer, you're pretty much guaranteed to hit traffic jams the nearer you get to town. There's a big car park by the port (av du Gaulle).

THE VILLAGE OF TORTOISES

About 20km north of Collobrières, the **Village des Tortues** *(tortupole.fr)* protects one of France's most endangered species, the Hermann tortoise *(Testudo hermanni)*. Once common along the Mediterranean coast, it is today found only in the Massif des Maures and Corsica. A viewing trail travels through the reserve (look out for vicious-looking models of the tortoise's ancestors lurking among the bushes). Along the way, you'll also visit the tortoise clinic, where wounded tortoises are treated before being released back into the wild, and the nurseries, where precious eggs are hatched and young tortoises spend the first three of their 60 to 100 years.

In summer, the best time to see the tortoises is in the morning and late afternoon. Hatching season is from mid-May to the end of June; from November to early March, they're all tucked up during hibernation.

DETOUR

Massif des Maures

Start: 06 Domaine du Rayol

A wild range of wooded hills rumpling the landscape inland between Hyères and Fréjus, the **Massif des Maures** is a pocket of surprising wilderness just a few kilometres from the summer hustle of the Côte d'Azur. Shrouded by pine, chestnut and cork oak trees, its near-black vegetation gives rise to its name, derived from the Provençal word *mauro* (dark pine wood). Traditional industries (chestnut harvests, cork, pipe-making) are still practised here, and the area is criss-crossed by hiking trails that offer wraparound views of the coastline. From June to September, access to many areas is limited due to the risk of forest fires, but at other times of year, it's a haven of peace and nature.

It can be approached from the east from St-Tropez along the D14, but a more entertaining route is to head inland from Rayol-Canadel-sur-Mer along the switchbacking D27, over the Col du Canadel and along the tortuous rte des Crêtes onto the D98.

If you want to extend the drive, you can follow the D41 north up to the leafy village of **Collobrières** (population 1910); it's renowned for its chestnuts and hosts its own chestnut festival in October. The tourist office offers guided forest walks and can point you in the direction of the **Châtaignier de Madame**, the biggest chestnut tree in Provence, measuring a mighty 10.4m round.

Alternatively, you can head south down the D41 and rejoin the coast road at Le Lavandou.

07 St-Tropez

Sizzling actress Brigitte Bardot came to St-Tropez in the '50s and transformed the peaceful fishing village into a jet-set favourite. Tropeziens have thrived on their sexy image ever since. At the **Vieux Port**, yachts like spaceships jostle for millionaire moorings, while out on the beaches, cashed-up kids dance until dawn and the restaurants are fabulous, as long as you aren't picking up the tab.

Swamped by more than 100,000 visitors a day in summer, outside the peak season St-Tropez rediscovers its soul. Now's the time to wander the cobbled lanes in the old fishing quarter of **La Ponche**, or sip a pastis and watch a game of pétanque (a variant of bowls) on lovely **place des Lices** – preferably with a generous slice of *tarte tropézienne,* the town's famous orange-perfumed cake. Whenever you come, don't miss the **Citadelle de St-Tropez** *(saint-tropez.fr/culture/citadelle),* a 17th-century fortress that offers dazzling views from its hillside perch just east of the centre. Its dungeons are home to the excellent **Musée de l'Histoire Maritime**, an interactive museum with a focus on Provence's seafaring history.

THE DRIVE: Back onto our old friend again, the D559, through Port-Grimaud and Ste-Maxime, along the coast, and into Fréjus after 38km. Allow more time than you think you'll need; traffic is inevitable. St-Raphaël is just round the bay.

08 Fréjus & St-Raphaël

They might not be quite on a par with many of Provence's Roman ruins, but the little town of **Fréjus** is still worth a detour if you're an archaeology enthusiast, as it includes the remains of an amphitheatre, Roman theatre and various arches and portals. Even if you're not looking for ruins, the old town is lovely: make sure you stop in at heavenly **Le Palais du Fromager** for a gourmet tour of local cheeses. Just along the coast is Fréjus' sister town, **St-Raphaël**, a beachy, boaty kind of place and a good overnight base.

THE DRIVE: Zip along the A8 before exiting onto the D1555 and heading northwards towards Draguignan. Turn off onto the D955 before you reach town, which will take you via the Gorges de Châteaudouble, and stay on the road all the way to Comps-sur-Artuby. Here you turn left onto the D71 and enter the wild, sky-high world of the Gorges du Verdon.

09 Moustiers-Ste-Marie

From the coast, it's time to head inland into the hills of the **Haut-Var**, a rocky, wild landscape that feels a world away from the chichi towns of the coast. Dry and sparsely populated, studded with hill villages and riven by gorges, it makes for spectacular driving. Your ultimate destination is the majestic **Gorges du Verdon**, sometimes called Europe's Grand Canyon, but it's worth making a detour via one of the lesser-known valleys, like the **Gorges de Châteaudouble**, 12km north of the military town of Draguignan.

From the coast, it's about a 1½-hour drive before you enter the gorges near Comps-sur-Artuby, then climb past the impressive **Pont d'Artuby**, Europe's highest bridge, and track the southern side of the gorges along a route that's sometimes known (appropriately enough) as **La Corniche Sublime** (D955 to D90, D71 and D19). The drops are dizzying and it's single-file most of the way, but there aren't many more memorable drives. Eventually, you'll pass the emerald-green waters of the Lac de Ste-Croix before reaching the journey's end in **Moustiers-Ste-Marie**.

Moustiers- Ste-Marie
DIEGOMARIOTTINI/SHUTTERSTOCK

Atelier BON
LA MAISON PROVENCALE

26

★ BEST FOR

HIKES

Nothing beats the hike down the 'king's staircase' in Bonifacio.

PROVENCE & SOUTHEAST FRANCE

SOUTHERN CORSICA

DURATION: 10 DAYS

DISTANCE: 260KM / 160 MILES

GREAT FOR: FAMILIES, HISTORY & CULTURE

BEST TIME TO GO: SPRING OR LATE SUMMER TO BEAT THE CROWDS AND THE HEAT.

IMPORTANT: SNOW TYRES/CHAINS/SOCKS REQUIRED 1 NOVEMBER – 31 MARCH

Escalier du Roi d'Aragon

Starting with your foot on the pedal in the Corsican capital, this 10-day journey ducks and dives along the island's most dramatic coastal roads and mountain passes in southern Corse (Corsica). Mellow green hikes, gold-sand beaches and crisp turquoise waters to break the drive and stretch your legs are never far away, and for archaeology buffs there's the added bonus of some of France's most extraordinary prehistoric sites.

LINK YOUR TRIP

24 Riviera Crossing
Pop your car on the ferry in Bastia and sail to Nice for more mountainous, hairpin-laced corniches (coastal roads) with giant blue views.

27 Corsican Coast Cruiser
Completely smitten? Motor north from Ajaccio and up to Île Rousse to cruise the island's west coast.

01 Ajaccio

Napoléon Bonaparte's hometown and the capital of France's ravishing Île de Beauté (aka Corsica), this charismatic city on the sea thoroughly spoils with fine art in **Palais Fesch – Musée des Beaux-Arts** *(musee-fesch.com)* and a beautiful bay fringed with palm trees. After sampling these delights, hike 12km west to **Pointe de la Parata** to watch the sunset turn the **Îles Sanguinaires** (Bloody Islands) vivid crimson. Later, savour drinks beneath the stars on a trendy waterfront terrace at **Port Tino Rossi**.

THE DRIVE: From Ajaccio port, pick up the N193 and subsequent T40 to Bonifacio. After 12km turn right onto the D302, direction Pila Canale (a brown sign reads 'Filitosa'), and prepare for the sudden grand view of Ajaccio city below as the road climbs. Bear right onto the D255 and wind along peaceful green

DANIEL_GAUTHIER/SHUTTERSTOCK

lanes via the D55, D355, D757 and D57 to Filitosa.

02 Filitosa

Nowhere is more evocative of ancient Corsican civilisation than this **archaeological site** *(filitosa.fr)* ripe with olive trees, pines and the intoxicating scent of maquis (herbal scrub). Visit around noon when the sun casts dramatic shadows on the carved statues and menhirs woven around trees and circling sheep pastures.

Corsica developed its own megalithic faith around 4000 to 3000 BCE, and many of the stones at Filitosa date from this period. The menhirs are particularly unusual, including some with detailed faces, anatomical features like rib cages, even swords and armour.

THE DRIVE: Wind your way back to the D57 and meander south to the sea along the D157 to join the southbound T40 just north of Propriano. Count on about 40 minutes to cover the 30km trip to Sartène.

03 Sartène

With its ramshackle granite houses, shaded shabby streets and secretive alleys, this sombre town evokes the rugged spirit of rural Corsica, notorious for banditry and bloody vendettas in the 19th century.

A colourful time to motor in is on Good Friday during the **Procession du Catenacciu**, celebrated since the Middle Ages. Barefoot, red-robed and cowled, the Catenacciu (literally 'chained one'; penitent) lugs a massive 35kg wooden cross through town in a re-enactment of Christ's journey to Calvary. The rest of the year, the cross and 17kg penitent chain hang inside **Église Ste-Marie**.

Don't leave town without filling your picnic hamper with cheese, sausage, honey and wine from **La Cave Sartenaise** *(lacavesartenaise.com)*.

THE DRIVE: From Sartène it is an easy one-hour drive along the southbound T40 to Bonifacio. Slow down along the final leg – coastal views are glittering and you might well want to jump out for a dip.

04 Bonifacio

With its glittering harbour, incredible clifftop perch and stout citadel teetering above the cornflower-blue waters of the **Bouches de Bonifacio**, this Italianate port is an essential stop. Sun-bleached townhouses, dangling washing lines and murky chapels secreted in a postcard-worthy web of alleyways hide within the old citadel, while down at the harbour, kiosks tout must-do boat trips through gin-clear waters to **Îles Lavezzi**.

Park at the harbour and walk up **montée du Rastello** and **montée St-Roch** to the citadel gateway with its 16th-century drawbridge. Inside is the 13th-century **Bastion de l'Étendard** *(bonifacio.fr/visite-decouverte/bastion-de-letendard)* with a history museum. Stroll the ramparts to place du Marché and place de la Manichella for jaw-dropping views of the legendary cliffs. Then hike down the **Escalier du Roi d'Aragon** *(bonifacio.fr)*, a steep staircase cut into the southern cliff face to the water. Legend says its 187 steep steps were carved in

PHOTO OPPORTUNITY

The cliffs of Bonifacio from a boat.

a single night by Aragonese troops during the siege of 1420. In truth, the steps led to an underground freshwater well, in a cave on the seashore.

THE DRIVE: From the harbour, head north along the T10 towards Porto-Vecchio. Count on about 45 minutes to cover the 35km from Bonifacio to the Plage de Palombaggia turn-off, signposted on the large roundabout south of Porto-Vecchio town proper.

05 Plage de Palombaggia

When it comes to archetypal 'idyllic beach', immense Plage de Palombaggia is near impossible to top. This pine-fringed beach stars on most Corsica postcards, with sparkling turquoise water, long stretches of sand and splendiferous views over the **Îles Cerbicale**. Melting into its southern fringe are the equally picture-perfect expanses of sand and lapping shallow waters of **Plage de la Folacca**. This irresistible duo is sure to set your heart aflutter.

THE DRIVE: Follow rte de Palombaggia on its anti-clockwise loop around the peninsula, afterwards joining the busy T10 briefly for its final sprint into Porto-Vecchio. Spend a pleasant hour mooching along at a relaxed, view-savouring pace.

06 Porto-Vecchio

Shamelessly seductive and fashionable, Porto-Vecchio is the Corsican St-Tropez, the kind of place that lures French A-listers and wealthy tourists. Its picturesque backstreets, lined with restaurant terraces and designer shops, have charm in spades – presided over with grace by the photogenic ruins of an old **Genoese citadel**.

Small and sleepy by day, Porto-Vecchio sizzles in season when it dons its dancing shoes and lets rip for hot nights of partying. Cafes and bars are clustered on place de la République and along the seafront.

THE DRIVE: Leave Porto-Vecchio by the winding D368 and follow it through the heavily wooded Forêt de l'Ospédale – excellent walks and picnic spots – to the rural hamlet of L'Ospédale (1000m), 18km northeast. Continue on the same road through more forest and loads more exhausting wiggles to Zonza, 20km north again. It'll take a good hour for the entire journey.

07 Zonza

The chances are you've had a temporary surfeit of superb seascapes, so take a couple of days out to explore the **Alta Rocca** wilderness, a world away from the bling and glitz of the coast. At the south of the long spine that traverses Corsica, the area is an exhilarating combination of dense, mixed evergreen–deciduous forests and granite villages strung over rocky ledges.

No mountain village plunges you more dramatically into its heart than Zonza, a hamlet overshadowed by the iconic **Aiguilles de Bavella** (Bavella Needles), granite pinnacles like shark's teeth that jab the skyline at an altitude of more than 1600m. Hiking is the thing to do in this wild neck of the woods.

THE DRIVE: Allow up to 20 minutes for the go-slow, bend-laced D268 that climbs slowly and scenically up from Zonza to the mountain pass at 1218m, 9km north.

DETOUR

Prehistoric Corsica

Start: 07 Zonza

This short but startling detour dives into the heart of ancient Corsica. To create a perfect weekend, combine it with an overnight stay at the island's best boutique-farm spa.

From Zonza drive 9km south along the D268 to **Levie**, unexpected host to the **Musée de l'Alta Rocca** *(isula.corsica/patrimoine/Musee-de-l-Alta-Rocca_a72.html)*, a local history and ethnographical museum.

Continue south along the D268 and after 3km turn right onto rte du Pianu (D20), a narrow lane signposted 'Cucuruzzu Capula Site Archéologique'. Soon after, you arrive at **A Pignata** *(apignata.com)*, a chic mountain retreat where you can gorge on Alta Rocca mountain views crossed by swirling clouds from a poolside chaise longue. Fronted by brothers Antoine and Jean-Baptiste, the farmhouse spa with vegetable garden and pigs (and the most mouth-watering charcuterie) is first-class. Its 18 rooms are contemporary and its restaurant is the best in southern Corsica. For heaven on earth, go for the impossibly romantic treehouse for two.

Next morning, continue along the same D20 road for five minutes to the **Site Archéologique Cucuruzzu Capula** *(isula.corsica/musees)*, 3.7km in all from the D268. Allow two hours to explore the archaeological site. Enthralling for kids and adults alike, an evocative 3km

Bonifacio (p195)
TROYEAH/SHUTTERSTOCK

interpretive trail takes you on foot between giant boulders coloured bright green with moss to the Bronze Age *castelli* (castles) of Cucuruzzu and Capula. Along the way, kids can duck into the earliest natural-rock shelters used by prehistoric humans (who were small in stature) and poke around the remaining rooms of a stronghold where, a few centuries later, they butchered wild boar, cooked broth, spun wool and fashioned thongs from stretched animal skins.

Backtrack to the D268 and turn left (north) back to Levie and beyond to Zonza.

08 Col de Bavella

No number of hairpins or sheer drops can prepare you for the spectacular drama that awaits you atop the Bavella Pass (1218m), the perfect perch for marvelling close-up at the **Aiguilles de Bavella**. Depending on the time of day and weather, these gargantuan granite spikes glimmer red, gold, crimson, ginger or dark broody burgundy.

Short and long hikes are a dime a dozen, and when you've finished savouring the outdoor action and intoxicating alpine views, there is unforgettable feasting on roasted baby goat and wild pig stew at the **Auberge du Col de Bavella** *(auberge-bavella.com)* on the pass. If you want to stay overnight, this Corsican inn has dorm beds.

THE DRIVE: Steady your motoring nerves for relentless hairpins on the perilously steep descent along the D268 from the Col de Bavella to the Col de Larone, 13km northeast, and onwards north through the hills to Solenzara on the coast. Allow at least an hour for the entire 30km trip.

09 Solenzara

The town itself is not particularly postcard-worthy. What gives this seaside resort on Corsica's eastern coast natural appeal is its handsome spread of sandy beaches and the journey to the resort – one of the most stunning (and nail-biting) drives on Corsica. So steep and narrow is the road in places that it's not even single lane, while hazy views of the tantalising Mediterranean far below pose an unnerving distraction. Once through the thick pine forest of the **Forêt de Bavella**, the road drops across the **Col de Larone** (608m) to eventually meet the banks of the **River Solenzara**. When the extreme driving gets too much, pull over and dip your toes in the crystal-clear river water – there are swimming and picnic spots aplenty.

River Solenzara

WESTEND61 GMBH/ALAMY

STAY AWHILE

ZONZA

BY ANNA RICHARDS

Hiking boots are pretty much a uniform in Zonza. From here, it's possible to test out a section of the **GR20** *(le-gr20.fr)*, the legendary hiking trail that crosses the entire, mountainous spine of the island over 180km and is generally tackled over 16 days. Many consider it to be the toughest hiking trail in Europe – and it left physical (and mental) scars on my legs when I through-hiked it – but from Zonza you can get a flavour of the (marginally) easier southern section.

Two of the best, challenging hikes are the four-hour there-and-back route to **Punta di u Pargulu**, or a seven-hour loop right through the craggy **Aiguilles de Bavella**; though, note, it's for experienced hikers only, and many sections require scrambling. Easier routes go up to a viewpoint at **Croix de Leccia**, or to **Refuge de Paliri**, one of the *refuges* (mountain huts) on the GR20, where you can spend the night in the heart of the mountains.

Vasques, natural rock pools formed by Corsica's inland rivers and waterfalls, are wonderful ways to spend the day alternating between icy dips and drying off, lizard-like, on flat rocks. Multiple businesses run canyoning trips to up the adrenaline, including **ABC Roberto Canyon** *(canyoningcorse.fr)*, which operates out of Quenza, a 15-minute drive away.

A tough day of hiking calls for a slap-up meal. At **L'Eternisula** *(leternisula.com)* enjoy mountain hospitality and tuck into plenty of local culinary specialities, including wild boar terrine, charcuterie platters and sheep's cheese cannelloni.

LINK YOUR TRIP

26 **Southern Corsica** Stop at Zonza for a hike on this trip along Corsica's southern coast.

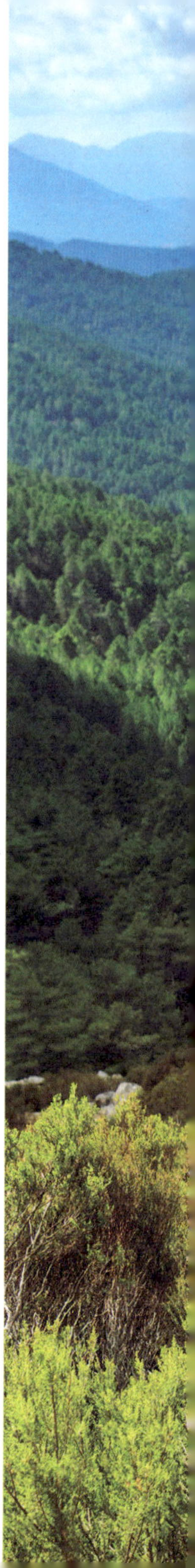

Left: Refuge de Paliri; Right: GR20

PLACES TO STAY

Most of the accommodation in Zonza is in self-catered *gîtes,* but there are a few campsites.

- **Camping Bavella Vista**
  Among the best, with wooden *roulottes* (caravans), a handful of wooden chalets and pitches, all set amid an abundance of leafy foliage. *(campingbavellavista.fr)*

- **Le Pré aux Biches**
  In the middle of a forest just outside town, it has Mongolian yurts and a trapper tent, plus wild swimming on the doorstep. *(lodges-yourtes-corse.com)*

- **Auberge Sole e Monti**
  Fifteen minutes away in Quenza, this place has belonged to the same family since it opened in the 1960s. The rooms are simple, but there's a positively enormous garden and the restaurant is excellent. *(solemonti.com)*

27

PROVENCE & SOUTHEAST FRANCE

CORSICAN COAST CRUISER

DURATION: 5 DAYS

DISTANCE: 185KM / 115 MILES

GREAT FOR: FAMILIES, NATURE

BEST TIME TO GO: APRIL TO JULY AND SEPTEMBER FOR QUIET ROADS AND BLUE-SKY VIEWS.

Keep both hands firmly on the wheel during this high-drama ride along Corsica's hairpin-laced west coast. Dangerously distracting views out the window flit from glittering bay and bijou beach to sawtooth peak, blazing-red rock and maquis-cloaked mountain. Meanwhile, the road – never far from the dazzling big blue – gives a whole new spin to the concept 'go slow': you won't average much more than 35km/h for the duration of the trip.

LINK YOUR TRIP

25 Var Delights
Sail by car ferry to Marseille and enjoy the coastal treasures of the Var.

26 Southern Corsica
Corsica is so seductive you might well find yourself extending your trip with this 10-day motor from Ajaccio around the island's southern tip to Porto-Vecchio on the east coast and beyond.

01 Île Rousse

Sun-worshippers, celebrities and holidaying yachties create buzz in this busy beach town straddling a long, sandy curve of land backed by mountains and herb-scented maquis.

Begin the day on Île Rousse's central tree-shaded square, **place Paoli**, overlooked by the 21 classical columns of the Greek-temple-styled **food market**, built around 1850. Get lost in the rabbit warren of old-town alleys around the square, and at noon sip a pre-lunch apéritif on the terrace of venerable **Café des Platanes** *(balagne-corsica.com/cafe-des-platanes)* and watch people play boules.

Later, take a sunset stroll past a Genoese watchtower and lighthouse to the russet-coloured rock of **Île de la Pietra**, from which the town, founded by Pascal Paoli in 1758, gets its colourful name. **Sea kayaking** *(balagne-corsica.com/commerce-et-service/crystal-paddle)* around the promontory and its islets is an outdoor delight.

TRAVEL - FR/SHUTTERSTOCK

★ BEST FOR

BOAT TRIPS

Set sail from Porto for some of Corsica's most breathtaking coastal scenery.

Algajola beach

THE DRIVE: From the roundabout at the western end of town, pick up the T30 towards Calvi; buy fresh fruit for the journey from the open-air stall signposted 'Marché Plein Air' on the roundabout.

02 Algajola

This gloriously old-fashioned, bucket-and-spade address makes a great base. Its golden-sand beach is one of Corsica's longest and loveliest, and budget accommodation options are superb. If your idea of luxury is drifting off to the orchestra of crashing waves and frolicking on the sand in pyjamas fresh out of bed at dawn, there is no finer place to stay.

Next morning, jump aboard the *trinighellu* (trembler), aka the **Tramway de la Balagne**, a dinky little seaside train that trundles along sand-covered tracks between Île Rousse and Calvi, stopping on request only at hidden coves and bijou beaches en route.

THE DRIVE: Continue towards Calvi on the coastal T30 and in the centre of Lumio, 6km south of Algajola, turn right following signs for 'Plage de l'Arinella'. Twist 2.6km downhill past leafy walled-garden *residences secondaires* (holiday homes) to where the turquoise water laps Plage de l'Arinella.

03 Plage de l'Arinella

If there is one crescent of sand in Corsica you must not miss, it's this serene, rock-clad cove with one of the island's finest beach restaurants and dramatic views of the citadel of Calvi. Lunch here is a trip highlight.

From the stylish, shabby-chic interior of **Le Matahari** *(lematahari.com)* to the big windows looking out to Calvi beyond the waves, this hip beach spot is one very special hideaway. Wooden tables, strung on the sand and topped with straw parasols, immediately evoke a tropical paradise, while cuisine is creative – think penne *à la langouste* (lobster), squid, fresh *morue* (codfish) or a simple tuna steak pan-fried to pink perfection.

THE DRIVE: Motor back up the hill to join the coastal T30 and continue south for another 15 minutes, around the Golfe de Calvi, to Calvi. The best spot to park is at the top of town, across from the entrance to the citadel.

04 Calvi

Basking between the fiery orange bastions of its 15th-century citadel and the glittering waters of a moon-shaped bay, Calvi feels closer to the chichi sophistication of a French Riviera resort than a historic Corsican port. Palatial yachts and private cruisers jostle for space along its harbourside, while high above the quay the watchtowers and battlements of the town's Genoese stronghold stand guard, proffering sweeping views inland to Monte Cinto (2706m).

Set atop a lofty promontory, Calvi's massive fortified **citadel** has fended off everyone down the centuries, from Franco-Turkish raiders to Anglo-Corsican armies. Wraparound views from its five feisty bastions certainly have the wow factor, and **Chez Tao** *(instagram.com/cheztao)*, a wildly hip and lavish music bar around since 1935, is the spot to lap them up, cocktail in hand.

THE DRIVE: Across from the citadel, pick up the coastal road D81B signposted 'Rte de Porto – Bord de Mer'. Before driving off, don't miss the old shabby square shaded by rare ombu trees with gnarled and knotted trunks, and sweet honey-producing flowers.

05 Pointe de la Revellata

Within seconds of leaving town, you're deep in the hot sun-baked maquis, with a low stone wall being the only separator between white-knuckled passenger and green drop down to emerald water below. After 4km the magnificent cape of Pointe de la Revellata – the nearest Corsican point to the French mainland – pops into view, with a toy-like white lighthouse at its tip and dusty walking trails zigzagging between the scrub and the ocean. Park and indulge in a signposted 1.5km hike to **Chapelle Notre Dame de la Serra**, where drop-dead views of the peninsula, its beaches and the mountains of Corsica's interior unfold.

THE DRIVE: Continue south on the D81B. After the *champ de tir* (military shooting range), savour a brief reprieve from the big coastal views as the road ducks inland

The citadel, Calvi

RAFAL MICHAL GADOMSKI/SHUTTERSTOCK

between the mountainous 703m hulk of Capu di a Veta and fields of grazing sheep. At the first road fork, 35km south of Calvi, bear right along the D81 signposted 'Galeria 5km, Porto 49km', and at the second fork, bear left.

SASHA64F / SHUTTERSTOCK

Girolata

06 Col de la Croix

Having driven for a good hour around relentless hairpins, you might be tempted to stop on **Col de Palmarella** (405m), a mountain pass with fine views of the W-shaped bay of the Golfe de Girolata far below. Pull over to photograph the blazing blue Mediterranean ensnared by the flaming-red rock of **Punta Rossa**, the dollhouse-sized hamlet of **Girolata** tucked in the crook of the bay, and the menacing dark green of forested **Capo d'Osani**. But save the picnic lunch and sun-fuelled siesta for Col de la Croix (260m), about 10km further south.

Park in the car park and pick up the dusty footpath behind the snack bar signposted 'Panorama – Table d'Orientation'. Climbing gently uphill for 20 minutes through typical Corsican maquis, the path suddenly staggers out of the Mediterranean bush into a mind-blowing panorama of fiery red and smouldering black-green capes, blue bay and the spaghetti road you've successfully navigated to get here. An orientation table tells you what's what.

Back at the roadside *buvette* (snack bar), longer walking trails lead downhill to the seaside hamlet of **Girolata** (1¾ hours, 7km) and **Plage de Tuara** (45 minutes, 3km).

THE DRIVE: Count on a good half-hour of relentlessly bend-laced motoring to cover the 25km from Col de la Croix south to Porto. The final five minutes reward you with a sudden narrowing of the road and dramatic roadside rock formations that flame a brilliant red. Go even slower than slow.

07 Porto

The crowning glory of the west coast, Porto sits sweet at the foot of a thickly forested valley trammelled on either side by crimson peaks. Split by a promontory, the village itself is topped by a restored **Genoese tower** built in the 16th century to protect the gulf from Barbary incursions. Scale the russet-coloured rocks up to the square tower, take in the tiny local-history exhibition inside, then stroll to the bustling marina, where a footbridge crosses the estuary to a eucalyptus grove and pebble beach. From April to October, boats sail from the marina to the shimmering seas around the magnificent, UNESCO-protected marine reservation of **Réserve Naturelle de Scandola**.

THE DRIVE: Cruise 12km south along the same coastal D81 towards the village of Piana. When you see red, you'll know you've hit the next stop.

DETOUR

Gorges de Spelunca

Start: 07 Porto

If you crave a break from the blue, head inland into the hills to reach **Ota** and **Évisa**, a twin set of enigmatic mountain villages that dangle defiantly above a plunging canyon blanketed with thick woods of pine, oak and chestnut. Quintessentially Corsican, these magical mountain hideaways are a haven for hikers, positioned halfway along the **Mare e Monti hiking trail** and within striking distance of Corsica's answer to the Grand Canyon, the unforgettable **Gorges de Spelunca**.

Until the D84 was carved into the mountainside, the only link between the two villages was a tiny mule track via two Genoese bridges, the **Ponte Pianella** (also called Ponte Vecchju) and **Ponte Zaglia**. The trail between the villages is a fantastic day hike (five hours return), winding along the valley floor past the rushing River Porto and soaring orange cliffs, some more than 1km high. Or follow the shorter two-hour section between the bridges; pick up the trail at the arched road bridge 2km east of Ota.

Carpeting the slopes east of Évisa is **Forêt d'Aïtone**, home of Corsica's most impressive stands of *laricio* pines. These arrow-straight, 60m-high trees once provided beams and masts for Genoese ships.

South of Porto, the D84 wiggles direct to Évisa, 22km east and a good 30 minutes of go-slow, blind-bend driving. Or opt for the narrower, slower D124 to the north that detours to the village of Ota before hooking up with the same D84.

08 Les Calanques de Piana

No amount of hyperbole can capture the astonishing beauty of these sculpted cliffs teetering above the Golfe de Porto. Rearing up from the sea in staggering scarlet pillars, teetering columns, towers and irregularly shaped boulders of pink, ochre and ginger, Les Calanques flame red in the sunlight and are among Corsica's most iconic, awe-inspiring sights. And as you sway around switchback after switchback along the rock-riddled 12km stretch of the D81 south of Porto towards the village of **Piana**, one mesmerising vista piggybacks another.

For the full technicolour experience of this natural ensemble of gargantuan proportion, park up and savour Les Calanques on foot. Several trails wind their way around these dramatic rock formations, which are uncannily shaped like dogs' heads, dinosaurs and all sorts; trails start near **Pont de Mezzanu**, a road bridge on the D81 about 3km north of Piana. Afterwards, splurge on lunch at Corsica's most mythical hotel, **Les Roches Rouges** *(lesrochesrouges.com)*.

THE DRIVE: The driving drama is done with: it's a relatively easy 70km drive south along the D81 to the Corsican capital of Ajaccio.

09 Ajaccio

Corsica's capital is all class – and seduction. Commanding a lovely sweep of the bay, the city breathes confidence and has a real whiff of the Côte d'Azur. Mosey around the centre with its mellow-toned buildings and vibrant cafe culture, stroll the marina and trendy beach-clad rte des Sanguinaires area, and congratulate yourself on arriving in the city – several hundred hairpin bends later – in one piece!

Napoléon Bonaparte was born here in 1769, and the city is dotted with sites relating to the diminutive dictator. You can visit his childhood home, which is now a museum, the **Maison Bonaparte** *(musees-nationaux-malmaison.fr)*. Though little of the original decor remains, it has interesting memorabilia – including a glass medallion containing a lock of the general's own hair.

The Oscar for most fascinating museum goes to Ajaccio's fine-arts museum, established by Napoléon's uncle, inside **Palais Fesch** *(musee-fesch.com)*. France's largest collection of Italian paintings outside the Louvre hangs here.

Les Calanques de Piana
EVANNOVOSTRO/SHUTTERSTOCK

PHOTO OPPORTUNITY

Snap blazing-red rock formations at Les Calanques de Piana.

28

PROVENCE & SOUTHEAST FRANCE

THE CAMARGUE

★ BEST FOR

ROMANTICS

Dinner by the hearth in the timber-beamed 17th-century kitchen of Le Mas de Peint.

DURATION: 4 DAYS

DISTANCE: 190KM / 118 MILES

GREAT FOR: FAMILIES, NATURE

BEST TIME TO GO: SPRING AND EARLY AUTUMN ARE IDEAL FOR VIEWING HUGE FLOCKS OF MIGRATORY BIRDS.

Réserve Nationale de Camargue (p210)

Leave Arles and the highway behind and suddenly you're surrounded by the Camargue's great yawning green and an equally expansive sky. It won't be long until you spot your first field of cantering white horses or face off with a black bull. This is not a long trip, but one that will plunge you into an utterly unique world of cowboys, fishers, beachcombers, the Roma, and all their enduring traditions.

LINK YOUR TRIP

22 Roman Provence
Slot in the Camargue trip's loop south from either Nîmes or Arles.

23 Lavender Route
From Arles, take the 570N and the D28 (direction Châteaurenard), then the D900 to Coustellet.

01 Arles

Befitting its role as gateway to the Camargue, Arles has a delightfully insouciant side. Long home to bohemians of all stripes, it's a great place to hang up your sightseeing hat for a few languorous hours (or days). Soak it in from the legendary bar at the **Hôtel Nord-Pinus** *(nord-pinus.com)*, with its bullfighting trophies and enthralling photography collection, or pull up a table on lively **place Paul Doumer**, where Arles' new generation makes its mark. Make a beeline for the Saturday-morning **market** and pack a Camargue-worthy picnic basket with local goat's cheese, olives and *saucisson d'Arles* (bull-meat sausage), or do likewise on Wednesday mornings on bd Émile Combes.

There's precious little parking within the old town, though you will find ample free parking near the train station off rue Pierre-Louis Rouillard.

VADIM PETRAKOV/SHUTTERSTOCK

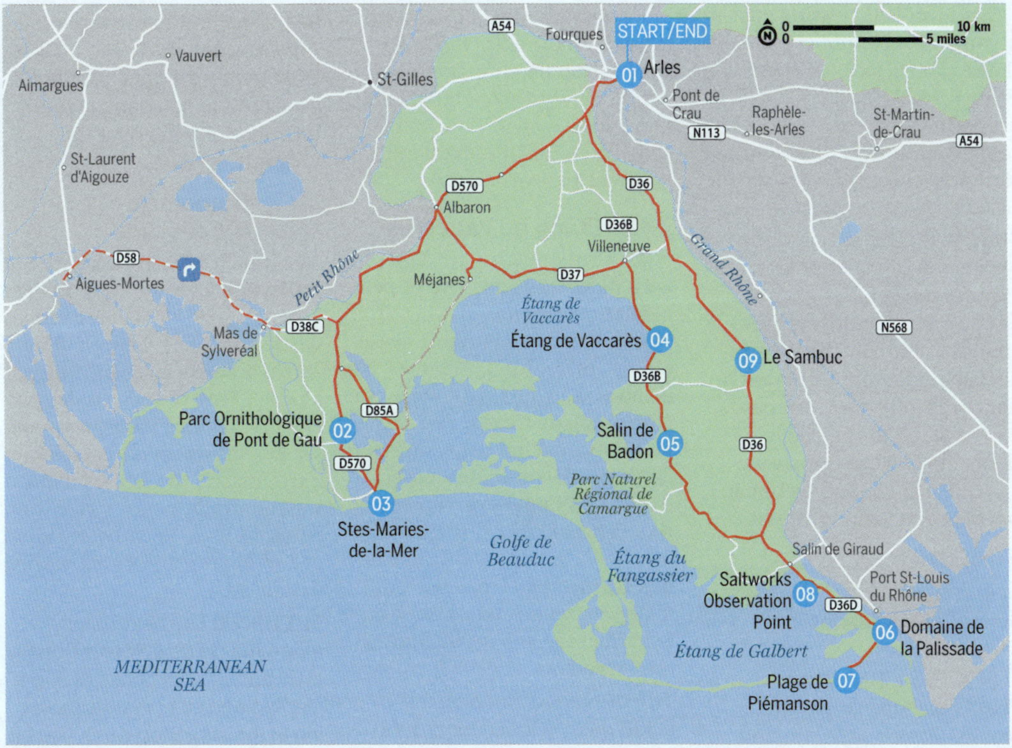

THE DRIVE: Take the D35A across the Grand Rhône at the Pont de Trinquetaille, then follow signs to the D570 – you'll soon be in no doubt you've entered the Camargue. Continue south on the D570 until Pont de Gau, 4km before you hit the coast, around 30 minutes all up.

02 Parc Ornithologique de Pont de Gau

Itching to get in among all that green? **Parc Ornithologique de Pont de Gau** *(parcornithologique.com)*, a 60-hectare bird park, makes for a perfect pit stop. As you meander along 7km of trails, flamingos pirouette overhead; the pink birds can't help playing diva. Secreted away in the marshes, though, is every bird species that calls the Camargue wetlands home, including herons, storks, egrets, teals and raptors.

THE DRIVE: Continue south on the D570. The last stretch of road into Stes-Maries-de-la-Mer is dotted with stables – this is little-white-horse heaven, so get out your camera.

03 Stes-Maries-de-la-Mer

Apart from a stretch of fine-sand beaches – some 30km long – the main attraction at this rough-and-tumble beach resort is the hauntingly beautiful **Église des Stes-Maries** *(sanctuaire-des-saintesmaries.fr)*, a 12th-century church that's home to a statue of Sara-la-Kali, or black Sara. The crypt houses her alleged remains, along with those of Marie-Salomé and Marie-Jacobé, the Maries of the town's name. Shunned by the Vatican, this palaeo-Christian trio has a powerful hold on the Provençal psyche, with a captivating backstory involving a boat journey from Palestine and a cameo from Mary Magdalene. Sara is the patron saint of the *gitans* (Roma people), and on 24 and 25 May each year, thousands come to town to pay their respects and party hard. Don't miss the ex-voto paintings that line the smoke-stained walls, personal petitions to Sara that are touching and startlingly strange in turns.

This town is the easiest spot to organise *promenades à cheval* (horse riding); look for Fédération Française d'Equitation (FFE) accredited places, such as the friendly **Cabanes de Cacharel** *(camargueacheval.com)* on the easterly D85A.

THE DRIVE: The scenic D85A rejoins the D570. After 10 minutes or so, turn right onto the D37. Stop at Méjanes for supplies or to visit the legendary fish restaurant **Le Mazet du Vaccarès** *(mazet-du-vaccares.fr)*. The D36B dramatically skims the eastern lakeshore; it's a 20-minute journey but is worth taking your time over.

DETOUR

Aigues-Mortes

Start: 03 Stes-Maries-de-la-Mer

Located over the border from Provence in the Gard, Aigues-Mortes sits a winding 28km northwest of Stes-Maries-de-la-Mer at the Camargue's far western extremity. Its central axis of streets often throngs with tourists, and shops spill out Camargue-themed tack, but the town is nonetheless magnificent, set in flat marshland and completely enclosed by rectangular ramparts and a series of towers. Come sundown, things change pace, and its squares are lovely places to join locals for a relaxed *apéro* (predinner drink). It was established by Louis IX in the mid-13th century to give the French crown a Mediterranean port, and it was from here that the king launched the seventh Crusade (and persecuted Cathars). The **Tour de Constance** *(aigues-mortes-monument.fr)* once held Huguenot prisoners; today it's the start of the 1.6km wall-top circuit, a must-do for heady views of salt mountains and viridian plains. Park on bd Diderot, on the outside of the northeastern wall.

04 Étang de Vaccarès

This 600-sq-km lagoon, with its watery labyrinth of peninsulas and islands, is where the wetlands are at their most dense, almost primordial. Much of its tenuous shore forms the **Réserve Nationale de Camargue** and is off-limits, making the wonderful nature trails and wildlife observatories at **La Capelière** *(snpn.com/reservedecamargue)* particularly precious. The 1.5km-long **Sentier des Rainettes** (Tree-Frog Trail) takes you through tamarisk woodlands and the grasses of brackish open meadows.

THE DRIVE: Continue on the D36B past Fiélouse for around 10 minutes.

05 Salin de Badon

Before you leave La Capelière, grab your permits for another outstanding reserve site, once the **royal saltworks**. Around the picturesque ruins are a number of observatories and 4.5km of wild trails – spy on flamingos wading through springtime iris. Avid birdwatchers mustn't miss a night in the **gîte** *(snpn.com/reservedecamargue)* here, a bare-bones cottage in a priceless location.

THE DRIVE: Continue south until you meet the D36, turning right. Stop in Salin de Giraud for bike hire and fuel (there's a 24/7 petrol station on av Joseph Imbert) or visit the saltworks. The D36 splits off to cross the Rhône via punt, but you continue south on the D36D, where it gets exciting: spectacular salt pans appear on your right, the river on your left.

06 Domaine de la Palissade

Along the D36D, **Domaine de la Palissade** *(palissade.fr)* organises horse treks and kayaking excursions where you'll find yourself gliding across brackish lakes and through a purple haze of sea lavender. You can also explore the lagoons and scrubby glasswort on foot; pick up a free map of the estate's marked walking trails, which range from 1.5km to 8km. Book horse-riding or kayaking excursions at least one day ahead.

THE DRIVE: The next 3.7km along the rte de la Mer is equally enchanting, with flocks of birds circling and salt crystals flashing in the sun. Stop when you hit the sea.

07 Plage de Piémanson

Just try to resist the urge to greet the Med with a wild dash into the waves at this lovely, windswept beach anchoring the southern end of rte de la Mer. Located just west of the mouth of the Rhône, the sands stretch for 6km, which means it's not hard to find your own private space. Head 1km east for the popular nudist beach. There's ample free parking and lifeguards in July and August, but no facilities of any kind, so bring food and drinks (the nearby village of Salin de Giraud has all the essentials).

THE DRIVE: Backtrack north along the D36D. Just before Salin de Giraud, look for a signed turn-off on your left,

PRILL/SHUTTERSTOCK

PHOTO OPPORTUNITY

Saltworks Observation Point for its pink-tinged backdrop and flocks of flamingos taking flight.

Saltworks Observation Point

which leads to a small car park and viewing spot.

08 Saltworks Observation Point

This lookout provides a rare vantage point to take in the stunning scene of pink-stained *salins* (salt pans) and soaring crystalline mountains. As fruitful as it is beguiling, this is Europe's largest saltworks, producing over 340,000 tonnes per year. A microalgae gives the water its pinkish hue and also provides nourishment for the shrimp. This also gives the pinkish colour to the flamingos, which feed upon the shrimp.

THE DRIVE: Heading north on D36 for 20 minutes, Le Mas de Peint is on your right before Le Sambuc, while the fork-and-trowel shingle of La Chassagnette is on the left to its north.

09 Le Sambuc

This sleepy town's outskirts hide away one of the region's most luxurious places to stay and one of its best restaurants. **Le Mas de Peint** *(masdepeint.com)* is owned by the Bon family, who have been in the *gardian* (cowboy) business for decades. Along with superb Provençal food and lovely rooms, the 500-hectare estate also offers flamenco, bull-herding and birdwatching weekends.

THE DRIVE: Continue north on the D36, where you'll remeet the D570 heading to Arles, a 25km stretch in all.

10 Arles

Back in Arles, the last stop is **Les Arènes** (Amphithéâtre; *arenes-arles.com*), the town's incredibly well-preserved Roman amphitheatre. Dating from around 90 CE, this great arena would once have held more than 21,000 baying spectators, and it's still used for many events. The structure itself hasn't survived the centuries entirely intact, but it's still an evocative insight into the Roman psyche. Entry is on the northern side.

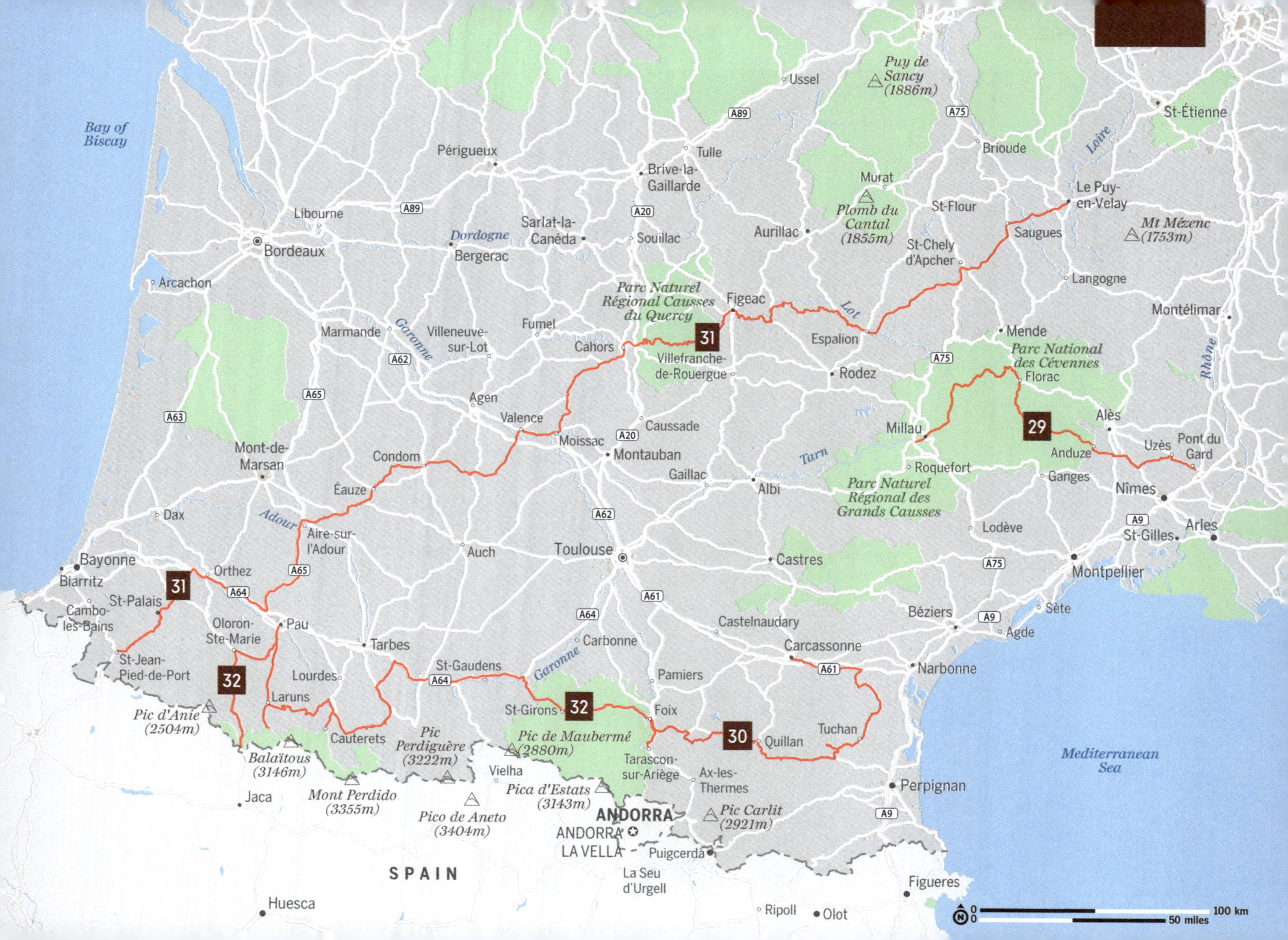

Bay of Biscay
Mediterranean Sea
SPAIN
ANDORRA
ANDORRA LA VELLA
Bordeaux
Toulouse
Montpellier
Périgueux
Brive-la-Gaillarde
Tulle
Ussel
Puy de Sancy (1886m)
Brioude
St-Étienne
Le Puy-en-Velay
Mt Mézenc (1753m)
Murat
Plomb du Cantal (1855m)
St-Flour
Saugues
St-Chely d'Apcher
Langogne
Montélimar
Aurillac
Libourne
Arcachon
Dordogne
Bergerac
Sarlat-la-Canéda
Souillac
Parc Naturel Régional Causses du Quercy
Figeac
Lot
Espalion
Mende
Parc National des Cévennes
Florac
Rhône
Loire
Marmande
Garonne
Villeneuve-sur-Lot
Fumel
Cahors
Villefranche-de-Rouergue
Rodez
Millau
Alès
Uzès
Pont du Gard
Anduze
Ganges
Nîmes
Arles
St-Gilles
Agen
Valence
Moissac
Caussade
Montauban
Tarn
Roquefort
Parc Naturel Régional des Grands Causses
Gaillac
Albi
Lodève
Condom
Éauze
Mont-de-Marsan
Dax
Adour
Aire-sur-l'Adour
Auch
Castres
Sète
Agde
Béziers
Bayonne
Biarritz
Orthez
St-Palais
Cambo-les-Bains
Oloron-Ste-Marie
Pau
Tarbes
Lourdes
St-Gaudens
Carbonne
Castelnaudary
Carcassonne
Narbonne
St-Jean-Pied-de-Port
Laruns
Pamiers
Foix
St-Girons
Cauterets
Pic d'Anie (2504m)
Balaïtous (3146m)
Pic Perdiguère (3222m)
Pic de Maubermé (2880m)
Tarascon-sur-Ariège
Ax-les-Thermes
Quillan
Tuchan
Perpignan
Vielha
Pica d'Estats (3143m)
Pic Carlit (2921m)
Jaca
Mont Perdido (3355m)
Pico de Aneto (3404m)
Puigcerdà
La Seu d'Urgell
Figueres
Huesca
Ripoll
Olot
A89
A75
A20
A62
A65
A63
A64
A61
A9
29
30
31
32
0
100 km
50 miles

THIERRY64/GETTY IMAGES

Florac (p218)

PYRENEES & SOUTHWEST FRANCE

EXPLORE

PYRENEES & SOUTHWEST FRANCE

Both geographically and culturally remote from Paris, the region of Occitania comprises the areas formerly known as Languedoc-Roussillon and Midi-Pyrénées. It's a land of immense fortifications that once protected the Cathars (a Christian sect persecuted for heresy); of snowcapped peaks where the language and culture can be more similar to that of Spain's Catalonia, just over the border; and of ancient caves and caverns where Roquefort cheese silently matures. As these delightful routes will prove, this is prime driving country – from the wine-producing plains of the Bas-Languedoc to the high passes and gleaming mountain lakes *(ibóns)* of the Pyrenees.

Toulouse

Toulouse, the largest hub town in these parts, is known as 'La Ville Rose' (the Pink City) for its attractive, coral-coloured streetscapes. France's fourth-largest city, it's served by Toulouse-Blagnac International Airport, which offers flights to centres in France, Europe and North Africa. You can easily traverse the 7km between the airport and the city centre on the Navette Aéroport shuttle, which stops at the main bus and train stations via place Jeanne d'Arc.

Toulouse's excellent range of accommodation is partly compromised by high occupancy rates among low-budget options (due to a scarcity of rental stock) and high demand during the week (prices sometimes fall at weekends). A hub for the produce and gastronomy of the surrounding areas, it's a wonderful place to eat and stock up for the nearby 'Cathar Trail', 'Cheat's Compostela' and 'Pyrenees' trips. TGV and Intercity trains run from Gare Matabiau to Paris, Bordeaux, Marseille, Albi, Carcassonne and other destinations, and car rental is easily found at the airport, the train station and dotted throughout town.

WHEN TO GO

April to June is a good time to visit: the Cévennes and Haut Languedoc are in bloom, and things are still relatively quiet. July and August can see very high temperatures, with beaches and accommodation oversubscribed in places. The shoulder months of September and October, when the weather is mild, the crowds thin and the wine grapes are harvested, are ideal.

Montpellier

Founded in the 10th century by the Count of Toulouse, Montpellier is an easy-going, multicultural beach town with lovely streetscapes, great museums and gardens, and easy access to the 'Pont du Gard to Viaduc de Millau' and 'Cathar Trail' routes. The centre is blessed with beautiful places to stay, many with parking in nearby public spaces.

Nearby Montpellier-Méditerranée Airport connects to limited French, European and North African destinations; you may find it more convenient to get here by train from elsewhere in France. Montpellier Sud-de-France TGV Station offers three-hour connections with Paris, while Montpellier St-Roch has trains for Carcassonne, Narbonne, Nîmes and Perpignan. Car rental is available at the airport, both stations and in the city centre.

Nîmes

An important city in the Roman province of Transalpine Gaul, the handsome contemporary city of Nîmes retains vestiges of its past, including France's best-preserved Roman amphitheatre. It's a pleasant place to base yourself for both the 'Pont du Gard to Viaduc de Millau' and 'Cathar Trail' drives. There's good accommodation in the city centre, but you may need to park your car in a public space.

Nîmes Alès Camargue Cévennes Airport handles only a few routes – you're more likely to arrive by TGV from Paris Gare de Lyon. Local trains spread out to Arles, Avignon, Montpellier and beyond. Car rental and grocery supplies are easily found.

TRANSPORT

Toulouse, Montpellier and Nîmes are all linked to Paris and Charles de Gaulle Airport by fast TGV trains. Other services connect with centres including Marseille, Lyon and Bordeaux. Toulouse-Blagnac and (to a lesser extent) Montpellier-Méditerranée Airports are the only real options for flying directly to the region.

NOTE: A Crit'Air sticker is required in Toulouse and Montpellier. See p287 for more details.

WHERE TO STAY

Villa du Taur, near the wonderful Romanesque Basilica of St-Sernin, is one of central Toulouse's most stylish and well-priced options. **Carcassonne Townhouse** is a superior B&B in a 19th-century riverside townhouse affording awe-inspiring views of the medieval Cité de Carcassonne. Close to the city's Roman amphitheatre, **Appart' City Nîmes Arènes** is a well-priced, modern hotel occupying a grand 19th-century Hausmann-style building. **L'Abbaye de Camon** offers luxury accommodation in a 12th-century Benedictine abbey, and might just be the most fairy-tale accommodation in the Pyrenees. Just outside Lourdes, **Eth Béryè Petit** is a delightful 18th-century farmhouse with three great-value rooms.

RESOURCES

- **Visit Toulouse**
  An excellent source of information on the city's restaurants, events and attractions. *toulouse-tourisme.com*
- **Tourism Aveyron**
  Helps you pinpoint the best gastronomy and essential sights of this lesser-known region. *tourisme-aveyron.com*
- **Montpellier Tourism**
  Focuses on green options. *montpellier-france.com*
- **Cathar Castles**
  For history and castle geeks. *catharcastles.info*

WHAT'S ON

- **Fête de la Violette**
  Since the 19th century, Toulouse has turned violet every February to celebrate the city's favourite flower.
- **Festival de Carcassonne**
  Over 200,000 people attend this sprawling festival, which brings over 120 musical, theatrical and dance acts to Carcassonne between June and August.
- **Festival Hestiv'Òc**
  The palm-lined promenades and pretty parks of Pau come alive for three days of free music and performances in mid-August.

29

★ BEST FOR

FAMILIES

Canoeing beneath the towering cliffs of the Gorges du Tarn.

PYRENEES & SOUTH-WEST FRANCE

PONT DU GARD TO VIADUC DE MILLAU

DURATION: 5 DAYS

DISTANCE: 223KM / 139 MILES

GREAT FOR: FAMILIES, NATURE

BEST TIME TO GO: APRIL TO JULY FOR WARM, SUNNY DAYS.

Stand-up paddleboarding, Gorges du Tarn (p218)

Languedoc is known for its fine coastline and even finer wines, but on this trip you'll explore a different side of this peaceful corner of France. Inland, the landscape climbs into the high hills and river ravines of the Parc National des Cévennes, beloved by walkers, kayakers and nature-lovers alike. The scenery is truly grand, but keep your eyes on the tarmac, as some of the roads are hairy.

LINK YOUR TRIP

22 Roman Provence
The tour through southern France's Gallo-Roman legacy also passes through Pont du Gard, so it's a perfect add-on.

31 Cheat's Compostela
The Chemin de St-Jacques drive is an ideal route to the Atlantic coast. It starts 180km northeast of Millau in Le Puy-en-Velay.

01 Pont du Gard

The trip begins 21km northeast of Nîmes at the **Pont du Gard** *(pontdugard.fr)*, France's finest Roman aqueduct. At 50m high and 275m long, and graced with 35 arches, it was built around 19 BCE to transport water from Uzès to Nîmes. A museum explores the bridge's history. You can walk across the tiers for panoramic views over the Gard River, but the best perspective of the bridge is from downstream, along the 1.4km **Mémoires de Garrigue** walking trail.

For a different take on the Pont du Gard, try seeing it from the water. Canoe and/or kayak rental companies are plentiful.

There are large car parks on both banks of the river, a 400m level walk from the Pont du Gard. Early evening is a good time to visit, as admission is cheaper and the bridge is stunningly illuminated after dark.

SARAH_DIAS/SHUTTERSTOCK

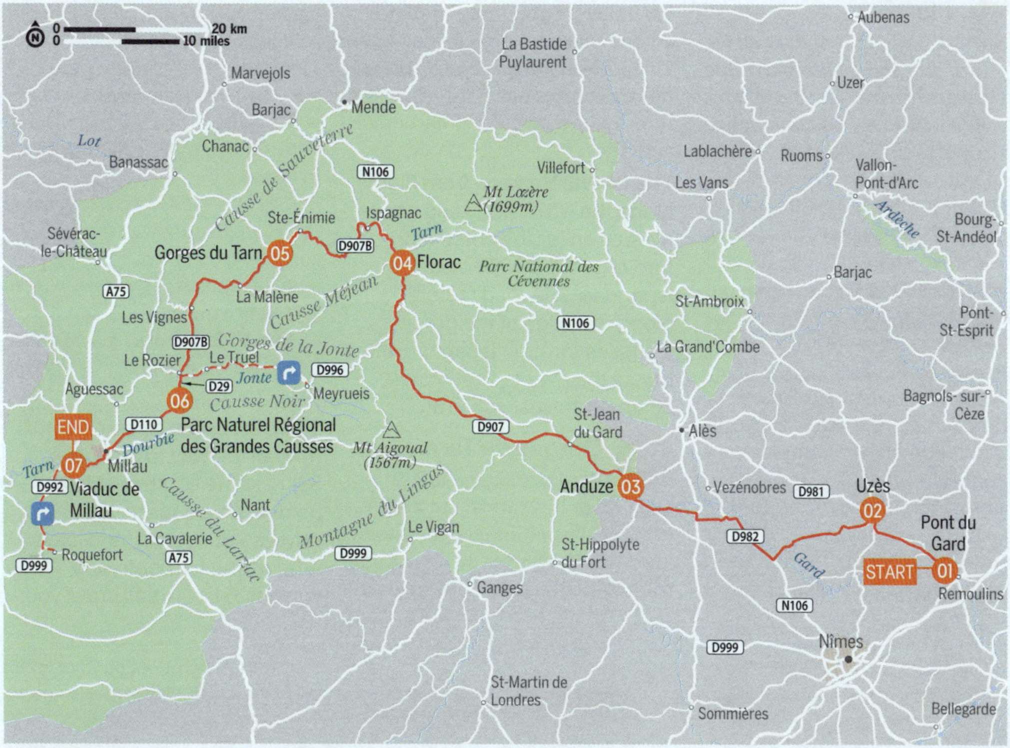

THE DRIVE: Drive northwest from the Pont du Gard along the D981 for 15km to Uzès.

02 Uzès

Northwest of the Pont du Gard is Uzès, a once-wealthy medieval town that grew rich on the proceeds of silk, linen and liquorice. It's also home to the **Duché Château** *(uzes.com)*, a castle that belonged to the powerful Dukes of Uzès for more than 1000 years. You can climb 135 steps to the top of the Tour Bermonde for a magnificent view across the town's rooftops.

Built in 1090 on the site of a Roman temple, Uzès' **Cathédrale St-Théodont** was partially destroyed in both the 13th and 16th centuries and stripped during the French Revolution. All that remains of the 11th-century church is its 42m-high round tower, **Tour Fenestrelle**, the only round bell tower in France, which resembles an upright Leaning Tower of Pisa.

If you've got a sweet tooth, don't miss the nearby **Musée du Bonbon Haribo** (Sweets Museum; *museeharibo.tickeasy.com*), a confectionary museum belonging to the Haribo brand. Join in with a tasting session, or just pick up some treats for the road.

THE DRIVE: From Uzès, travel 44km west on the D982 and D907 to Anduze; the Train à Vapeur des Cévennes is well signposted.

03 Anduze

If you fancy a break from driving, a trip aboard the **Train à Vapeur des Cévennes** *(trainavapeur.com)* is just the ticket. This vintage steam train chugs 13km between Anduze and St-Jean du Gard, a journey of 40 minutes each way. En route, you'll stop at a 150-year-old bamboo garden, the **Bambouseraie de Prafrance** *(bambouseraie.com)*.

THE DRIVE: The 74km stretch between Anduze and Florac along the D907 follows the river and slowly loops up through the forested hillsides into the high Cévennes. Petrol stations are few and far between, so remember to fill your tank.

04 Florac

It's a long, winding drive up into the **Parc National des Cévennes** *(causses-et-cevennes.fr)*. Created in 1970, this is a wild range of rumpled hills, forested ravines and quiet hamlets. Famously featured in Robert Louis Stevenson's classic 1878 travelogue, *Travels with a Donkey in the Cévennes,* it's still a remote and sparsely populated landscape, home to rare species including vultures, beavers, otters, roe deer and golden eagles. Since 2011, it has formed part of one of France's largest UNESCO World Heritage Sites, the Causses and Cévennes.

The riverside town of Florac makes an ideal base, draped along the west bank of the Tarnon River, a tributary of the Tarn. There's not much to see in town, but it's a good place to stretch your legs: Florac's **Maison du Parc National des Cévennes** has comprehensive information on hiking and other activities.

THE DRIVE: Head on from Florac along the N106, and keep your eyes open for the sharp left turn onto the D907B towards Ispagnac. The road teeters along the edge of the gorge as it passes through Ispagnac and tracks the river to Ste-Énimie, 28km northwest of Florac.

05 Gorges du Tarn

West of Florac, the rushing Tarn River has carved out a series of sheer slashes into the limestone known as the Gorges du Tarn. Running southwest for 50km from Ispagnac, this spectacular ravine provides one of Languedoc's most scenic drives. In summer the cliff-side road becomes one long traffic jam, though – you'll find spring or autumn are more relaxing times to travel.

Until the road was constructed in 1905, the only way through the gorges was by boat. Piloting your own kayak is still the best way to experience the scenery; the villages of **Ste-Énimie** and **La Malène** both have lots of companies offering river trips.

THE DRIVE: The cliff-side D907B runs all the way to Le Rozier, 36km to the southwest of Ste-Énimie. It's a superbly scenic drive, so don't rush, and leave ample time for photo ops. When you get to Le Rozier, crawl your

Kayaking, Pont du Gard (p216)

PHOTO OPPORTUNITY

The Pont du Gard Roman aqueduct from the water below.

TOMAS MAREK/SHUTTERSTOCK

way up the hairpin bends of the D29 and turn left onto the D110 to La Cité des Pierres, another 9km.

06 Parc Naturel Régional des Grandes Causses

Around the gorges of the western Cévennes, the Tarn, Jonte and Dourbie Rivers have created four high *causses* ('plateaux' in the local lingo): Sauveterre, Méjean, Noir and Larzac, each slightly different in geological character. You could spend several days touring the tangled roads that cut between them, but the D996 along the **Gorges de la Jonte** is particularly detour-worthy.

South of Le Rozier is the **Cité des Pierres** *(lacitedepierres.com)*, where centuries of erosion have carved out a landscape of amazing limestone formations, often given fanciful names, such as the Sphinx and the Elephant. Several walking trails cover the site, or you can cheat and catch a tourist train instead.

THE DRIVE: Continue along the narrow D110 towards Millau, 18km to the southwest. There are a couple of great roadside lookouts on the way, as well as a trail to the top of the local peak known as Puncho d'Agast.

DETOUR

Gorges de la Jonte

Start: 06 Parc Naturel Régional des Grandes Causses

The 20km-long Gorges de la Jonte cleave east–west from Meyrueis to Le Rozier, dividing Causse Noir from Causse Méjean. They're much more lightly trafficked – though busy enough in summer – than the more famous Gorges du Tarn, and make for a spectacular loop drive in combination with their better-known neighbour. Just west of Le Truel on the D996, more than 200 reintroduced vultures have taken up residence on the limestone cliffs. You can watch them gliding above the Gorges de la Jonte from the viewing point at the **Maison des Vautours** *(maisondesvautours.fr)*, which also has a live video feed from the nesting sites.

07 Viaduc de Millau

Finish your road trip with a spin over the gravity-defying Viaduc de Millau, the famous road bridge that hovers 343m above the Tarn River. Designed by the British architect Norman Foster, the bridge contains over 127,000 cu metres of concrete and 19,000 tonnes of steel, but somehow still manages to look like a gossamer thread, seemingly supported by nothing more than seven needle-thin pylons.

It's such a wonderful structure, it's worth seeing twice. Begin with the drive across: head north of Millau on the D911, and then turn south onto the A75 motorway.

Once you've crossed the bridge, turn off at exit 46 and loop back to Millau along the D999 and D992, which passes directly underneath the bridge and gives you an unforgettable ant's-eye view. En route, you'll pass the bridge's visitor centre, **Viaduc Expo** *(leviaducdemillau.com)*.

DETOUR

Roquefort

Start: 07 Viaduc de Millau

The village of Roquefort, 25km southwest of Millau via the D992 and the D999, is synonymous with its famous blue cheese, produced from the milk of local ewes who live in natural caves around the village. Marbled with distinctive blue-green veins caused by microscopic mushrooms known as *Penicillium roquefort*, this powerfully pungent cheese has been protected by royal charter since 1407, and was the first cheese in France to be granted AOC (Appellations d'Origines Contrôlées) status in 1925.

There are seven AOC-approved producers in the village, three of which (La Société, Gabriel Coulet and Papillon) offer cellar visits and tasting sessions. The cellars of four other producers aren't open to the public, but they all have shops where you can sample the village's illustrious cheese.

30

★ BEST FOR

HISTORY

Go in search of the Holy Grail in Montségur.

PYRENEES & SOUTH-WEST FRANCE

THE CATHAR TRAIL

DURATION: 3 DAYS

DISTANCE: 247KM / 153 MILES

GREAT FOR: HISTORY & CULTURE, NATURE

BEST TIME TO GO: SEPTEMBER AND OCTOBER WHEN THE SUMMER HEAT HAS PASSED.

Château de Montségur (p222)

The parched land between Perpignan and the Pyrenees is known as Le Pays Cathare (Cathar Land), a reference to the Christian order that escaped persecution here during the 12th century. Its legacy remains in a string of hilltop castles, flanked by sheer cliffs and dusty scrubland. Most can be reached after a short, stiff climb, but this is wild country and fiercely hot in summer, so be sure to pack a hat and plenty of water.

LINK YOUR TRIP

31 Cheat's Compostela
Make a longish detour off our version of the Chemin de St-Jacques by driving northwest of Carcassonne for 165km to Moissac, with an optional stop in Toulouse en route.

32 The Pyrenees
Foix sits on the eastern edge of the Pyrenees, so our Pyrenean tour makes a natural next stage – although you'll have to do it in reverse.

01 Carcassonne

Jutting from a rocky spur of land and ringed by battlements and turrets, the fortress of **Carcassonne** was one of the Cathars' most important strongholds. After a notorious siege in August 1209, the castle crumbled into disrepair, but it was saved from destruction in the 19th century by Viollet-le-Duc, who rebuilt the ramparts and added the turrets' distinctive pointy roofs.

Carcassonne is one of the Languedoc's biggest tourist draws, and its cobbled streets can feel uncomfortably crowded in summer. Try to time your visit for early or late in the day when it's at its most peaceful.

THE DRIVE: From Carcassonne, take the A61 east for 36km towards Narbonne. Turn off at exit 25, signed to Lezignan-Corbières, and follow the D611 across the sun-baked

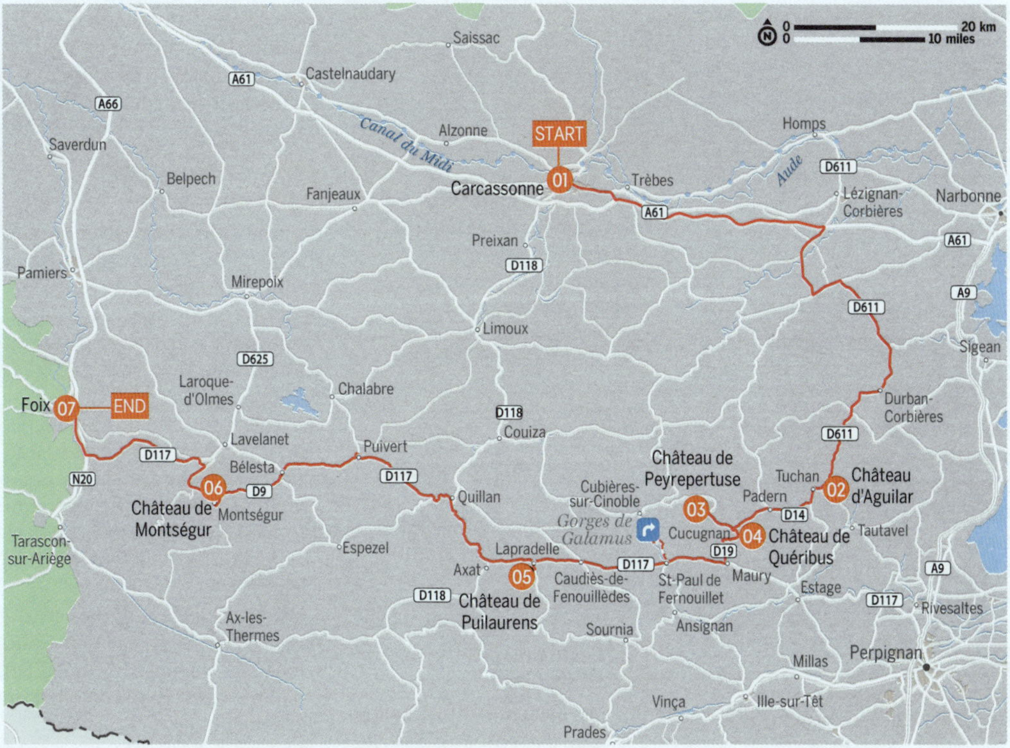

COLIBRI VISION/SHUTTERSTOCK

countryside for 46km. Just before you reach Tuchan, look out for a white sign with a blue castle pointing to 'Aguilar'. Drive up this minor track to the car park.

02 Château d'Aguilar

When the Albigensian Crusade forced the Cathars into the mountains between France and the province of Aragon, they sought refuge in a line of frontier strongholds. The first of these is the **Château d'Aguilar** *(tuchan.fr)*, which squats on a low hill near the village of Tuchan. It's the smallest of the castles and is crumbling fast – but you can still make out the corner turrets along with the hexagonal outer wall.

THE DRIVE: Take the D611 through Tuchan, emerging from the narrow streets onto dry, vine-covered slopes. You'll reach a roundabout; turn left onto the D14, signed to Padern and Cucugnan. (After 15km, note the turn-off to the Château de Quéribus on the D123 as you bypass Cucugnan; you'll be returning here following your next stop.) Continue 9km northwest towards Duilhac-sous-Peyrepertuse.

03 Château de Peyrepertuse

The largest and perhaps most dramatic of the Cathar castles is **Peyrepertuse** *(peyrepertuse.com)*, spanning a narrow ridge with a dizzying drop of 800m on either side. Several of the original towers and many sections of ramparts are still standing. In mid-August, the castle holds falconry displays and a two-day medieval festival, complete with knights in armour.

THE DRIVE: Take the turn-off onto the D123 near Cucugnan. The road twists and turns steeply into the dusty hills. Keep your eyes peeled for the Quéribus turn-off as you drive another 3km uphill.

04 Château de Quéribus

Perilously perched 728m up on a rocky hill, **Quéribus** *(cucugnan.fr)* was the site of the Cathars' last stand in 1255. Its interior structure is fairly well preserved: the **Salle du Pilier** inside the central keep still features its original Gothic pillars, vaulting and archways. There's also a small house that has been converted into a theatre, which shows a film documenting the story of the castle through the eyes of one of the castle's curates.

The top of the keep is reached via a narrow staircase and offers a truly mind-blowing view stretching to the Mediterranean and the Pyrenees on a clear day.

THE DRIVE: Drive back down to the turn-off, and turn left. Continue along this road (the D19) for 8km to the small town of Maury. Take the D117 for 25km to Puilaurens. The next castle is signed from here, another 3km south.

DETOUR

Gorges de Galamus

Start: 04 Château de Quéribus

Languedoc's soft limestone has created plenty of eye-popping gorges, but for heart-in-the-mouth views, the Gorges de Galamus near the village of St-Paul-de-Fenouillet are hard to beat. Gouged out by the River Agly, the gorge is spanned by a terrifyingly narrow road, cut by hand into the cliff face at the end of the 19th century. There are car parks at either end, from where you can hike up to the photogenic Ermitage St-Antoine de Galamus, clinging halfway up the cliff face. If you don't feel like walking, in summer, electric shuttles called *diablines* can be hired for €1.30 per person each way.

Look out for the turn-off to the right near St-Paul-de-Fenouillet as you drive along the D117 from Quéribus towards Puilaurens.

TOP TIP

PASSEPORT DES SITES DU PAYS CATHARE

The **Passeport des Sites du Pays Cathare** *(payscathare.org)* gives a €1 reduction off 21 local sites, including medieval abbeys at St-Hilaire, Lagrasse and Villelongue. Pick it up for €4 at tourist offices throughout the region.

05 Château de Puilaurens

If it's the classic hilltop castle you're after, **Puilaurens** *(chateau-puilaurens.com)* is it. With its turrets and lofty location, it's one of the most visually striking of the Cathar fortresses, with all the classic medieval defences: double defensive walls, four corner towers and crenellated battlements. It's also said to be haunted by the White Lady, a niece of Philippe le Bel.

THE DRIVE: Backtrack to the D117 and follow it west for 49km to Bélesta, skirting through hills, fields and forests. As you drive through town, spot signs onto the D9 to 'Fougax et B/Querigut/Château de Montségur'. The village is another 14km further along this road; follow it through the village to the castle's roadside car park.

06 Château de Montségur

For the full Monty Python medieval vibe – not to mention a good workout (bring your own water) – tackle the steep 1207m climb to the ruins of the **Château de Montségur** *(montsegur.fr)*. It was here, in 1242, that the Cathar movement suffered its heaviest defeat; attacked by a force of 10,000 royal troops, the castle fell after a gruelling nine-month siege, and 220 of the defenders were burnt alive when they refused to renounce their faith.

Montségur has also been cited as a possible location for the Holy Grail, which was supposedly smuggled out of the castle in the days before the final battle.

The original castle was razed to rubble after the siege, and the present-day ruins largely date from the 17th century.

THE DRIVE: Continue on the D117, turning onto the busy N20 to Foix, 32km northwest.

07 Foix

Complete your trip through Cathar country with a visit to the **Château de Foix**, nestled among the foothills of the Pyrenees. It's in a more complete state of repair than many of the Cathar fortresses you've seen, and gives you some idea of how they may have looked in their medieval heyday.

Carcassonne (p220)

JORRISGWW/SHUTTERSTOCK

PHOTO OPPORTUNITY

The view from the ramparts of Carcassonne.

31

PYRENEES & SOUTH-WEST FRANCE

★ BEST FOR

CULTURE

Comparing churches in Condom, Cahors and Moissac, each with a grand carved tympanum (decorative arch).

CHEAT'S COMPOSTELA

DURATION: 7 DAYS

DISTANCE: 710KM / 440 MILES

GREAT FOR: HISTORY & CULTURE

BEST TIME TO GO: MAY TO SEPTEMBER, TO MAKE THE MOST OF THE SUMMER SUNSHINE.

IMPORTANT: SNOW TYRES/CHAINS/SOCKS REQUIRED 1 NOVEMBER – 31 MARCH.

Estaing

Known in French as the Chemin de St-Jacques, the 'Camino' or 'Way of St-James' is one of Europe's greatest pilgrimages. It was originally undertaken on foot by those seeking credit in the afterlife. We can't promise equal spiritual merit if you're driving, but this classic French branch-route does present many lovely villages, iconic churches and historic cities, plus a giant iron statue of the Virgin Mary on a tower of volcanic rock.

LINK YOUR TRIP

32 The Pyrenees
For fantastic mountain scenery, join our Pyrenees trip at Pau, just 12km off the A65/64 junction that you'll pass between Condom and St-Jean Pied de Port.

38 The Lot Valley
Between Figeac and Cahors you can combine this itinerary with the most beautiful section of the Lot Valley trip.

01 Le Puy-en-Velay

Your journey begins at the striking town of Le Puy-en-Velay, where pilgrims would traditionally have earned a blessing at the **Cathédrale Notre-Dame** *(cathedraledupuy.org)* with its Romanesque archways and Byzantine domes. Older and much more distinctive is the 10th-century **Chapelle St-Michel d'Aiguilhe** *(rochersaintmichel.fr)*, perched on top of a remarkable 85m-high needle of volcanic rock. Its cave-like interior and 12th-century frescoes create an otherworldly atmosphere. On another rocky crag is an enormous cast-iron statue of the Virgin Mary, aka **Notre Dame de France**. A creaky spiral staircase winds its way to the top of the 835-tonne structure, which is 22.7m tall if you include the pedestal. Peep through portholes for dizzying vistas over the town.

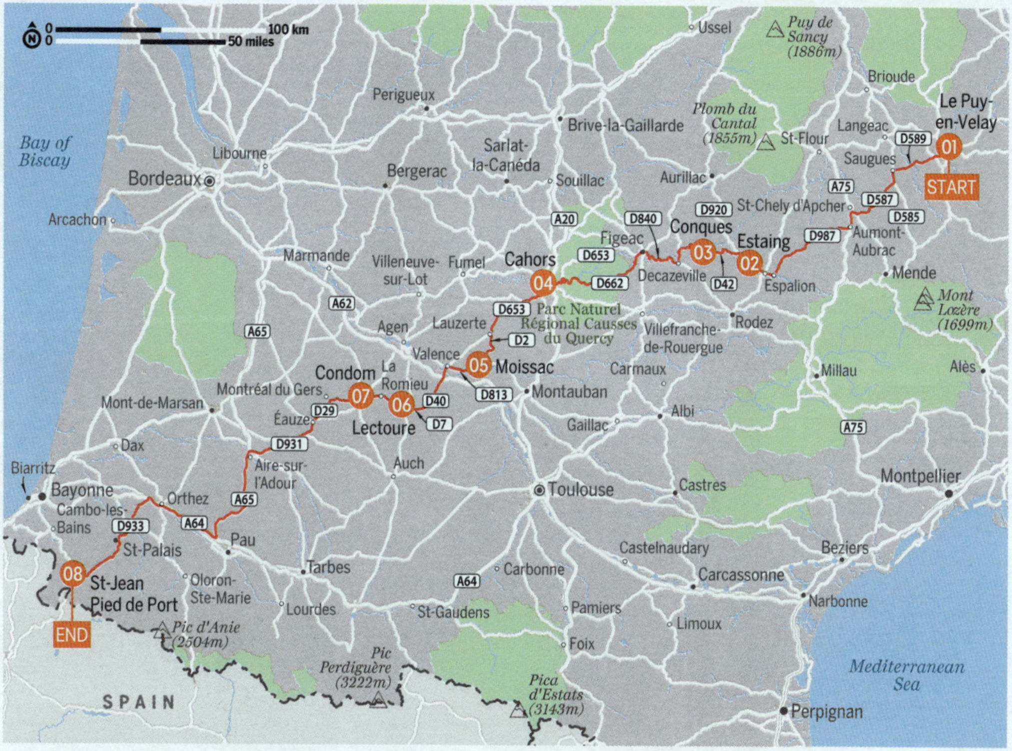

LEOKS/SHUTTERSTOCK

THE DRIVE: From Le Puy, it's a memorable day's drive of around 160km to Estaing, with plenty of village stops en route. The D589 winds down across the Allier Valley just bypassing Monistrol-d'Allier, where a pilgrims' chapel is set into a cliffside. The D589 continues west to Saugues, famed for its sheep market and the tall, if stunted, Tour Anglais fortress tower. From there head south on the D585 to castle-hamlet Esplantas, then southwest on the D587. On the A75 motorway, zip one exit south to Aumont Aubrac, from which the D987 closely follows the Camino via charming pilgrim villages Nasbinals, Aubrac and (with a small detour) St-Chely d'Aubrac. At lovely St-Côme-d'Olt, you finally reach the River Lot, which you follow downstream through Espalion, with its 14th-century bridge.

02 Estaing

Especially memorable when seen reflected across the river, Estaing is a pyramidal cluster of old stone buildings enfolding a Tolkienesque 15th-century church. Inside are the relics of St Fleuret, a 5th-century miracle-working bishop.

THE DRIVE: For the 42km route to Conques, follow the Lot downstream. Turn left across the river at the second dam, zigzagging up the narrow D135 to hilltop Golinhac with its panoramic viewpoint. Go 1.5km west on the D519, dogleg 150m south on the D904, then continue west to Conques (24km) on the similarly narrow, winding D42 via Espeyrac and Senergues.

03 Conques

The next major stop for medieval pilgrims would have been the magical hillside-village of Conques – or more specifically, the **Abbey Church of Ste-Foy**, built to house the holy relics of its namesake saint. It's a classic example of a pilgrimage church: simple and serene, with few architectural flourishes except for the carved

PHOTO OPPORTUNITY

Le Puy's emormous statue of the Virgin Mary.

tympanum (decorative arch) above the main doorway depicting the Day of Last Judgment.

THE DRIVE: Head northwest on the D901, recrossing the Lot River in a beautiful wide valley. Follow signs to Decazeville (21km), where you turn west onto the D840. Around 50km from Conques you reach Figeac, whose medieval heart is a fine place to spend at least half a day. From there, it's a slow but delightful 75km drive to Cahors along the Lot Valley. A faster alternative is via the D13 and D653, which takes about an hour from Figeac.

04 Cahors

Now best known for its rich red Malbec wines, the city of Cahors sits on an excentric loop of the Lot River. In the Middle Ages it was a rare crossing point on the wide river and its fortified 14th-century bridge, the **Pont Valentré**, formed part of its defences with three soaring towers that give the UNESCO-listed structure an unmistakable grandeur.

Cahors also retains an impressive Romanesque cathedral, the **Cathédrale St-Étienne**. Consecrated in 1119, the cathedral's airy nave is topped by two huge cupolas which, at 18m wide, are the largest in France. The tympanum of the cathedral's north portal sees an ascending Christ surrounded by fluttering angels and swooning saints.

THE DRIVE: The lovely 61km route to Moissac crosses a sparsely populated area of gently rolling fields and woodlands. Leave central Cahors on the southbound D620,

Notre Dame de France, Le Puy-en-Velay (p224)

ROLF G WACKENBERG/SHUTTERSTOCK

FRANCK - A/SHUTTERSTOCK

Chapelle St-Michel d'Aiguilhe, Le Puy-en-Velay (p224)

CHEMIN DE ST-JACQUES

In 9th-century Spain, a hermit named Pelayo stumbled across what he believed to be the tomb of the Apostle James, brother of John the Evangelist. Ever since, the Galician town of Santiago de Compostela has been one of Christendom's holiest sites. In the Middle Ages, millions of pilgrims were inspired to walk there from the far corners of Europe. Their arduous journey, known as the 'Camino' (*Chemin de St-Jacques* in French), was an act of piety and penance that might earn a reduced spell in purgatory after death. As the centuries proceeded, plague, wars and changing religious ideas meant that numbers waned significantly. Barely 3000 souls undertook the journey in 1987, the year that Paolo Coelho wrote about the experience in his reflective classic *The Pilgrimage,* but since then its popularity has ballooned – in 2025, numbers surpassed 500,000.

Today, walkers or horse riders who complete the final 100km to Santiago aren't promised merit in heaven but do qualify for a Compostela Certificate, issued on arrival at the cathedral. Cyclists need to complete 200km. Within France, there are four main routes starting at Paris, Vézelay, Arles and notably Le Puy-en-Velay, a route known as the Via Podensis and marked as the GR65 hiking route. Find out more at *webcompostella.com* and *chemindecompostelle.com/gr-65-voie-du-puy-en-velay*.

turning right onto the D653 after 4km at a poorly signed suburban roundabout. After 39km, consider detouring up into the pretty little hill town of Lauzerte for a coffee on the arcaded central square. Then head south on the D2, forking right on the D16 and entering Moissac on the D957.

05 Moissac

Moissac is a large riverside town, partly on an 'island' formed between the Tarn and the Garonne Canal. Its one crowning glory is the UNESCO-listed **Abbaye St-Pierre** *(abbayemoissac.com)*, a monumental abbey church built from a curious mixture of brick, stone and wood cladding. Its Gothic interior was repainted in the 1960s to recreate the original wallpaper-like effect and contains the superb 15th-century *Mise au Tombeau,* a large polychrome wooden sculpture of Jesus' body being placed in the tomb. Above the south portal, the 1130 **tympanum** depicts St John's vision of the Apocalypse. Behind the abbey's main entrance you can access the 'world's oldest' **cloister**, which was completed in 1100. Its slender stone columns are topped with carved capitals, many of them depicting animals, plants and biblical scenes, such as Samuel pouring holy oil over a kneeling David.

THE DRIVE: Head westbound on the D813 through flat, agricultural lands following the canal to forgettable Valence. Cross the canal on the D116, then the Garonne on the D953, which becomes the D88 south of the motorway. Turn right at Masonville onto the D40, then head west on the D7 to reach the arty citadel-village of Lectoure, in total 57km from Moissac.

06 Lectoure

This fortified hilltop town retains an almost complete set of medieval lower ramparts and quite a few stone mansions dating back to the 13th-century era of English rule. The colonnades and painted chapel of the **former lords' palace** are now filled with bric-a-brac stalls, with artists' workshops in the cellars below. There's also a scattering of other craft, antique and decor shops dotted around town. The giant **cathedral-church of St-Gervais**, built on the site of an ancient pagan temple, holds the relics of St-Clair of Aquitaine, the first bishop of Albi.

THE DRIVE: By the D7, Condom is a straight 24km drive from Lectoure. However, pilgrims follow a prettier 34km route via tiny Marsolan, with its glorious panorama point, and La Romieu, with a superb former abbey church and charming gardens.

07 Condom

Despite its giggle-inducing name, Condom actually has nothing to do with contraceptives – its name dates from Gallo-Roman times, when it was known as Condatomagus. The town's Flamboyant Gothic **Cathédrale St-Pierre** was the main point of interest for pilgrims, who could take wet-weather protection in the covered cloisters. Condom's other claim to fame is as the home of Armagnac, a potent brandy brewed since medieval times, originally as a medicinal tonic. The **tourist office** has a list of local producers in the surrounding area that offer tastings.

THE DRIVE: The last day's drive is 230km, 100km of that on motorway, because for part of the way roads don't really parallel the footpaths of the true Camino. Leave Condom via the citadel-hamlet of Laressingle (9km) and the beautifully preserved *bastide* (fortified town) of Montreal-du-Gers. The D29 then leads southwest to cathedral-town Éauze, from which the N524 and D931 take you to Air sur-l'Adour. Air's distinctive, UNESCO-listed Church of Ste-Quitterie honours a 4th-century Visigoth princess who was decapitated for refusing to give up Christianity. From here take the A65 and A64 toll highways to junction 7, then head south on the D933, which rejoins the original pilgrim route at Ostobat. The final 22km to St-Jean Pied de Port passes through the attractive Basque town of St-Jean-le-Vieux.

08 St-Jean Pied de Port

St-Jean Pied de Port wows with cobbled lanes, impressive ramparts, stone-and-whitewash houses and a Vauban citadel all set amid pretty green foothills. Here, three important branches of the Camino converge before crossing into Spain via the Roncevalles Pass, 8km away. While you might be ending your drive here, spare a thought for the real pilgrims who still have another 800km to walk before journey's end at Santiago de Compostela's famous cathedral.

Antiques, Lectoure
PERNELLE VOYAGE/SHUTTERSTOCK

Peinture
sur Masques

STAY AWHILE

CAHORS

BY ANNA RICHARDS

Cahors was once an important town: the 14th-century bridge, **Pont Valentré**, was the first (and for a long time, only) way to cross the Lot River. Much of the vast, Romanesque cathedral was built in the 12th century, one of Cahors' richest periods, but the Hundred Years' War and several outbreaks of Black Death decimated the town, and it has become one of France's forgotten treasures. Today it's best known for the masses of châteaux and vineyards producing Malbec wine in close proximity.

Most winemakers in the Cahors area are happy for you to drop by for tastings, but a call 30 minutes in advance is always appreciated. Alongside tastings, many winemakers have launched into the world of oenotourism. At **Château de Haute-Serre** *(hauteserre.fr)* you can take e-scooter tours of the vineyard, while **Château Lagrézette** *(chateau-lagrezette.com)* offers history-themed tours, and has accommodation among the vines in a 17th-century water mill.

The Lot River has some of the calmest waters for kayaking and paddleboarding. **Nautinéa** *(nautinea.fr)*, based in Douelle (12km upriver from Cahors), organises guided or unguided river descents to Cahors by SUP or kayak, returning to base on e-bikes. The river winds past several châteaux, including one belonging to the Danish royal family, **Château de Cayx** *(chateau-de-cayx.com)*. There are wine tastings of their own vintages at the on-site boutique for €10.

LINK YOUR TRIP

31 Cheat's Compostela Step off the track for a short break halfway along this trip.

Left: Pont Valentré;
Right: Château de Cayx

FROM LEFT: ANIBAL TREJO/SHUTTERSTOCK; MOREL/ANDIA/ALAMY

PLACES TO STAY

Inside the old city, **Hôtel Jean XXII** *(hotel-jeanxxii.com)* is the most atmospheric place to stay. It's set inside a 13th-century palace, but since our idea of luxury has changed somewhat in the intervening eight centuries, the nine rooms are very simply furnished, but very good value. Many of the surrounding châteaux also have on-site accommodation.

As well as the water mill at Château Lagrézette, it's possible to sleep in a converted barn in the vineyard at **Domaine la Paganie** *(domainelapaganie.com)*, and take a tour in a 2CV too (if you're not yet tired of driving).

32

PYRENEES & SOUTH-WEST FRANCE

THE PYRENEES

DURATION: 7 DAYS

DISTANCE: 522KM / 324 MILES

GREAT FOR: FAMILIES, NATURE

BEST TIME TO GO: JUNE TO SEPTEMBER, WHEN ROADS ARE SNOW-FREE. OCTOBER FOR AUTUMN COLOURS.

IMPORTANT: SNOW TYRES/CHAINS/SOCKS REQUIRED 1 NOVEMBER – 31 MARCH.

★ BEST FOR

OUTDOORS

Hiking to the Lac de Gaube or Refuge Wallon near Cauterets.

Lac de Gaube (p235)

They might not have the altitude of the Alps, but what the Pyrenees do have is an unsurpassed beauty. The mountains are laced with deep, green valleys punctuated by pretty stone villages. With every valley and massif offering something new, it's a thrilling region to travel through and even the most hardened driver will feel the urge to get out of the car and take to a hiking trail.

LINK YOUR TRIP

30 The Cathar Trail
From Foix, it's only a short drive from the mountains before you reach the heart of the Cathar lands and their amazing châteaux.

33 Basque Country
This Pyrenean trip makes a natural extension of our themed trip through the French Basque country. From St-Jean Pied de Port, it's 71km to Oloron-Ste-Marie, or 103km to Pau.

01 Pau

Palm trees might seem out of place in this mountainous region, but Pau (rhymes with 'so') has long been famed for its mild climate. In the 19th century this elegant town was a favourite wintering spot for the wealthy, and their legacy is visible in the town's grand villas and smart promenades.

Its main sight is the **Château de Pau** *(chateau-pau.fr)*, built by the monarchs of Navarre and transformed into a Renaissance château in the 16th century. It's home to a fine collection of Gobelins tapestries and Sèvres porcelain.

Pau's tiny old centre extends for around 500m around the château, and boasts many attractive medieval and Renaissance buildings.

Central street parking in Pau is mostly *payant* (chargeable), though there's limited free parking at the central Stadium de la Gare.

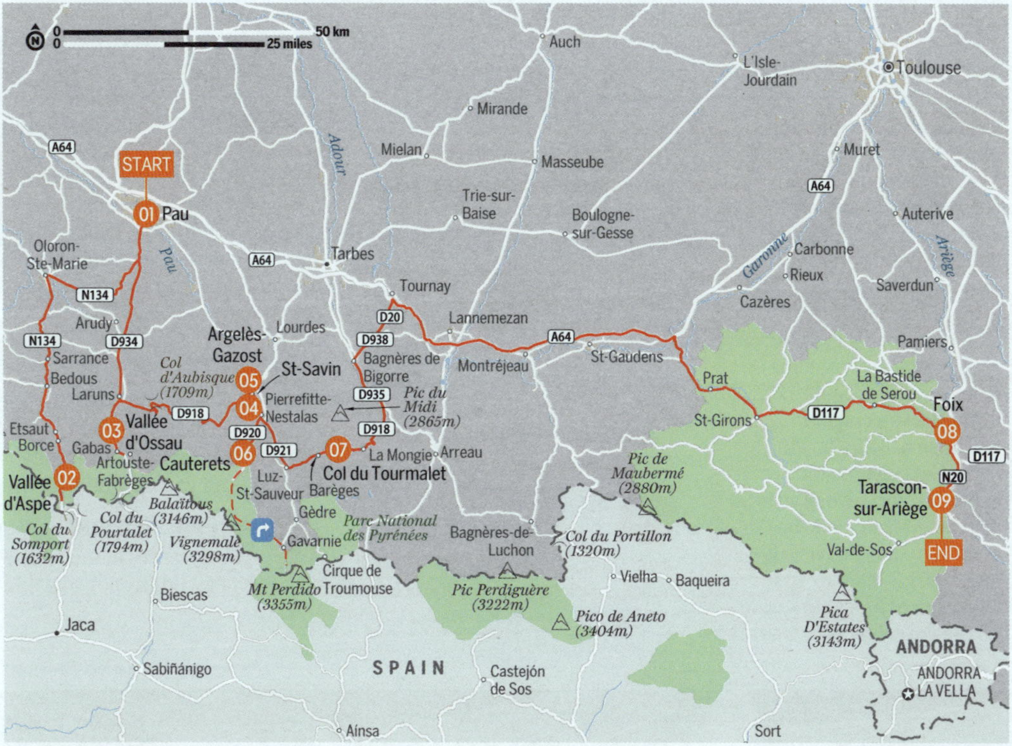

VACLAV VOLRAB/SHUTTERSTOCK

THE DRIVE: To reach the Vallée d'Aspe from Pau, take the N193 to Oloron-Ste-Marie. The first 30km are uneventful, but over the next 40km south of Oloron the mountain scenery unfolds in dramatic fashion, with towering peaks stacking up on either side of the road.

02 Vallée d'Aspe

The westernmost of the Pyrenean valleys makes a great day trip from Pau. Framed by mountains and bisected by the Aspe River, it's awash with classic Pyrenean scenery. Allow yourself plenty of time for photo stops, especially around pretty villages such as **Sarrance**, **Borce** and **Etsaut**.

Near the quiet village of **Bedous**, it's worth detouring up the narrow road to **Lescun**, a tiny hamlet perched 5.5km above the valley, overlooking the peak of **Pic d'Anie** (2504m) and the **Cirque de Lescun**, a jagged ridge of mountain peaks that close out the head of the valley.

The return drive to Pau is just over 80km.

THE DRIVE: To reach the Vallée d'Ossau from Pau, take the N134 north of town, veering south onto the D934 towards Arudy/Laruns. From Pau to Laruns, it's about 42km.

03 Vallée d'Ossau

More scenic splendour awaits in the Vallée d'Ossau, which tracks the course of its namesake river for a spectacular 60km. The first part of the valley as far as Laruns is broad, green and pastoral, but as you travel south the mountains really start to pile up, before broadening out again near Gabas.

Halfway between Arudy and Laruns, you can spy on some of the mightiest birds of the western Pyrenees, griffon vultures, at the **Falaise aux Vautours** (Cliff of the Vultures; *falaise-aux-vautours.com*). Live CCTV images are beamed from their nests to the visitors centre in Aste-Béon. Griffon vultures are common throughout the western part of the Pyrenees. Much rarer cousins include the Egyptian vulture and the massive lammergeier.

The ski resort of **Artouste-Fabrèges**, 6km east of Gabas, is linked by cable car to the **Petit Train d'Artouste** *(artouste.fr)*, a

THE TRANSHUMANCE

If you're travelling through the Pyrenees between late May and early June and find yourself stuck behind a cattle-shaped traffic jam, there's a good chance you may have just got caught up in the Transhumance, in which shepherds move their flocks from their winter pastures up to the high, grassy uplands.

This ancient custom has been a fixture on the Pyrenean calendar for centuries, and several valleys host festivals to mark the occasion. The spectacle is repeated in October, when the flocks are brought back down before the winter snows set in.

miniature mountain railway built for dam workers in the 1920s. The train is only open between June and September; reserve ahead and allow four hours for a visit.

THE DRIVE: The D918 between Laruns and Argelès-Gazost is one of the Pyrenees' most breathtaking roads, switchbacking over the lofty Col d'Aubisque. The road feels exposed, but it's a wonderfully scenic drive. You'll cover about 52km, but allow yourself at least 1½ hours. Once you reach Argelès-Gazost, head further south for 4km along the D101 to St-Savin.

04 St-Savin

After the hair-raising drive over the Col d'Aubisque, St-Savin makes a welcome refuge. It's a classic Pyrenean village, with cobbled lanes, cafes and timbered houses set around a fountain-filled main square.

It's also home to one of the Pyrenees' most respected hotel-restaurants, **Le Viscos** *(hotel-leviscos.com)*, run by celeb chef Jean-Pierre St-Martin, known for his blend of Basque, Breton and Pyrenean flavours (as well as his passion for foie gras). After dinner, retire to a cosy country-style room and watch the sun set over the snowy mountains.

THE DRIVE: From St-Savin, travel back along the D101 to Argelès-Gazost. You'll see signs to the Parc Animalier des Pyrénées as you approach town.

05 Argelès-Gazost

The Pyrenees has a diverse collection of wildlife, but spotting

Le Viscos, St-Savin

IVOHA/ALAMY

it in the wild isn't always simple. Thankfully, **Parc Animalier des Pyrénées** *(parc-animalier-pyrenees.com)* does all the hard work for you. It's home to endangered Pyrenean animals including wolves, marmots, lynxes, ravens, vultures, beavers and a few brown bears (whose limited presence in the Pyrenees is highly controversial).

THE DRIVE: Take the D921 south of Argelès-Gazost for 6km to Pierrefitte-Nestalas. Here, the road forks; the southwest branch (the D920) climbs up a lush, forested valley for another 11km to Cauterets.

06 Cauterets

For alpine scenery, the century-old ski and spa resort of Cauterets is perhaps the signature spot in the Pyrenees. Hemmed in by mountains and forests, it has clung on to much of its fin de siècle character, with a stately spa and grand 19th-century residences.

To see the scenery at its best, drive through town along the D920 (signed to the 'Pont d'Espagne'). The road is known locally as the **Chemins des Cascades** after the waterfalls that crash down the mountainside; it's 6.5km of nonstop hairpins, so take it steady.

At the top, you'll reach the giant car park at **Pont d'Espagne**. From here, a combination *télécabine* (cable car) and *télésiege* (chair lift) ratchets up the mountainside, allowing access to the area's trails, including the popular hike to sapphire-tinted **Lac de Gaube** and the even more beautiful but longer walks to the **Refuge Wallon** (four hours return) and **Refuge Oulette de Gaube** (five to six hours return).

THE DRIVE: After staying overnight in Cauterets, backtrack to Pierrefitte-Nestalas and turn southeast onto the D921 for 12km to Luz-St-Sauveur. The next stretch on the D918 is another mountain stunner, climbing up through Barèges to the breathtaking Col du Tourmalet.

ROAD PASSES IN THE PYRENEES

The high passes between the Vallée d'Ossau, the Vallée d'Aspe and the Vallée de Gaves are often closed during winter. Signs are posted along the approach roads indicating whether they're *ouvert* (open) or *fermé* (closed). The dates given below are approximate and depend on seasonal snowfall.

Col d'Aubisque
(1709m, open May-Oct) The D918 links Laruns in the Vallée d'Ossau with Argèles-Gazost in the Vallée de Gaves. An alternative that's open year-round is the D35 between Louvie-Juzon and Nay.

Col de Marie-Blanque
(1035m, open most of year) The shortest link between the Aspe and Ossau valleys is the D294, which corkscrews for 21km between Escot and Bielle.

Col du Pourtalet
(1795m, open most of year) The main crossing into Spain generally stays open year-round except during exceptional snowfall.

Col du Tourmalet
(2115m, open Jun-Oct) Between Barèges and La Mongie, this is the highest road pass in the Pyrenees. If you're travelling east to the Pic du Midi (for example from Cauterets), the only alternative is a long detour north via Lourdes and Bagnères de Bigorre.

DETOUR

Cirque de Gavarnie
Start: 06 Cauterets

For truly mind-blowing mountain scenery, it's well worth taking a side trip to see the **Cirque de Gavarnie**, a dramatic glacially formed amphitheatre of mountains 20km south of Luz-St-Sauveur. It's a return walk of about two hours from the village, and you'll need to bring sturdy footwear. There's another spectacular – and quieter – circle of mountains 6.5km to the east, the **Cirque de Troumouse**. It's reached via a hair-raising 8km toll road (open April to October). There are no barriers and the drops are really dizzying, so drive carefully.

07 Col du Tourmalet

At 2115m, Col du Tourmalet is the highest road pass in the Pyrenees, and it usually only opens between June and October. It's often used as a punishing mountain stage in the Tour de France, and you'll feel uncomfortably akin to a motorised ant as you crawl up towards the pass.

From the ski resort of La Mongie (1800m), a cable car climbs to the top of **Pic du Midi** *(picdumidi.com)*. This high-altitude observatory commands otherworldly views – but it's often blanketed in cloud, so

♥ WHY I LOVE THIS TRIP

STUART BUTLER, WRITER

The craggy peaks of the Pyrenees are home to some of France's rarest wildlife and most unspoilt landscapes, and every twist and turn in the road seems to reveal another knockout view. I've spent the past two decades living at the western foot of these mountains and still never tire of exploring them. For me, there is simply no more beautiful mountain range on earth. This west-to-east drive through the mountains showcases some of its finest, and most easily accessible, sights, views and experiences.

make sure you check the forecast before you go.

THE DRIVE: The next stage to Foix is a long one. Follow the D918 and D935 to Bagnères de Bigorre, then the D938 and D20 to Tournay, a drive of 40km. Just before Tournay, head west onto the A64 for 82km. Exit onto the D117, signed to St-Girons. It's another 72km to Foix, but with twisting roads all the way and lots of 30km/h zones, this last part takes at least 1½ hours.

08 Foix

Looming above Foix is the triple-towered **Château de Foix**, constructed in the 10th century as a stronghold for the counts of the town. The view from the battlements is wonderful and a refurbishment has spruced up the displays on medieval life. There's usually at least one daily tour in English in summer.

Afterwards, head 4.5km south to **Les Forges de Pyrène** *(forges-de-pyrene.com)*, a fascinating 'living museum' that explores Ariège folk traditions. Spread over 5 hectares, it illustrates traditional trades such as glass blowing, tanning, thatching and nail making, and even has its own blacksmith, baker and cobbler.

THE DRIVE: Spend the night in Foix, then head for Tarascon-sur-Ariège, 17km south of Foix on the N20. Look out for brown signs to the Parc de la Préhistoire.

09 Tarascon-sur-Ariège

Thousands of years ago, the Pyrenees were home to thriving communities of hunter-gatherers, who used the area's caves as shelters and left behind many stunning examples of prehistoric art.

Near Tarascon-sur-Ariège, the **Parc de la Préhistoire** provides a handy primer on the area's ancient past. It explores everything from prehistoric carving to the arts of animal-skin tent making and ancient spear-throwing.

About 6.5km further south, the **Grotte de Niaux** *(sites-touristiques-ariege.fr)* is home to the Pyrenees' most precious cave paintings. The centrepiece is the **Salon Noir**, reached after an 800m walk through the darkness and decorated with bison, horses and ibex. The cave can only be visited with a guide. From April to September there's usually one daily tour in English at 1.30pm. Bookings are advisable.

Cirque de Gavarnie (p235)

CHRISTOPHE FAUGERE/SHUTTERSTOCK

PHOTO OPPORTUNITY

Posing in the imposing Cirque de Gavarnie.

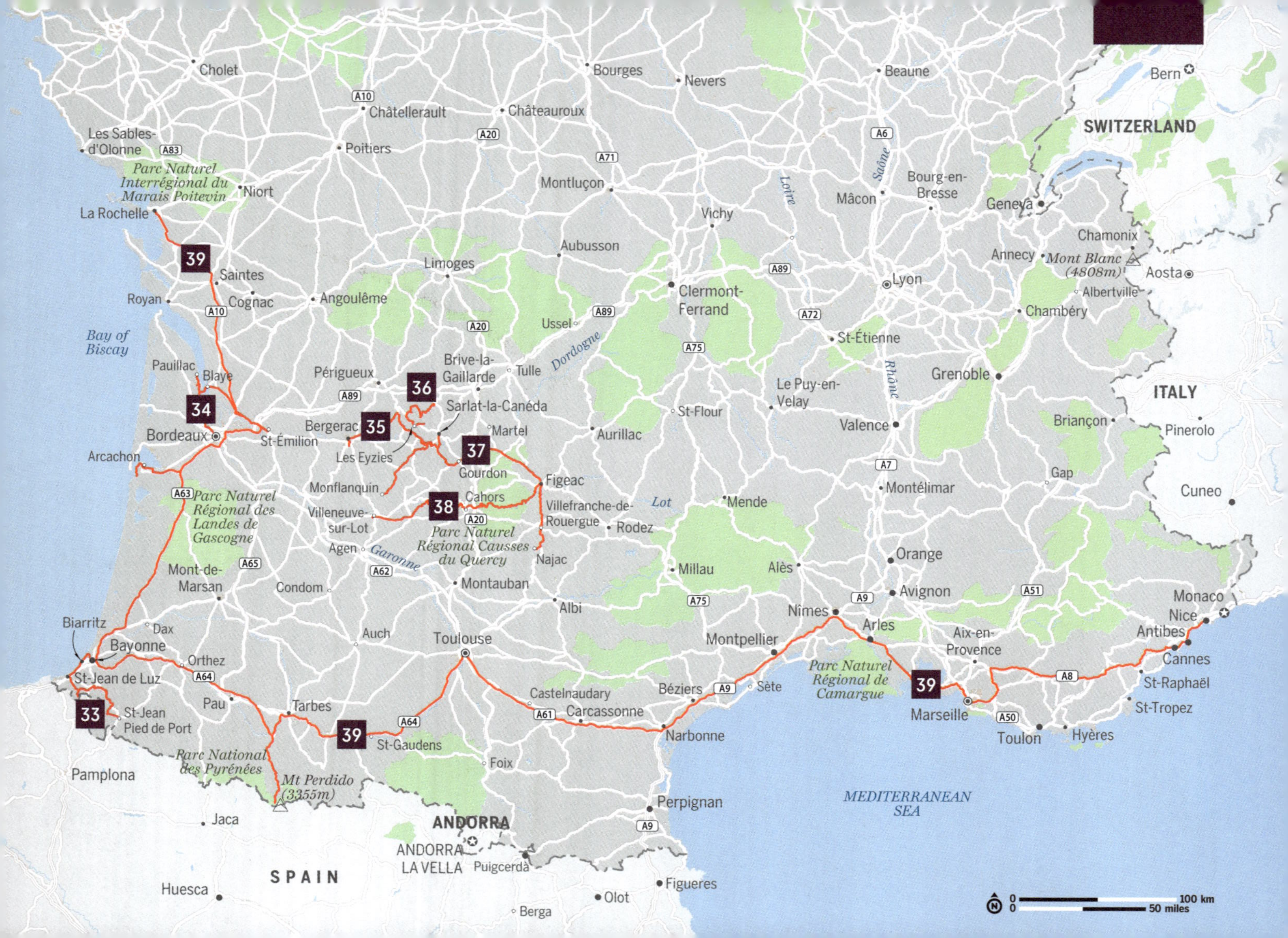

SWITZERLAND
ITALY
SPAIN
ANDORRA
Bay of Biscay
MEDITERRANEAN SEA
33
34
35
36
37
38
39
Bern
Geneva
Chamonix
Mont Blanc (4808m)
Aosta
Albertville
Annecy
Chambéry
Beaune
Bourges
Nevers
Cholet
Châtellerault
Châteauroux
Les Sables-d'Olonne
Poitiers
Parc Naturel Interrégional du Marais Poitevin
Niort
La Rochelle
Montluçon
Mâcon
Bourg-en-Bresse
Loire
Saône
Vichy
Aubusson
Limoges
Saintes
Royan
Cognac
Angoulême
Clermont-Ferrand
Lyon
St-Étienne
Ussel
Dordogne
Tulle
Brive-la-Gaillarde
Périgueux
Pauillac
Blaye
Bordeaux
St-Émilion
Bergerac
Sarlat-la-Canéda
Les Eyzies
Martel
Gourdon
Figeac
Aurillac
St-Flour
Le Puy-en-Velay
Rhône
Grenoble
Valence
Briançon
Pinerolo
Cuneo
Gap
Montélimar
Arcachon
Monflanquin
Cahors
Villeneuve-sur-Lot
Villefranche-de-Rouergue
Rodez
Lot
Mende
Parc Naturel Régional des Landes de Gascogne
Parc Naturel Régional Causses du Quercy
Agen
Garonne
Najac
Montauban
Mont-de-Marsan
Condom
Millau
Alès
Orange
Avignon
Albi
Nîmes
Arles
Aix-en-Provence
Monaco
Nice
Antibes
Cannes
St-Raphaël
St-Tropez
Biarritz
Dax
Bayonne
Auch
Toulouse
Montpellier
Parc Naturel Régional de Camargue
Marseille
Toulon
Hyères
Orthez
St-Jean de Luz
Pau
Tarbes
Castelnaudary
Carcassonne
Béziers
Sète
Narbonne
St-Jean Pied de Port
St-Gaudens
Foix
Parc National des Pyrénées
Pamplona
Mt Perdido (3355m)
Jaca
Perpignan
Andorra La Vella
Puigcerdà
Huesca
Figueres
Olot
Berga
A10
A20
A83
A71
A6
A89
A72
A75
A7
A63
A65
A62
A64
A61
A9
A51
A8
A50
0
100 km
0
50 miles

CHRISATPPS/SHUTTERSTOCK

Pujols (p276)

ATLANTIC COAST

EXPLORE

ATLANTIC COAST

From the surfing magnet of Biarritz on the Atlantic coast to the culturally unique enclave of the French Basque Country, the vineyards and hilltop villages of the Lot Valley, and the splendid food and wine of Bordeaux, the southwestern corner of France promises pleasure in abundance. These itineraries take you to medieval river ports that grew fat on the wine trade, to cave systems decorated with Europe's earliest art, to the feet of the mighty Pyrenees and even on a grand tour from the Atlantic to the Mediterranean. Buckle up for the best of southwest France.

Bordeaux

Bordeaux is the main hub for the southwestern Atlantic seaboard, and France's sixth-largest city. It's also the world's largest urban World Heritage Site – 18 sq km of harmonious architecture, photogenic boulevards and museums. Among all that, you'll find a good spread of accommodation across all budgets, with some excellent central options (book ahead in spring and summer). Bordeaux' restaurants, wine shops and groceries all support the city's stellar gastronomic reputation – you won't lack supply options.

Bordeaux–Mérignac Airport, 12km west of town, serves over 25 airlines flying to French, European and North African destinations. Buses run the 40-minute route to the city centre and train station every 10 minutes between 6am and 11pm. Just six hours from London on the Eurostar and two to three hours from Paris on the ultrafast TGV, Bordeaux is also a hub for regional trains to Bayonne and Biarritz, the winemaking centre of St-Émilion and other destinations. Car-rental offices can be found at the airport, at St-Jean train station and north of the central place de la Bourse.

Bayonne

The appealing seaside city of Bayonne is the capital of the French Basque Country and the ideal base from which to begin our 'Basque Country' drive. Situated at the confluence of the Adour and Nive Rivers, filled with colourful

WHEN TO GO

Atlantic spots like Biarritz overflow with visitors in July and August, when the weather is hottest. The shoulder months (April to June and September) see temperatures, crowds and prices decline. Things are at their least expensive from October to April, when black truffles also appear in Dordogne markets; however, many restaurants and hotels close or operate reduced hours.

half-timbered buildings, museums and medieval walls and churches, it's also worth spending some time here. The covered market and abundance of groceries and supermarkets allow you to stock up for the road, and there's good accommodation to be had in the lower and midrange price brackets.

Nearby Aéroport Biarritz Pays Basque is also convenient for Biarritz and the coast, Bayonne is linked to Paris by high-speed TGV trains, and car-rental offices can be found at the airport, near the station and in the centre of town.

Bergerac

Gourmands and history lovers might consider making Bergerac their touring base for the 'Gourmet Dordogne', 'Heritage Wine Country', 'Cave Art of the Vézère Valley', 'Dordogne's Fortified Villages' and 'Lot Valley' drives. A pleasant town of some 28,000, it offers a mix of charming and functional hotels, a healthy spread of groceries and supermarkets, and car-rental offices at the airport and train station. Bergerac Dordogne Périgord Airport offers only limited and seasonal connections, but the town is served by frequent regional trains running between Bordeaux and Sarlat.

TRANSPORT

Flying into Bordeaux-Mérignac or Biarritz Pays Basque is the most direct way to enter this region. If no scheduled routes suit your purposes, you can always fly into Paris, Toulouse or Marseille and make use of their high-speed TGV rail connections with Bordeaux. Bordeaux, Toulouse, Bayonne, Bergerac and other hubs are also well served by slower regional trains.

NOTE: A Crit'Air sticker is required in Bordeaux, Toulouse, Montpelier, Marseille and Nice. See p287 for more details.

WHERE TO STAY

Perhaps Bayonne's most luxurious hotel, **Hôtel & Restaurant les Basses Pyrénées** is built into the 17th-century ramparts in the heart of the old town. Foodies will love it. **Maison Brisson**, located in the southern suburbs of Bordeaux, will please book-lovers on a tight budget. **Domaine des Bories** offers rural eco-cottages of varying sizes in the heart of the Dordogne, while **Churchill Hôtel** in the historic St-Seurin neighbourhood of Bordeaux is a good-value 14-room haven with stylish decor. **Hôtel Mercure Figeac Viguier du Roy** is a luxury hotel sensitively created from the historic palace that was home to the King's Magistrate in Figeac for four centuries.

RESOURCES

Vins Saint-Émilion
Provides a full guide to the wines of this UNESCO-listed region. *vins-saint-emilion.com*

En Pays Basque
Essential for anyone seeking to research the French Basque Country before they visit. *en-pays-basque.fr*

Lascaux II
Provides background to and practical details of the prehistoric treasures of the Lascaux Caves. *lascaux-ii.fr*

WHAT'S ON

Fest'Oie
The goose, revered in the gastronomy of the Dordogne, is celebrated in Sarlat-la-Canéda over two days every March.

Bordeaux Wine Festival
For four days in June or July this annual *fête du vin* sees the city's historic quays illuminated with bonhomie and salutes to the local vintages.

St-Émilion Jazz Festival
This celebration of music and merrymaking comes to the ancient wine-producing town of St-Émilion for three days every July.

33

ATLANTIC COAST

BASQUE COUNTRY

DURATION: 7 DAYS

DISTANCE: 117KM / 73 MILES

GREAT FOR: FAMILIES, FOOD & DRINK, HISTORY & CULTURE

BEST TIME TO GO: SEPTEMBER AND OCTOBER OFFER THE BEST COMBINATION OF WEATHER AND LOW CROWDS.

IMPORTANT: SNOW TYRES/CHAINS/SOCKS REQUIRED 1 NOVEMBER – 31 MARCH

★ BEST FOR

CULTURE

Absorbing the Basque spirit of old Bayonne.

Bayonne

Driving into the village of Espelette you'll be struck by how different everything is from other parts of the country. The houses are all done up in the red and white of Basque buildings, streamers of chilli peppers hang from roof beams, and from open windows comes a language you don't recognise. As you'll discover on this tour, being different from the rest of France is exactly how the proud Basques like it.

LINK YOUR TRIP

31 Cheat's Compostela
From St-Jean Pied de Port work your way in reverse through our cheat's version of this ancient spiritual journey.

34 Heritage Wine Country
From Bayonne it's a 192km pine-tree-scented drive to the capital of wine, Bordeaux, and the start of our wine tour.

01 Bayonne

Surrounded by sturdy fortifications and splashed in red and white paint, Bayonne is one of the most attractive towns in southwest France. Its perfectly preserved old town and riverside restaurants are an absolute delight to explore, but the town is best known to French people for producing some of the nation's finest chocolate and ham.

Inside the **Musée Basque et de l'Histoire de Bayonne** *(musee-basque.com)*, you can explore the seafaring history, traditions and cultural identity of the Basque people.

Also worth a visit is Bayonne's Gothic **Cathédrale Ste-Marie** *(cathedraledebayonne.com)*, whose twin towers soar elegantly above the old town.

THE DRIVE: Bring a towel because you're taking the 13km (25-minute) beach-bums route to Biarritz. Follow the

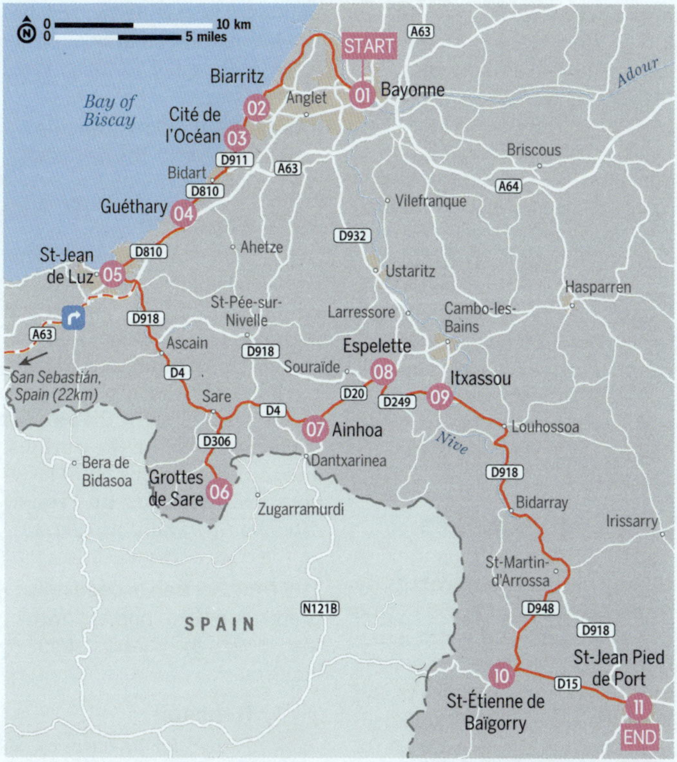

BOTOND HORVATH/SHUTTERSTOCK

Adour River out of Bayonne down allées Marines and av de l'Adour. At the big roundabout turn left onto bd des Plages and take your pick from any of the beaches along this stretch. This road will eventually lead into Biarritz.

02 Biarritz

As ritzy as its name suggests, this stylish coastal town took off as a resort in the mid-19th century when Napoléon III and his Spanish-born wife, Eugénie, visited regularly. Along its rocky coastline are architectural hallmarks of this golden age, and the Belle Époque and art deco eras that followed. Although it retains a high glamour quotient (and high prices to match), it's also a magnet for vanloads of surfers, with some of Europe's best waves.

Biarritz' raison d'être is its fashionable beaches, particularly the central **Grande Plage** and **Plage Miramar**, which are lined end to end with sunbathers on hot summer days.

For a look under the waves, check out the **Aquarium de Biarritz** *(aquariumbiarritz.com),* rich in underwater life from the Bay of Biscay and beyond.

For life further afield, have a poke about the stunning museum collection of Asian art at **Asiatica** (Musée d'Art Asiatique; *musee-asiatica.com*).

THE DRIVE: It's a 35-minute, 2.6km walk or a 10-minute drive south out of Biarritz along rue de Madrid to the Cité de l'Océan. On the way you'll pass some fantastic stretches of sand just calling for you to dip a toe in the sea or hang ten on a surfboard.

03 Cité de l'Océan

We don't really know whether it's fair to call Biarritz' showpiece **Cité de l'Océan** *(citedelocean.com)* a mere 'museum'. At heart it's a museum of the ocean, but in reality this is entertainment, cutting-edge technology, theme park and science museum all rolled into one spectacular attraction. Inside the eye-catching building you'll learn how the ocean was born, surf like a pro and join an underwater expedition to study Polynesian grey sharks.

THE DRIVE: It's an often painfully congested drive 7km south down the D911 (av de Biarritz) and D810, passing through the village of Bidart, to the ocean views of pretty Guéthary.

04 Guéthary

Built onto cliffs overlooking the ocean south of Biarritz, this red-and-white seaside village has gained a reputation as the Basque Country's chichi resort of choice for the jet set. The pebble beach below the village offers safe bathing for all the family, while the offshore reefs offer some exceptional surf for the brave.

THE DRIVE: It's another seriously traffic-clogged 7km south along the D810 to St-Jean de Luz. This short 6km hop should only take 10 minutes, but it rarely does! Sadly, there's no worthwhile alternative route.

05 St-Jean de Luz

If you're searching for the quintessential Basque seaside town – with atmospheric narrow streets and a lively fishing port pulling in large catches of sardines and anchovies that are cooked up at authentic restaurants – you've found it.

St-Jean de Luz' beautiful banana-shaped sandy **beach** sprouts stripy bathing tents from June to September. The beach is sheltered from Atlantic swells and is among the few child-friendly beaches in the Basque Country.

With plenty of boutique shops, bijou cafes and pretty buildings, walking the streets of the pedestrianised town centre is a real pleasure. Don't miss the town's finest church, **Église St-Jean Baptiste** *(paroissespo.com/eglise-st-jean-baptiste-st-jean-de-luz)*, which has a splendid interior with a magnificent Baroque altarpiece.

THE DRIVE: The 15km, 20-minute drive down the D918 and D4 to Sare is a slow road through the gorgeous gentle hills of the pre-Pyrenees. From the village of Sare, which is well worth a wander, pick up the D306 for a further 6km (12 minutes) to the Grottes de Sare.

DETOUR

San Sebastián, Spain

Start: 05 St-Jean de Luz

Spain, and the elegant and lively city of San Sebastián, is just a few kilometres along the coast from St-Jean de Luz. Put simply, San Sebastián is not a city you want to miss out on visiting. The town is set around two sickle-shaped beaches, at least one of which, **Playa de la Concha** (Paseo de la Concha), is the equal of any city beach in Europe. But there's more to the city than just looks. With a whole heap of Michelin-starred restaurants, and arguably the finest tapas in Spain, many a culinary expert has been heard to say that San Sebastián is possibly the world's best food city.

By car from St-Jean de Luz, it's just a short 20-minute motor south along the A63 (and past an awful lot of toll booths!), or you can endure the N10, which has no tolls but gets so clogged up that it will take you a good couple of hours to travel this short distance.

06 Grottes de Sare

Who knows what the first inhabitants of the **Grottes de Sare** *(grottesdesare.fr)* – who lived some 20,000 years ago – would make of today's whizz-bang technology, including lasers and holograms, during the sound-and-light shows at these caves. Multilingual 45-minute tours take you through a gaping entrance via narrow passages to a huge central cavern adorned with stalagmites and stalactites.

THE DRIVE: To get to the next stop, Ainhoa, 13.5km northeast, retrace your steps to Sare to pick up the D4. Count 20 minutes for the journey. If you're feeling adventurous, you could weave your way there on any number of minor back roads or even cross briefly into Spain and drive via the lovely village of Zugarrmurdi.

07 Ainhoa

Beautiful Ainhoa's elongated main street is flanked by imposing 17th-century houses, half-timbered and brightly painted. The fortified church has the Basque trademarks of an internal gallery and an embellished altarpiece.

THE DRIVE: It's 6km down the D20 to Espelette, the next tasty port of call.

08 Espelette

The whitewashed Basque town of Espelette is famous for its dark-red chillies, an integral ingredient in traditional Basque cuisine. In autumn, the walls of the houses are strung with rows of chillies drying in the sun. To learn more about the chillies, and to taste and buy chilli products, visit **L'Atelier du Piment** *(atelier-du-piment-espelette.fr)* on the edge of town.

THE DRIVE: It's an exceedingly pretty 6km (10 minutes) down the D249 to the cherry capital, Itxassou.

09 Itxassou

Famed for its cherries, as well as the beauty of its surrounds, Itxassou is a classic Basque village that well rewards a bit of exploration. The cherries are used in the region's most famous cake, gateau Basque, which is available pretty much everywhere you look throughout the Basque Country.

THE DRIVE: It's 28km (about 30 minutes) down the D918 and D948 to St-Étienne de Baïgorry. On the way you'll pass the village of Bidarry, renowned for its white-water rafting, and some pretty special mountain scenery.

10 St-Étienne de Baïgorry

The riverside village of St-Étienne de-Baïgorry is tranquillity itself. Like so many Basque settlements, the village has two focal points: the

PHOTO OPPORTUNITY

Looking across Grande Plage in Biarritz from the southern headland.

Grande Plage (p243), Biarritz

church and the **fronton** (court for playing *pelota,* the local ball game). It's the kind of place to while away an afternoon doing nothing very much at all.

THE DRIVE: It's a quiet 11km (20-minute) drive along the rural D15 to our final stop, St-Jean Pied de Port. The thirsty will be interested to know that the hills around the village of Irouléguy, which you pass roughly around the halfway point, are home to the vines that produce the Basque Country's best-known wine.

11 St-Jean Pied de Port

At the foot of the Pyrenees, the walled town of St-Jean Pied de Port was for centuries the last stop in France for pilgrims heading south over the Spanish border and on to Santiago de Compostela in western Spain. Today it remains a popular departure point for hikers attempting the same pilgrim trail.

St-Jean Pied de Port isn't just about hiking boots and pilgrimage, though; its old core, sliced through by the Nive River, is an attractive place of cobbled streets and geranium-covered balconies. Specific sights worth seeking out include the **Église Notre Dame du Bout du Pont**, which was thoroughly rebuilt in the 17th century. Beyond Porte de Notre Dame (the main gate into the old town) is the photogenic **Vieux Pont** (Old Bridge), the town's best-known landmark.

STAY AWHILE

BAYONNE

BY ANNA RICHARDS

Bayonne is Basque and proud of it. It's best known for the **Fêtes de Bayonne** *(fetes.bayonne.fr)*, a positively raucous summer celebration of Basque culture, food and music started by local rugby players in 1932. More than a million people attend each year!

You don't need to visit during the festival to see how important Bayonne's Basque heritage is, though. Throughout the summer, the city organises initiations in *pelota* every Thursday afternoon on **place Paxta**, which are open to both adults and kids. It's similar to squash, using basket-like scoops rather than rackets. If you'd prefer to watch the pros rather than participate, seek out a match happening in the region; the vast majority take place in **St-Jean Pied de Port**, an hour inland on the Spanish border.

The proximity to Spain is tangible in Bayonne's cuisine. *Pinxtos* are a mainstay. These bar snacks, typically smaller than tapas, are served on toothpicks. Look out for *jambon de Bayonne* (Bayonne ham), squid and *tortilla de patatas* (potato omelette).

Walk it all off at **Caradoc Park**, a vast urban park spread over several hectares a short distance outside the city. When the summer heat kicks in, it's a great place for a picnic in the shade of maple trees, agapanthus and redwoods, and it has lovely views of the Pyrenees. **Kaxu Galerie** *(kaxu.fr)*, a street art gallery, is also well worth a visit for temporary exhibitions and workshops where you can give graffiti a go yourself.

LINK YOUR TRIP

33 **Basque Country** Spend some time in the most Basque of towns before taking on this road trip.

Left: St-Jean Pied de Port;
Right: Fêtes de Bayonne

FROM LEFT: BEPSY/SHUTTERSTOCK; DELPIXEL/SHUTTERSTOCK

PLACES TO STAY

There's no shortage of places to stay in Bayonne, but reserve as far in advance as possible if visiting for the Fêtes de Bayonne (late July or early August), when the city bursts at the seams. At other times of the year, try a floating bed on board **Péniche Djebelle** *(penichedjebelle.hotelbayonne.net)*, a houseboat with two rooms on the Adour River, where breakfast is served on deck. **Hôtel et Restaurant des Basses Pyrénées Grand Bayonne** *(hotel-bassespyrenees-bayonne.com)* is central and has oodles of character, with a terrace in the ramparts and exposed stone walls in every room.

34

ATLANTIC COAST

HERITAGE WINE COUNTRY

★ BEST FOR

FOODIES

Slurping fresh oysters at Bordeaux' Marché des Capucins.

DURATION: 5 DAYS

DISTANCE: 257KM / 160 MILES

GREAT FOR: FOOD & DRINK, HISTORY & CULTURE

BEST TIME TO GO: SEPTEMBER AND OCTOBER: THE GRAPE HARVEST TAKES PLACE AND OYSTERS ARE IN SEASON.

Oysters, Marché des Capucins

10am: the southern sun warms your face and you're standing in a field surrounded by vines heavy with ready-to-burst grapes. 1pm: cutlery clinks, tummies sigh in bliss and you're on a gastronomic adventure in a top-class restaurant. 7pm: toes in the sand and Atlantic breezes in your hair and you down an oyster in one. All this and more awaits you on this refined culinary trip.

LINK YOUR TRIP

33 Basque Country
From Arcachon drive 182km through the forests of Les Landes to Bayonne and our Spanish-flavoured Basque Country tour.

35 Gourmet Dordogne
Slip some truffle hunting into your wine tour. From St-Émilion it's a mere 100km to Périgueux and the Gourmet Dordogne drive.

01 Bordeaux

Gourmet Bordeaux is a city of sublime food and long, lazy sun-drenched days. Half the city (18 sq km) is UNESCO-listed, making it the largest urban World Heritage Site – and an absolute delight to wander around. Barista-run coffee shops, on-trend food trucks, an inventive dining scene and more fine wine than you could ever possibly drink make it a city hard to resist.

Wine aficionados will adore **La Cité du Vin** *(laciteduvin.com)*, a stunning contemporary building designed to resemble a modern wine decanter on the banks of the River Garonne. The curvaceous gold building glitters in the sun and its 3000 sq metres of exhibits inside, dedicated to immersing visitors in the complex world of wine, are equally sensational. Tours end with a glass of wine in the panoramic **Latitude 20** wine bar on the 8th floor.

The **tourist office** *(bordeaux-tourisme.com)* runs a packed program of city tours in English, including gourmet and wine tours, river cruises in the warmer months, and child-friendly tours. All tours take a limited number of participants; reserve ahead.

THE DRIVE: It's a 24km trip along the D1 from Bordeaux to La Winery in Arsac. Technically this should take around 40 minutes, but traffic around Bordeaux can be dreadful so allow longer.

02 La Winery

Part giant wine shop, part wine museum, **La Winery** *(winery.fr)* is a glass-and-steel wine centre just off the D1215 that mounts concerts and contemporary-art exhibits alongside various fee-based tastings, including innovative ones that determine your *signe œnologique;* advance reservations are required. The boutique stocks over 1000 different wines.

Should you leave with an urge to taste more fine wine in the company of exceptional food and picture-postcard vineyard views, follow smart local gastronomes to **Nomade** *(restaurant-nomade.fr)*, squirrelled away into the teeny former train station building in the village of Labarde. Young Pauillac-born chef Thibault Guiet, with partner Manon Garret, serves a sensational modern cuisine, firmly rooted in local seasonal products.

THE DRIVE: It's a 15-minute drive (11km) east from La Winery to Labarde along the rural D208 and D105E1. From here, it's 35 minutes (25km) north along the scenic D2 via Margaux to Pauillac. Bages is 2km south of the latter.

> ☑ TOP TIP
>
> ### OYSTERS AT CAPUCINS
>
> A classic Bordeaux experience is a Saturday morning spent slurping oysters and chilled white wine from one of the seafood stands at **Marché des Capucins** *(marchedescapucins.com)*. Afterwards you can peruse the stalls while shopping for the freshest ingredients to take on a picnic.

03 Pauillac

Northwest of Bordeaux, along the western shore of the Gironde Estuary – formed by the confluence of the Garonne and Dordogne Rivers – lie some of Bordeaux' most celebrated vineyards. On the banks of the muddy Gironde, the port town of Pauillac is at the heart of Bordeaux wine country, surrounded by the distinguished Haut-Médoc, Margaux and St-Julien appellations. Extraordinary châteaux pepper these parts, including prestigious **Château Margaux**, with cellars designed by Lord Norman Foster in 2015; they cannot be visited.

The Pauillac wine appellation encompasses 18 *crus classés* in all, including the world-renowned Mouton Rothschild, Latour and Lafite Rothschild. The town's tourist office houses the **Maison du Tourisme et du Vin** *(pauillac-medoc.com)*, with information on châteaux and how to visit them; advance reservations are essential.

Memorable and delicious is lunch at **Café Lavinal** *(jmcazes.com/en/cafe-lavinal),* a 1930s-styled village bistro in Bages with retro red banquet seating, a zinc bar and revisited French classics cooked up by a duo of local Médoc chefs.

THE DRIVE: Count on no more than 15 minutes to cover the 9km between Bages and the next stop. Follow the D2 south out of Pauillac for almost 7km, turn right towards Lachesnaye, and continue for another 1.5km, then turn right to Château Lanessan.

04 Château Lanessan

There are so many châteaux around here with such a confusing web of opening times and visiting regulations that it can be hard to know where to begin. One of the easiest to visit is **Château Lanessan** *(lanessan.com),* a neoclassical castle with English-style gardens and a 19th-century greenhouse. You can tour just the wine cellar; visit the impressive stables built in the shape of a horseshoe in 1880 with marble feed troughs, a pine-panelled tack room and a museum of 19th-century horse-drawn carriages; or do both. The property also offers vertical wine tastings and two-hour wine-blending workshops.

THE DRIVE: Getting to Blaye involves splashing over the Gironde River on a car ferry. Return to the D2 and head south to Lamarque where you hop on board the small **TransGironde ferry** *(gironde.fr/deplacements/les-bacs-girondins-ferries/ligne-des-bacs-blaye-lamarque)* for the short 4.5km, 20-minute crossing to Blaye. It's 11km from the château to the ferry.

05 Blaye

If you want a lesson in how to build a protective citadel, then spectacular **Citadelle de Blaye** is about as good an example as you could hope to find. Largely constructed by that master fortress builder Vauban in the 17th century, it was a key line of defence protecting Bordeaux from naval attack. It was inscribed onto the UNESCO World Heritage List in 2008.

St-Émilion

PHOTO OPPORTUNITY

Red roofs of St-Émilion from place des Créneaux.

NORIOX/SHUTTERSTOCK

THE DRIVE: From Blaye to St-Émilion is a 50km drive. From Blaye take the D137 towards St-André de Cubzac, where you join the D670 to Libourne. After a bit of time stuck in traffic, you continue down to St-Émilion. It should take an hour, but traffic means it will probably take longer.

DETOUR

Cognac

Start: 05 Blaye

On the banks of the Charente River amid vine-covered countryside, the picturesque town of Cognac, home of the double-distilled spirit that bears its name, proves that there's more to southwest France than just wine.

The best-known Cognac houses are open to the public, running tours of their cellars and production facilities, and ending with a tasting session. The **tourist office** *(destination-cognac.com)* can give advice on the current opening hours of each Cognac house.

It's 85km from Blaye to Cognac, much of which is along the A10 highway. From Cognac you can reach St-Émilion in two hours on the D731 followed by the busy N10.

06 St-Émilion

The medieval village of St-Émilion perches above vineyards renowned for producing full-bodied red wines and is easily the most alluring of all the region's wine towns.

The only way to visit the town's most interesting historical sites is with one of the tourist office's varied **guided tours**.

The tourist office also organises two-hour afternoon **château visits**, and runs various events throughout the year, such as **Les Samedis de l'Oenologie**, which combines a vineyard visit, lunch, a town tour and a wine-tasting course on Saturdays.

For a fun and informative introduction to wine tasting, get stuck into a themed tasting at the wine school inside the **Maison du Vin** *(maisonduvinsaintemilion.com)*.

THE DRIVE: To get to the next stop you've simply no option but to endure the ring road around Bordeaux – avoid rush hour! Head towards Bordeaux on the N89, then south down the A63 following signs to Arcachon and then Gujan Mestras. It's a 100km journey that should, but probably won't, take an hour.

07 Gujan Mestras

Take a break from the grape and head to the seaside to eat oysters in the area around Gujan Mestras. Picturesque oyster ports are dotted around the town, but the best one to visit is **Port de Larros**, where locally harvested oysters are sold from wooden shacks. To learn more about these delicious shellfish, the small **Maison de l'Huître** *(maison-huitre.fr)* has a display on oyster farming, including a short film in English.

THE DRIVE: It's 10 sometimes-traffic-clogged but well-signposted kilometres from Gujan Mestras to Arcachon.

08 Arcachon

The seaside town of Arcachon has lured bourgeois Bordelaises since the end of the 19th century. Its four little quarters are romantically named for each of the seasons, with villas that evoke the town's golden past amid a scattering of 1950s architecture.

Arcachon's sandy beach, **Plage d'Arcachon**, is flanked by two piers. Lively **Jetée Thiers** is at the western end. In front of the eastern pier, **Jetée d'Eyrac**, stands the

ON THE WINE TRAIL

The 1000-sq-km wine-growing area around the city of Bordeaux is, along with Burgundy, France's most important producer of top-quality wines. The Bordeaux region is divided into 57 appellations, grouped in turn into seven families, then subdivided into a hierarchy of designations; *premier grand cru classé* is the most prestigious. Most of the region's reds, rosés, sweet and dry whites and sparkling wines include the abbreviation AOC (Appellation d'Origine Contrôlée) on their labels, indicating that the contents have been grown, fermented and aged according to strict regulations governing viticultural matters.

Bordeaux has more than 5000 châteaux, referring not to palatial residences but rather to the estates where grapes are grown, picked, fermented and matured as wine. A handful are open to visitors, by advance reservation only. Many close during the *vendange* (grape harvest) in October.

Whet your palate with wine-tasting workshops organised by the Bordeaux tourist office or an introductory two-hour workshop at the highly regarded **École du Vin** (Bordeaux Wine School; *ecoleduvindebordeaux.com*).

☑ TOP TIP

OYSTER TASTE TEST

Oysters from each of the Bassin d'Arcachon's four oyster-breeding zones hint at subtly different flavours.

See if you can detect these:
Banc d'Arguin – milk and sugar
Île aux Oiseaux – minerals
Cap Ferret – citrus
Grand Banc – roasted hazelnuts

town's turreted **Casino de la Plage**, built by Adalbert Deganne in 1953 as an exact replica of Château de Boursault in the Marne. Inside, it's a less-grand blinking and bell-ringing riot of poker machines and gaming tables.

On the tree-covered hillside south of the Ville d'Été, the century-old **Ville d'Hiver** (Winter Quarter) has over 300 villas ranging in style from neogothic through to colonial.

For a different view of Arcachon and its coastline, take to the ocean waves on one of the boat cruises organised by **Les Bateliers Arcachonnais** (UBA; *bateliers-arcachon.com*). It offers daily, year-round cruises around **Île aux Oiseaux**, the uninhabited 'bird island' in the middle of Arcachon bay. It's a haven for terns, curlews and redshanks, so bring your binoculars. In summer there are day excursions to the **Banc d'Arguin**, the sand bank off the Dune du Pilat.

THE DRIVE: Dune du Pilat is 12km south of Arcachon down the D218. There are restrictions on car access in summer for the last part of the route.

09 Dune du Pilat

This colossal sand dune (sometimes referred to as the Dune de Pyla because of its location in the resort town of Pyla-sur-Mer) stretches from the mouth of the Bassin d'Arcachon southwards for almost 3km. Already the largest in Europe, it's spreading eastwards at 4.5m a year – it has swallowed trees, a road junction and even a hotel.

The view from the top – approximately 114m above sea level – is magnificent. To the west you can see the sandy shoals at the mouth of the Bassin d'Arcachon, and dense dark-green pine forests stretch from the base of the dune eastwards almost as far as the eye can see. The only address to have a drink or dine afterwards is **La Co(o)rniche** *(lacoorniche.com)*, a 1930s hunting lodge transformed by French designer Philippe Starck into one of France's most stunning seaside restaurants.

Dune du Pilat
STANISLAV SIMONYAN/SHUTTERSTOCK

35

ATLANTIC COAST

GOURMET DORDOGNE

★ BEST FOR

FOODIES

Drooling at the wonderful open-air markets.

DURATION: 2 DAYS

DISTANCE: 113KM / 70 MILES

GREAT FOR: FOOD & DRINK

BEST TIME TO GO: SEPTEMBER AND OCTOBER FOR HARVEST MARKETS; DECEMBER AND FEBRUARY FOR TRUFFLES.

Outdoor market, Sarlat-la-Canéda

If you enjoy nothing better than soaking up the sights, sounds and smells of a French market, you'll be in seventh heaven in the Dordogne's picturesque villages and history-draped towns. Immersing yourself in this region's culinary culture is one of the best – and tastiest – ways to experience life in rural France. Note that for some of the best tasting experiences, calling ahead is advisable.

LINK YOUR TRIP

34 Heritage Wine Country
The hallowed vineyards of Bordeaux lie 96km to the west of Bergerac along the D936.

37 Dordogne's Fortified Villages
At the castle village of Castelnaud-la-Chapelle, this route intersects our trip visiting the Dordogne's best *bastides* (fortified market-towns).

01 Sarlat-la-Canéda

Start in the honey-stoned town of Sarlat-la-Canéda, the beautifully preserved medieval town that's the central hub of tourism in the Dordogne. It hosts a busy **outdoor market** on Saturday mornings, with a more subdued version on Wednesdays. Local farm stalls selling seasonal treats such as cèpe mushrooms, duck terrines, foie gras and walnuts fill the central place de la Liberté and radiate out into virtually every space in the town centre. There's also an atmospheric **night market**.

Even if you're not here on market day, you can shop for fine produce at Sarlat's **Marché Couvert** (Covered Market), housed in a former church, imaginatively converted by French star architect Jean Nouvel. A lift takes visitors to the tower-top for panoramic views across Sarlat's multi-spired slate rooftops.

You might choose to stay two nights in Sarlat and return here after the first day's drive: distances are short.

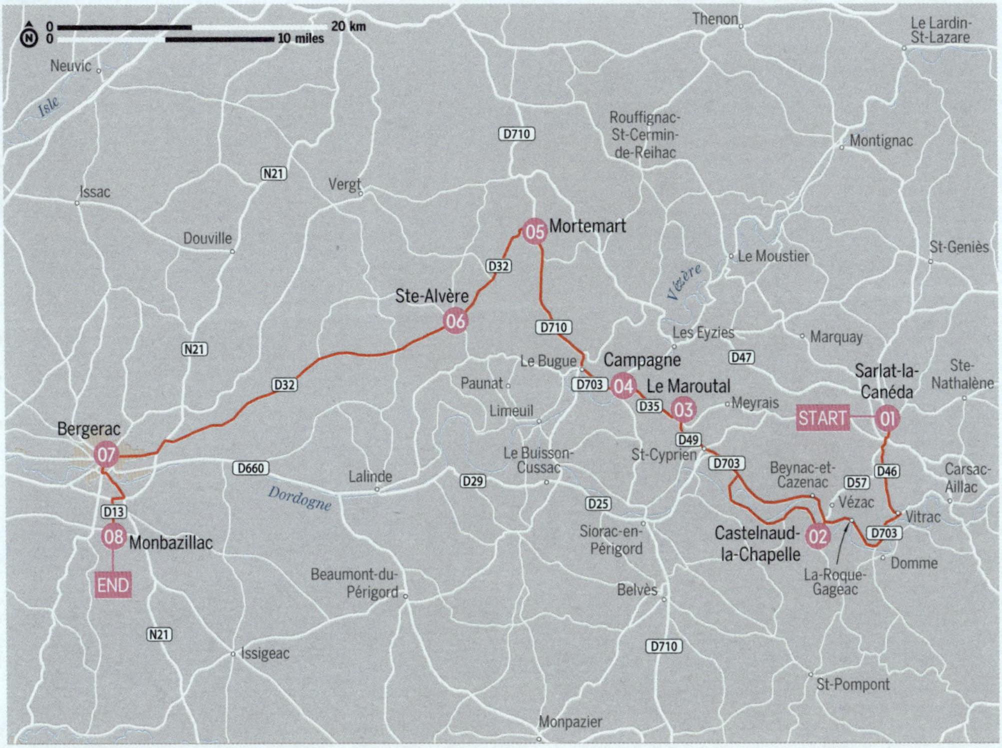

THE DRIVE: Though there's a more direct route (13km via Vézac), it's worth taking your time and an extra 6km to admire the Dordogne Valley's signature stretch of majestic castle-crowned scenery. Start by heading south to Vitrac, then turn west, approximately following the river's north bank. You'll drive right through the classic cliff-backed village of La-Roque-Gageac, a picture-perfect place to sip a waterside coffee, and for boating, canoeing or kayaking depending on your energy levels. Continuing, you pass the base of the remarkable topiary gardens of **Marqueyssac** *(marqueyssac.com)* as an unforgettably impressive trio of castles comes into view. Cross the bridge and climb through Castelnaud, initially following signs to the castle and upper car park, then turning left just after the bus park on a signed lane to the Eco-Musée de la Noix du Perigord.

02 Castelnaud-la-Chapelle

The humble *noix* (walnut) has been a prized product of the Dordogne for centuries, and remains widely used in liqueurs and many local recipes, not just the ubiquitous dessert, *gâteau de noix* (walnut cake). Set in a pretty hillside orchard, the **Eco-Musée de la Noix du Perigord** *(ecomuseedelanoix.fr)* is part farm shop, part museum at which you can watch fragrant walnut oil being made on an antiquated original mill-contraption. Lots of nut-based goodies are available. Barely 800m away, don't miss the medieval **Château de Castelnaud** *(castelnaud.com)* with its superb museum of historical weaponry.

THE DRIVE: The 19km drive northwest from Castelnaud is the same distance via either bank of the Dordogne. The north route takes you right past the domineering **Château de Beynac** *(chateau-beynac.com)*, an archetypal medieval fortress crowning the clifftop above delightful Beynac village. The south route is partly on tiny country lanes and passes the more homely **Château des Milandes** *(milandes.com)*, once home to

1920s music-hall star and civil rights activist Josephine Baker (1906–75). The two routes converge as the D703 to St-Cyprien where, opposite the station, you turn right onto the D49. Just 200m after it converges with the D35, veer right following signs to the Domaine de la Voie Blanche.

03 Le Maroutal

This part of the Dordogne isn't generally known for its wines, but **Domaine de la Voie Blanche** *(domaine-voie-blanche.com)* is a special case, and a pioneer in using earthenware amphorae instead of barrels to mature its sophisticated all-organic reds. This is a small family operation so it's worth calling ahead, but in summer the farm's tasting room is generally open.

THE DRIVE: Backtrack southwest to the D35, then follow that road to Campagne. In Campagne the postcard-perfect local castle is now an occasional exhibition centre set in a glorious park of lawns, streams and giant mature trees: entrance is free so it's well worth stretching the legs. About 1km further, the D35 crosses the river: after the bridge turn very sharp left and follow the Grolière signs for 700m.

04 Campagne

Alongside black truffles, the Dordogne is also famous for its foie gras (fattened goose liver). You'll see duck and goose farms dotted all over the countryside, many of which offer tours and a *dégustation* (tasting). A much-lauded producer, **Grolière** *(foiegras-groliere.com)*, has shops in several tourist centres, but its farm base is in a soothingly rural spot in Malmussou, across the Vézère River from Campagne, with honking geese and an enticing shop. Given a little advance notice, they'll also show you a five-minute film explaining foie gras production and let you visit the cannery.

THE DRIVE: Drive the D703 through the bustling town of Le Bugue then follow Périgueux signs onto the D710, continuing 13km north to Mortemart. If you'd rather give the boar farm a miss, an alternative, slightly circuitous route to Ste-Alvère starts off heading southwest from Le Bugue, taking in the

Château de Castelnaud (p255)

LE SIMON/SHUTTERSTOCK

SLOWMOTIONGLI/SHUTTERSTOCK

Truffle-gathering

TRUFFLE SECRETS

Few ingredients command the same culinary cachet as the *truffe noire* (black truffle), variously known as the *diamant noir* (black diamond) or, hereabouts, the *perle noire du Périgord* (black pearl of the Dordogne). The gem references aren't just for show, either: a high-end truffle crop can fetch as much as €1200 per kg.

A subterranean fungus that grows naturally in chalky soils (especially around the roots of oak trees), this mysterious mushroom is notoriously capricious; a good truffle spot one year can be bare the next, which has made farming them practically impossible. The art of truffle-hunting is a closely guarded secret; it's a matter of luck, judgement and experience, with specially trained dogs (and one lone pig) to help in the search.

In season (December to February), special truffle markets are held around the Dordogne, notably at Sarlat and Ste-Alvère.

lovely hilltop village of Limeuil, then swinging northwest via Paunat with its austere abbey church and great restaurant.

05 Mortemart

For a token fee, you can see wild boars being raised in the semi-freedom of fenced fields and woodlands at **Les Sangliers de Mortemart** *(elevage-sangliers-mortemart.com)*. These porky cousins of the modern pig are fed a rich diet of *châtaignes* (chestnuts), which gives the meat a distinctive nutty-gamey flavour. Boar meat is a key ingredient in the hearty stew known as *civet de sanglier,* as well as pâtés and country terrines. The farm's shop sells a range of home-produced boar-themed goodies.

THE DRIVE: From Mortemart, it's a lovely 12km drive through classic Dordogne countryside on the D32 to Ste-Alvère.

06 Ste-Alvère

The charming little village of Ste-Alvère has lots of genuine rustic character, and is famed as another centre for truffles. In midwinter, time your arrival for the brief but much-celebrated Monday morning **truffle market** *(truffe-perigord-noir.com)*. At other times, displays in the little **tourist office** offer insights into truffle cultivation and there are signposted walks in the nearby truffle woods. The village has two good restaurants, a cafe-bar and a foie-gras merchant.

THE DRIVE: Continue to Bergerac on the D32. Some 24km from Ste-Alvère, just before you arrive at the N21 junction, a short detour south brings you to the famed **Chateau de Tiregand winery** *(chateau-de-tiregand.com),* which offers tastings, though you can't enter the palatial castle itself. Otherwise continue 6km into Bergerac and park at Le Forail, one of the city's few free car parks. Walk 500m west along rue Junien Rabier to find the old town.

07 Bergerac

Vineyards carpet the countryside around Bergerac, producing rich reds, fragrant whites, fruity rosés and particularly famous honeyed dessert wines. With 13 Appellations d'Origines Contrôlées (AOCs), and more than 1200 growers, the choice is bewildering. Thankfully, the **Quai Cyrano** *(quai-cyrano.com)* knows all the best vintages, offers free tastings and can help you target vineyards to visit. You could happily spend at least another couple of days touring the local wineries using Bergerac as a base.

THE DRIVE: Monbazillac is 8km south of Bergerac via the D936E and then the D13.

08 Monbazillac

Of all the wines produced around Bergerac, none is more instantly recognisable than the sweet, liquid sunshine of Monbazillac. The name is also synonymous with the iconic **Château de Monbazillac** *(chateau-monbazillac.com),* a grand 16th-century château that surveys row after row of neatly planted vines on a steep slope south of Bergerac. However, the tour-bus crowds can be oppressive here and there are plenty of alternatives nearby to taste not just dessert wines but also Bergerac AOC dry whites and structured Pécharmant reds (from north of Bergerac). Family-run **Château Montdoyen** *(chateau-montdoyen.com)* is a good, offbeat choice whose wines take curious catch-phrase names.

Château de Monbazillac

SERGEY KELIN/SHUTTERSTOCK

PHOTO OPPORTUNITY

Monbazillac's conical château turrets rising above endless neat rows of vines.

36

ATLANTIC COAST

CAVE ART OF THE VÉZÈRE VALLEY

★ BEST FOR

FAMILIES

Le Thot's 'prehistoric' zoo hosts bison, reindeer and ibex.

DURATION: 3 DAYS

DISTANCE: 79KM / 50 MILES

GREAT FOR: FAMILIES, HISTORY & CULTURE

BEST TIME TO GO: APRIL TO JUNE, WHEN MOST SITES ARE OPEN, BUT THE SUMMER CROWDS HAVEN'T ARRIVED.

Musée National de Préhistoire, Les Eyzies

This trip feels like opening a time capsule into the prehistoric past. Hidden deep underground in murky caves around the Vézère Valley, Cro-Magnon people left behind a remarkable legacy of ancient artworks, ranging from rock sculptures to multicoloured murals – and this is one of the few places in the world where it's possible to see their work up close. Best of all, the caves are set in beautiful rural countryside that makes for lovely driving.

LINK YOUR TRIP

35 Gourmet Dordogne
Lascaux IV is 27km north of Sarlat-la-Canéda, the start of our Gourmet tour, which also passes through Campagne, just 6km southwest of Les Eyzies.

38 The Lot Valley
From Sarlat-la-Canéda, it's another 10km drive to either Beynac or Domme, both on the Fortified Villages route.

01 Les Eyzies

Hugging an overhanging curl of cliff, this attractive little tourist village, 20km northwest of Sarlat-la-Canéda, is the ideal starting point for exploring the Vézère Valley. Most major caves are within half-an-hour's drive, but tickets for some are in short supply, so both timing and planning are important. Think ahead by prebooking online for Lascaux (day 3). Then on day 1, dash straight for the ticket booth at Fond de Gaume, joining the early morning queue. Hopefully, you'll be able to score tickets to Comberelles as well as Font de Gaume; both have extremely limited availability, online booking is impossible and tickets must be bought on the day of your visit and in person (so you can't send just one of your group to buy for everyone). While you're here, you could also buy the Cap Blanc ticket to get a reduced combo-price for the three entrances. If you've started late and no tickets remain, consider rerouting your driving trip and then

MAXIME VILLAEYS/MUSÉE NATIONAL DE PRÉHISTOIRE

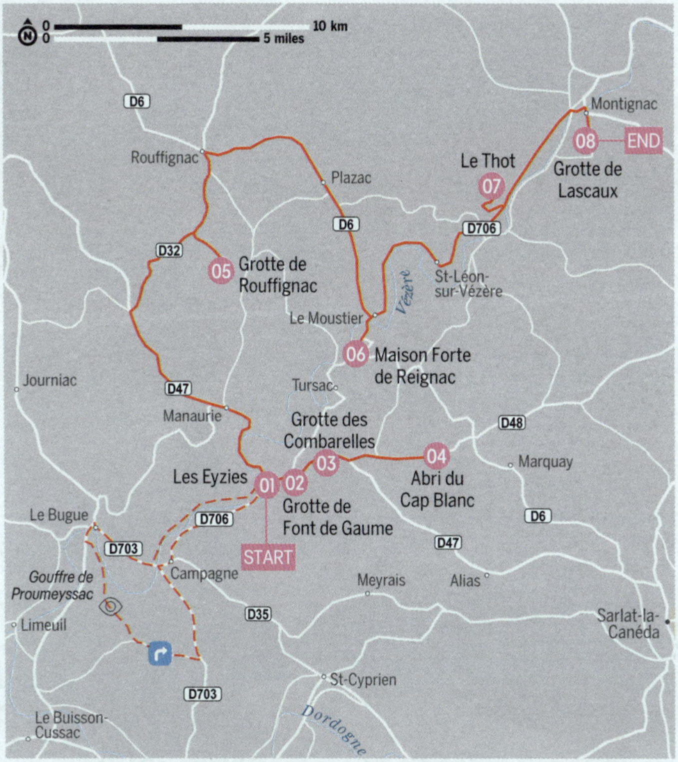

trying again early next morning. Once your tickets are arranged, you'll probably have some time before (or between) your visiting slots. So head back into Les Eyzies and acquaint yourself with the cultures of the prehistoric human cave-artists through brief film-presentations at **PIP** (Pôle Internationale de la Prehistoire; *pole-prehistoire.com*), a free, modernist exhibition centre. To learn a whole lot more, walk 400m west from PIP along a pretty, pedestrian lane to the **Musée National de Préhistoire** *(musee-prehistoire-eyzies.fr)*, home to France's most comprehensive collection of prehistoric artefacts from Stone Age tools and jewellery to animal skeletons and original rock friezes taken from the caves. Allow an hour or two to do it justice.

THE DRIVE: Font de Gaume is barely 1km east along the D47.

DETOUR

Gouffre de Proumeyssac

Start: 01 Les Eyzies

If you find you've got to wait a day for another shot at getting Font de Gaume tickets, why not visit a very different type of cave that's attractive for its sheer beauty rather than its ancient art? The **Gouffre de Proumeyssac** *(gouffre-proumeyssac.com)*, 22km southwest of Les Eyzies, displays its magnificent 'cathedral' of stalactites through a very professional sound-and-light show and offers the unique opportunity (extra fee) of descending into the gaping space on an 11-person dangling basket. Booking an arrival slot is wise, online in July and August, or by phone at other times. The audioguide is a very worthwhile extra.

02 Grotte de Font de Gaume

Now you've got the background, it's time to see some real cave art. **Font de Gaume** *(sites-les-eyzies.fr)* is a particularly celebrated underground cavern as it contains the only original multicoloured cave paintings that are still open to public view in their original state. Its full 'gallery' contains over 230 animal images and includes reindeer, horses, mammoths, bisons and bears, though only limited sections are visited, illuminated solely by the guide's torch. Of the six daily tours (each maximum 13 people) just the 11.15am and/or 4pm tours are usually in English.

THE DRIVE: Continue along the D47 for 1km from Font de Gaume and turn off at the brown sign for the Grotte des Combarelles. Be sure to arrive at least 10 minutes before the time slot on the ticket, which you'll need to have prepurchased at Font de Gaume earlier that day.

03 Grotte des Combarelles

The narrow, very long **Grotte des Combarelles** *(sites-les-eyzies.fr)* is renowned for animal designs that are engraved rather than painted. Squint in the guide's lamp-light to make out scratched forms of mammoths, horses, reindeer and human figures, as well as a fantastic mountain lion that seems to leap from the rock face. Claustrophobes beware.

THE DRIVE: Travel 1km further east of Combarelles, then turn left onto the twisty D48 into a pleasant wooded valley.

K

Continue for 7km, following the road up the hillside towards the Cap Blanc car park. The museum entrance is a short walk downhill along a rough track.

GRANGER - HISTORICAL PICTURE ARCHIVE/ALAMY

04 Abri du Cap Blanc

This ancient **sculpture gallery** *(sites-les-eyzies.fr)* makes a fascinating comparison with Combarelles. It's a cliff-overhang that was used as a natural shelter 14,000 years ago by Cro-Magnon people, who left behind an amazing 40m-long frieze of horses and bison, carved directly into the rear wall of the site using flint tools. Originally the cave would have been open to the elements, but it's now fronted by a modern museum.

THE DRIVE: Backtrack to Les Eyzies (10km) and stay overnight. Next morning start early, cross the river and follow the pleasant but busy D47 northwest. Initially the route is squeezed between cliffs and the Vézère as you pass the Grotte de Grand Roc cave entrance. Then it climbs the Manaurie Valley, paralleling the railway. Around 11km from Les Eyzies, 250m after you pass the big viaduct beside the farmstead of La Loulie, fork right onto the narrower D32. That road climbs through woodlands onto an agricultural plateau, where after 5km you'll need to turn right. A brown sign says 'Grotte Préhistorique de Rouffignac 2km' but it's easy to miss.

05 Grotte de Rouffignac

The astonishing **Grotte de Rouffignac** *(grottederouffignac.fr)* is often known as the 'Cave of 1000 Mammoths' thanks to its plethora of painted pachyderms. The paintings are spread along the walls of a subterranean cavern system that stretches over 8km in total, though you won't see all of that and the visit is made easier thanks to a rickety electric train: no chance of getting lost. Along the way, a highlight is a frieze of 10 mammoths in procession. You'll also see many hollows in the cave floor, scratched out by long-extinct cave bears. Tickets are sold at the cave entrance.

Lascaux IV (p264)

FREEPROD33/SHUTTERSTOCK

Cave painting, Grotte de Rouffignac

PREHISTORY 101

The earliest cave art around the Vézère dates from approximately 20,000 BCE, during the last ice age. The artists were early modern humans, known to history as Cro-Magnon people after the cave where their first remains were discovered. They lived a hunter-gatherer lifestyle using the mouths of caves as temporary hunting shelters, though why they ventured much deeper inside to paint the walls remains a mystery: it's assumed that the images held some kind of magical, religious or shamanic significance. Designs range from geometric forms and occasional stylised humans to depictions of the various animals that the artists hunted, notably mammoths, woolly rhinoceros, reindeer and aurochs – ancestors of the modern cow. Some were scratched, a few were chipped as sculptures and many more were painted using mineral pigments, including charcoal (black), ochre (red/yellow) and iron-ore (red). The painting seems to have ceased around 11,000 BCE, about the same time that temperatures rose, many predators became extinct, and humans settled down to a more fixed lifestyle of farming and agriculture.

THE DRIVE: From the Grotte de Rouffignac, retrace your route 2km north then turn right, taking the D32 to the roundabout in Rouffignac, a large village whose lack of old buildings is a result of WWII destruction – German reprisals for the daring of the French Resistance. Take the D6, curving back south on a pretty route that descends a ridge through Plazac to rejoin the Vézère Valley at Le Moustier (15km total). Neanderthal bones have been found near here. As you cross the river, a cliff rising to the left is incised with a very long abri (cliff-overhang shelter) known as La Roque St-Cristophe. Keep ahead, however, and continue 2.5km south (towards Les Eyzies) for the Maison Forte de Reignac.

06 Maison Forte de Reignac

Three-storey medieval **Maison Forte de Reignac** *(maison-forte-reignac.com)* was built straight into the cliff face using abri-caves that once sheltered prehistoric humans. Now the mansion is kitted out with period furnishing and displays of everything from prehistoric finds to medieval weaponry. Even if you don't go in, it's photogenic when seen from outside.

THE DRIVE: If you missed out on Font de Gaume earlier, you could nip back from here to Les Eyzies and try again for a ticket tomorrow. Otherwise, head northwest towards Montignac through the pretty village of St-Léon-sur-Vézère with its dainty mini-castle in a walled, riverside garden. Le Thot is 1.8km off the main D706.

07 Le Thot

Head to **Le Thot** *(parc-thot.fr)* to meet 3D beasts that were depicted by prehistoric artists. Some, including reindeer, stags, horses, ibex and European bison, live in the park. Others – like woolly mammoths – have fibreglass stand-ins since the real animals are long extinct. Combo tickets including Lascaux IV can save a little money.

THE DRIVE: Get back onto the D706 and head for Montignac (7km), an attractive riverside town, to explore, dine and sleep. Next morning, head to the hilltop 1km south of town, where you'll find the entrance to Lascaux IV.

08 Grotte de Lascaux

Sometimes nicknamed the Sistine Chapel of cave art, the Lascaux caves are home to France's most famous – and finest – prehistoric paintings. Though the original cave has been closed for its protection since 1963, **Lascaux IV** (International Centre for Cave Art; *lascaux.fr*) is a cutting-edge copy. Using laser technology and 3D printing, the exact contours, engravings and nearly 600 paintings have been reproduced to the millimetre, and the result feels remarkably like a real cave – it's damp, dark and chilly, and the whole experience can be spine-tingling.

After the hour-long cave visit, you're turned loose with a tablet to explore the excellent **Lascaux Studio**, where life-size renderings of all the major scenes are given context with superimposed images, and there's a multimedia show, a 3D film and an interactive gallery examining relationships between prehistoric and modern art.

Online reservations (advisable) can be made up to two days ahead. A certain number of same-day tickets are sold on-site, so if you show up bright and early you might still get in.

Maison Forte de Reignac
PACK-SHOT/SHUTTERSTOCK

PHOTO OPPORTUNITY

A fortified mansion squeezed into the cliff-overhang at Reignac.

37

ATLANTIC COAST

DORDOGNE'S FORTIFIED VILLAGES

DURATION: 5 DAYS

DISTANCE: 230KM / 143 MILES

GREAT FOR: HISTORY & CULTURE

BEST TIME TO GO: APRIL OR OCTOBER, WHEN RESTAURANTS ARE OPEN, BUT TOURIST NUMBERS ARE MANAGEABLE.

★ BEST FOR

HISTORY

The superb museum of medieval armour within the classic castle at Castelnaud.

Château de Castelnaud (p268)

The Dordogne Valley may be a picture of tranquillity now, but during the Hundred Years' War it often marked the military frontier between antagonistic English and French forces. The area's many châteaux and fortified villages are a reminder of this war-torn past and especially distinctive features are *bastides,* whose square-grid street plans are focused on a central marketplace, originally encircled by defensive walls and ramparts.

LINK YOUR TRIP

35 Gourmet Dordogne
In Beynac you can link up with our gastronomic road trip around the Dordogne.

38 The Lot Valley
This trip meets our route along the Lot Valley at the enchanting medieval town of Figeac.

01 Monflanquin

Founded in 1256, beautifully preserved Monflanquin crowns a hilltop, its roads forming the gridlike street layout of a classic *bastide* but with an unusual slope to its market square, the **place des Arcades**. That's lined by impressive *passages couverts* (covered shopping arcades) and buildings in a picturesque mixture of architectural styles. Here you'll find a **tourist office** *(coeurdebastides.com)* that doubles as a museum about *bastides,* and four very tempting dining options in differing price ranges. Thursday is market day year-round, plus in July and August there's a **musical night market**.

THE DRIVE: Start east along the D150 signed to Salles. After 4km turn north on the narrow D235 via Paulhiac. Much of the drive is through forest but after 11km you'll spot the impressive castle

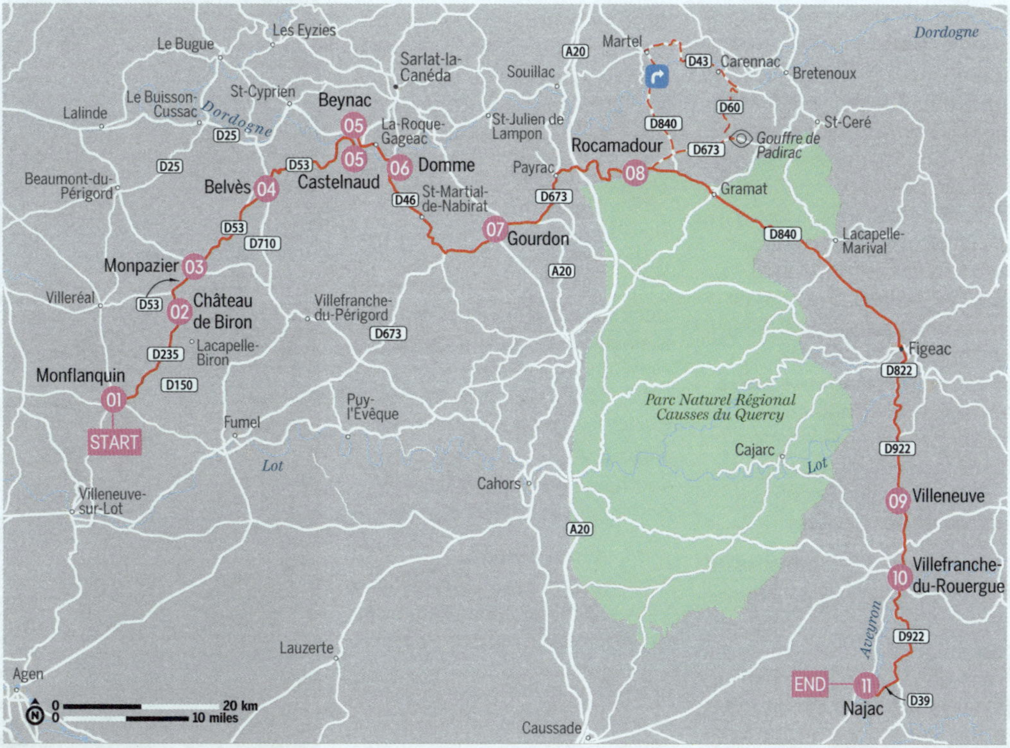

AURELIEN KEMPF-PIKSL/SHUTTERSTOCK

ahead across fields. Turn left at the D53 crossroads.

02 Château de Biron

Looming agressively on a prominent hilltop, the much-filmed **Château de Biron** *(chateau-biron.fr)* is one of the most formidable fortresses in the region. It's a glorious mishmash of styles, having been fiddled with by eight centuries of successive heirs. You'll get a pretty good idea of the place from walking round the photogenic hamlet outside, but paying for an entry ticket allows you inside to see regularly changing exhibitions of contemporary art along with some grand fireplaces and a double loggia staircase supposedly modelled on one at Versailles. Ticket sales end one hour before closing.

THE DRIVE: Monpazier is around 8km from Biron; head north then northeast.

03 Monpazier

Monpazier is perhaps the best example of *bastide* architecture in southwest France. It's criss-crossed by arrow-straight streets, some barely a shoulder's width, and retains gateway towers from the fortifications that would once have surrounded it. The arcaded **place Centrale** is a gem with an ancient-timbered market hall in one corner complete with a trio of original grain measures.

Despite its small size, Monpazier has several restaurants, pottery workshops, a glass-blowing studio, a hatter, an unexpectedly contemporary barista coffee shop and a superb British-run microbrewery all within a couple of minutes' walk.

THE DRIVE: Take the D53 northeast from Monpazier, and follow it for 16km. Much of the route is through lichen-bearded woodlands.

04 Belvès

Another of the Dordogne's great hilltop fortress-towns, Belvès is an atmospheric hodge-podge of medieval tower-houses and fine viewpoints with a reasonable assortment of eating and drinking options.

The beautiful old-wooden **market hall** remains almost intact, with just a few 'golden' beams replacing a small area of fire damage. A neck-ring from a former pillory is still attached to one upright.

Half a dozen subterranean former **cave dwellings** can be visited by arrangement with the tourist office.

THE DRIVE: The most direct route to Beynac (22km) is north up the D710, then along the Dordogne Valley on the D703. For confident drivers, a lovely alternative uses much smaller (indeed at times minuscule) back lanes wiggling northeast across country to the garden-set Château de Milandes (16km). Further tiny lanes cross the ridge to the Château de Castelnaud (5km). Beneath Castelnaud village you can cross the river and backtrack another 5km to Beynac.

05 Beynac & Castelnaud

The **Château de Beynac** *(chateau-beynac.com)* is surely the most dramatic of all the medieval fortresses that guard the Dordogne's cliff-edged banks. Mostly built during the 12th and 13th centuries, it is perched above a picture-perfect village that featured in the Lasse Hallström movie *Chocolat* (2000). From the ramparts you gaze upriver across one of France's most magical landscapes, dotted with several other castles. The most notable (4.5km southwest) is the **Château de Castelnaud** *(castelnaud.com)*, hosting a particularly impressive museum of medieval warfare. Facing it across the river, the **Jardins de Marqueyssac** *(marqueyssac.com)* are superb topiary gardens high atop a river-view promenade.

THE DRIVE: The route from Beynac to Domme follows the meandering Dordogne through its most classic castle-dotted section and past the ultra-photogenic village of La Roque Gageac, pressed magically into the cliff side by the river: a fine place for boat rides or kayaking. Cross the river to Cenac and wind steeply up to Domme. In summer you'll generally need to park outside the walls and walk in.

06 Domme

Combining panoramic views across the Dordogne Valley with 13th-century ramparts, original fortified gateways and plentiful cafes and souvenir shops, Domme is a well-preserved *bastide* high on a prominent outcrop. While deservedly popular, the tourist crowds can get overwhelming in summer.

THE DRIVE: The D46 heads southeast through St-Martial-de-Nabirat to Gourdon (25km).

07 Gourdon

Bigger, less complete, but far less visited than Domme, Gourdon has a compact medieval core that slopes up steeply from a ring avenue of cafes. Follow charming rue de Majou past tall, old buildings to the sturdy central church, then take the stairway up to an esplanade with a 360-degree panorama of vast proportions. This was once the site of one of the region's great hilltop castles, but that was completely dismantled after 1619 as a punishment for the lord of Gourdon's disobedience towards French king Louis XIII. Nothing remains but the viewpoint.

THE DRIVE: Pick up the twisty D673, which crosses underneath the A20 motorway, winding on with fine views across the Ouysse River and the cliffs around Rocamadour after 30km. There are car parks at the top and bottom of Rocamadour and several more in L'Hospitalet, around 1km beyond, but the village itself is pedestrianised.

Rocamadour (p271)

PAOLO BUGNONE/GETTY IMAGES

PHOTO OPPORTUNITY

Rocamadour at dusk seen across the valley.

08 Rocamadour

Clinging precariously to a rocky cliff side, the holy town of Rocamadour looks like something out of *The Lord of the Rings*. It's been an important pilgrimage destination since the Middle Ages thanks to the supposedly miraculous powers of its Vierge Noire (Black Madonna), which is now housed in the Chapelle de Notre Dame, one of several chapels that make up the town's holy hub, the **Sanctuaires** (Sanctuaries). These are accessed up a long stairway (or lift) from the one commercial street that overflows (just as in the pilgrims' day) with souvenir shops and touristy restaurants. One of the medieval gateways is still standing at the end of this 'Grande Rue'.

Alternatively, from the Sanctuaires you can climb to the clifftop via a switchback footpath/stairway following the Stations of the Cross and emerging next to Rocamadour's dinky little 14th-century **château**. During the Middle Ages, pilgrims would have climbed the route on their knees as a demonstration of piety. These days you can cheat by catching a funicular.

THE DRIVE: A 45km drive southeast brings you to historic Figeac, which is well worth a stop to explore, have lunch and consider an overnight stay. From there, head due south on the D822: it's an attractive 23km run once you're clear of the industrial zone on Figeac's upper southern edge.

DETOUR

Martel & Carennac

Start: 08 Rocamadour

Historic **Martel**, 22km north of Rocamadour, was the ancient capital of the Vicomte de Turenne. It's locally famed for its seven (fairly modest) towers, including Tour Tournemire (once a prison) and Tour des Cordeliers (the last remnant of a 13th-century Franciscan monastery). Most memorable is the central square with its covered market hall (active Wednesday and Saturday), within a stone's throw of which are several great places to drink and eat: don't miss the wonderfully rustic farm shop-restaurant **Au Hasard Balthazar** *(auhasardbalthazar.fr)*.

From Martel, follow the D43 18km east along the Dordogne to idyllic **Carennac**, a tiny riverside village that wraps stone buildings so tightly around its former castle that the latter is virtually invisible. It contains a church with a magnificent tympanum and cloister plus a small museum section. With a minor detour you can loop back to Rocamadour (26km) via the **Gouffre de Padirac** *(gouffre-de-padirac.com)*, a mineral-spangled cave system with an underground lake that you visit by boat.

09 Villeneuve

Worth a 10-minute stop as you whizz by, Villeneuve is an oval lozenge of historical fortified village complete with two portcullis gates.

THE DRIVE: Villefranche is 11km south of Villeneuve. Driving into the heart of the old centre is impractical, but several metered car parks are well placed along the diamond-shaped inner ring road (the first hour is free).

10 Villefranche-de-Rouergue

Once you get through its sprawling outskirts, Villefranche's mostly pedestrianised centre reveals itself as a beautifully preserved *bastide* grid. At its centre is the **place Notre Dame**, host to one of the region's most authentic weekly markets (Thursdays). The square's wide stone arcades are broken in the northeast corner by the arch-base tower of the city's main church, the **Collégiale Notre Dame**. Inside, the wooden choir stalls are ornamented with a menagerie of comical and cheeky figures. Two blocks southwest via rue du Sergent Bories, **place Grifol** (place de la Fontaine) is a sunken square centred upon an octagonal 1336 fountain that was once the city's public laundry.

THE DRIVE: The D922 continues south towards Najac, 23km from Villefranche.

11 Najac

If you were searching for a film set for Camelot, you've found it. Najac's long, wide village square is memorable enough for its medieval cottages. But what's so special is the photo-perfect view from its western end, where the cascade of descending antique buildings perfectly frames a medieval **castle** that tops the next hillock along. Straight from the pages of a fairy tale, the austere tower flutters with flags and pennants, while on either side dizzyingly steep slopes plunge into the Aveyron River far below.

The main access footpath (unsuitable for those with limited mobility) passes the **Maison du Gouverneur** *(maisondugouverneur-najac.fr)*, a powerfully built 13th-century stone mansion with exhibits about local history.

In winter, most dining options close, but a cafe-bar and a *boulangerie* (bakery) are open year-round.

Najac

MEHDI33300/SHUTTERSTOCK

38

ATLANTIC COAST

THE LOT VALLEY

★ BEST FOR

FAMILIES

Paddling down the Lot River in a kayak from Bouziès.

DURATION: 3 DAYS

DISTANCE: 176KM / 109 MILES

GREAT FOR: FAMILIES, NATURE

BEST TIME TO GO: MARCH TO MAY, WHEN THE VALLEY IS AT ITS MOST TRANQUIL.

Kayaking, Bouziès

For river scenery, the Lot is right up there alongside the Loire and the Seine. Over countless millennia, it's carved its way through the area's soft lemon-yellow limestone, creating a landscape of canyons, ravines and cliffs, best seen on the zigzagging 80km-odd section between Faycelles and Cahors. It's a journey to savour: take your time, pack a picnic and soak up the vistas.

LINK YOUR TRIP

31 Cheat's Compostela
This route intersects with our road-trip version of the Chemin de St-Jacques at Cahors and Figeac.

37 Dordogne's Fortified Villages
Figeac is also on our *bastide* and fortress tour, which begins at Monflanquin around 20km north of the Lot Valley.

01 Figeac

Riverside Figeac is packed with gems of medieval and Renaissance architecture, yet has a lived-in authenticity trumping that of many more tourist-centric places. Founded by Benedictine monks, the town was later an important medieval trading post, a leather-making centre and a pilgrim stopover.

Figeac is also famous as the birthplace of François Champollion (1790–1832), the Egyptologist and linguist whose efforts in deciphering the Rosetta Stone provided the key for cracking hieroglyphics. Explore his story at the engrossing **Musée Champollion** *(musee-champollion.fr)* in the heart of the old town.

THE DRIVE: The corkscrew drive west of Figeac along the D662 is a classic, descending steeply from the pretty hamlet of Faycelles, then tracking the course

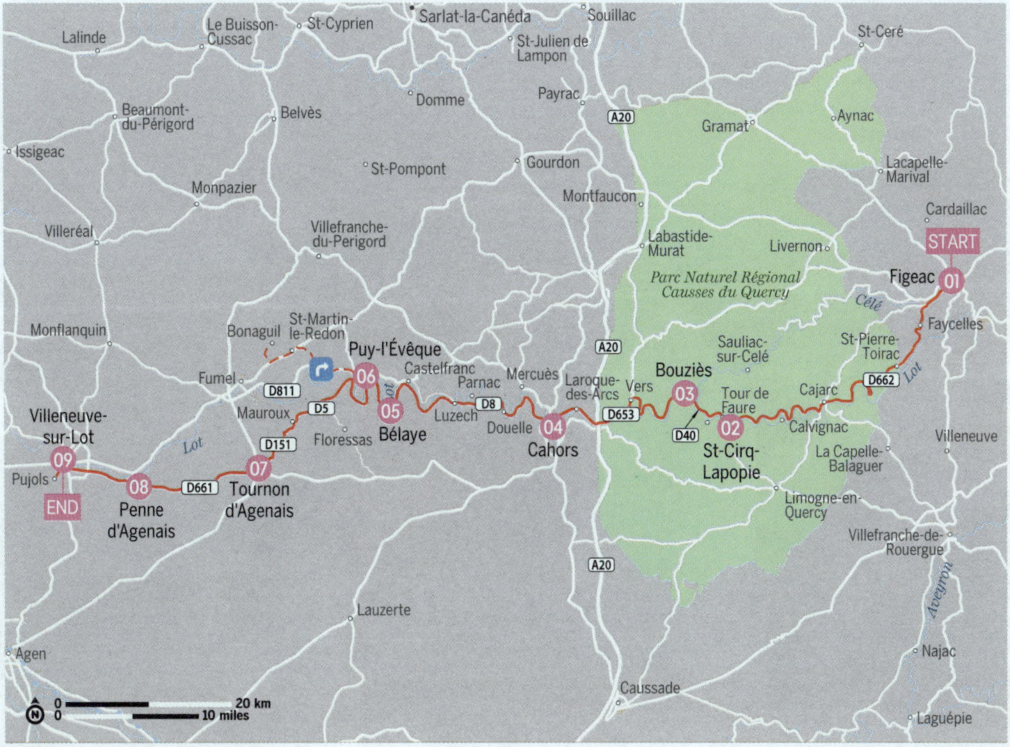

of the Lot River all the way to Cahors. The 48km stretch of road to St-Cirq-Lapopie is particularly scenic, at some points cut directly into the cliff side, at others snaking along the peaceful riverbanks. Take it slowly and enjoy the drive, making regular stops at a whole series of delightful villages en route. Don't miss a brief glimpse of the cliff-side castle in Larroque-Toriac, consider a meal stop in Cajarc and admire the serrated village silhouette of Calvignac topping a ridge across the river – especially dramatic at sunset. At Tour de Faure cross the bridge and climb 3km west to St-Cirq.

02 St-Cirq-Lapopie

This famously photogenic hilltop village teeters at the crest of a sheer cliff, high above the Lot. It's a delightful tangle of red-roofed houses, cobbled streets and medieval buildings, many of which now house potters' and artists' studios. The village is essentially one long, steep main street; at the top is the ruined **château**, which has a magnificent viewing terrace that overlooks the whole Lot Valley. It's a magical setting, but be warned: if it's peace and tranquillity you're looking for, you won't find it in high summer when the access lanes can get jammed with visitors. Car parks ring the village at a discreet distance.

THE DRIVE: Leave St-Cirq heading east, being careful not to miss a poorly signed right-hand turn after 1.1km. Descend steeply for 5km and you'll reach the river at Bouziès.

03 Bouziès

In front of Bouziès' very functional Hotel Les Fallaises, **Les Croisères de St-Cirq-Lapopie** *(croisieres-saint-cirq-lapopie.com)* runs regular river cruises on its small fleet of boats, including aboard an open-topped *gabarre,* a traditional flat-bottomed barge. A narrow suspension bridge crosses the Lot from Bouziès village, joining the main D662 beneath a curious cliff side. Closer inspection shows that it is riddled with little caves that had once been fortified into ancient retreat-shelters.

PHOTO OPPORTUNITY

Standing on top of St-Cirq-Lapopie's ruined sky-top château.

Around 1km east, **Kalapca** *(kalapca.com)* hires out kayaks and canoes, perfect for experiencing the gorgeous river scenery at your own pace. It also has a zip line right across the valley to take in the scene from the air.

Some 6.5km north of here via Cabarets is the entrance to the 1200m-long **Grotte du Pech Merle** *(pechmerle.com)* with prehistoric art from painted mammoths to hand tracings. Booking ahead online is recommended year-round and essential on summer weekends.

THE DRIVE: The twisty 28km riverside route to Cahors is a gently appealing drive. En route, tiny Laroque-des-Arcs is worth a brief stop to photograph its small chapel on a rock pillar. In Cahors there is free parking on place Charles de Gaulle, or a free half-hour by meter close to Pont Valentré if you just want snaps of the famous bridge.

04 Cahors

Nestled in a U-shaped bend in the Lot, Cahors is the area's main city with a thoroughly charming historic core and the **Pont Valentré**, one of France's most iconic medieval bridges. Built as part of the city's 14th-century defences, the bridge has three tall defensive towers that give it a distinctive form.

It's also worth stepping inside the **Cathédrale St-Étienne**, Cahors' beautiful 12th-century cathedral, most notable for the mixture of swooning saints and barbaric stabbings on its sculpted north portal.

Cahors brands itself the Capital of Malbec: don't miss sampling a selection of the region's splendidly rich reds at the **Malbec Lounge** attached to the city centre tourist office. If these appeal, there are plenty of wineries to visit, especially once you reach Puy-l'Évêque.

THE DRIVE: Head west of town via the D8, following signs to Luzech. A short detour into Parnac, on a peninsula of the Lot, reveals a dazzling wealth of vines from the Cahors AOC. The route crosses a neck of the Lot at Luzech, with its single medieval street, fortress tower and riverfront tea shop-lunch stop, Quai N°5. The road roughly parallels the river's south bank, passing close to Castelfranc where, just across the suspension bridge, there's a delightfully 'real' cafe-bar. As the road swings south again, a 2km hairpin detour zigzags up to Bélaye, 35km total drive from Cahors.

05 Bélaye

The hamlet of Bélaye is tiny and its ancient fortifications are very much a series of ruins, partly recycled into local houses. It's worth the short detour for the viewpoint with its magnificent panorama across a bend in the Lot. It's right beside a seasonal cafe, which essentially opens on holidays and whenever the sun shines.

THE DRIVE: The drive to Puy-l'Évêque via Grézels is just 10km, but wine buffs might consider adding an extra 13km loop via Floressas to take in two very different Malbec wine-tasting experiences. In a lovely hilltop setting 1km east of the village, **Château Chambert** *(chambert.com)* is easy as a drop-in site with an impressive welcome room that becomes a bistro in summer. Right in Floressas, **Château Laur** *(vignobles-laur.fr/en)* is a smaller outfit that's unique in using its deeply coloured Malbec grapes not just for full-bodied reds but also to make sparkling and dry white wines. Floressas to Puy-l'Évêque is 9km.

06 Puy-l'Évêque

On a rocky hillside above the northern bank of the Lot, Puy-l'Évêque was once one of the most important medieval ports in the Lot Valley. The former quays are lined with once-grand merchants' houses and the old town climbs a steep, deep-cleft valley topped with a fortress tower (now the town hall) and many medieval stone mansions, mostly tumbledown and decaying. The scene is best appreciated from the main road bridge that spans the Lot. For touring the Cahors wineries, Puy-l'Évêque is an ideal base. Around 4km southwest at Bru near Vire-sur-Lot, try comparing the Malbecs at suave **Clos Triguedina** *(famille-baldes.com)*, where there's a museum and guided-tour option, with those at next-door **Château Nozières** *(chateaunozieres.com)*, a merrily unpretentious family place offering free tasters, some dispensed directly from the inox tanks to your glass via petrol-style pumps.

THE DRIVE: Head southwest through classic river-valley wine country then climb into the hills on the D5 via Mauroux to Tournon (18km).

St-Cirq-Lapopie (p273)

JON CHICA/SHUTTERSTOCK

DETOUR

Bonaguil

Start: 06 Puy-l'Évêque

If you have some extra time, or don't fancy touring the wineries, an easy detour from Puy-l'Évêque takes you on narrow back lanes to the tiny hamlet of **St-Martin-le-Redon** with its impressive midsized Romanesque church. Continuing northwest, the road reveals the first breathtaking view of the **Château de Bonaguil** between trees. It's a fine example of late-15th-century military architecture, incorporating towers, bastions, loopholes, machicolations and crenellations. Although ruined, the powerful walls that remain are extremely impressive. There's a couple of places at which to eat at the base of the castle and just down the lane is a historic *lavoir* (village washing point).

07 Tournon d'Agenais

The region is pimpled with impressive hilltop *bastides,* but unlike many, Tournon is a little off the tourist trail so you're likely to have the sweeping rampart views pretty much to yourself. The cosy central square has a hotel, a small restaurant and a *brocante*-cafe, but facilities are otherwise limited.

THE DRIVE: Driving west to Penne d'Agenais (16km) you're fired down a series of long straight roads through undulating fields and classic French countryside.

08 Penne d'Agenais

The old core of Penne crowns a high, steep ridge looking down on the Lot. The town's most visible landmark is the silvered dome of a 19th-century neo-Byzantine **pilgrims' church**, and there's plenty of charm in the climb that takes you there from the main square up a doglegged lane past several older buildings.

THE DRIVE: Villeneuve is a straight run 11km west on the D661.

09 Villeneuve-sur-Lot

Villeneuve should be a great discovery – a 1253 *bastide* retaining two prominent gatehouse towers and a gridlike city plan curiously cut in half by the river. There's a 13th-century bridge, a market square and a soaring brick church (1930s), but sadly the overall feel is slightly downtrodden and you'd do best to hurry 3km south through the sprawling suburbs to contrastingly charming **Pujols**. In a cute medieval hamlet on a ridgetop with extensive views, here you'll find a free museum-shop of handmade wooden toys, a bell tower/gateway, several arts studios and a couple of restaurants.

Penne d'Agenais

CHRISATPPS/SHUTTERSTOCK

39

ATLANTIC COAST

ATLANTIC TO MED

★ BEST FOR

FAMILIES

La Rochelle, with child-friendly attractions and boats.

DURATION: 10 DAYS

DISTANCE: 1498KM / 931 MILES

GREAT FOR: FOOD & DRINK, HISTORY & CULTURE

BEST TIME TO GO: SPRING OR AUTUMN, FOR WARM WEATHER SANS THE CROWDS.

IMPORTANT: SNOW TYRES/CHAINS/SOCKS REQUIRED 1 NOVEMBER – 31 MARCH.

La Rochelle

In May the film starlets of the world pour into Cannes to celebrate a year of movie-making. Let them have their moment of glam – by the time you've finished scaling Pyrenean heights, chewing Basque tapas, acting like a medieval knight in a turreted castle and riding to the moon in a spaceship, you too will have the makings of a prize-winning film.

LINK YOUR TRIP

10 Breton Coast
The windswept coast of Brittany is a wild tonic to the south's refined atmosphere. Drive three hours north of La Rochelle to start the trip in Vannes.

24 Riviera Crossing
Starting in Nice, this drive takes you through the glitzy, glam French Riviera.

01 La Rochelle

Known as La Ville Blanche (the White City), La Rochelle is home to luminous limestone facades, arcaded walkways, half-timbered houses and gargoyles glowing in the coastal sunlight. A prominent French seaport from the 14th to the 17th centuries, it remains one of France's most attractive seafaring cities.

There are several defensive towers around the **Vieux Port** (Old Port), including the lacy **Tour de la Lanterne** *(tours-la-rochelle.fr)* that once served to protect the town at night in times of war. Scale their sturdy stone heights for fabulous city and coastal views.

La Rochelle's number-one tourist attraction is its state-of-the-art **aquarium** *(aquarium-larochelle.com)*. Equally fun for families is the **Musée Maritime** (Maritime Museum; *museemaritime.larochelle.fr*), with its fleet of boats to explore, and a

SGR WILDLIFE PHOTOGRAPHY/SHUTTERSTOCK

trip out to sea with **Croisières Inter-Îles** *(inter-iles.com)* to admire the unusual iceberg of an island fortress, Fort Boyard.

THE DRIVE: Using the main A10 toll road it's 187km (about 2½ hours) to St-Émilion. Turn off the A10 at exit 39a, signed for Libourne. Skirt this industrial town and follow the D243 into St-Émilion.

DETOUR

Île de Ré

Start: 01 La Rochelle

Bathed in the southern sun, drenched in a languid atmosphere and scattered with villages of green-shuttered, whitewashed buildings with red Spanish-tile roofs, Île de Ré is one of the most delightful places on the west coast of France. The island spans just 30km from its most easterly and westerly points, and just 5km at its widest section. But take note: the secret's out and in high season it can be almost impossible to move around and even harder to find a place to stay.

On the northern coast, about 12km from the toll bridge that links the island to La Rochelle, is the quaint fishing port of **St-Martin-de-Ré**, the island's main town. Surrounded by 17th-century fortifications (you can stroll along most of the ramparts) constructed by Vauban, the port town is a mesh of streets filled with craft shops, art galleries and sea-spray ocean views.

The island's best beaches are along the southern edge – including unofficial naturist beaches at **Rivedoux Plage** and **La Couarde-sur-Mer** – and around the western tip (northeast and southeast of Phare-des-Baleines). Many beaches are bordered by dunes that have been fenced off to protect the vegetation.

From La Rochelle it's 24km and a half-hour drive to St-Martin-de-Ré via the toll bridge **Pont de l'Île de Ré** *(pont-ile-de-re.com)*.

GUPPY
PA
S.N.C.A.N
NORD 1101

02 St-Émilion

Built of soft honey-coloured rock, medieval St-Émilion produces some of the world's finest red wines. Visiting this pretty town, and partaking in some of the tours and activities on offer, is the easiest way to get under the (grape) skin of Bordeaux wine production. The **Maison du Vin de St-Émilion** *(maisonduvinsaintemilion.com)* runs wine-tasting classes and has a superb exhibition covering wine essentials.

Guided tours of the town and surrounding châteaux are run by the **tourist office** *(saint-emilion-tourisme.com);* reserve ahead in season. Several tours include tastings and vineyard visits.

THE DRIVE: Leave St-Émilion on the D243 to Libourne, cross the town, then pick up the D1089 signposted 'Agen, Bergerac, Bordeaux'. Continue on the N89 towards Bordeaux until you see signs for the A630 toll road – at which point sit back and hit cruise control for the remaining 226km to Biarritz. Count 240km and about 2½ hours in all.

03 Biarritz

This coastal town is as ritzy as its name makes out. Biarritz boomed as a resort in the mid-19th century due to the regular visits by Napoléon III and his Spanish-born wife, Eugénie. Along its rocky coastline are architectural hallmarks of this golden age, and the Belle Époque and art deco eras that followed.

Biarritz is all about its fashionable beaches, especially the central **Grande Plage** and **Plage Miramar**. In the heat of summer you'll find them packed end to end with sun-loving bathers.

THE DRIVE: It's 208km (2¾ hours) to the village of Gavarnie. Take the A63 and A64 toll roads to exit 11, then the D940 to Lourdes (worth a look for its religious Disneyland feel). Continue south along the D913 and D921.

04 Cirque de Gavarnie

The Pyrenees doesn't lack impressive scenery, but your first sight of the Cirque de Gavarnie is guaranteed to raise a gasp. This breathtaking mountain amphitheatre is one of the region's most famous sights, sliced by thunderous waterfalls and ringed by sawtooth peaks, many of which top out at over 3000m.

♥ WHY I LOVE THIS TRIP

NICOLA WILLIAMS, WRITER

I simply cannot resist the big blue or fine wine, so this tasty seafaring trip is right up my alley. Feasting on fresh oysters on the seashore aside, I strongly advise a long lazy lunch at La Terrasse Rouge near St-Émilion. This spectacular vineyard restaurant was borne out of Jean Nouvel's designer revamp of Château La Dominique's wine cellars: dining on its uber-chic terrace overlooking a field of dark-red glass pebbles is the ultimate French road-trip reward.

There are a couple of large car parks in the village of Gavarnie, from where it's about a two-hour walk to the amphitheatre. Wear proper shoes, as snow lingers along the trail into early summer.

THE DRIVE: Retrace your steps to Lourdes, then take the N21 towards Tarbes and veer onto the A64 to reach Toulouse. It takes nearly three hours to cover the 228km.

05 Toulouse

The vibrant southern city of Toulouse is dubbed 'La Ville Rose', a reference to the distinctive blushing-pink brickwork of its classic architecture. Its city centre is tough to navigate by car, but there's a paying car park right beneath Toulouse's magnificent central square, **place du Capitole**, the city's literal and metaphorical heart. South of the square, walk the tangle of lanes in the historic **Vieux Quartier** (Old Town). Then, of course, there are the soothing twists and turns of the nearby Garonne River and mighty Canal du Midi – laced with footpaths to stretch your legs.

Having a car is handy for visiting two out-of-town sights celebrating modern Toulouse's role as an aerospace hub: the gigantic museum of Airbus, **Aeroscopia** *(musee-aeroscopia.fr),* just north of the airport; and, across town, **Cite de l'Espace** *(cite-espace.com),* which brings this interstellar industry vividly to life through a shuttle simulator, a planetarium, a 3D cinema, a simulated observatory, and so on. Both have free parking.

THE DRIVE: It's an easy 95km (one hour) down the fast A61 to Carcassonne. Notice how the vegetation becomes

Aeroscopia
ANIBAL TREJO/SHUTTERSTOCK

suddenly much more Mediterranean about 15 minutes out of Toulouse.

06 Carcassonne

Perched on a rocky hilltop and bristling with zigzagging battlements, stout walls and spiky turrets, from afar the fortified city of Carcassonne is most people's perfect idea of a medieval castle. Four million tourists a year stream through its city gates to explore La Cité, visit its **keep** *(remparts-carcassonne.fr)* and ogle at stunning views along the city's ancient ramparts.

THE DRIVE: Continue down the A61 to the Catalan-flavoured town of Narbonne, where you join the A9 (very busy in summer) and head east to Nîmes. From there the A54 will take you into Arles. Allow just over two hours to cover the 223km and expect lots of toll booths.

07 Arles

Arles' poster child is the celebrated impressionist painter Vincent van Gogh. If you're familiar with his work, you'll be familiar with Arles: the light, the colours, the landmarks and the atmosphere, all faithfully captured. But long before Van Gogh rendered this grand Rhône River locale on canvas, the Romans valued its worth. Today it's the reminders of Rome that are probably the town's most popular attractions. At **Les Arènes** (Amphithéâtre; *arenes-arles.com*) enslaved people, criminals and wild animals (including giraffes) met their dramatic demise before a 20,000-strong crowd during Roman gladiatorial displays.

THE DRIVE: From Arles take the scenic N568 and A55 route into Marseille. It's 88km (an hour's drive) away.

DETOUR

Aix-en-Provence

Start: 07 Arles

Aix-en-Provence is to Provence what the Left Bank is to Paris: an enclave of bourgeois-bohemian chic. Art, culture and architecture abound here. A stroller's paradise, the highlight is the mostly pedestrian old city, **Vieil Aix**. South of cours Mirabeau, **Quartier Mazarin** was laid out in the 17th century, and is home to some of Aix' finest buildings. Central place des Quatre Dauphins, with its fish-spouting fountain (1667), is particularly enchanting. Further south, locals play pétanque beneath plane trees in peaceful **Parc Jourdan**. From Arles it's a 77km (one-hour) drive down the A54 toll road to Aix-en-Provence. To rejoin the main route take the A51 and A7 for 32km (30 minutes) to Marseille.

08 Marseille

With its history, fusion of cultures, *souq*-like markets, millennia-old port and *corniches* (coastal roads) along rocky inlets and sun-baked beaches, Marseille is a captivating and exotic city. Ships have docked for more than 26 centuries at the colourful **Vieux Port** (Old Port) and it remains a thriving harbour. Guarding the harbour are **Bas Fort St-Nicolas** and **Fort St-Jean**, founded in the 13th century by the Knights Hospitaller of St John of Jerusalem. A vertigo-inducing footbridge links the latter with the stunning **Musée des Civilisations de l'Europe et de la Méditerranée** (MuCEM, Museum of European & Mediterranean Civilisations; *mucem.org*), the icon of modern Marseille.

From the Vieux Port, hike up to the fantastic history-woven quarter of **Le Panier**, a mishmash of steep lanes hiding *ateliers* (workshops) and terraced houses strung with drying washing.

THE DRIVE: To get from Marseille to Cannes, take the northbound A52 and join the A8 toll road just east of Aix-en-Provence. It's 181km and takes just under two hours.

09 Cannes

The eponymous film festival only lasts for two weeks in May, but thanks to regular visits from celebrities, the buzz and glitz are in Cannes year-round. The imposing **Palais des Festivals et des Congrès** (Festival & Congress Palace; *palaisdesfestivals.com*) is the centre of the glamour. Climb the red carpet, walk down the auditorium, tread the stage and learn about cinema's most prestigious event on a 1½-hour guided tour run by the **tourist office** *(cannes-france.com)*.

THE DRIVE: Leave the motorways behind and weave along the D6007 to Nice, taking in cliffs framing turquoise Mediterranean waters and the yachties' town of Antibes. It's 31km and, on a good day, takes 45 minutes.

10 Nice

You don't need to be a painter or an artist to appreciate the extraordinary light in Nice. The likes of Matisse and Chagall spent years lapping up the city's startling luminosity, and for most visitors here, it is this magical light that seduces. The city has several world-class sights, but the star attraction is the seafront **Promenade des Anglais**. Stroll and watch the world go by.

Fort St-Jean, Marseille

SERGII FIGURNYI/SHUTTERSTOCK

TOOLKIT

Left: Sanctuaires (p271), Rocamadour
JUANJE PEREZ PHOTOGRAPHY/SHUTTERSTOCK

ARRIVING

Aéroport de Charles de Gaulle in Paris is the most common long-haul entry point. RER trains, buses and night buses take you to the city centre. Aéroport d'Orly is closer to Paris, and Metro Line 14 links it straight to the city centre. By Eurostar, you'll exit at Gare du Nord with Metro connections for Paris plus trains heading elsewhere in France. Alternatively, you might come by ferry or train from elsewhere in Europe.

AIRPORT CAR RENTAL

Prebook your car hire; it's essential during peak periods when stocks are low. All the major international rental agencies are at the airport. Some operators offer one-way hires, saving you the return journey (road tolls do add up).

At Paris Charles de Gaulle Airport's Terminal 1, the car-hire desk location is well signposted; less so if you arrive at Terminal 2.

Have your hire-company phone number on hand, especially if your flight is delayed, as most counters close by midnight (sometimes earlier). After-hours returns are usually possible here via a drop box.

Paris Charles de Gaulle Airport is around 30km northeast of Paris. You'll save time, money and hassle by not driving into Paris. On-street parking is between €4 and €6 per hour (depending on the *arrondissement* (city district); it's time-limited to two hours (from 9am to 8pm). Private car parks charge around €25 per day and are open 24/7.

AIRPORT TO CITY CENTRE

	CHARLES DE GAULLE	ORLY	GARE DU NORD
TRAIN	35min €14	30min €2.55	5min €2.55
BUS	45min €4.99	30min €2	30min €2.05
TAXI	25min from €56	15min from €45	10min €15

WI-FI

Wi-fi (pronounced 'wee-fee' in French) is available at airports, train stations, hotels, most museums and tourist offices. Get a burner email to protect your privacy when using public wi-fi.

BORDER CROSSINGS

The EU's new entry/exit system (EES) means non-EU visitors may need to provide biometric details such as fingerprints and photos. Implementation has begun, and it is likely to be in place at all border crossings from April 2026.

SAFE TRAVEL

Robberies and muggings have occurred on the RER trains from/to Paris airports. Stay abreast of local news and consider an alternative route.

POLICE

The police have a prominent presence on the ground in France. They have considerable powers and can ask for proof of identity (i.e. your passport documents) at any time. Stay calm and polite.

GETTING AROUND

ROAD DESIGNATIONS

There are different types of intercity road in France. *Autoroutes* (A roads) are multi-lane highways usually with tolls *(péages)*. They're well maintained with regular rest stops (with toilets and picnic tables) and fuel stations.

Routes Nationales (N or RN in the name) are national highways, sometimes with divider strips. Routes Départementales (or D roads) are local roads, while Routes Communales (C or V) are minor rural roads.

Overtaking lanes are well respected (move aside quickly for faster travelling vehicles).

DRIVING INFO

Drive on the right

130

Speed limits: 130km/h on motorways (110km/h in the rain)

.05

Blood alcohol limit is 50mg/100mL

TRAIN TRAVEL

SNCF trains *(sncf-connect.com)* are clean and efficient, making train travel the best way to zip between regions, where it's then possible to rent a car locally. You can also get up-to-the-minute timetable information from apps like *trainline.com*.

CRIT'AIR RULES

In a bid to reduce air pollution in city centres, many cities in France are now subject to Crit'Air restrictions, which ban heavily polluting vehicles from driving in the city centre. If bringing your own vehicle to France visit *certificat-air.gouv.fr/certificat* to obtain a Crit'Air rating and sticker (€3.11 plus postage). Routes that pass through a ZFE (*zone à faibles émissions*, or low emissions zone), subject to Crit'Air rules, are noted in the book.

ELECTRIC VEHICLES (EVS)

Electric recharge stations are prevalent here and 30% of new cars are electric. Chargemap (website and app) allows you to filter by vehicle and connector type. Use the Izivia or KiWhi apps to pay for top-up.

COMPARE ROAD COSTS

Make informed toll-road decisions with **Via Michelin** *(viamichelin.com)*, which gives you the average fuel cost for a journey, plus tolls, coupled with journey times. Faster roads mean higher tolls but less time and usually fewer kilometres.

PÉAGE ROAD TOLLS

Avoid the lanes for *télépéage* tag owners (marked with a lower-case 't'); instead head for booths with either a green arrow or a card/cash sign. Generally you collect a paper ticket at the start of the tollway and pay at a booth as you leave.

TRAVEL COSTS

Car rental
€80–180/day

Petrol
Approx €1.80/litre

Tolls from Paris to Lyon
Approx €40

ACCOMMODATION

HOW MUCH FOR A NIGHT IN A...

campsite
€20

self-catering apartment
€80–150

room in a five-star château
€200+

BOOK AHEAD

From fairy-tale châteaux to boutique hideaways, France has accommodation to suit every taste and pocket. If you're visiting in high season reserve ahead – the best addresses on the coast fill up months in advance, including camping grounds. For families, book a double with an extra bed at hotels, rather than a triple room. Groups of four or more are best served by self-catering options.

CAMPING

Camping is hugely popular here; there are hundreds of well-equipped campgrounds around the country, especially popular for family holidays *(campingfrance.com)*. Most are near rivers, lakes and the coast, and are open from April to late September (book well ahead for peak summer). An *emplacement* (site) has space for a tent and car parking. Pitching your tent in non-designated camping *sauvage* (camping spots) is illegal.

NEW-WAVE HOSTELS

France has plenty of new-wave design-driven hostels where you'll find visitors working on laptops (or scrolling their phones) in shared lounge-like spaces over coffee or light bites. As well as single beds in dorms, double rooms and family rooms are usually available; there's usually also English-speaking staff.

MEMORABLE SLEEPS

Looking for a night or two in a truly memorable accommodation? To look up unusual places to stay, from treehouses to floating cabins on ponds, transparent domes, teepees and yurts, head to *cabanes-de-france.com*. You can search by region and punctuate your road trip with a night sleeping with views of the stars or a morning waking up amid birdsong in the branches of a tree.

SHORT-TERM RENTALS

There has been cross-party talk about better regulation of short-term rentals, particularly in cities such as Paris, Lyon and Bordeaux, to ensure there is adequate housing available for locals. If that goes ahead, fewer properties for holiday-makers means prices will rise.

Transferring of poorly insulated homes from long-term rentals (where environmental upgrades such as insulation and energy efficiency are required) to the short-term rental market is another loophole to close.

When weighing up the cost of traditional accommodation such as hostels and hotels against locals' apartments, it's worth keeping this in mind.

PRICE BRACKETS

Budget accommodation can mean basic hotels without breakfast or small family-run places where shared language is less of a barrier thanks to online translations. Midrange usually includes a few extra creature comforts: elevators, quality soap and towels, and in-room tea-making facilities. Top-end places stretch from luxury five-star palaces with swimming pools and Michelin-starred restaurants to boutique-chic alpine chalets.

CARS

CAR RENTAL

Airports and major train stations are well serviced with car-rental companies, including major international players, plus local outfits such as **Rent a Car** *(rentacar.fr)* and **DLM** *(dlm.fr)*. Local agencies aren't always open on the weekend.

You need to be over 21 and have had a driving licence for at least a year (sometimes three) plus an international credit card. Drivers under 25 often have to pay a daily surcharge.

Collision-damage waivers (CDW) vary. You can usually reduce or cancel the excess fee by paying a daily insurance 'supplement'. However, your travel insurance or credit card may cover CDW – check with your providers before you book.

Automatic transmission is the exception and is more expensive.

HOW MUCH TO HIRE A CAR?

Small car
€60 per day

Campervan
€90–150 per day

EV
€60–80 per day

EVS

France is at the forefront of the switch to electric; however, EV and hybrid rental vehicles are less available outside cities. Rentals, from the Toyota C-HR to the BMW X5 eDrive SUV, come at a premium (but with a lower carbon footprint).

Route planning is imperative when touring by EV. Some recharge stations are only suitable for specific vehicles. Pre-register your vehicle with your app before you depart. Also check your app to ensure recharge points are not out of order. Crawling in traffic, especially in a city like Paris, will drain your batteries – leave plenty of buffer time.

Recharging overnight at hotels, or around supermarket shopping or meal times, will save time on the road.

OTHER GEAR

Extras such as infant or child seats, additional drivers, roadside assistance packages and an on-demand telephone concierge service all come at an extra cost per day. Be sure to prebook child seats ahead of time, although it may be cheaper (and safer) to bring your own.

COLUMBO.PHOTOG/SHUTTERSTOCK

RESPONSIBLE TRAVEL

RESPONSIBLE TRAVEL

CLIMATE CHANGE & TRAVEL

Lonely Planet urges all travellers to engage with their travel carbon footprint, which will mainly come from air travel. While there often isn't an alternative, travellers can look to minimise the number of flights they take and use cleaner ground transport, such as trains.

One proposed solution – purchasing carbon offsets – unfortunately does not cancel out the impact of individual flights. While most destinations will depend on air travel for the foreseeable future, for now, pursuing ground-based travel where possible is the best course of action.

The **UN Carbon Offset Calculator** shows how flying impacts a household's emissions.

The **ICAO's carbon emissions calculator** allows visitors to analyse the CO_2 generated by point-to-point journeys.

Clef Verte
laclefverte.org
Environmentally friendly hotels and restaurants.

Crit'Air
certificat-air.gouv.fr
Implementing restrictions based on vehicle emissions.

Gold Standard
goldstandard.org
Reduce and offset your carbon footprint.

LOCAL PRODUCE

Food air miles? Pffftt. Nearly every village has a local butcher (who will often make pâtés and *saucisson* – sausage), local *boulangeries* (bakeries), and a weekly food market selling fresh local produce and cheeses.

CYCLING

Cycling is *très cool*, with more and more *pistes cyclables* (bike paths) in cities and the countryside. Plan routes using *francevelotourisme.com* to see more of France's gorgeous countryside on two wheels.

WWOOF!

For longer stays, consider WWOOFing *(wwoof.fr/en)*. Learn more of the language, enjoy organic homegrown produce, and develop new skills such as caring for animals, growing a vegetable garden and learning permaculture basics.

SAFE TRAVEL

HEALTH CARE

Health care is readily available throughout France. Pharmacies – look for an illuminated green cross outside indicating a pharmacy is open – are extremely helpful and sell a wide range of medicines without prescription *(ordonnance)*. Details of the closest *pharmacie de garde* open at night and on Sundays are displayed in pharmacy windows.

CAR BREAKDOWN

Make sure you have breakdown and accident cover with a phone number to call (ask if there's an English-speaking option) with your rental outfit. If that's not available, find out what cover is offered by your travel insurers, or your own home-country automobile associations. Keep all phone numbers at the ready, as it's harder to look them up in an emergency situation.

THEFT

Never leave anything valuable in an unattended car. Watch out for pickpockets and bag-snatchers, especially around train stations, cash points and major tourist areas. Thieves often work in groups – one will distract you while another robs you. Don't keep your passport, credit cards and phone in one place. Split these between bags/pockets so that if one gets stolen you're not completely stuck.

SNOW

Between 1 November and 31 March, it's a legal requirement to have a vehicle equipped with winter tyres, or to carry either snow chains or snow socks in your car in mountainous parts of France (34 departments in total).

DRUG LAWS

On-the-spot fines of €200 are issued if you're caught smoking cannabis. In 2021 the government approved the over-the-counter sale of CBD products with a THC content of less than 0.3%, but in 2024 banned products containing the more potent HHC. Meanwhile, a limited trial of medical cannabis has been extended until March 2026.

NATURAL DISASTERS

Forest fires are increasing in southern France during the summer months due to hotter, drier weather. Familiarise yourself with the emergency procedures and stay abreast of local developments, including road closures and evacuation plans. There's also increasing risk of floods in France – check weather conditions and follow local advice. Avalanches are a risk in mountainous areas.

IN CASE OF EMERGENCY

15
Ambulance (SAMU)

17
Police

18
Fire

112
General emergency (Europe-wide)

NUTS & BOLTS

GOOD TO KNOW

Time zone
Central European Time, GMT/UTC+1

Country code
33

Emergency number
112

CURRENCY: EURO (€)

BANKCARDS

Bankcards with an embedded chip work virtually everywhere, including at *autoroute* toll plazas. You may also need to insert your card and key in your PIN at, for example, unstaffed petrol stations or if you're over your daily pay-wave limit. Beware: international fees on individual transactions charged by most banks add up.

ATMS

Automated teller machines (ATMs) – known as *distributeurs automatiques de billets* (DAB) or *points d'argent* in French – are the cheapest and most convenient way to get euros. ATMs connected to international networks are situated in all cities and large towns and usually offer decent exchange rates.

CASH

Cash is best for smaller transactions, tipping staff and cash-only businesses. Leave a cash tip for service at hotels and restaurants and for tour guides. There's no need to tip at bars or cafe counters (only for table service).

OPENING HOURS

Opening hours are erratic and complex – if important, check first. Expect shops and banks to be closed from noon to 1.30pm. Restaurants are open noon to 2.30pm and then 7pm to 9pm.

STRIKES

Strikes have played a strong part in French political life, even more so in recent years. These can cause travel disruptions, so keep abreast of local news before – and during – your stay, and be prepared to make contingency plans.

HOW MUCH FOR...

a dozen market oysters
€15–30

a bistro lunch
€15–20

a glass of wine
€6–12

museum admission
€free–22

ELECTRICITY

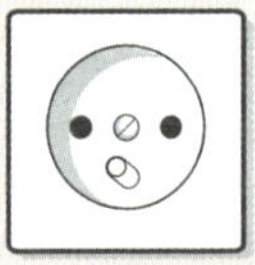

Type E
220V/50Hz

TOILETS

Public toilets, signposted WC (short for 'water closet'; pronounced veh-seh), or *toilettes,* are not plentiful outside the big cities. Self-cleaning toilet pods *(sanisettes)* are usually open 24 hours. Unisex toilets are common.

INDEX

Drives 000

Map pages **p000**

THE WRITERS

This is the 5th edition of Lonely Planet's *Best Road Trips: France* guidebook, updated with new material by Anna Richards.

Writers on previous editions whose work also appears in this book are included below.

Anna Richards

Anna is an award-winning travel and adventure writer who has been living in Lyon, France, since 2021, drawn by proximity to the mountains. Her work takes her road tripping all over the country in her battered Clio, often with two large, hairy dogs in tow. Occasionally she gets to ride in style, when her partner, a keen motorcyclist, hires a Royal Enfield.

Contributing writers

Alexis Averbuck, Joel Balsam, Oliver Berry, Celeste Brash, Stuart Butler, Jean-Bernard Carillet, Gregor Clark, Mark Elliot, Steve Fallon, Anita Isalska, Catherine Le Nevez, Christopher Pitts, Daniel Robinson, Regis St Louis, Ryan Ver Berkmoes, Tasmin Waby, Nicola Williams

Send us your feedback

We love to hear from travellers – your comments keep us on our toes and help make our books better. Our well-travelled team reads every word on what you loved or loathed about this book. Although we cannot reply individually to your submissions, we always guarantee that your feedback goes straight to the appropriate writers, in time for the next edition.

BEHIND THE SCENES

This book was produced by the following:

Destination Editor
Darren O'Connell

Coordinating Editor
Gabrielle Innes

Production Editor
Will Allen

Image Researcher
Fabrice Robin

Cartographer
Anita Banh

Assisting Editors
Melanie Dankel, Anne Mulvaney, Vicky Smith

Cover Researcher
Sam Ubinas

Thanks to
Ailson Killilea, Saralinda Turner

Product Development
Sofie Andersen, Melinda Anderson, Marc Backwell, Alison Killilea, Darren O'Connell, James Smart, Robin Yule

Acknowledgments

Digital Model Elevation Data
Contains public sector information licensed under the Open Government Licence v3.0 website nationalarchives.gov.uk/doc/open-government-licence/version/3/

Cover photographs
Front: Les Calanques de Piana (p206); Philip Lee Harvey/Lonely Planet
Back: Château de Monbazillac (p258); Richard Semik/Shutterstock

Visit **lonelyplanet.com/contact** to submit your updates and suggestions or to ask for help. Our award-winning website also features inspirational travel stories and news.

Note: We may edit, reproduce and incorporate your comments in Lonely Planet products such as guidebooks, websites and digital products, so let us know if you are happy to have your name acknowledged. For a copy of our privacy policy visit **lonelyplanet.com/legal**

lonely planet

Published by Lonely Planet Global Limited
CRN 554153
Digital Depot, Roe Lane off Thomas Street, Dublin
D08 TCV4, Ireland (EU authorised representative)
5th edition – Sep 2026
ISBN 9781806530427

10 9 8 7 6 5 4 3 2 1
Printed in China